The most amazing haunted & mysterious places in Britain

PUBLISHED BY
THE READER'S DIGEST ASSOCIATION, INC.
LONDON • NEW YORK • SYDNEY • MONTREAL

The most amazing haunted & mysterious places in Britain

Contents

Introduction

Restless ghosts, mischievous sprites and dark legends are an elemental part of Britain's supernatural heritage. Explore the shadowy side of England, Scotland and Wales and discover a world of wicked deeds, strange tales and inexplicable events.

By most accounts, Britain is the most haunted nation in the world. From the earliest times, its inhabitants have carried with them a wealth of supernatural beliefs, each generation spinning its own – often more fanciful – versions of the old myths and legends to explain the stranger aspects of the human and natural world. For them, spirits walked with the living, the wicked tormented the innocent and suffered torment in return, and the land's wild reaches were places of great wonder and fear.

Drawn from traditional stories and centuries of local lore, many of the accounts in this book hark back to a time when wizards appeared to command the elements, the Devil made mischief on a regular basis and the unhappy dead clung to the world of the living.

As a populous group of isles with a long and bloody history, it is no surprise that Britain has more spectres than its neighbours, but not all hauntings are historic. Many mysteries continue to baffle and intrigue, and many ghoulish apparitions are distinctly modern. No one claims to see dragons in the sky today; strange lights may be described by observers as alien spacecraft or at the very least, Unidentified Flying Objects. Phantom buses have supplanted spectral coaches on the streets, and real black cats – rather than demonic black dogs – prowl the countryside. Ancient Roman Legionaries may still march over hillsides, but spectral soldiers on manoeuvres are just as likely to have come from the Second World War.

Shetland Islands

Orkney Islands

SCOTLAND
212-247

NORTHEAST ENGLAND
174-191

NORTHWEST ENGLAND
158-173

CENTRAL ENGLAND
128-157

EAST ANGLIA
104-127

WALES
192-211

LONDON
88-103

SOUTHERN ENGLAND
48-87

Channel Islands

SOUTHWEST ENGLAND
8-47

How to use this book

Wherever you travel in Britain, you can be sure you are never far from the site of an unexplained event, a place of ancient myth or the home of a disconsolate ghost. *The Most Amazing Haunted & Mysterious Places in Britain* offers a comprehensive guide to Britain's strange phenomena by location. The book is divided by region into nine chapters: Southwest England, Southern England, London, East Anglia, Central England, Northwest England, Northeast England, Wales and Scotland (see left). At the beginning of each chapter is a map of the region, divided by county, or in the case of Wales and Scotland, by area. Numbers on the map show the geographical location of the entries in the following chapter. The map serves as a useful aid to planning trips and excursions, and directions at the end of each entry lead you by road or landmark to each destination.

Out and about

There are more than 600 entries in this book. All are accessible by car, on foot, and in the case of certain islands, by ferry. Some are in the centre of towns and cities, others require a walk, varying from a gentle ramble to a strenuous hike.

To reach places in remote areas, you should always be well prepared. Take an up-to-date map and a compass, wear walking boots and suitable weatherproof clothing, check the weather report before you set out and always tell someone where you are going.

The majority of the featured houses, castles, stately homes and inns are accessible to the public. Many are run by national organisations, others by private individuals. Where properties are not accessible to the public (for example where an inn has become a private house), always respect the occupants' privacy. Do not trespass on to their land to view or photograph the property.

Useful websites

Much of the British countryside together with older buildings in towns or cities are owned or controlled by heritage organisations. All the organisations listed below run supernatural-themed events and ghost tours at selected properties at certain times of the year, particularly around Halloween, 31 October.

www.english-heritage.org.uk – English Heritage provides ghost tours for adults and children at selected properties
www.cadw.wales.gov.uk – Cadw (Welsh Historic Monuments) celebrates Halloween with fireworks and events at Caerphilly Castle and Rhuddlan Castle
www.nationaltrust.org.uk – The National Trust organises Halloween ghost walks, talks, tours, fancy dress and craft activities for children at selected properties
www.nts.org.uk – The National Trust for Scotland cares for a number of properties said to have resident ghosts. Halloween tours and activities are organised each year

KEY

1 Main entry
County boundary
Motorway
Principal A road

1

2 Ilfracombe

Barnstaple

Bideford

4

A39

A39

A377

A386

23

DEVON
24-31

Bude

A39

Okehampton

22

A30

A39

21

22

Launceston

23

A386

16

18

20

Bodmin
Moor

29

A30

28

31

Tavistock

20

Dartmoor
National
Park

Padstow

A39

24

19

Bodmin

27

30

17

Newquay

CORNWALL
10-23

Liskeard

A38

16

St Austell

A390

A38

Plymouth

A30

14

18

26

25

15

Truro

19

A390

5

6

4

3

A394

Penzance

Falmouth

2

10

8

7

1

11

9

Helston

12

Isles of Scilly

13 Tresco

St Mary's

Southwest England

Piskies, mermaids and giants mingle with saints and sinners in the southwest, where fading remnants of folklore co-exist with some very modern mysteries. Big cats and strange hounds stalk the lonely moors, while ancient lanes, hillforts and henges are best avoided after dark.

Bristol

Weston-super-Mare

Minehead

Exmoor National Park

Bath

Mendip Hills

Frome

Somerset Levels

Bridgwater

Glastonbury

SOMERSET
38–45

Taunton

Tiverton

Shaftesbury

Yeovil

Honiton

Blandford Forum

DORSET
32–37

Exeter

Lyme Regis

Dorchester

Poole

Bournemouth

Exmouth

Weymouth

Swanage

Torquay

Dartmouth

Salcombe

Alderney

Guernsey

Herm

St Peter Port

Sark

CHANNEL ISLANDS
46–47

Jersey

St Helier

CORNWALL

Rocky coastlines, untamed moors and relics of a pagan past have given Cornwall an air of otherworldliness that modern life has done little to dispel. It remains one of the most haunted places in the country.

❶ Land's End

The fertile land of Lyonesse, with its mythical city of Lyons, once stretched from Land's End to the Isles of Scilly until, some 900 years ago, it was suddenly engulfed by the sea. Just one man survived the dramatic flood. His name was Trevilian and he escaped by riding a white horse to high ground and safety. The Trevilian family arms acknowledge this feat of daring and good fortune, depicting a horse rising from the sea. The legend of Lyonesse persists in the area, and Mount's Bay fishermen insist that drowned buildings can sometimes be seen beneath the waves around the Seven Stones reef.

▶ *9 miles SW of Penzance on A30. Seven Stones Reef lies 20 miles W of Land's End.*

❷ Whitesand Bay

It may be that the dark spirit whose despairing cries can still be heard above the autumn gales in this remote spot between Land's End and the Lizard were once attributed to a Celtic god. But from the mid 17th century at least, Cornish tales have identified it with the soul of Jan Tregeagle, doomed to eternal torment for the sins he committed in life. There is little doubt that Jan Tregeagle existed. In the early 1600s, he was a stern and unpopular local magistrate who used his position to amass a considerable fortune. His body was buried in St Breock's churchyard, after which his grizzly legend grew. Magistrate became murderer in the stories of the locals, and he was vilified as the

WHITESAND BAY

killer of his wife and children and thief of an orphan's estates.

Within a few short years, Tregeagle was summoned from the grave to bear witness against a debtor in Bodmin court and, once raised, his spirit could not be laid to rest. Priests and exorcists set him seemingly impossible tasks, convinced that while he was working at these, his soul would be safe from the Devil. Eventually, they bound Tregeagle to weaving ropes of sand at Gwenvor Cove and there he is said to remain, in continuous struggle. Now, when a northerly wind destroys his work, his howls of anguish and rage can be heard reverberating across Whitesand Bay.

▶ *On minor roads off A30, 1 mile N of Land's End.*

❸ Carn Kenidjack

The reputation of this rocky outcrop is of a sombre, haunted place, and an old tale suggests it was once the site of a demonic wrestling match. Many years ago, two miners were walking past it after dark, on their way home from the hamlet of Morvah, when they were overtaken by a black-robed horseman. The rider invited them to watch a wrestling match and, feeling compelled to follow him, the terrified miners found they had joined a party of fearsome demons, commanded by the horseman, who was the Devil himself. During the first fierce bout, one of the wrestlers was thrown against a rock and appeared to be dying. The two miners, overcome by a sense of Christian charity, ran to him and whispered a prayer in his ear. At once the earth trembled and the whole party vanished shrieking in a black cloud. The miners, petrified with fear, hid on the carn until dawn.

▶ *1 mile NE of St Just along minor roads off A3071.*

❹ Trewellard

During the early 1950s, at the height of newspaper reports of 'flying saucers' across Britain and America, UFO sightings were plentiful in West Cornwall. Most were subsequently explained away as natural phenomena, such as meteors (small chunks of debris that burn up in the Earth's atmosphere), or as military aircraft tests conducted by the Ministry of Defence. But on the night of Thursday, September 8, 1977, a sighting on an altogether different level occurred in clear skies above the lonely hamlet of Trewellard, 2 miles north of St Just. Around 9.00pm, while taking an evening stroll, Chris Sabine, his fiancée, Jane Eddy, and four members of her family all saw what they took to be a spotlight floating about 90m (300ft) above the Carne – a local patch of high ground. A glance through binoculars showed the object to be spinning, with two red lights on one side and a single green light on the other. As it passed over the group's heads, the object was seen to be circular in shape and emitted a faint hum. After a few minutes, it flew off to the south towards Mount's Bay.

Remarkably, some 15 minutes later, the Waters family of Newlyn saw 'a brilliant white light, much bigger than a star' hovering in the southeastern sky over the Bay. It rose vertically as it came towards them, revealing a 'red light on one side and green light on the other while a third light flashed underneath'. The family heard 'a faint humming sound' as it passed overhead, after which the light disappeared off to the northwest. According to the Waters, it was visible for about 10 minutes – a fact later confirmed by friends who had seen the light while strolling along Newlyn Promenade.

The extraordinary similarity between the two accounts suggests that the objects seen by Chris Sabine's group and the Waters family were one and the same. The presence of red and green lights (the international convention for indicating port and starboard) points to some form of helicopter or vertical take-off aircraft, yet no such craft in existence – either then or now – operates so noiselessly as to emit a 'faint hum'. No other plausible explanation for the sighting has ever been put forward.

▶ *On B3306, 2 miles N of St Just.*

❺ Zennor

A chorister at the local church, squire's son Matthew Trewella, sang so beautifully that his voice attracted a mermaid from the sea. Using all her charms, she lured him back to her deep domain, from where he never returned. His voice, so legend says, can still be heard echoing up from beneath the waves. The mermaid, with long flowing hair, a mirror and a comb can be seen today, carved on a 15th-century bench end in Zennor church.

▶ *On B3306, 4 miles W of St Ives.*

SOUTHWEST ENGLAND

❻ Trencrom Hill

Also known as Trecobben, an Iron Age hillfort commands stunning views over St Ives, Hayle and Mount's Bay. The story goes that, long ago, Trecobben was a fortress of the giants who used to inhabit Cornwall. One rock formation, the Giant's Cradle, is cited as evidence. This is where these huge people would drag their enemies and murder them. Other tales are told about the Giant's Cave at Lamorna and the Giant's Chair 3 miles southeast of Land's End. While historians may prefer the theory that the giants were merely tall Saxon invaders, who appeared enormous to the much shorter Celts, there is no doubt that the legendary stories are far more colourful.

▶ *On minor roads 2 miles S of St Ives. Lamorna is 5 miles SW of Penzance off B3315 and the Giant's Chair is 3 miles SE of Land's End.*

❼ Mawnan

In 1976, the picturesque village of Mawnan beside the Helford river near Falmouth became the scene of an extraordinary sighting when two girls camping in the woods beside the ancient parish church claimed to have seen a hideous apparition outside their tent. According to one of the pair, Sally Chapman, her attention was caught by a hissing sound. When she turned round, she was confronted by what looked like a cross between a man and an owl, with a bird's head, wings instead of arms, and human-like legs with huge black pincers for toes. The creature took off, violently shaking the branches of the surrounding trees as it did so. Over the next two years several witnesses claimed to have seen the creature, including two sisters who reported a feathered 'bird man' hovering above Mawnan church. The flight of the so-called 'Owl Man of Mawnan' might easily have been dismissed as one of pure fancy were it not for an anonymous letter written to a local newspaper some 20 years later by a woman claiming to be a student from Chicago. It appeared that she, too, had seen the Owl Man while on a visit to the area, describing it as having 'a ghastly face, wide mouth, glowing eyes and pointed ears' as well as 'clawed wings'. Intriguingly, the appearance of the Owl Man coincided with strange glowing lights seen floating above the ground within the immediate vicinity of Mawnan church.

▶ *On minor roads 5 miles SW of Falmouth.*

❽ Praa Sands

Just inland from the beach, a fortified manor house, the tower of which dates back to the late 15th century, has earned a reputation for being one of the most haunted castles in Britain. This is Pengersick. Wilder claims that the grounds are patrolled by a 'demon dog' and were once the meeting place for devil-worshippers are dismissed by the current owners as the invention of smugglers, keen to discourage visitors. Countless less dramatic appearances have been recorded over the years, though, including a monk in a wide-brimmed hat, a lady in white and the figure of a dancer who is said to skip noiselessly across the floor of the castle's Solar Room. At such times, the temperature inside the building plummets inexplicably. The castle has also been implicated in the wreck of the *St Anthony*, a Portuguese ship that foundered off the coast at Gunwalloe in 1527 and was lost with a cargo of treasure exceeding £18,000. Artefacts from the wreck are in the possession of the Pengersick Trust.

▶ *¹/₂ mile S of Germoe on A394, 7 miles W of Helston and 10 miles E of Penzance.*

STRONGHOLD OF GIANTS CUT OFF BY THE TIDE

❾ Mount's Bay

The sizeable bite taken out of the Cornish coastline by the English Channel in the vicinity of Penzance appears to be something of a hotspot for UFO sightings. Almost 20 years to the day after the Trewellard incident (see page 11), on September 13, 1997, Phillip Gillet, the Town Crier of Penzance, awoke in the early hours of the morning and happened to glance out to sea through his bedroom window. To his amazement, he spied an orange-yellow light shaped like a rugby ball hovering silently above the water. According to Gillett, the object 'shimmered like a jelly' but appeared to remain stationary for about 20 minutes. Then, suddenly, it vanished – 'almost as if someone had switched off a light' – leaving the bewildered Gillett to ponder over what he had just witnessed.

In January 2008, another mysterious sighting took place over the Bay when Kelvin Barbery, a respected member of the local Search and Rescue team, photographed a cigar-shaped object in broad daylight hovering over a pair of coastal tankers. And in July of the same year, an anonymous local resident reported seeing a pair of bright lights move slowly and silently towards each other across the Bay, where they hovered together for 2 or 3 minutes before rising up into the sky in the direction of Marazion and fading from view.

▶ *S and E of Penzance and Marazion, which are on the A30 and A394.*

❿ St Michael's Mount

The Cornish name for St Michael's Mount is 'Carrick luz en cuz', which means 'the ancient rock in the wood', and at low tide the fossilised remains of the forest that once covered this part of the coast are still visible. According to local myth a giant named Cormoran and his wife Cormelian lived there. Cormoran was intent on building a stronghold of white granite, and sent his wife to find the great boulders and carry them back in her apron. One day, Cormelian, seeing her husband asleep, decided it would be easier to collect greenstone instead, which was nearer to hand. Unfortunately, Cormoran awoke and saw her. Enraged, he broke her apron strings and the greenstone crashed to the ground. A block of it still stands on the causeway to St Michael's Mount, which is said to be Cormoran's fortress.

Cormoran finally met his death at the hands of Jack the Giant Killer. Jack crept to the Mount one night and dug a deep pit, covering it with sticks and straw. Then, placing his horn to his lips, he awoke Cormoran. The giant rushed out and fell into the hole. Jack raised his axe and struck at the giant's head, killing him with a single blow. In gratitude, the local people presented Jack with a magnificent sword, and a belt embroidered with gold.

Within the present castle is a rough-cut stone seat, known as Michael's Chair. St Keyne, on a pilgrimage to the Mount, is believed to have endowed the seat with the same power that she gave to her holy well at the village of St Keyne, near Liskeard. If either the bride or groom is the first to sit in Michael's Chair, that partner will henceforth dominate the marriage.

▶ *St Michael's Mount is off Marazion, S of A394, 4 miles E of Penzance. Reached on foot via causeway at low tide, or ferry (summer only) at high tide.*

SOUTHWEST ENGLAND

⑪ Trewoofe

Now a farm, Trewoofe (pronounced 'trove') was once the manor house of the powerful Lovelis family. One evening, more than 300 years ago, Squire Lovelis gave chase to a white hare, which disappeared into an ancient stone-lined passage, or fougou, at nearby Boleigh. The squire and his pack followed, only to find that the hare had turned into a witch, and the passage contained an evil coven led by a demon. Lovelis recognised the demon as a stranger who had come to the village years before and seduced his wife. The squire swore angrily at him and at once the grisly group turned on Lovelis. When he finally emerged, his friends found him singing wildly and totally demented. Squire Lovelis and his dogs are said to haunt the district to this day.
▶ *Just N of Boleigh on the B3315, 5 miles SW of Penzance.*

⑫ Porthgwarra

South of Land's End, the hamlet of Porthgwarra was once known as Sweetheart's Cove. Many years ago, Nancy, the daughter of a farmer, fell in love with a sailor, William. Her parents disapproved of him and the lovers were forbidden to meet. Just before William joined his ship, the pair managed one last meeting in this cove. They vowed that they would be true to one another forever and, living or dead, they would meet again.

No news came from the sailor for many months and Nancy, growing more melancholy every day, watched for his ship from nearby Hella Point, which became known as Nancy's Garden. Eventually, she became quite mad and did little but lament the loss of her lover.

One moonlit night, an old woman sitting on the clifftop saw Nancy walk down to the cove and sit on a rock that was partially surrounded by water. The tide began to rise but the girl continued to gaze out to sea. The old woman, seeing the danger the girl was in, decided to go down and warn her of the rising water. When she arrived on the beach, she was surprised to see a sailor beside the young girl with his arm round her. Believing Nancy to be safe, the old woman sat down to watch. But the lovers did not move and, with increasing concern, the old woman called out to them. Neither heeded her warning. Suddenly they appeared to float off over the sea and then vanish. Nancy was never seen again, and next day word came that William's ship had gone down with all hands.

▶ *At end of minor road S from Polgigga on B3315, 2 miles SE of Land's End.*

⑬ Scilly Isles

Bishop Rock Lighthouse was an amazing feat of engineering when it was built towards the end of the 19th century to warn shipping of the treacherous Western Rocks. This is where *The Nancy* foundered in a terrible storm in 1784 with the loss of all on board, including Ann Cargill and her baby. Ann Cargill was an actress and singer, famous in her day as much for her scandalous behaviour as her theatrical prowess. She had gone to India with her lover, John Haldane, a captain with the East India Company, taken Bombay and Calcutta by storm, and was returning with a reputed fortune in jewels and cash. Her body was washed up on Rosevear, one of the smaller islands, still clutching her child. They were buried together on the island, but when it was realised who she was, the bodies were exhumed and reburied on St Mary's, the main island in the group.

A hundred years later, the construction workers employed to build the lighthouse were housed on Rosevear. They reported many strange happenings and believed the ghostly woman's voice they heard singing a lullaby was that of Ann Cargill. So the legend grew and Ann's lonely spirit still reputedly roams the desolate shore. In 2007, after some 200 years of searching, a wreck believed to be that of *The Nancy* was found on the Western Rocks.

▶ *Lying 28 miles SW of Land's End, the islands can be reached by helicopter, plane or boat.*

⑭ St Agnes

The ghost of Dorcas is still remembered around St Agnes. This unfortunate woman committed suicide in Polbreen Mine and her wraith remained in the mine's dark galleries. She took perverse pleasure in calling men from their work and wasting their time. Once, though, she saved a man's life. On hearing his name, he went to investigate. At that moment, a fall of rock crashed on to the spot where he had been standing.

▶ *At junction of B3277 and B3285, 3 miles W of A30. Polbreen Mine is at the foot of St Agnes Beacon, 1 mile W of the village.*

⑮ Chapel Porth

A cavity in the cliffs at Chapel Porth marks the spot where the mighty giant Bolster collapsed and died for love of St Agnes. The giant incessantly proclaimed his love for her but he was a married man and the virtuous missionary would only lecture him for his impropriety. At last, patience exhausted, the saint asked him to prove his love. His task was to fill the cavity with his blood. Bolster, convinced that it would not take much to fill such a small hole, plunged his knife into a vein and held his arm over the hollow. But St Agnes knew that the shaft was bottomless and could never be filled, and the giant bled to death. A red stain remains to show where his blood once flowed down the rocks into the sea.

▶ *At end of minor road 2 miles SW of St Agnes.*

ANN'S LONELY SPIRIT IS BELIEVED TO ROAM THE DESOLATE SHORE

SCILLY ISLES

16 Penhale Sands

According to legend, Penhale Sands was once the site of Langarroc, a beautiful town with seven fine churches. Mining made the town rich, but with wealth came a sad moral decline. So evil were its ways that, one night, a storm arose and buried the town and its people beneath a sand dune. Even now, says the legend, when the night is stormy, the bells of the seven churches can be heard above the roar of the sea.

The story has a grain of truth, for sand certainly did engulf the region. During excavations in the mid 19th century several human skeletons were uncovered near the ruins of a medieval church, together with a graveyard and a 9th-century cross. They stand close to the site of a 6th-century oratory – one of the earliest-known Christian buildings in Britain. It is believed to mark the spot where St Piran, patron saint of tin miners and of Cornwall itself, landed from Ireland.

▶ *Penhale Sands are N of Perranporth on B3285, off A3075.*

LANDING PLACE OF CORNWALL'S PATRON SAINT

ST PIRAN'S CROSS

⑰ Newquay

More usually associated with fun-loving holidaymakers and weatherbeaten surfers, this North Cornish town nevertheless enjoys a considerable reputation as a site of supernatural goings-on. The north wing of nearby Trerice Manor, a splendid Tudor edifice built by the Arundel family in 1573, is reputedly home to the ghost of a young serving girl who took her own life after being made pregnant by the lord. Sightings of her are apparently accompanied by a sudden drop in temperature and a smell of lilac.

The original north wing, where 'wicked' Lord Arundel had his chambers, lay derelict for more than a century, allegedly because no one could bear to live in it. A short walk from the town, on the estuary of the River Gannel, locals speak of the 'Gannel Crake' – a terrifying screaming noise that is described as the cries of tormented souls.

Along the coast, the splendid Victorian Grade II listed Headland Hotel is said to echo with the voices of wounded RAF servicemen who were hospitalised there during the Second World War. At the 500-year-old Albion public house in nearby Crantock, the ghosts of a pirate smuggler and an old man pace the route of a secret tunnel that was built to connect the pub with the beach. Even the Newquay golf club is not immune from ghostly visitations – appearances include an old man who sits watchfully in the corner of the snooker room.

▶ *At end of A392, 8 miles W of A30 from Indian Queens junction.*

⑱ St Allen

This village near Truro is the setting for an odd tale of a little boy who wandered into a copse near his home to pick wild flowers. When his mother called him for supper, he was nowhere to be seen. Three days of frantic searching by the villagers ended when he was found sleeping peacefully at the place where his mother had last seen him. He appeared quite ignorant of the time that had elapsed. He said that while picking flowers, he had heard a bird singing so beautifully that he was compelled to follow it deep into the woods. Night fell and stars were shining. Suddenly he realised that each star was, in fact, a pisky. These fairy folk led the boy to a marvellous cave of crystal pillars studded with jewels of every colour. Here he was fed on the purest honey before the piskies sang him to sleep. When he awoke, he found himself back in the copse by his home.

▶ *On minor roads between A30 and A39, 4 miles N of Truro.*

⑲ Truro

It used to be the custom for wassailers in Truro to circulate the city at New Year, drinking beer or cider from a gaily decorated bowl in order to ward off evil spirits. The Old English word wassail means 'be of good cheer' and latterly the idea has been to collect money for charity. Less happy is the story of Comprigney, just outside the town. Reports of spectres and rattling chains are a grim reminder of the site's history – in Cornish, 'Gwel Cloghprenyer' means 'the field of the gibbet'.

Truro has its fair share of ghosts. The Wig & Pen pub is reputedly haunted by a young girl, phantom monks have been seen around the cathedral and uncarthly presences have been reported on both wharfsides, which were rough places in the days when Truro was a thriving port. Several murders were committed there.

▶ *At junction of A39 and A390.*

⑳ St Teath

Anne Jeffries was born here in 1626. At the age of 19, she went to work as a servant for the family of a Mr Moses Pitt. One day, while sitting in her employer's garden, she encountered a group of tiny men, whom she befriended. One of them touched her eyes and suddenly she found herself flying through space until she came to a strange and beautiful country. Returning at last to the garden, she found herself surrounded by the anxious household, who thought she had fallen into a fit.

This was the first of many meetings with the 'airy people', as she called them, who also taught her the arts of healing and herbal lore. Understandably, she was accused of witchcraft, and committed to Bodmin jail by the notorious Jan Tregeagle, then the local magistrate (see pages 10–11 and 23). She refused all food, saying the little people would feed her. Eventually she was still released for lack of evidence. Records of the trial and letters from Moses Pitt to the Bishop of Gloucester, describing her experiences, are in the Bodleian Library at Oxford.

▶ *Just W of A39, 7 miles NE of Wadebridge.*

SOUTH-WEST ENGLAND

㉑ St Nectan's Glen

A secluded waterfall cascades 12m (40ft) into a circular rock basin known locally as the Kieve. St Nectan, on his deathbed, threw his silver chapel bell into this torrent, and it vanished into the rocks. He vowed that it would reappear only when true religion had been restored to what, in the 5th century, was a dissident Church. His body, together with the sacramental plate, was placed in a chest, and this too was hidden beneath the rocks in the Kieve. Centuries later, miners tried to blast their way through to the treasure, but after many fruitless attempts they were astonished to hear the ringing of a silver bell. It was accompanied by a solemn voice that proclaimed, 'The child is not yet born who shall recover this treasure.' Work stopped immediately, and the fulfilment of St Nectan's prophecy is awaited still.

▶ *On footpath from Trethevey on B3263, 1½ miles NE of Tintagel.*

㉒ Tintagel

Uther Pendragon seduced the beautiful Igerna at Tintagel, and she later gave birth to the boy who became King Arthur. The region is steeped in Arthurian lore, but the castle was in fact built by Reginald of Cornwall, the illegitimate son of Henry I, in 1141 – long after the historical Arthur lived. At one time it belonged to the Black Prince, but by 1540 it was a ruin. Below the castle, in the echoing recesses of Merlin's Cave, the wizard's ghost is said to wander. A local belief is that Arthur himself lives on in the form of the Cornish chough, a bird that may occasionally be seen perched on the wave-lashed ledges of the cliffs.

▶ *On coast, 17 miles S of Bude, along B roads, 5 miles W of A39.*

㉓ Altarnun

The ancient village of Altarnun, a few miles west of Launceston, is named after the 5th-century saint, St Non (also 'Nun' and 'Nonna'). She was the mother of St David, the patron saint of Wales, who built a monastery there at a time when he was making his way to Britanny from Pembrokeshire. The entrance to the village church has one of the finest Celtic crosses in Cornwall, which may date back to the time of St Non herself. But a far greater mystery lies in the rectory fields, just a short walk away – a holy well that for centuries was said to cure the sick and the insane. In his 1602 *Survey of Cornwall*, Richard Carew writes of the well's use as a 'bowsenning pool' into which unfortunate 'frantic' individuals were plunged and then beaten until their symptoms subsided. After their ducking they were carried to the church for a service of thanksgiving to St Non. Ominously, Carew also mentions that persistent sufferers would be 'bowsenned again and again, while there remained in them any hope of recovery.'

▶ *Just N of Fivelanes junction on A30, 9 miles SW of Launceston.*

CENTRE OF
ARTHURIAN
LEGEND
TINTAGEL CASTLE

㉔ Rillaton

A burial mound at Rillaton on Bodmin Moor was plagued by a ghostly druid priest. The phantom would waylay any passer-by and offer him a magic potion from a golden cup that could never be drained. One day a drunken hunter threw the dregs in the spectre's face. Shortly afterwards, both the hunter and his horse were found dead at the bottom of a ravine. In 1837, workmen looking for building material opened a stone-lined vault and found it to contain a gold cup and a human skeleton. As treasure trove, the cup became the property of the crown and remained in use in the royal household until the death of George V in 1936. Then the Rillaton cup, as it became known, was loaned to the British Museum where it is now on display. It is thought to date from 1700–1500 BC.
▶ *On minor roads between B3254 and B3257, 7 miles NE of Liskeard.*

㉕ Talland

Parson Dodge, vicar of Talland in the early 18th century, enjoyed considerable local fame as an exorcist. His services were employed by the vicar of nearby Lanreath, who had been upset by the manifestation of a spectral coach with demon driver and headless horses. At the sight of Dodge, the demon wailed in terror and the entire equipage vanished for ever. Local people were afraid to approach Talland church at night for fear they should meet the parson driving evil spirits before him down Bridle Lane to the sea. It has been suggested that Dodge was actually in league with Polperro smugglers and that he encouraged the tales about himself to keep people away while contraband was moved.
▶ *On minor road, 1 mile S of A387, 2.5 miles W of Looe.*

㉖ Polperro

A cavern below Chapel Hill on the western side of the harbour is known as Willy Willcocks' Hole. Willy Willcocks was a fisherman. When exploring the cave, he lost his way in the maze of tunnels behind the entrance and his restless spirit still roams the passages seeking a means of escape, his cries mingling with the wind on dark nights.
▶ *On minor road, $^1/_2$ mile S from end of A387, 6 miles SW of Looe.*

㉗ Bodmin

There are few more atmospheric buildings in Cornwall than Bodmin Jail, constructed in 1776 during the reign of George III to house the country's most nefarious criminals, and the first jail in Britain to have fully walled single-person cells. Some 55 executions by hanging took place in Bodmin Jail, the last in 1909. In 1844 no less than 20,000 people packed themselves within the prison's walls to witness the public execution of Matthew Weeks for the murder of his girlfriend, Charlotte Dymond, although there is some doubt about whether he committed the crime. Charlotte's body was found at Roughtor, near Camelford, and her ghost is said to haunt the spot. Now the trial is re-enacted in Bodmin's restored court house, the Shire Hall, and the paying public acts as jury.

The last prisoner was released from Bodmin Jail in 1927, but during the Second World War both the Crown Jewels and the Domesday Book were taken there for safekeeping. Today the Jail welcomes visitors as a museum, bar and restaurant. As well as the cold spots and light anomalies that characterise haunted buildings, several groups of paranormal investigators have reported being scratched or bruised by small

PARANORMAL INVESTIGATORS HAVE REPORTED BEING BRUISED BY SMALL STONES
BODMIN JAIL

stones that appeared to be 'fired' out of the thick stone walls like air-rifle pellets. A team from the BBC found that the temperature of the walls was unusually high, suggesting that the phenomenon might be the result of some unknown heat source below the ground.

Nearby Lanhydrock House, a magnificent country mansion rebuilt in the 1880s after the original 17th-century manor house was destroyed in a terrible fire, is another favourite location for paranormal investigators. Among its most famous ghosts is a grey lady who is seen regularly in the Long Gallery and the Drawing Room. In 2004, a group of researchers who held an overnight vigil in the house reported that they had all experienced some form of supernatural occurrence by the time dawn broke.
▶ *Just W of A30, 7 miles SE of Wadebridge and 13 miles W of Liskeard.*

㉘ Bolventor

Immortalised in Daphne Du Maurier's 1936 novel of the same name, Jamaica Inn nestles within the brooding slopes of Bodmin Moor on the Launceston-Bodmin road. It was built as a coaching inn in the mid 18th century with money supplied by the local Trelawney family, two of whom had served as Governors of Jamaica. As well as providing shelter for many a traveller caught unawares by the Moor's unpredictable weather, the inn played host to plenty of less salubrious characters and was a notorious haunt of highwaymen, smugglers and other assorted villains until well into the 19th century.

The inn's chequered past and remote location have since helped it to acquire a reputation as an eerie, haunted place, and the fact that it is now popular with tourists has done nothing to diminish its uncanny atmosphere. Among Jamaica Inn's most famous ghosts is that of a young sailor who sits on a wall gazing warily at vistiors before vanishing into thin air. Legend has it that he was summoned outside one night by a stranger and his lifeless body was found on the Moor the following day. Reports of heavy footsteps on the staircases and landings, invisibly slammed doors and inexplicable knocking sounds are too many to be dismissed. Room number 5 appears to be especially prone to ghostly visitations and is a favourite overnight stay for couples with an interest in the supernatural. Amateur ghost-hunters regularly record 'orbs' – light anomalies visible only on digital video and still cameras – and the sudden drops in temperature that are said to presage the presence of a spirit.
▶ *On A30 as it crosses Bodmin Moor, 10 miles NE of Bodmin.*

TRISTAN AND ISEULT

DURING THE 6th CENTURY, Cornwall was ruled by a villainous king named Mark. While reluctantly seeking a wife, Mark found a long golden hair and vowed to marry the girl to whom it belonged. He sent his nephew Tristan on a quest to find the maiden, and Tristan set sail for Ireland.

Years before, Tristan had been wounded in combat with the Irish king's brother-in-law and was secretly nursed back to health by Iseult the Fair, the king's daughter. Now, on his return to Ireland, the young warrior slayed a troublesome dragon. So grateful was the king, he promised Tristan his daughter's hand in marriage. But the golden hair belonged to Iseult, and ever dutiful, Tristan prepared to take her back to Cornwall as his uncle's bride. On the voyage, Tristan and Iseult mistakenly drank a love potion intended for Iseult and Mark, binding them even closer together. Although Iseult married Mark, the lovers met in secret. Eventually, though, they decided Iseult should honour her marriage vows, and she assumed her place by Mark as queen.

Years later, Tristan was again wounded in battle. Now married in a new kingdom, he nevertheless sent for Iseult to nurse him and told his messenger to hoist a white sail on the returning ship if she was on board, and a black one if not. As the ship approached, his jealous wife told him she could see only a black sail, whereupon Tristan died. Iseult, on arrival, died of a broken heart. At Castle Dore near Fowey, possibly the site of Mark's castle, an ancient stone marks Tristan's grave.

BODMIN MOOR

㉙ Bodmin Moor

Confronted by the wild and windswept granite tors of Bodmin Moor, it is easy for the casual tourist to imagine all manner of strange apparitions lurking in the shadows of its countless streams and rocky outcrops. The area's small farmers, however, who eke a living from the stony soil, are not normally given to flights of fancy. So it came as some surprise when sightings of a large wild animal – quickly dubbed the 'Beast of Bodmin Moor' – first hit the local newspaper headlines in the summer of 1983. Described as being 'dark and panther-like', with a body between 1–1.5m (3–5ft) long, the animal appeared to have much in common with other British big-cat sightings, notably the so-called 'Surrey Puma' (see page 77), which allegedly stalked the Home Counties during the 1960s.

By the early 1990s, numerous sightings of the Beast, together with the remains of livestock that it had allegedly taken as prey, prompted the Ministry of Agriculture, Fisheries and Food to launch an investigation. In July 1995, the report concluded that 'no evidence of such a beast existed'. In the same year, the skull of a puma found in the local River Fowey was examined by the Natural History Museum in London, who decided that it had been stripped from a puma-skin rug and was probably a hoax.

Yet the sightings continued, culminating in the release of a 20 second video in 1998 that clearly shows a black, cat-like creature roaming across the Moor's heather-strewn slopes. According to local Newquay zookeeper Mike Thomas, it is 'the best evidence yet' that some unknown species of big cat is at large in the area. Thomas believes that the creatures could be the descendents of wild cats that escaped captivity as long ago as Roman times and have subsequently lived undetected. Others think that a more likely explanation for the Beasts lies in the one-time fashion for exotic pets that resulted in a number of big cats and reptiles being released into the wild during the 1960s and '70s after their owners found them too much to handle.

Meanwhile, Moor-dwellers dismiss suggestions that their sheep have been taken by semi-wild dogs as 'utter rubbish'. 'It has a foul scream like a woman's,' reported local farmer Rosemary Rhodes, who claimed to have lost ten ewes to the Beast out of a flock of 100. 'You'll know when the Beast's there,' insisted her neighbour, John Goodenough. 'There'll be no rabbits or foxes about and the birds stop singing. That's the call for caution.'

▶ *Lies both sides of A30 as it runs between Launceston and Bodmin.*

㉚ Goonzion Downs

With a mining tradition dating back to the Bronze Age and a golden age of tin mining that lasted from the Middle Ages until the 19th century, it is hardly surpising that myths and legends of haunted mines abound in Cornwall. In common with ancient mining communities around the world, these supernatural occurrences are often attributed to impish mine spirits – known collectively in Cornwall as 'Knockers'. Described in legend as thin-limbed and hook-nosed, the Knockers were thought to be largely benevolent and would often guide miners to a new lode by tapping out a code on the rock. One long-disused tunnel at the Goonzion Mine on Bodmin Moor acquired the nickname 'The Roaring Shaft' after numerous bangs, cracks and other mysterious noises were heard emanating from it. The sounds were said to be a warning from a local group of Knockers, the Kobolds. They were not considered to be dangerous unless a tinner upset them. Whistling would offend them and bring ill luck. If their favours were not rewarded with food or tallow, the offender might find himself in bad trouble. On one occasion, Tom Trevorrow, a confirmed sceptic, refused to share his meal with the Knockers – the following morning, his tools were crushed beneath a fall of rock and he was nearly killed. Misfortune continued to dog him until he left the mines.

At Wheal Vor, near Helston, the spectre of a white hare would appear before an accident, and in many mines a spectral hand would clasp the ladder as a miner climbed down the shaft. This, too, was a warning of imminent misfortune.

▶ *Goonzion Downs lie just W of St Neot on a minor road N of A38, 9 miles E of Bodmin.*

㉛ Dozmary Pool

The ghost of Jan Tregeagle was doomed to empty this supposedly bottomless lake with a perforated limpet shell (see pages 10–11). He was kept at his work by a pack of headless demon hounds, waiting to carry him off if he ever ceased his labours. Now they pursue him relentlessly as he runs away across Bodmin Moor, shrieking in rage and torment.

Several hot, dry summers have exposed Dozmary's granite bed, dispelling the myth that it's bottomless, but the pool is still regarded as the domain of the Lady of Lake, guardian of King Arthur's sword. It was into these dark waters that Sir Bedivere flung Excalibur, and from here that King Arthur began his journey to Avalon.

▶ *Beside minor road, 2 miles S of Bolventor, on A30 running across Bodmin Moor.*

SOUTHWEST ENGLAND

DEVON

The peaceful green countryside and coastal attractions of glorious Devon are belied by the abundance of supernatural activity that is witnessed there, from wailing apparitions to UFOs.

❶ Lundy Island

Before the lighthouses on Lundy were automated in the 1990s, keepers often reported seeing a young girl walking dangerously near the cliff edge. She is supposed to be a widow who threw herself from the cliffs when her husband died.

During most of its early history Lundy was occupied by a succession of piratical owners who preyed upon Bristol-bound ships. This freebooting tradition continued into the early years of the 19th century when the lease-holder, Thomas Benson, offloaded shipments of tobacco there to avoid import duty. When he obtained the government contract for transporting convicts to the colonies, many got no farther than Lundy, where they were used as slaves in construction projects and on the land. Having insured an old brigantine, Benson unloaded her cargo on Lundy before scuttling the vessel within sight of another ship. He collected the insurance, but was betrayed by a drunken sailor and spent the rest of his life in exile.

▶ *11 miles off Hartland Point, in Bristol Channel. Sea crossings from Bideford and Ilfracombe in summer, helicopter service from Hartland Point in winter.*

❷ Woolacombe

Sir William de Tracy, one of the four knights who murdered St Thomas Becket at Canterbury, lived at Mortehoe, near Woolacombe. After his sensational crime, numerous legends associated with the family began to circulate in the surrounding villages. At Woolacombe, his ghost endlessly attempts to spin a rope from sand. If he seems likely to succeed, a black dog appears with a ball of fire in its mouth and burns through the flimsy cord. In rough weather, Sir William is said to ride up and down the sands wailing, in accordance with the saying that the Tracys 'had ever the wind and the rain in their faces'.

▶ *At end of B3343, 4 miles W of A361, 2 miles S of Ilfracombe.*

❸ Exmoor

All over the world, people associate Exmoor with R.D. Blackmore's novel *Lorna Doone*, the story of an outlaw family that terrorised the district in the 17th century, and of the heroic farmer, John Ridd, who defeated them. Fiction and fact have become intertwined, for the real Doones were equally villainous. Having been expelled from Perthshire in 1620, they settled in a ruined Celtic monastery on Exmoor and made a living by blackmail and extortion. Oare Church is still pointed out as the place where Lorna Doone was shot on her wedding day, although no one seems to know whether the incident was based on fact or not. Another character in the novel, who certainly existed, was the highwayman, Tom Faggus. Born at South Mokon and hanged at Taunton, Faggus had a horse that was so well trained it was believed to be his familiar spirit. Some said that Faggus would never have been captured if his horse had not been shot first. As for John Ridd, whether fictional or not, several local people still claim descent from him.

▶ *Exmoor lies S of the A39 which runs along the N coast of Devon and Somerset. Oare Church is on minor roads just S of A39, 5 miles E of Lynton.*

❹ Chittlehampton

At the eastern end of the North Devon village of Chittlehampton lies a well that is associated with the shrine of St Urith, a christian martyr who was cut to pieces with scythes by Saxon villagers early in the 8th century at the instigation of her stepmother. Her remains disappeared from the local church during the Reformation of the 16th century, by which time the cult of St Urith was prevalent throughout Devon and Cornwall and the sick came from miles around to be cured by the healing waters of the well. Water from it is still presented in church on St Urith's Day, July 8.

▶ *Just N of B3227, which runs between A361 and A377, 8 miles SE of Barnstaple.*

THE WELL OF ST URITH

ST URITH, CHITTLEHAMPTON

⑤ Axminster

Now a ruin, Newnham Abbey was founded by Reginald de Mohun in 1247. Ten years later, as he lay dying, he dreamt of a boy 'more radiant than the sun' who walked from the abbey font to its altar. This dream was believed to represent de Mohun's saintliness and his acceptance into the next world. Confirmation of this was received 75 years later when the paving over his grave was removed for repair. Beneath the stones lay his body, perfectly preserved and exuding a fragrant odour. Several medieval saints were reputedly distinguished by this sweet, floral aroma, which became known as the 'odour of sanctity'.

▶ *At junction of A35 and A358, 10 miles E of Honiton. Newnham Abbey is SW of the town centre.*

⑥ Uplyme

A cottage in the village was once plagued by the phantom of a large black dog. One day, in desperation, the farm worker who lived there took a poker and chased the ghost into his attic where it leapt through the roof. Hitting at the thatch, the man discovered a hoard of Stuart coins. With his new-found wealth, he bought another house in the village and converted it into an inn, naming it 'The Black Dog' in gratitude to his ghostly benefactor. The inn is now a B&B, and the dog continues to haunt the neighbourhood, particularly the lane behind the inn. Its last recorded appearance was in 1959, when it was seen by three holidaymakers simultaneously one evening.

▶ *On B3165 1 mile NW of Lyme Regis.*

WAS FAMED FOR HEALING
CHITTLEHAMPTON

❼ Southleigh

By the crossroads to Beer and Southleigh, on the south side of the A3052, stands the Hangman's Stone. The story goes that a sheep-stealer once came past carrying a heavy carcass on a rope over his shoulder. The weight had made him so weary that he decided to take a rest in this quiet spot. Setting the dead sheep on the stone, he sat down with his back against the rock. He fell asleep and, as he slept, the carcass slipped off the stone and pulled the cord tight around the thief's neck, strangling him to death.

▶ *Hangman's Stone is at junction of A3052 and B3174, 9 miles W of Lyme Regis. Southleigh is on minor road 2 miles N of junction.*

❽ Exeter

In 1941, an air raid reduced much of the old part of the city to rubble. Fortunately, the cathedral survived, although it was badly damaged, and repairs were begun as early as 1943. While these were being carried out, an extraordinary collection of wax models was discovered in a cavity on top of the stone screen surrounding the choir. They included representations of human and animal limbs, part of a horse's head and the complete figure of a woman. Almost certainly, these were votive offerings that were once placed on the tomb of Bishop Edmund Lacy, who died in 1455. During his lifetime, the bishop was said to have shown much saintliness and, after he died, sick pilgrims used to kneel by his tomb to pray for recovery, either for themselves or for their sick animals. As a mark of faith, they would leave behind them a wax image of the ailing limb or animal. At the Reformation in 1538, the zealous dean cleared the cathedral of all images and relics. These wax offerings probably survived because some faithful pilgrim deliberately hid them. They are now kept in the cathedral library.

Just outside the city is the well and chapel of St Sidwell, who was martyred in the 6th century. The story goes that her stepmother coveted some land the girl had inherited and bribed two harvesters to murder her. As she knelt in prayer in a field, they decapitated her with scythes and, where her head fell, a spring gushed forth.

▶ *Off Junction 30 of M5, 80 miles SW of Bristol. The parish of St Sidwell is NE of the city centre.*

EXETER CATHEDRAL

9 Dawlish

In February 1855, the seaside town of Dawlish and its surrounding countryside became the scene of one of the most baffling mysteries in the history of South Devon. The town awoke after a heavy snowfall to discover thousands upon thousands of cloven hoofprints stretching in every direction, appearing to pass through solid walls and haystacks as well as over the roofs of barns and outbuildings. A set of prints was even seen to stop at the River Exe and continue on the other bank, as if the creature who made them had walked across the water (which was not frozen at the time).

Local clergymen decided that the prints were the work of the devil, while scientists struggled to find a more rational explanation. The prints were all set 21.5cm (8½in) apart and alternated in a way that suggested a bipedal, rather than a four-legged, animal. Hopes of finding an answer were briefly raised when a zookeeper in nearby Sidmouth announced that 'several kangaroos' had recently escaped, but in fact the prints bore no resemblance to kangaroo tracks.

Another theory held that the prints were made by the trailing ropes of a stray balloon that had somehow made its way over the town during the night, yet no balloon was ever found. Sir Richard Owen, a distinguished biologist and one of the founders of London's Natural History Museum, maintained that the prints were nothing more than badger tracks that had become distorted as the snow thawed and then froze again, although he was at a loss to explain why there were so many tracks, scattered over so wide an area.

Similar phenomena have been recorded in other parts of the world, where they are nearly always associated with electrical storms. Perhaps the 'Devil's Footprints', as they are known, were indeed the work of a freak atmospheric condition that has yet to be explained.

▶ *On A379 14 miles S of Exeter.*

10 Milber

Reverend William Keble Martin took charge of this new parish near Newton Abbot in 1931, despite there being no permanent church. One night, the curate dreamt of a strange church that had three naves converging fan-wise towards the altar, so that the whole congregation had an uninterrupted view of the sacrament. An architect told Keble Martin that the scheme was feasible and the church was built to this unique design. It has been known ever since as 'The Dream Church'.

▶ *Just E of A380, 1 mile SE of Newton Abbot.*

11 Berry Pomeroy

This rambling and ruined castle was once the home of the powerful Pomeroy family, who settled there shortly after the Norman Conquest. Legend says that for the Pomeroys' part in the religious rebellion in 1549, Edward VI ordered that the castle's fortifications should be reduced. The family refused to obey and when royal troops arrived to enforce the order, two Pomeroy brothers put on their armour, blindfolded their horses, and rode over the ramparts to their deaths.

The story is told of two medieval Pomeroy sisters, Eleanor and Margaret. Both loved the same man and Eleanor, insanely jealous of her beautiful sister, imprisoned Margaret and starved her to death. Margaret's ghost is said to walk the ramparts and anyone who sees her will die shortly afterwards.

Another ghost that is supposed to presage death is the spectre of a 13th-century woman – a Pomeroy – who had an incestuous relationship with her father. It is said that because she smothered her child, her troubled spirit can find no rest.

▶ *1 mile E of Totnes on minor road N of A385.*

12 Totnes

A curious legend tells that Brutus, the leader of the survivors of the Trojan garrison, got as far as England. He sailed up the River Dart, stepped ashore on a rock and announced to all who cared to listen:

Here I am and here I rest,
And this town shall be called Totnes.

He found the country around to be inhabited by giants, and having captured a pair of them, named Gog and Magog, he took the two to London where they stood guard outside his palace. Effigies of these two giants still stand in the Guildhall, replacements for earlier figures that were destroyed by fire during the Second World War. The Brutus Stone – the stone on which the Trojan leader is supposed to have stood to proclaim his arrival – is set into the pavement in Fore Street, Totnes, near the East Gate.

▶ *At junction of A385 and A381, 6 miles W of Paignton.*

⓭ Torbay

On May 26, 2004, Torquay's local media were flooded with reports from residents of the Torbay area claiming to have seen a cigar-shaped object floating in the sky. One witness even managed to capture footage of the sighting on his mobile phone. The absence of clouds in the sky at the time helped observers to pick out the object, but made it hard to estimate its size. Some estimates put it at about 60m (200ft) in length. Data released under the Freedom of Information Act by the Ministry of Defence shows that there have been 12 reported sightings of UFOs in Torbay since 1998.

▶ *Reached from A380, 25 miles S of Exeter.*

⓮ Brixham

On April 28, 1967, the coastguard on Berry Head reported a mysterious flying object, which later hovered over the town at a height of around 490m (1,600ft) for about an hour. Since it appeared just before midday, observers were able to see it in detail, and the sighting is well documented. The UFO was described as huge and dome-shaped, with a door in the side. Eventually, it climbed rapidly and vanished.

▶ *S end of Tor Bay, 7 miles S of Torquay.*

⓯ Buckfastleigh

Overlooking Buckfast Abbey, perched on an outcrop of rock at the summit of a flight of 196 steps, stand the ruins of Holy Trinity church. A short distance away, a large and mysterious-looking building has a four-way pent roof and no apparent opening within its walls save for a grille of iron bars, behind which lies a tomb covered by a great stone slab. The tomb is the final resting place of Squire Richard Cabell, a 17th-century local nobleman who, in addition to being inordinately fond of hunting, had such a reputation for cruelty and immorality that he was said to have sold his soul to the Devil. When Cabell died on July 5, 1677, he was interred to the sound of a pack of ghostly hounds baying for him from across the wilds of Dartmoor. From that time onwards, on the anniversary of his death, Cabell is said to lead the phantom beasts across the moor in search of his lost soul. Local villagers constructed the 'pent house' around the tomb in a vain attempt to keep Cabell's demonic spirit at bay, but apparently to no avail.

During the 19th century, the lonely church allegedly became the haunt of grave-robbers until the spire was struck by lightning. In 1884, it was fully restored, only to be seriously damaged again in a fire five years later. During the Second World War, the church lost many of its stained-glass windows to a blast from a stray German bomb. And in 1992 it was completely destroyed in another fire, which, according to local rumour, was started by Satanists during a ritual at the tomb.

Almost directly beneath the tomb lies a system of caves in which is located the 'Little Man' – a joined-up stalactite and stalagmite that bears an uncanny resemblance to a Satanic figure that is thought to represent Cabell himself. The exploits of the evil squire may also have been the inspiration behind Sir Arthur Conan Doyle's famous Sherlock Holmes story *The Hound of the Baskervilles*.

▶ *On A38, 22 miles SW of Buckfastleigh. Buckfast Abbey and ruins of Holy Trinity church are N of the town centre.*

⓰ Dartmoor

Separated by a broad band of Devonshire farming country, the uplands of Dartmoor and Exmoor are quite different in character. Dartmoor is a craggy inland plateau of rough moorland, treacherous bogs and rocky outcrops, while Exmoor curves gently across heather and pasture, to drop steeply from over 300m (1,000ft) to the sea.

In a remote northern part of Dartmoor lies Cranmere Pool. Now drained, it was once a notorious bog to which evil spirits were consigned. The most famous of these was Bengie Geare, a former mayor of Okehampton, whose phantom still makes occasional appearances, in the guise of a black pony.

On Fox Tor, Childe's Tomb marks the place where a 10th-century Saxon noble died. Lost in a blizzard, he cut open his dead horse and crawled inside for warmth. Before he expired, he wrote his will in the horse's blood on a nearby rock.

▶ *Lies NE of Plymouth, roughly bounded by A386, A30 and A38. B3212 runs across the moor from Moretonhampstead in the NE to Yelverton in the SW.*

⓱ River Dart

According to superstition, the swift-flowing River Dart claims one human life each year. Understandably, a drowning in early spring removed a great deal of anxiety from the rest of the community. A local rhyme goes:

'River Dart, River of Dart:
Every year thou claimest a heart.'

Moorland travellers might be plagued by pixies, which were believed to disorientate people deliberately so that they would fall into one of the many bogs that riddle the moor.

▶ *Rising at the centre of Dartmoor, the river flows SE through Postbridge and Bellever to meet its western branch at Dartmeet. It flows on through Buckfastleigh and Totnes to the sea at Dartmouth.*

⓲ Postbridge

Motorists and cyclists are advised to beware while traversing the lonely stretch of the B3212 from Two Bridges to Postbridge on Dartmoor, in case a pair of ghostly hands covered in thick hair seize control of their vehicle and force them off the road. The legend of the 'Hairy Hands' may sound far-fetched, but tales of their appearance were remarkably persistent throughout the early part of the last century. The tales began in the early 1900s, with reports that cyclists' handlebars had been wrenched away from them, causing them to crash. In 1921, a doctor from Princeton was killed and his children pitched out of his motorcycle's sidecar in an apparently inexplicable accident. A few months later an Army officer reported that his motorcycle had been forced off the road by 'hairy, muscular hands' that clamped themselves over his own. In 1925, the tale took an even more sinister turn when a woman staying in a caravan beside the road reportedly woke up to find a dismembered hand clawing at the window. The very next day, a car was found in a ditch nearby with its driver dead at the wheel.

▶ *5 miles NE of Princeton on B3212, running SW to NE over Dartmoor.*

DARTMOOR'S ROCKY OUTCROPS

⑲ Yelverton

Hanging on the wall of Buckland Abbey near Yelverton is a drum belonging to the great Elizabethan sailor, Sir Francis Drake, who took it with him on his voyages around the world in the *Golden Hinde* between 1577 and 1580. The drum is said to contain Drake's soul and to beat spontaneously at momentous times in the nation's maritime history. It was allegedly heard when the Pilgrim Fathers left Plymouth for America, when Nelson was given the freedom of the City of Plymouth, when Napoleon was briefly a prisoner in the city, en route to St Helena, and, most recently, in 1940 when the British army was successfully evacuated from the beaches of Dunkirk. The drum at Buckland is the subject of a famous poem by Sir Henry Newbolt, and survived the blaze that partly destroyed Buckland Abbey in 1938.
▶ *On A386 10 miles N of Plymouth.*

⑳ Tavistock

Fitzford Gate is all that remains of an ancient mansion that once stood on the west side of the town. Several times a year, the ghost of Lady Howard is supposed to ride out from the gate in her coach of bones, drawn by headless horses and preceded by a black hound with one eye in its forehead. This gruesome cortege travels to Okehampton church where the coach stops and Lady Howard descends. She picks a blade of grass from the churchyard, presses it sadly to her bosom, and then rides back to Fitzford Gate. The reason for this curious pilgrimage is said to be that Lady Howard, who was born in 1596 and was twice widowed before she reached the age of 16, murdered all four of her husbands. The legend can be no more than three-quarters true at best, since her fourth husband outlived her.
▶ *At junction of A386 and A390 to W of Dartmoor.*

㉑ Chagford

A ghostly echo of the English Civil War is to be found at the Three Crowns Hotel in Chagford – a building that is believed to date back to the 13th century. The ghost in question is that of a 33-year-old Cavalier named Sydney Godolphin, whose family were among King Charles I's most ardent supporters. Godolphin

was the MP for Helston in Cornwall, but he made an unlikely soldier. A noted romantic poet, he was described by his commander as being 'as absolute a piece of virtue as ever our Nation bred'. On the night of February 7, 1643, a party of Royalist horsemen waylaid a troop of Parliamentary soldiers who were staying at the Three Crowns, and in the ensuing skirmish, Godolphin took a bullet in the leg. He died on the stone floor of the porch. His ghostly likeness has been seen many times since then, most notably in 1980, when his appearance at the dining-room door caused a surprised chef to drop a large tray of food.

Down the road, at the Whiddon Park Guest House, another tragic tale concerns a bride who was murdered there by a former suitor on her wedding day – July 10. Dressed in black, she can still be seen at the entrance to the bedroom where the murder took place on the anniversary of her death.
▶ *On B3206 1 1/2 miles from A382, 12 miles SE of Okehampton.*

OKEHAMPTON CASTLE

㉓ Shebbear

In the village square, beneath an ancient oak, rests a large boulder. Every November 5, the church bell-ringers assemble by the stone and, using crowbars, lever it until it turns over. Then they return to the church and ring a peal on its bells. One reason for this is that Satan was once thought to lie beneath the stone, and the ritual ensures that he is kept down for another 12 months. The Shebbear stone is said to have been the foundation stone of Henscott church across the River Torridge, but the Devil moved it.

▶ *On minor roads between A386 and A388, 12 miles S of Bideford.*

㉒ Okehampton

Situated on Dartmoor, just off the road from Okehampton to the Army Camp, and marked by the remains of a heavily weathered granite cross, Fitz's Well is shrouded in mystery. Legend has it that the cross was erected by a grateful couple who had been 'piskie led' – led astray on the Moor by the fairy folk – until they drank at the well and broke the spell. A more likely explanation is that the well was the work of 16th-century local lawyer Sir John Fitz, who also has a similar well named after him near Tavistock (also called Fice's Well). The cross may have originally belonged to St Michael's Chapel at Halstock, which is believed to have fallen into disrepair at around the same time.

▶ *Just off A30 to the N of Dartmoor.*

㉔ North Tawton

Bathe Pool is a grassy hollow in a privately owned field near Cottle's Wood. At times of national crisis, or when a public figure is about to die, the usually dry hollow allegedly fills with water. The phenomenon has been reported on several occasions. Apparently, it prophesied the deaths of Nelson, Wellington and Edward VII, and was seen just before the First World War. The town gets its name from the River Taw, which is Celtic for 'silent river'.

▶ *1 mile N of A3072, 7 miles E of junction with A386, 6 miles N of Okehampton.*

㉕ Zeal Monachorum

The home of the Oxenham family, this village sprang to fame in 1635 when, during an outbreak of disease, all Oxenhams who were not going to recover were visited by a bird with a white breast, which fluttered over their beds. Previous deaths had been marked by similar instances, when the bird was seen nearby, and Charles Kingsley used the occurrence in his book *Westward Ho!* The bird appeared to dying Oxenhams on several occasions during the 20th century, and does not seem to be confined to Devon. On one occasion, it was seen in Kensington, West London.

▶ *On minor roads between A377 and A3072, 16 miles NW of Exeter.*

SOUTHWEST ENGLAND

SATAN WAS HELD AT BAY BY THE SHEBBEAR STONE
SHEBBEAR

DORSET

Behind the Heritage coastline, which stretches from Lyme Regis to Christchurch, lies Thomas Hardy's Wessex, a county rich in archaeological sites, unspoilt countryside and ghostly visitations.

❶ Shaftesbury

In this ancient hilltop town, where King Canute died in 1035, stand the remains of a ruined abbey. Shortly before the Dissolution in 1539, the last abbess is said to have ordered a monk to hide the abbey treasures. Only he knew their whereabouts, but before he could tell the abbess, he had a stroke and took his secret with him to the grave. To this day, no one has ever found the treasure, but the monk's ghost has often been seen walking round the abbey before vanishing through a wall. Perhaps he is still trying to find the abbess to tell her where the treasure is hidden. The ghost is invisible from the knees downwards, which may suggest that ground level was once lower than at present.

▶ *At junction of A350 and A30, 11 miles N of Blandford Forum.*

❷ Kingston

An 18th-century inn situated in this small village is said to be haunted. The Scott Arms' ghost is that of an old woman who has been seen sitting with her back to the bar after closing time, drinking from a mug. During the summer of 1970, a couple staying at the inn saw her hazy figure standing at the foot of their bed. No one knows who the ghost is.

▶ *5 miles W of Swanage on B3069.*

❸ Blandford Forum

The ancient market town of Blandford Forum is home to a number of ghosts, some of which are still making their presence felt. At the Crown Hotel, a woman in a black crinoline dress can be observed pacing the upstairs corridors. A member of the cleaning staff once saw her disappear into a room that was subsequently found to be empty. Meanwhile, the ghost of a highwayman is said to haunt the hotel's courtyard. Over at the neighbouring Nelson's Ale House, the troubled spirit of a woman once incarcerated in the building has been known to propel bottles across the room, and children's voices are heard to emanate from the upstairs. At the nearby Army Royal Signals Museum, a ghost called Mary is thought to be responsible for a wide range of supernatural activity. She is believed to be the spirit of a young girl who was due to marry an American serviceman during the Second World War, but who was murdered on the eve of her wedding close to the place where the Museum now stands. Curiously, the ghost was previously known as 'Fred'.

▶ *24 miles NE of Bournemouth at junction of A350 and A354.*

❹ Badbury Rings

Sited on a hilltop within the grounds of Kingston Lacy House are the concentric earthworks of the Iron Age hillfort known as Badbury Rings. Recent excavations show the area to have been inhabited for almost 10,000 years, but it is traditionally known as the place where the legendary Celtic king Arthur defeated the invading Saxons in the 6th century.

The hill has always been popular with lovers, whose trysts in more recent times have been disturbed by a variety of phantoms and ghostly beings. Among them is a dwarf-like creature with a hideously disfigured face who has a habit of peering into cars parked in the field at the entrance to the rings. There have also been reports of the sound of ghostly soldiers fighting, and of a scar-faced warrior on horseback who chases away night-time visitors to the site.

Meanwhile, on the nearby Wimborne road, the phantom of a gigantic Irish Wolfhound is said to spring out in the path of unsuspecting drivers in a bid to find its lost master. The 'Shapwick Monster', a legend associated with the neighbouring village of the same name, has

a more plausible explanation. The story goes that the body of the 'monster' was discovered after a travelling fishmonger had set up his stall in the area. It turned out to be a particularly fine example of a king crab, which in spite of their proximity to the sea, none of the villagers had ever seen before!

▶ *Off B3082 6 miles SE of Blandford Forum.*

❺ Wimborne Minster

The ruin of Knowlton church, a few miles North of Wimborne Minster, is one of the most atmospheric places in Dorset, not to mention reputedly one of the most haunted. The church was originally constructed in the 12th century within the earthworks of a Bronze Age Neolithic fort dating back to roughly the same time as Stonehenge. As a result, the church is surrounded by a ditch, which legend states is there to keep the spirits in, rather than intruders out, and may have been built with stones taken from a henge that once stood on the site. The village of Knowlton thrived until the late 15th century, when the Black Death finally reached it, wiping out the inhabitants. The church remained in use until the 18th century, after which it fell into disrepair. Countless stories are told of supernatural occurrences, both inside and outside the building. One involves the ghostly tolling of the bell, which was stolen and either sent to one of the neighbouring villages or accidentally dropped in the river.

▶ *Knowlton church is 7 miles N of Wimborne Minster on B3078.*

A GHOSTLY BELL TOLLS IN THE TOWER
KNOWLTON CHURCH

❻ Poole

When it received its charter from the Earl of Salisbury in 1248, this town was an important fishing and trading port.
The earl's name is immortalised in the small, disused lock-up or prison still called 'The Salisbury', situated near the Georgian Customs House. In 1965, it was a new shop in the High Street that was the scene of a suspected haunting – frightened customers ran out after seeing objects being moved by some invisible agency. Another haunting was reported in 1966 during alterations to the Crown Hotel. A piano repeatedly sounded a single note, and heavy but invisible objects were dragged about the upper floors. Later, three witnesses saw a 'fluorescent mist' drift across the stable-yard.

In the same area, the road to Upton is said to be haunted. Four headless men are alleged to carry a coffin along the road and then disappear through the hedgerow.
▶ *S of A35, 6 miles W of Bournemouth.*

❼ Studland Bay

Sailors anchored in the Bay who venture ashore for a well-earned pint at the nearby Bankes Arms pub had best beware of the apparition that appeared on the path leading up from the beach on two separate occasions in August 2004 and August 2008. Two completely independent groups of people both insist that they encountered a woman in a white jacket and trousers with hair down to her shoulders, who announced that 'she had just been for a swim' before melting away before their eyes. The uncanny similarities between the two sets of stories defy all rational explanation.

The Bankes Arms is a quaint old building, little changed for 100 years or more. Its history includes a landlord suspected of involvement in smuggling, which flourished in the area in the 19th century.
▶ *N of village of Studland on B3351 3 miles N of Swanage. Ferry from Sandbanks, 5 miles SW of Bournemouth.*

HOME TO A PHANTOM LEGION

❽ St Alban's Head

High on the cliffs of the Isle of Purbeck stands St Aldhelm's Chapel, a building with tragic origins that became known as the 'Devil's Chapel'. Apparently, in 1140 a bride and groom were sailing around the headland watched by the bride's father when a storm blew up and the boat capsized. The desolate father built the chapel in memory of the drowned couple, and decreed that a light was always to be left burning there as a warning to sailors.

In more recent times, it may be that the chapel earned its Satanic soubriquet due to the work of wreckers, who allegedly enticed unwary mariners onto the rocks.

Local traditions suggest that a girl can find a husband by dropping a pin through a hole in the pillar supporting the roof, and that wishes may be granted by sticking a pin in the wall.
▶ *Access from South West Coast Path, 6 miles SW of Swanage.*

❾ Flower's Barrow

The site of a fine defensive Iron Age earthwork, Flower's Barrow lies at the western end of the Purbeck Hills. The strategic importance of the place led the Romans to establish a fort there, and some maintain that the garrison continues to carry out its duties. In 1678, a phantom legion was seen marching along the Ridgeway, and it has been reported on several occasions since then, usually in times of national crisis. One such sighting occurred just before 1939, and the ghostly columns were seen several times during the Second World War. The last sighting was in 1970, when an old lady saw the legion at Knowle Hill, near Corfe.
▶ *Reach on foot from South West Coast Path, 1 mile S of East Lulworth on B3070, 6 miles SW of Wareham.*

❿ Wool

Woolbridge Manor, a Jacobean house that stands by the River Frome, was once the property of the Turberville family. The story goes that a spectral coach-and-four drives from the manor at twilight, but can be seen only by those of Turberville blood, for whom it foretells disaster. Some years ago, the driver of a local bus refused to move his vehicle until 'this there coach be gone through they there doors'. For the legend to be correct, the bus driver must have had Turberville antecedents.

Thomas Hardy adapted the family name for his novel *Tess of the D'Urbervilles*, in which Tess believes she has seen the coach, and disaster does indeed follow.
▶ *5 miles W of Wareham on A352.*

⓫ Bovington Camp

At the Armoured Vehicle Museum at Bovington Camp, staff have frequently reported seeing the ghost of a German tank commander whose Tiger tank is one of the most popular exhibits. Down in the village, Clouds Hill Cottage was the last home of Colonel T.E. Lawrence – better known as Lawrence of Arabia – who was killed in a road accident nearby. It is said that the sound of his Brough Superior motorcycle can still be heard in the surrounding lanes on the anniversary of his death on May 19, 1935. The Antelope public house in nearby Dorchester, a favourite of Lawrence's, also reports having a ghost of the famous First World War hero, dressed in his motorcycling gear.
▶ *On minor road 1 mile N of A352, 4 miles W of Wareham.*

SOUTH-WEST ENGLAND

⑫ Moigns Down, Holworth

One of the most famous UFO sightings in Britain took place in October 1967, when a local man named Brooks got caught in a force 8 gale while out walking his two dogs. Having taken shelter in a hollow, Mr Brooks stared up and noticed a strange craft in the sky, which he described as circular, with one 'girder' pointing forwards like a fuselage and three similar girders pointing to the rear. As he watched, the girders rearranged themselves to form a cross shape around a central disc, which began spinning. After about 20 minutes, the girders resumed their original position and the craft sped off. According to Mr Brooks's eye surgeon, who had recently given him a cornea implant, the phenomenon could be explained by a tiny piece of skin travelling across his eye. Yet, strangely, two days earlier, two Devon policemen had reported following a cross-shaped flying object for several miles in their car, as it travelled above the countryside bordering Devon and Dorset.
▶ *On minor road 1 mile S of A352, 11 miles W of Wareham.*

⑬ Bincombe

Bincombe Hill and Bincombe Down were extensively settled during the Stone and Bronze Ages, evidence of which is provided by the many burial mounds, or barrows, in the district. However, tradition insists that these hillocks, known locally as the Music Barrows, are actually the houses of the fairy folk, and anyone putting an ear to the top of one of them at midday may hear the sound of a fairy orchestra.
▶ *1 mile E of A354, 4 miles S of Dorchester.*

⑭ Isle of Portland

Phantoms of great black dogs, or 'shucks', are said to be a common sight all over the county of Dorset. Among the most well known is the 2m (6ft) high apparition that goes by the name of the 'Tow' or 'Row' Dog. Manifesting without warning all over the Isle of Portland, the beast is unusual for a shuck in that it never seeks to harm those it accosts but merely blocks their path – assuming they are brave enough not to run. A supernatural

occurrence of quite a different kind took place early one morning in May 1976 when a local man named Murphy was out walking his dog. For a few seconds, Mr Murphy found himself surrounded by American GIs and armoured vehicles from the Second World War, before the scene melted away to leave both dog and owner stunned. It was suggested that the experience was a flashback to the time of Allied preparations for the D-Day landings.
▶ *6 miles S of Weymouth on A354.*

⑮ Athelhampton

Visitations by a headless man are among the eerie incidents that have occurred in Athelhampton House, parts of which are more than 500 years old. The headless man was reportedly often seen in the 19th century. In the 20th, a Grey Lady seems to have been active, and a Black Monk appeared. The Martyn family, who lived in the house between 1350 and 1595, were devout Catholics, and this ghost may be that of an itinerant priest.

Legend tells of a pet ape being accidentally walled up in a priest's hole, and its phantom, too, is alleged to roam about the house.
▶ *On minor road just S of A35, 7 miles NE of Dorchester.*

⑯ Cerne Abbas

Lying in a hollow in what was once the parish graveyard, St Austin's (or St Augustine's) Well is unique among Dorset's holy wells in having once been part of a shrine. The well's origins are thought to date back to the middle of the 7th century, when it was known as the Silver Well and was attributed to St Edwold – a member of the royal family of Mercia, the Saxon kingdom to the north – who became a holy man and established a hermitage nearby. By the 11th century, the monks of Cerne felt the need to attach a more colourful past to their well and concocted a story that it had been established by St Augustine, a century before Edwold, as a reward to a group of temperate shepherds who professed to prefer water to beer. A shrine, now long since demolished, was erected over the spring and it acquired a reputation not only for healing powers, but for granting wishes and foretelling the future through the reflections in its waters. It is said that anyone who gazed into the well on the morning of Easter Sunday would see the faces of those fated to die within the year. In times past, village girls drank the water and prayed to St Catherine to help them to find a husband.

Cerne Abbas is also famous for its giant, a mighty chalk man wielding a club – and wearing nothing but a belt. Many believe the 54m (180ft) figure to have been carved in prehistoric or Roman times – one theory is that he represents the Roman god Hercules – but there is no written record of the giant before 1694. This leads some to suspect that he was carved as a caricature of Oliver Cromwell. Whatever his origins, at one time women who wanted to conceive would spend a night on the hillside, ideally on the giant's impressive member.
▶ *8 miles N of Dorchester on A352.*

⑰ Halstock

The Quiet Woman House in Halstock was once an inn, with a sign that showed a woman with her head beneath her arm. It represented a 7th-century saint named Juthware or Judith, who used to help pilgrims on their way to a shrine at Halstock. Her jealous stepmother and brother resented the constant presence of strangers in the house, and one day her brother became so angry that he decapitated her with his sword. To his consternation, she at once picked up her head and carried it to the altar of the local church before finally expiring. Now her ghost, carrying her head under her arm, haunts the lane on Judith Hill in Halstock.
▶ *18 miles NW of Dorchester on minor roads between A37 and A356.*

⑱ Bettiscombe

An ancient human skull, kept in the privately owned Bettiscombe Manor, reputedly has the power to bring disaster to both building and occupants if it is removed. One tenant in the early 19th century tried to get rid of it by throwing it into a nearby pond. For days the house was shaken by screams and tremors, until the tenant was forced to retrieve the grisly relic.

According to tradition, an 18th-century slave who served the owner of Bettiscombe, was buried, against his dying wish, in the local churchyard and not in his native land. Hideous shrieks from his grave were silenced only after the body was removed to the manor. Now just the skull remains.

In fact, analysis has shown that the skull is about 2,000 years old, and is that of a woman in her twenties. It is believed to have come from Pilsdon Pen, a Celtic sanctuary on manor land.
▶ *9 miles NE of Axminster, close to junction of B3165 and B3164.*

⑲ Lyme Regis

The Duke of Monmouth raised his standard here in 1685 at the start of his ill-fated West Country uprising. In one of the aptly named Bloody Assizes, after the rebellion was crushed, Judge Jeffreys condemned 12 Lyme Regis people. The night before the hangings, the judge reputedly dined in the Great House, which once stood in Broad Street. His ghost is reputed to haunt the spot to this day – some say, gnawing a bloody bone.
▶ *On A3052, 2 miles S of its junction with A35, 10 miles W of Bridport.*

HEADLESS GHOSTS, BLACK DOGS AND AMERICAN SOLDIERS HAUNT THE COUNTY'S QUIET LANES
DORSET

SOMERSET

Belief in devils and fairies once flourished in the 'summer land' of the Saxons, but more recent and bloody history gives restless souls ample excuse to revisit the scenes of their demise.

❶ Bristol Channel

Somewhere between Somerset and Pembrokeshire lie the Green Meadows of Enchantment – fairy islands not usually visible to humans, and certainly not to those who seek them, since they can disappear at will, although it has been reported that they may be seen from the air. Fairy folk from the islands used to visit Laugharne Market in Carmarthenshire, and during the 19th century some sailors claimed to have landed and joined the fairy revels. However, when the sailors re-embarked on their vessel and looked back, they found that the islands had vanished.

▶ *Lies N of coast of Devon and Somerset and S of coast of Wales.*

❷ Locking

Tales abound in the West Country about fugitives from the battle of Sedgemoor in 1685, which ended in crushing defeat for Charles II's illegitimate son, the Duke of Monmouth, who had planned to oust his uncle James II from the throne. One story concerns John Plumley, who was the owner of Locking Manor. He fled back home and hid close to Locking, but his dog gave away his hiding place and he was caught and hanged. His wife swept the dog up in her arms and, wild with despair, plunged to her death in Locking Well. Her distraught ghost, still carrying the dog, is said to haunt the district to this day.

▶ *3 miles E of Weston-super-Mare on A371.*

BRISTOL CHANNEL, NEAR PORLOCK

❸ Banwell Hill

Within the prehistoric earthwork of Banwell Camp lies a great cross constructed out of turf. The cross is raised about 0.6m (2ft) above the enclosed ground, and the four arms, each 1.2m (4ft) broad, point to the four quarters of the compass. No one knows who built it, or when or why, but local legend says that the Devil kept raising gales to blow down each upright cross that the villagers erected, so they finally foiled the Evil One by laying the cross on the ground.
▶ *5 miles E of Weston-super-Mare on A371.*

❹ Cheddar Gorge

Standing among the stalactites and stalagmites of the magnificent limestone caves at Cheddar Gorge, contemplating the cannibalistic rituals of the people who inhabited the site some 40,000 years ago, it is not hard to conjure up visions of supernatural spirits, dancing amid the shadows in the caves' dim light. Yet until a little more than 200 years ago, the Gorge was practically unknown, the track leading to it having been long abandoned by local people, following tales of ghostly attacks on passers-by by malevolent entities that emanated from the hillside. More recently, a group of researchers who spent the night on a vigil at nearby Cox's Mill reported a range of supernatural phenomena that included light anomalies, a sudden feeling of sickness and a face that appeared from the wood panelling around the main fireplace.
▶ *The Gorge is along the B3135 NE of Cheddar on A37, 14 miles SE of Weston-super-Mare.*

❺ Stanton Drew

A macabre tale is told about three prehistoric stone circles that stand close by the River Drew. One Saturday, a village wedding was followed by a party that continued into the night. As midnight struck, the devout piper, who did not want to play on a Sunday, refused to carry on. The bride swore she would find another piper to keep the party going, even if she had to go to Hell to fetch him. At that moment an old man appeared and offered his services, which were joyfully accepted. His music was so exhilarating that the dancers could not

stop – too late, they found that their musician was the Devil himself. The faster he played, the faster they danced. When morning came and the fiend returned to Hell, the villagers found that the wedding party had been turned to stone. The group of three stone circles is still known as 'The Devil's Wedding'.
▶ *On B3130 1 mile W of junction with A37, 6 miles S of Bristol.*

❻ Bath

The magnificent city of Bath, with its Roman ruins and splendid Regency architecture, is much loved by tourists and locals alike, and as might be expected for a place with such a vibrant and varied history, the city has its fair share of ghosts. Among its most famous phantom visitors is the 'Man in the Black Hat' – thought to be the figure of Admiral Phillip, the first Governor of New South Wales – who strides along Saville Row in full 18th-century garb, including a black tricorne hat. In the famous Royal Crescent, the appearance of a ghostly carriage is said to commemorate the elopement of Irish playwright and politician Richard Brinsley Sheridan and his lover, Elizabeth Linley, who lived at number 11. Sheridan fought a duel with a married man, Captain Thomas Mathews, for the hand of Miss Linley but was unfaithful to her, leaving her to die of tuberculosis at the age of 38.

Down at the Theatre Royal, the ghosts of an 18th-century married woman and her lover, who were murdered by the woman's jealous husband, are said to wander freely between the theatre and the next-door Garrick's Head public house. Legend also has it that a tortoiseshell butterfly mysteriously appears in the theatre in the middle of winter, at the start of the pantomime season.

At Popjoy's Restaurant in Saw Close, diners and staff have occasionally been surprised by the appearance of a 'solid-looking' woman, who is said to be the ghost of Juliana Popjoy, the mistress of Bath's most famous dandy, Beau Nash. And at the Beehive pub in Landesdown Road, a Victorian serving maid named 'Bunty' makes fleeting appearances, dressed in a blue-grey gown.

High above the town at Freezing Hill, the site of a battle during the Civil War, the air is reputed to echo to the sounds of Cavaliers and Roundheads engaged in bloody struggle.
▶ *12 miles SE of Bristol.*

SOUTH-WEST ENGLAND

❼ Shepton Mallet

Giles Cannard, a prosperous 18th-century Shepton Mallet innkeeper, owed much of his wealth to his dealings with sheep-stealers, smugglers and highwaymen. His downfall came when he was persuaded into an attempt to defraud the town of its common land. Somehow news leaked out and the angry townsfolk set out towards his inn with murder in their hearts. Rather than fall into the hands of the mob, the terrified man hanged himself. He was buried at the crossroads with a stake through his heart to prevent him from walking. However, the treatment does not seem to have been effective since his ghost was frequently seen in the vicinity of his old inn – long since vanished – and near his burial place.

Another story claims that Giles Cannard was the last man in England to be hanged for sheep stealing. The Cannards Grave Inn, by the hillside crossroads, once commemorated this event with a sign showing a corpse swinging from a gallows tree, but in the 1990s the name was changed to the Cannards Hotel and the sign removed.

In the hills north of Shepton Mallet, the walls of one particular cave in Ham Wood are said to bear the marks of a terrible visitation by the Devil. In the late 17th century, a former stocking knitter named Nancy Camel lived in the cave. Seeing her poverty, the Devil offered her riches and a life of ease in exchange for her soul. Nancy yielded to temptation, and although she continued to live in the cave, she never worked again and never appeared to lack for anything.

She grew old, and at last the time came for her to fulfil her part of the bargain. One terrifying stormy night, Satan brought a great horse and cart to carry her to Hell. People nearby claimed to hear piercing shrieks, the crack of a whip and the creaking of wheels. When they approached the cavern the next morning Nancy had vanished. The slab at the cave mouth was were stamped with the impression of a horse's hooves and the tracks of cartwheels, which remain faintly visible today at Nancy Camel's hole.

▶ *At junction of A361 and A37, 20 miles S of Bristol.*

❽ South Cadbury

An Iron Age hillfort near the village of South Cadbury has earthwork ramparts that enclose an area of almost 18 acres. The fort, known as Cadbury Castle, has been identified with Camelot since at least the 15th century. From here, Arthur allegedly led the Britons to victory against the Saxon invaders, and this is the setting for the medieval romances of Lancelot and Guinevere, and Galahad and the Holy Grail.

Even if it was never the 'many tower'd Camelot' of fable, archaeological evidence confirms that during the 6th century, the Arthurian period, the site was occupied by a British warrior chieftain, who reinforced the earth defences with stone and timber, converting the old hillfort into a powerful stronghold. Although the chieftain's name will probably never be known, local tradition has no trouble in identifying him as Arthur. According to legend, the hill is hollow, and there Arthur and his knights lie sleeping until such time as England call upon their services again. Every seven years, on Midsummer Eve, a great door in the hillside opens, and the gallant band rides out to water the horses at a spring near Sutton Montis church. Queen Camel, a village near the foot of Cadbury Hill, is one of several places that has been suggested as the site of the Battle of Camlann, in which Arthur was mortally wounded by his nephew, Mordred.

▶ *On minor roads 2 miles E of A359, 9 miles N of Yeovil.*

❾ Buckland St Mary

Red-clothed fairies were seen in Somerset for the last time at Buckland St Mary, so the story goes. They were defeated in a pitched battle with the pixies, so that everywhere west of the River Parret is now Pixyland. These pixies can easily be recognised by their red hair, pointed ears and green clothing. The fairies are thought to have fled to Ireland, although a few may have settled in Devon and Dorset.

▶ *Just N of A303 6 miles SW of Ilminster.*

THE HILLFORT HAS LONG BEEN LINKED TO CAMELOT
CADBURY CASTLE

⑩ Blackdown Hills

The Holman Clavel Inn, near Culmhead, is home to Chimbley Charlie, a hearth spirit who sits on the wooden beam, or 'clavey', above the fireplace. The beam is made of holly, or 'holman' as it is called locally.

One story tells of a dinner party being prepared for a local farmer. The table had been laid in the dining room when one of the staff remembered that the farmer had scoffed at Charlie – a dangerous thing to do. They shut the door and hoped for the best, but just before the guests arrived, staff members went to make sure that everything was all right. Inside, they found the table bare – tankards were hanging up, the silver had been put away and the table linen neatly folded. It was a sure sign that Charlie did not like the farmer, and the dinner was cancelled.

▶ *The Blackdown Hills lie 8 miles SW of Taunton. The Holman Clavel Inn, near Culmhead, is W of B3170, 8 miles S of Taunton.*

⑪ Croydon Hill

Some time in the 19th century, so legend tells, a Croydon ploughboy went to Rodhuish to have a plough-blade repaired. The talk at the smithy turned to tales of the Croydon Hill Devil, a horned beast that was supposed to lurk in the lane over the hill. The butcher's boy thought he would frighten the other lad by imitating the Devil and waylaying him. As the Croydon boy approached the lane, he saw a horned monster, which bellowed furiously at him.

In terror, the ploughboy lashed out with the plough-blade and then ran. All that was found later by the villagers was a bullock's hide with a great gash in it – but the butcher's boy was never seen again. It is said the Devil took him, and the boy can be heard howling on Croydon Hill on stormy nights as his and other lost souls are hounded by demons.

▶ *4 miles S of Minehead on minor road off A396.*

PITCHFORK REBELS

ONE OF THE MOST HARROWING episodes in the history of the West Country echoes down the years in ghostly stories of unquiet spirits. When the rebel Duke of Monmouth – the illegitimate son of Charles II – landed at Lyme Regis on June 11, 1685, with just a handful of men, thousands of West-countrymen rallied to his cause. Poorly armed and poorly disciplined, they were no match for James II's troops, and Monmouth had no money to equip or pay his troops.

Nevertheless, for almost a month, the rebels ruled Somerset, and Monmouth was proclaimed king in Taunton market place. Then, on the night of July 5, on the moonlit lowlands of Sedgemoor, the rebels fought and lost the battle on which their hopes, and lives, depended. Monmouth fled from the battlefield a broken man, and was soon captured – allegedly found cowering in a ditch. He was taken to London and brought before King James, and on July 15 beheaded on Tower Hill.

The king sent the Judge Jeffreys – a man famous for his terrible temper – down to Taunton to mete out justice to the rebels, which he did swiftly and brutally in a series of 'Bloody Assizes'. More than 200 were hanged and their remains displayed around the country, while 800 were transported to sugar plantations in the West Indies. Heddon Oak near Crowcombe is one of the trees still pointed out as a gallows tree. Sometimes, it is said, the clank of chains and the gasps of choking men can still be heard there, and at Taunton Castle, the tramp of James's soldiers bringing prisoners to trial still echoes through the sombre corridors.

SOUTHWEST ENGLAND

The ancient isle of Avalon

Glastonbury Tor dominates the landscape, rising from a mist of Arthurian legend, Christian myth and New Age magic.

There is something different about Glastonbury. Even before reaching the bustling little Somerset town, which has an unusually large proportion of New Age shops offering all manner of alternative therapies, visitors cannot fail to be struck by the geography of the place. The 158m (520ft) high cone of Glastonbury Tor, topped by the roofless St Michael's Tower, rises out of the surrounding countryside rather like an island amid a sea of green. With half-closed eyes it is not hard to imagine it as it was 7,000 years ago, when the Tor was indeed surrounded by water; today it stands as a monument to another time and another world – a world of pagan mystery, legend and spirituality that still casts a long shadow.

Arthur's ancient tomb

The 12th-century author Geoffrey of Monmouth was among those drawn by the power of Glastonbury's aura, which in those days was greatly augmented by the town's claim to be the site of the oldest Christian church in the western world. It was Geoffrey who, in his *History of the Kings of Britain*, stated that Glastonbury was 'the ancient and blessed Isle of Avalon', where the legendary King Arthur first acquired his sword *Calibum* (Excalibur) and where Arthur was later taken, mortally wounded, after his confrontation with the evil King Mordred.

Some 50 years after the publication of Geoffrey's book, in or around 1193, the monks of Glastonbury Abbey claimed to have recovered from the grounds a massive wooden coffin and a lead cross inscribed with the words *Hic jacet sepultus inclitus rex Arthurus in insula Avalonia* – 'Here lies the renowned King Arthur in the island of Avalon'. Inside the coffin were the bodies of a giant man and a woman – said to be Arthur and his queen Guinevere. The find became the talk of the country, attracting pilgrims to Glastonbury by the thousand; both bodies were eventually reburied in 1278 at a religious ceremony attended by the then-king, Edward I and his queen Eleanor.

Cynics have since pointed out that the affair was more likely to have been a medieval publicity stunt, devised by the monks of Glastonbury to ensure a continuing lucrative flow of pilgrims in the face of stiff competition from the shrine of Archbishop Thomas Becket in Canterbury, who had been murdered in 1170. There is no other evidence linking the town with Arthur, the 7th-century warrior who defended Celtic Britain from the invading Saxons – although why the monks would have bothered is not clear, for the foundation of their own church is the subject of an altogether more intriguing legend. According to the late 12th-century French poet Robert de Boron, it was Joseph of Arimathea, the man who donated his own tomb for the burial of Christ, who first brought the gospel to Glastonbury long before the foundation of the church of Rome. Arriving by sea in the company of 11 fellow evangelists, Joseph is said have carried with him the Holy Grail – the vessel used by Christ at the Last Supper. Upon his arrival, Joseph reputedly struck the ground with his staff, bringing into being the equally legendary Glastonbury Thorn – a hybrid of the hawthorn tree that flowers once in spring and once in midwinter, and which grows only in and around the confines of the ruined abbey. (Although the original tree is long since dead, the winter blossom from one of its cuttings is traditionally presented by the town to the ruling monarch on Christmas Day.)

Controversy surrounds Joseph's supposed journey to Glastonbury, which over the centuries grew more intertwined with Arthurian legend, as well as acquiring embellishments of its own – one version states that Joseph actually visited the area in the company of the boy Jesus. However, it is known that the nearby Bristol Channel lay on an established Phoenician trade route, and that connections between Celtic Britain and the Holy Land pre-date Christianity by several centuries – the Phoenicians trading cloth, dyes and spices for much-prized Cornish tin. Perhaps therein lie the origins of the story, which has persisted in spite of the pre-eminence of the Roman Catholic church over the older Celtic Christian church from the 7th century onwards.

Spiritual energy

In more recent times, Glastonbury has again become a focus for those in search of a more spiritual life. Visitors are in part drawn by the town's legends, but also attracted by Glastonbury's reputation as a source of earth energies. In 1935, one of the first of them, a woman named Katherine Maltwood, had a vision in which she pictured the topography of Glastonbury and its surrounding villages to trace out the 12 signs of the zodiac – the so-called 'Glastonbury Zodiac'. Like so much connected with this mysterious place, it is an ethereal concept, intertwined with the remnants of ancient beliefs. But for New Age truth seekers this only adds to the enigma.

Like the story of Avalon itself, Glastonbury's mystique refuses to die. Each year a new generation is drawn – like their medieval ancestors before them – to experience the town's enduring power.

A lone tower marks
the spot of the oldest
Christian church in the
western world, founded
1,600 years ago to
counter pagan powers

ST MICHAEL'S TOWER, GLASTONBURY TOR

⑫ Minehead

A famous Minehead ghost is that of 17th-century Mrs Leakey, who during her lifetime was beloved by all. After death, however, her spirit underwent a terrible change. Haunting the Minehead waterfront, it conjured – or 'whistled' up storms, sank ships and attacked travellers on lonely roads. Exorcism provoked fresh violence and in 1637 Charles I's Privy Council sent a Royal Commission to investigate the affair. The presiding bishop managed to quell the phantom by resolutely refusing to believe in its existence. The story was popularised 160 years later by Sir Walter Scott, who described the ghost in his epic poem 'Rokeby' in 1813.

Despite the scorn of the bishops, the ghost remains the subject of local speculation and is said to haunt the picturesque Culver Cliffs.
▶ *Off A39, 26 miles W from the M5 near Bridgwater.*

⑬ Stogumber

When Sir Francis Drake wooed Elizabeth Sydenham, her noble family, aware of the great sailor's humble origins, refused to permit the match. Sadly, Drake went back to sea, and Elizabeth, tired at last of waiting for her roving lover, became betrothed to a man of her parents' choice.

Legend says that on the wedding day, the guests assembled in Stogumber church and, as the bridal party approached the door, a blinding flash and a thunderous roar in the sky preceded the arrival of a huge cannonball that fell at the feet of the bride. Elizabeth was convinced that Drake had somehow found out about her marriage and had fired a shot across the world to show his anger. She refused to allow the ceremony to continue and, in due course, Drake returned to claim her. The couple were married in 1585.

A meteorite, which is nearly as big as a football, and is kept in the hall at Coombe Sydenham House, is said to be the 'cannonball'.
▶ *On minor roads off A358 5 miles S of Watchet.*

⑭ Stogursey

Wick Barrow, a Bronze Age burial mound, has long been associated with the pixies. Once, a ploughman working nearby heard the voice of what he took to be a small child crying in the bushes on the mound. The voice was complaining that it had broken its peel – a type of flat wooden shovel once used for putting loaves into old-fashioned baking ovens. When the ploughman went to look, he could find nothing but a tiny wooden peel with its handle broken. Thinking the child was hiding in the bushes but would eventually return for its toy, he mended the peel and left it where he found it. When his work was over, he went to see if the toy had been taken. It was gone, and in its place lay a beautiful cake, hot from the pixies' oven, as his reward.
▶ *On minor roads 3 miles N of A39, 7 miles W of Bridgwater.*

⑮ Bridgwater

Travellers on the A39 between Bridgwater and Street should be aware that they are on a stretch of road patrolled by Dorset's most famous highwayman – Thomas Pocock, who terrorised the county around the turn of the 18th century. Reputedly, he appears on a black horse that gallops frantically without going anywhere. His body is slumped over the saddle as if his life is draining away. This may have something to do with the manner of his death – he was mortally wounded while attempting a robbery. Pocock was a Robin Hood-type figure, who robbed the passengers of smart carriages and distributed the money among the poor. According to legend, his hideout was a cave in the grounds of Chilton Priory, the ruins of which can be seen beside the main road. The most recent recorded sighting took place in 1999, when a mother and daughter claimed to have seen him materialise in the road before them.
▶ *10 miles NE of Taunton. Chilton Priory is 5 miles E of Bridgwater on A39.*

BITTER SPIRITS HANG AS BALLS OF LIGHT OVER THE BATTLEFIELD
WESTONZOYLAND

⑯ Westonzoyland

The battle of Sedgemoor was fought in 1685 on the outskirts of this quiet village, and the cruelty of that encounter and its bloody aftermath still haunt the memory of the West Country. The bitter spirits of slaughtered rebels are said to hang as balls of light over the battlefield, and strange shadows flit silently towards the River Cary, where they disappear. Phantom horsemen with their cloaks flying in the wind, ghostly troopers armed with pikes and staves, and even Monmouth himself, flee through the narrow lanes (see page 43).

In the late 19th century, a local farmer reported that, one foggy night on the moor, he heard what he took to be a drunk shouting, 'Come over and fight' – that was the last despairing cry of Monmouth's men as they were hit by cannon firing across the river.

Another disturbing sound that can apparently sometimes be heard near the village is of someone running accompanied by the pounding of a horse's hooves. The story goes that a famous runner, who was a follower of Monmouth's, was promised his life if he could outrun a horse. He was roped to a stallion and raced across Somerset beside it, but despite the horse tiring before he did, his captors broke their promise and hanged him anyway. The ghost of his sweetheart, who drowned herself in despair at his death, also reputedly haunts the area.

▶ *Battle site near Westonzoyland, 4 miles E of Bridgwater.*

⑰ Wookey Hole

Evidence of the limestone caves at Wookey being occupied by Stone Age hunters has been found in the form of human remains, pottery and crude jewellery. The caves are the result of millions of years of erosion by the River Axe, and where the river flows through the first three chambers, many weird stalagmite and stalactite formations may be seen. One enormous stalagmite is said to be the Witch of Wookey, who was turned to stone for her evil ways.

The witch was supposed to have lived in the caves with her familiars, a goat and its kid. She had been crossed in love, and out of vindictiveness she cast spells on the villagers of Wookey, who, in desperation, appealed to the Abbot of Glastonbury to rid them of the hag.

A monk was sent to the caves to confront the witch and, since she knew that evil cannot prevail against good, she tried to run away. But the monk sprinkled her with holy water, and she turned to stone in the place where she stands today, on the bank of the Axe in the Great Cave at Wookey Hole.

In another version of the legend, the witch was feared throughout Somerset, but her special malevolence was directed against lovers. The monk who turned her into stone had taken holy vows after the witch had, by her spells, wrecked his forthcoming wedding to a local girl.

In 1912, some substance was given to the legend when excavations in the caves revealed the bones of a Romano-British woman, and nearby were the bones of a goat and kid, together with a comb, a dagger and a round stalagmite like a witch's crystal ball. These relics are in the Wells and Mendip Museum.

Legend also tells that a giant conger eel, some 9m (30ft) long, lies hidden in Wookey Hole. The creature decided to swim up the Severn to become king of the river, but on his way he destroyed many salmon nets and flooded the countryside with his tremendous flounderings. Fishermen drove him back and forced him to swim up the narrow River Axe, where he squeezed into Wookey Hole, and remains stuck for ever.

▶ *On minor road 1 mile N of Wells.*

⑱ Wells

In addition to rumours of shadowy figures that drift silently down the corridors and spirits that knock over candles, the Crown Hotel has gained notoriety over the past ten years for manifesting apports – objects from the spirit world that acquire physical form in this one. In the case of the Crown, the apports take the unusual shape of black barley seeds, which first appeared in a room one day in the late 1990s and have reappeared in other rooms several times since then. No one has managed to come up with a satisfactory explanation for the strange organic appearances.

In a separate mystery, in the bar, a dark, man-like figure was captured on the hotel's security camera, only for staff to discover that the room was empty.

▶ *At junction of A39 and A371, 5 miles NE of Glastonbury.*

SOUTH-WEST ENGLAND

CHANNEL ISLANDS

Inhabited since prehistoric times, the Channel Islands are a hotbed of ghostly tales, many of which involve animal spirits and fairies. Less happily, Guernsey was the scene of some infamous witch trials.

GUERNSEY

❶ Le Catioroc, St Saviour

High on the bleak hill of Catioroc, close to the wild, rocky west coast and near the village of St Saviour, stands the most famous of Guernsey's megalithic tombs – the dolmen of Le Trépied. The site was first excavated in the early 19th century, when human bones were unearthed, along with arrowheads and other ancient artefacts. Yet long before the tomb gave up its secrets, it was renowned as a meeting place of the island's witches and warlocks, with sabbats reputedly held there every Friday night. Early in the 17th century, under the direction of the island's notorious witch-hunting Baillif, Amias de Carteret, one so-called witch was tortured into 'confessing' that Le Trépied was regularly visited by the Devil in the form of a black goat, which sat astride the tomb and pronounced itself to be *Baal Berith* – Hebrew for 'the Lord promises'. Even as late as the turn of the century, no respectable woman of Guernsey would be seen anywhere near the place after nightfall. The last witch trial on Guernsey took place in 1914, when a local woman was sentenced to eight years hard labour for her alleged association with the Devil.

▶ *5 miles W of St Peter Port on headland S of Perelle Bay.*

❷ Houmet

Le Creux des Fees, or Fairy Hollow, is a cave on the Houmet peninsula, between the bays of Vazon and Cobo. This granite cavern, which can only be approached at low tide, is – according to folklore – a popular haunt of fairies, and indeed, one of the entrances to fairyland. Deep in the cavern is said to be a passage to St Saviour's church, two miles away.

▶ *On minor road from coast road N of Vazon Bay, 3 miles NW of St Peter Port.*

❸ St Peter Port

In and around Guernsey's chief town of St Peter Port, locals tell of a phantom sow and her litter of piglets. The animals parade through the houses of wealthy townsfolk who have failed to give alms to the poor. Another sow – la coche du Vazaön – is said to haunt the sands of Vazon Bay, where she forages for acorns among the roots of long-submerged trees, while in the vicinity of Saint's Bay, villagers who gather seaweed from the shore may encounter a giant nanny goat.

▶ *On E coast of Guernsey. Reach by ferry from Jersey, Poole, Portsmouth and Weymouth. Also by air from UK airports.*

JERSEY

❹ Bouley Bay, Jersey

With its sweeping pebble beach and steep cliffs, Bouley Bay on the north coast of Jersey, between the villages of Trinity and St Martin, is one of the island's foremost beauty spots. According to local legend, however, it is also the stamping ground of one of Britain's most famous ghostly black dogs – Le Tchan du Bouôlé, or the Black Dog of Bouley Bay. Huge and menacing, with slavering jaws and burning eyes the size of saucers, it is said to patrol the beach and clifftops dragging chains behind it. Those who claim to have encountered the Black Dog say that it was the clanking of the chains that first alerted them, after which the beast appeared and ran around the terrified onlookers in ever-decreasing circles before suddenly vanishing. There are no records of the Black Dog ever harming anyone, but its appearance is said to presage the coming of a great storm. Herein may lie the story's origins, for Bouley Bay was once a favourite haunt of smugglers shipping contraband from France. What better way to discourage prying eyes than to concoct a legend that kept local villagers securely locked in their houses for fear of a change in the weather while the casks of brandy and sheaves of tobacco were brought ashore?

▶ *4 miles NE of St Helier.*

❺ Grouville, Jersey

Near to the village of Grouville lies the Neolithic site of La Hougue Bie, which dates back to around 3,500 BC and is one of the best-preserved cruciform passage graves in Europe. Although the 12m (39ft) high earthen mound is not known to have any supernatural associations, the fact that the passage of the tomb is precisely aligned with the Sun at the spring and autumn equinoxes suggests that it was once an important place of pagan worship. The ruins of a medieval chapel sit on top of the mound, which was excavated in the 1920s by the Société Jersiaise to reveal the bones of at least eight bodies. It was employed as a look-out post by the German occupying forces during the Second World War.

▶ *3 miles E of St Helier. La Hougue Bie NW of village at junction of B46 and B28.*

SARK

❻ La Coupée

Legends of black dogs abound throughout the Channel Islands, but the most famous – and fearsome – of all is that of the black dog of Sark. Said to be as big as a calf, it allegedly haunts the narrow isthmus of La Coupée, pursuing those about to die across the high ridge from Little Sark to Great Sark.

▶ *Reach Sark by ferry from Guernsey or Jersey.*

A PHANTOM BLACK
DOG PATROLS
SARK'S HIGH RIDGE
LA COUPÉE

Southern England

The green and pleasant southern counties harbour many strange secrets, from witchcraft and magic to devillish tricks and murder. Travellers should beware phantom horses and their deathly riders, and spectral girls on dark highways.

A40 Witney

9

A419
1
2 •Swindon

A429
A346
M4

A350 13
12
Chippenham• 3
4 Marlborough 6
5

A7
7

Devizes•

Trowbridge•
WILTSHIRE 82-87

A338
A303 17
16 A303 Andover•

A36
10 •Warminster 8
9
11

A303

A354

A338

•Salisbury

13

A36
M27

12

11 A31
10 New
Ringwood Fores
National

7
Lymington•

KEY

- ① Main entry
- — County boundary
- — Motorway
- — Principal A road

BEDFORDSHIRE 50-51

BUCKINGHAMSHIRE 54-57

HERTFORDSHIRE 64-66

OXFORDSHIRE 72-75

BERKSHIRE 52-53

HAMPSHIRE and Isle of Wight 58-63

SURREY 76-77

KENT 67-71

SUSSEX 78-81

The Chilterns

The North Downs

The South Downs

Bedford • Biggleswade

Milton Keynes

Buckingham

Leighton Buzzard

Luton • Stevenage • Hertford

Aylesbury

Tring • St Albans • Watford

Oxford

Didcot

High Wycombe

Maidenhead

Reading • Windsor

Basingstoke

Newbury

Woking • Guildford • Farnham

Dorking • Reigate

Haslemere • Crawley

Petersfield

Haywards Heath

Chichester • Bognor Regis • Worthing • Brighton

Portsmouth

Newport

Winchester

Southampton

Gravesend • Rochester • Chatham

Maidstone

Royal Tunbridge Wells

Crowborough

Ashford • Dover • Folkestone

Canterbury • Margate

Lewes • Eastbourne

Bexhill-on-Sea • Hastings • Rye

BEDFORDSHIRE

Soft chalk downlands and quiet water meadows fringing the River Ouse provide a tranquil setting for a whole host of spectral visitations and unsettling, devilish legends.

❶ Odell

Every hundred years, the ghost of Sir Rowland Alston appears in the village, riding a phantom horse. Several of the barons of Odell went by the same name, and memorials to them can be seen in the village church, but this particular lord sold his soul to the Devil. When the time came to complete the bargain, Sir Rowland took fright and sought sanctuary in the church. Five marks on the porch are said to be scratches left by the Devil as he shook the edifice in rage at being deprived of Sir Rowland's soul. The baron's next appearance is due in 2044.
▶ *On minor roads between A6 and A428, 7 miles NW of Bedford.*

❷ Bedford

The headquarters of the Panacea Society are located in the town of Bedford. This religious and charitable organisation maintains that 'war, disease, crime and banditry will increase until the bishops open Joanna Southcott's box.' Joanna Southcott (1750-1814) was a prophetess and her box, which is in the possession of the society, allegedly contains writings that will enable the human race to banish all those evils from the world. However, under the terms of Joanna's will the box can be opened only in the presence of 24 bishops, who have so far declined to cooperate.
▶ *10 miles NE of Junction 13 of M1 along A421.*

❸ Clophill

Just outside the village, at the top of Dead Man's Hill, stand the ruins of St Mary's church. Here, attempts to revive the Black Mass were evidently made in March 1963 and on Midsummer Eve 1969. On the first occasion, the tomb of an 18th-century apothecary's wife was opened, and her 200-year-old bones arranged in a circle about the gutted nave of the church. This may have been an experiment with necromancy, in which black magicians are supposed to summon and speak with the spirits of the dead. On the second occasion, tombs were again smashed and graves desecrated as part of some bizarre ritual.
▶ *On A6, 11 miles N of Luton.*

❹ Luton

Galley Hill was formerly known as Gallows Hill. The gibbet that once stood there caught fire one night in a fierce storm and a fearsome black dog was seen, revelling in the flames. For years after that, people gave the hill a wide berth, because the creature would occasionally reappear. During the 16th and 17th centuries, the hill was used as a burial ground for witches, and may also have been the centre of a secret witch cult. Excavations in 1962 exposed a horse's skull on top of which was placed a dice made of bone with the '6' uppermost. These objects are connected with ritual ceremonies and the weaving of spells.
▶ *2 miles E from Junction 10 of M1. Galley Hill E of A6, 2 miles N of the town centre.*

❺ Someries Castle

Built in the 15th century more as a fortified manor house than a castle, Someries was the home of Sir John Wenlock. During the Wars of the Roses, Sir John defected to the Yorkist side but, with a degree of bad timing, switched back to supporting the House of Lancaster in 1471. Shortly afterwards, the Lancastrian army, in which he held a command, was resoundingly defeated at the Battle of Tewkesbury and Sir John was killed, probably by his own leader, Edmund Beaufort, the Duke of Somerset. The remains of the house and grounds are reputedly haunted by Sir John's ghost, undeterred by the roar of passenger jets from nearby Luton Airport.
▶ *2 miles SE of Luton on minor road off B653.*

❻ Battlesden

The current Battlesden House stands on, or near, the site of a medieval manor house, and the grounds of this old house were once the province of a dishonest steward's ghost. In life, he used to overcharge for produce, and the apparition would rattle milk pails and recite:

> 'Milk and water I sold ever,
> Weight and measure I gave never,
> And I shan't rest, never, never!'

▶ *Off A4012, 6 miles NW of Dunstable.*

BIZARRE RITUALS AT THE TOP OF DEAD MAN'S HILL

ST MARY'S CHURCH, CLOPHILL

❼ Aspley Guise

Woodfield, a house in Weathercock Lane, was alleged to be haunted by Dick Turpin, his mare Black Bess and a pair of murdered lovers. The lovers had been walled up by the girl's father in the inn that once stood on the site, and Dick Turpin had stumbled on the guilty secret. Several witnesses reported the spectres flitting about the house and garden, and in 1947 the owner was said to have applied for a reduction in rates. The County Council was, apparently, unsympathetic, pointing out that Turpin was hanged in 1739, around 80 years before the house was built.

▶ *On minor roads from A5130 at Woburn Sands, 5 miles SE of Milton Keynes.*

❽ Marston Moretaine

The 15th-century church of St Mary's has a curious tower, which stands some distance away from the main building. According to local lore, the tower was detached by the Devil, who was trying to steal it. Finding it too heavy, he left it where it now stands.

In fact, the tower was probably built separately. It has especially thick walls at its base and may have been constructed as a watchtower, or as a refuge from flooding in the low-lying valley. One theory is that it was a place of safety for villagers escaping from marauding Vikings, who could well have sailed up the River Ouse as far as Bedford.

▶ *On A421, 6 miles SW of Bedford.*

WINDSOR CASTLE

BERKSHIRE

The county's regal connections are inseparable from its ghosts – kings and queens haunt the great houses while the old royal forest remains the domain of Herne, the ancient, mythical hunter.

❶ Bisham

Dame Elizabeth Hoby lived in Bisham Abbey during the 16th century, and her ghost has been seen several times in her former home. Her apparition has dark skin and a glaring white dress, like a photographic negative. A brilliant scholar and close friend of Elizabeth I, Dame Hoby is reputed to have beaten her young son William, thinking him dull-witted and lazy. In fact, the boy may have had a brain disease that, when aggravated by his mother's beatings, proved fatal. Dame Hoby's remorse lasted until her own death in 1609 and her troubled spirit has continued to manifest itself in the East Wing of the abbey. She is said to wander about, constantly trying to wash her bloodstained hands in a ghostly basin. Towards the end of the 19th century, the owner of Bisham Hall, Admiral Vansittart, was standing alone in the Great Hall where Dame Hoby's portrait still hangs. Although he did not believe the stories about the house being haunted, he suddenly felt that someone was standing behind him. He spun round and caught a glimpse of the spectral figure of Dame Hoby – and where her portrait should have been, there was only an empty frame.
▶ *S of River Thames, 1 mile S of Marlow.*

❷ Windsor

Since the mighty bastions of Windsor have protected monarchs from their subjects from the time of the Norman Conquest, it is not surprising that the ghosts within the castle are wholly royal. The quick, determined footsteps that hurry through the library are said to be those of Elizabeth I. By contrast, the steps in the cloisters are slow and halting. These may be echoes of Henry VIII, dragging his ulcerated leg through eternity. George III was sometimes confined to a room overlooking the parade ground, and several modern subalterns have been startled to see his face at the window, apparently summoned by the sound of men marching and drilling.

The ancient forest of Windsor Great Park is the province of Herne the Hunter. Festooned with chains, and with stag's antlers growing from his brow, he is most often seen at times of national crisis, near the place where a great oak once grew. According to legend, Herne was a royal huntsman in the service of Henry VII, Henry VIII or Richard II. In fact, Herne was associated with the park long before kings came to Windsor. His stag's antlers almost certainly identify him as Cernunnos, Celtic god of the underworld.
▶ *S of River Thames, 1 mile S of Junction 6 of M4.*

❸ Newbury

Belief in witchcraft lingered on in the Newbury area until well into the 20th century. A favourite meeting place for local covens was Cottington's Hill, a mile south of Kingsclere. When an investigation into local beliefs about witchcraft was carried out just before the First World War, several villagers from around Newbury claimed that, within living memory, three Berkshire witches had been buried alive with only their heads left above ground. All the accounts agreed that one of the three had lived longer than the others, because someone threw an apple core at her and she caught it in her mouth.

The most celebrated Newbury witch was captured by a troop of Cromwell's men in 1643. According to a contemporary pamphlet, the soldiers saw an elderly woman sailing on a plank down the River Kennet, seized her as a witch and tried to shoot her. But 'with a deriding and loud laughter at them, she caught their bullets in her hands and chewed them'. One of the soldiers slashed her forehead – an infallible method of rendering harmless even the most evil witch – and 'discharged a pistol underneath her ear, at which she straight sank down and died'.
▶ *On A4, 4 miles S of Junction 13 of M4.*

❹ Bucklebury

After the Reformation, the village of Bucklebury came under the control of the Winchcombe family, descendants of wool-merchant Jack of Newbury. In 1700, Frances Winchcombe married the first Lord Bolingbroke, Henry St John. Impeached by George I after Queen Anne's death in 1714, he fled to exile in France. His wife, left behind, finally pined away and died three years later. Lady Bolingbroke's ghost has been said to haunt the area ever since, riding in an open carriage drawn by black horses.
▶ *On minor roads N of A4, 5 miles NE of Newbury.*

SOUTHERN ENGLAND

BUCKINGHAMSHIRE

Dusk brings an uneasy peace to woods, fields and country lanes where those long gone are known to return, and where the roisterous goings-on in the notorious Hellfire Caves have left a haunting legacy.

❶ Calverton

Gib Lane, which takes its name from a long-gone gibbet, is supposedly haunted by the ghost of Lady Grace Bennett, a wealthy 17th-century widow who was well known for her miserly habits. Lady Bennett was murdered by Adam Barnes, a Stony Stratford butcher who had broken into her house in search of money. Barnes was convicted and hanged, and his body suspended in irons from the gibbet in the lane until it disintegrated. The site of the gibbet may be indicated by carvings on the barn that was built into the stone wall surrounding Manor House Farm orchard, next to the church. The carvings show two gibbets and bear the date 1693.

▶ *4 miles W of Milton Keynes on minor road off A5.*

❷ Woughton on the Green

Woughton on the Green lies close to the old Roman road of Watling Street and, during the 18th century, Dick Turpin often used the Old Swan Inn in the village, now part of Milton Keynes, as a convenient base. A local story tells how Turpin once stopped at the inn when he was being pursued after one of his hold-ups on the main highway. He quickly had his horse, Black Bess, re-shod so that her horseshoes pointed backwards, and then set out again, managing to escape when his pursuers rode off in the opposite direction. The ghosts of Dick Turpin and Black Bess have often been seen riding through the district at night.

▶ *1 mile S of Milton Keynes town centre.*

GHOSTLY
VICAR'S
PENANCE
FINGEST CHURCH

❸ Great Missenden

Abbey Mansion at Great Missenden incorporates part of the original Augustinian abbey, which was founded in 1133. Legend tells that Sir John de Plessis, the 9th Earl of Warwick and Lord of Missenden, ordered the monks of the abbey to bury him, seated on his white charger Principall, before the abbey's high altar. He died in 1263 and, despite his wish being carried out, the ghost of both Sir John and his horse can still be heard thundering across the nearby Chiltern Hills.
▶ *10 miles SE of Aylesbury on A413.*

❹ Penn

The countryside around the small village of Penn, near High Wycombe, was once haunted by the ghost of an 18th-century farm labourer, riding a phantom horse – and may still be. According to eyewitness accounts, the wraith gallops soundlessly out of the night and, with peals of laughter, vanishes into a grey mist.
▶ *On B474, 3 miles E of High Wycombe.*

❺ Hitcham

In Norman times, Hitcham Manor, near Taplow, was owned by two brothers named De Crispin, and both loved the same girl, daughter of the Lord of Dorney. She finally married one of the brothers, but this did not prevent her from providing loving comfort to the other. One day, her husband found her in his brother's arms and murdered her in a fit of jealous rage. He was ordered to make a pilgrimage to the Holy Land, but when he returned unrepentant, a curse was laid on him – that he and his descendants would never die peacefully. Ever since, says the legend, the bloody handprint of the murdered woman appears on the shield in the family's coat-of-arms whenever a De Crispin is about to die.
▶ *Hitcham Manor in Burnham, near Taplow, 2 miles NE of Maidenhead.*

❻ Hambleden

An 18th-century Hambleden girl, Mary Blandy, had the misfortune to fall in love with a married man, Captain William Cranstoun. Her father strongly disapproved and barred Cranstoun from his home. Shortly afterwards, Mr Blandy died from arsenic poisoning, and suspicion fell on Mary. At her trial, she admitted that she had given arsenic to her father – but only a small amount 'to change his mood'. Mary was found guilty of murder and hanged in 1752. Now her ghost, riding a phantom white horse, is said to haunt the lanes around Hambleden.
▶ *On minor road N of A4155, 4 miles W of Marlow.*

❼ Fingest

This parish, along with all the others in Buckinghamshire, once came under the jurisdiction of the Bishop of Lincoln. From 1320 to 1340, the incumbent was Henry Burghersh, who failed to endear himself to any of his parishioners, mainly because he set about enclosing common lands on the Church's behalf. As retribution for causing distress to the needy, his ghost is doomed to wander the countryside forever, and he has occasionally been seen riding in the woods near Fingest, dressed as a forester.
▶ *6 miles W of High Wycombe on minor road off B482.*

SOUTHERN ENGLAND

❽ West Wycombe

Set in the Chiltern countryside, West Wycombe Park is a National Trust-owned neo-classical mansion, surrounded by beautifully preserved landscaped gardens. In the grounds of the estate, the infamous Hellfire Caves are now a privately owned tourist attraction, but none the less creepy for that. In the 18th century they were reputed to be the scene of wild orgies and black-magic rituals.

In about 1755, Sir Francis Dashwood, owner of the Park, founded a private society, the Knights of St Francis of Wycombe. His secret brotherhood was limited to 24 men of high social standing. At first, they met at nearby Medmenham Abbey, where they conducted mock religious ceremonies and, reputedly, Black Masses. Before long, they became known as the Monks of Medmenham and, later, the Hellfire Club, adopting the motto 'Do what you will'.

Dashwood had already extended the chalk caves at West Wycombe, providing employment for the villagers during a time of bad harvests, and these chambers, connected by long and winding passages, deep underground, soon became the venue for the club's meetings. High-born ladies and prostitutes allegedly attended, dressed in costume and wearing masks. No one knows what took place in the Inner Temple cave. Rumours include all sorts of debauchery and Black Mass ceremonies. Apparently, once, when Dashwood produced a baboon, those present stampeded in terror, believing it to be the Devil.

The Hellfire Club gradually disbanded after 1763, but lurid tales of its sinister activities continued to flourish. The ghosts that allegedly haunt the caves today include Suki, a spectral bride, Paul Whitehead, a poet and steward of the Hellfire Club who died in 1774 and left his heart to Sir Francis, and a floating monk – no mention of Dashwood, who died in 1781 and presumably rests in peace in his specially constructed mausoleum on the estate.

▶ *2 miles W of High Wycombe off A40.*

❾ Lane End

In 1766, a young girl who always liked to dress in red died tragically two weeks before her wedding day. For a long time afterwards, according to local legend, her ghost roamed footpaths in the district. In 1943, the figure of a strange girl in a red dress and without a coat was seen crossing a field on a snowy December day, but she has not been reported since then.

▶ *4 miles W of High Wycombe on B482, just S of M40.*

❿ Haddenham

When Haddenham gardener Noble Edden witnessed two men stealing a sheep, he said nothing to the authorities. This was 1828 and the penalty for sheep-stealing was deportation or death. He knew the thieves, though, and could not resist the temptation to bleat like a sheep whenever he saw them in town. The two men, Tylor and Sewell, were thoroughly alarmed, and made sure of Edden's silence by murdering him one night. That same evening Mrs Edden, as she waited at home for her husband, had a vision of Tylor striking Edden with a stone. Edden's body was soon found, but it was not until the following year that the murderers were arrested. After Sewell confessed to the crime, both he and Tylor were hanged outside Aylesbury Prison on March 8, 1830. Noble Edden's ghost has been seen in a lane that branches off to Haddenham from the A418. It is said that whoever meets it will suffer bad luck.

▶ *On minor roads between A418 and A4129, 2 miles NE of Thame.*

⓫ Middle Claydon

Claydon House is the ancestral home of the Verney family, and it is supposed to be haunted by Sir Edmund Verney, Charles I's standard-bearer. His ghost appears whenever trouble threatens either his country or his family. Sir Edmund was killed in Warwickshire during the Battle of Edgehill in 1642, and died clutching the standard so tightly that his hand had to be hacked off. The hand was eventually returned to his family and is buried in the 13th-century All Saints church in the grounds of the estate. An elaborate monument to Sir Edmund and his family, commissioned by Sir Edmund's son, almost fills the south side of the chancel. Both the house and church are open to the public.

At Christmas 1642, several months after the battle, a host of spectral combatants appeared on the battle site at Edgehill (see page 154). Witnesses identified Sir Edmund as being among their number.

▶ *3 miles SW of Winslow off the A413, 6 miles SE of Buckingham.*

VERNEY'S MONUMENT, ALL SAINTS CHURCH

SACRED
To the Memory of the
Euer Honored
S.ᵗ EDMVND VERNEY who was
K.ᵗ MarShall 16 yeares
And Standard Bearer to Charles y.ᵉ firſt
In that memorable Battayle
of Edge Hill
where he was Slayne
on the 23 of October
1642.
Beinge then in the two and
Fiftieth yeare of his Age.
AND
in Honour of
Dame MARGARET his wife
Eldeſt Daughter of S.ʳ Thomas
Denton of Hellesdon K.ᵗ
by whome Hee had
Six Sonnes and Six Daughters.
She Dyed at London
on y.ᵉ 5.ᵗ and was buried here on y.ᵉ 7.
of Aprill 1641.
In the 47 yeare of
Her Age.

ALSO TO THE PERPETVALL HONOVR AND
MEMORY OF THAT MOST EXCELLENT AND
INCOMPARABLE PERSON DAME MARY SOLE
DAVGHTER & HEIRE OF IOHN BLACKNALL OF
ABINGDON IN Y.ᵉ COVNTY OF BERKES ESQ.ʳ AND
WIFE OF S.ʳ RAPHE VERNEY (ELDEST SONN OF
THE SAID S.ʳ EDMVND AND DAME MARGARETT)
BY WHOME SHE HAD THREE SONNES AND
THREE DAVGHTERS WHEROF ONLY EDMVND
AND IOHN ARE LIVEING. SHE DECEASED
AT BLOIS IN FRANCE, ON THE 10.ᵀᴴ DAY OF
MAY 1650 BEING ABOVT THE AGE OF 34 YEARES.
AND WAS HERE INTERRED ON THE 19.ᵀᴴ OF NOVEᴹ
FOLLOWING, WHERE HER SAID HVSBAND (AT WHOS
CHARGE AND BY WHOSE APPOINTMENT THIS MONV-
MENT WAS ERECTED) INTENDS TO BEE BVRIED:

HAMPSHIRE & ISLE OF WIGHT

There is no shortage of historical sites in Hampshire, or on its adjacent island, and no shortage of ghosts, either, from Tudor queens to chanting souls among the ruins of Beaulieu Abbey.

❶ Basing House

During the Civil War, Charles Paulet, Marquis of Winchester, held Basing House for three years against a siege by parliamentary troops. The Roundheads, under Oliver Cromwell himself, finally battered the house and its inhabitants into submission in 1645, and blew it up. Thought to be buried somewhere in the ruins is a golden calf, made from the Paulet family's melted-down gold plate and hidden during the siege. Apparently, Cromwell's ghost used to walk from the old tithe barn at Lyckpit across Plovers Dell, and at nearby Hook, the phantom of an unknown Cavalier, wearing a wide-brimmed hat, lace ruffles and a loose cloak, has been reported on the Common.
▶ *In Old Basing, 1 mile E of Basingstoke town centre.*

❷ Preston Candover

A wealthy man fleeing from plague-stricken London in 1665 died from the disease somewhere near the Preston gravel pits. The villagers, afraid to touch him, first shot his horse, and then with ropes and poles heaved the two corpses into the pits and buried them. At the same time, they buried the treasure that he was carrying, thinking that they would dig it up later when the risk of infection had passed. No records exist of the treasure's recovery, but the sound of a horse's hooves is reputed to echo on the path to the old pits.
▶ *On B3046, 7 miles S of Basingstoke.*

❸ Liphook

The spectre of a white calf haunts the countryside around Liphook, jumping hedges and trotting along the lanes. Sometimes it shrinks to the size of a cockerel, after which it vanishes completely. No explanation seems to be forthcoming, other than it being a fairy calf, but it may have some connection with Liphook's other phantom, a mysterious little boy who has been seen and heard playing a flute. He, too, haunts the Liphook lanes, and his music is occasionally heard coming from the tops of trees and from hedgerows.
▶ *Just S of A3, 8 miles NE of Petersfield.*

❹ Gosport

On stormy winter nights, the bones of Jack the Painter and the chains of his gibbet may be heard clanking in the wind on Blockhouse Point by Gosport, at the entrance to Portsmouth Harbour. Jack, alias James Aitken, started a fire in the harbour ropehouse in 1776. Whatever the reasons for his actions may have been – one theory is that he held anti-monarchist views and planned to destroy the fleet – he was caught, tried and hanged from the mizzen mast of a ship in the harbour. Afterwards, his corpse was gibbeted on Blockhouse Point, and for many years his rotting remains were a familiar warning to all who sailed with the Royal Navy.
▶ *S from M275 which leaves M27 at Junction 12.*

BEAULIEU ABBEY

❺ Owslebury

Marwell Hall, a mile south of Owslebury, belonged to the Church before Henry VIII gave it as a gift to the Seymour family. The Seymours were in favour because Henry had fallen in love with Jane, whom he married in 1536, shortly after the execution of his second wife, Anne Boleyn. Not much more than a year later Jane, too, was dead, never having recovered from the birth of her son, the future Edward VI. Now Jane's ghost haunts Marwell Hall, and a lady in white who sometimes drifts down an avenue of yew trees in the grounds is thought to be her predecessor.

Other ghostly visitors to the house are indicated by the sound of footsteps, supposedly made by guests searching for a missing bride. This story is associated with several country houses. During a game of hide-and-seek, the bride climbs into an old oak chest, the lid clicks shut and while the increasingly frantic guests search for her, she slowly suffocates. Many years later, the chest is found, prised open and her skeleton is discovered.

▶ *On minor roads 4 miles SE of Winchester.*

❻ Beaulieu

Beaulieu Abbey was founded in 1204 by Cistercian monks. The story goes that a group of the monks visited King John in 1201 to ask him for exemption from taxation. Their request so angered the king that he locked them up and ordered their trampling to death by horses the following morning. That night he dreamt that he was flogged for his cruelty, and when he awoke there were lash-marks on his back. So he released the monks and gave them the land at Beaulieu with permission to build an abbey. The Cistercians lived and worked there for 300 years until the Dissolution in 1538. In 1928, the ghost of a monk appeared to a woman at the abbey and told her to dig in a certain spot where she would find a coffer containing 'two round stones and some bones'. She found the coffer, and the bones were given a Christian burial. Since then, several visitors have reported hearing the devotional chanting of monks within the ruins of the abbey.

▶ *Junction of B3056 and B3054, 6 miles NE of Lymington.*

SOUTHERN ENGLAND

❼ Boldre

Early in the 20th century, Bywater House became the home of Mrs Gordon-Hamilton. She and her guests often heard the sound of rolling barrels and hurried footsteps in the house, and through a friend, who was a medium, she learnt that a young man had been murdered there in 1685. The house, which was much smaller in those days, was owned by a smuggler and the victim had lodged there overnight. He was carrying secret despatches for the Duke of Monmouth, who had just been defeated by the forces of James II in the Battle of Sedgemoor. The smuggler's daughter coveted the messenger's jewellery and persuaded her lover to murder him. They buried his body in the garden. In a photograph of Mrs Gordon-Hamilton, taken about 1920, the profile of a youth with Cavalier curls also appears. After seeing it, a friend dreamt that the young man took her to a place in the garden and told her to dig there, which she and Mrs Gordon-Hamilton did next day and discovered a well-preserved, but empty, secret chamber made of narrow, 17th-century bricks.

▶ *Just E of A337, 1 mile N of Lymington.*

❽ Gatcombe, Isle of Wight

Carved in oak on his tomb in Gatcombe church is the effigy of Edward Estur, a 14th-century crusader. In 1364, he went to the Holy Land accompanied by his mistress, Lucy Lightfoot. She stayed in Cyprus to await his return from the wars, but in Syria he suffered such severe head injuries that he forgot all about Lucy and returned to Gatcombe alone. They never saw one another again. In 1830, a young girl from Bowcombe became strangely infatuated with Edward's effigy. She constantly rode her horse to the church and spent hours gazing at the knight's tomb. Asked why she did this, she said, 'I love to be with him in my thoughts and dreams.' Just as she entered the church on the morning of June 13, 1831, a terrible storm blew up, which was accompanied by an eclipse of the sun. When the gale died down, the girl's horse was found, but she was never seen again. This girl, too, was named Lucy Lightfoot.

▶ *On minor roads 2 miles S of Newport.*

❾ Mottistone, Isle of Wight

Druid priests may have sacrificed white bulls beside the Long Stone on Mottistone Hill. The fact that there are really two stones, one horizontal and the other perpendicular, encourages speculation that Druids worshipped there. The perpendicular stone is said to represent a Druid god and the horizontal one a goddess. All that can be said for certain is that the barrow, or burial chamber, of which the Long Stone is a part, must be 4,000–5,000 years old. The name 'Mottistone' may suggest that the stone was a 'meeting stone' – it means 'the speaker's stone' in old English.

▶ *On B3399 5 miles SE of Yarmouth. The Long Stone is along footpaths N of the village.*

ANIMAL SACRIFICES TO A DRUID GOD AT LONG STONE
MOTTISTONE

⑩ Minstead

The Rufus Stone stands in a New Forest clearing, marking the spot where William II, nicknamed 'Rufus' because of his florid complexion, was killed on August 2, 1100, during a hunting expedition. The reason for his death has been variously attributed to a tragic accident, assassination and ritual sacrifice. According to the official version, Walter Tyrrel loosed off at a stag, missed and his arrow was deflected into William's heart. Tyrrel denied responsibility, and many contemporary accounts bear him out. William's youngest brother, Henry, reacted with suspicious alacrity. The king was killed at 7pm on Thursday evening, and his body was brought to Henry in Winchester on Friday morning. By midday William was buried and by afternoon Henry had seized the Treasury and was on his way to London to be crowned. Henry could easily have instigated his brother's murder.

However, there is another explanation. One of the most widespread of pagan beliefs, which may have persisted into the Christian era, was the idea of the Divine Victim, the king who was also a god, and who, when called upon, was expected to give his life and his blood to rejuvenate the earth. Several writers have theorised that Rufus was such a king. In support, they point out that he openly scoffed at Christianity and that, on the day he died, he made several remarks that indicated foreknowledge of his death. The date, too, was significant – August 2 was the day after Lugnasad, the Celtic harvest festival and a traditional time of sacrifice. Whatever the reason may have been, William Rufus was buried without ceremony, and refused the last rites of the Church.

All those present at the scene of William's death scattered, leaving his body lying alone in the approaching dusk. About 2 hours later, it was found by a charcoal burner, who loaded it on to his cart and carried it 20 miles to the town. As the cart bounced along, the king's blood is said to have watered the earth, and on every anniversary since his death, William's ghost follows the trail from the Rufus Stone in the quiet New Forest glade all the way to Winchester.

▶ *Just S of A31, 1 mile SW of Junction 1 of M27. The Rufus Stone is 1 mile NW of Minstead, just N of A31.*

⑪ Ellingham

Moyles Court in Ellingham was once the home of Dame Alice Lisle who, in 1685, was tried by the infamous Judge Jeffreys. Accused of sheltering two fugitives from the Battle of Sedgemoor, she was condemned to death by burning, despite being more than 70 years old. The unusual method of execution was later changed to beheading, and was carried out at Winchester the same year. Since then, her ghost may sometimes be heard in Moyles Court, and she has been seen riding down Ellingham Lane in a driverless coach drawn by two headless horses.

▶ *Just W of A338, 2 miles N of Ringwood.*

⑫ Breamore

On Breamore Down, three-quarters of a mile northwest of Breamore House, a curious labyrinth of interconnecting pathways has been cut into the turf. Called a miz-maze, it dates from medieval times and is one of seven such constructions scattered throughout England. One possibility is that it was associated with an Augustinian priory that once stood nearby. As a form of penance, the monks were made to crawl on their knees to the centre of the maze, and then to crawl out again.

▶ *On A338 7 miles S of Salisbury.*

⑬ Braishfield

Windmill Cottage in Dark Lane, Braishfield, is said to be haunted. Early in the 20th century, a wealthy woman in the area became obsessed with the fear that her money would be stolen, so she buried it secretly somewhere near the cottage. Shortly afterwards, she died without revealing the hiding place of the hoard. Her ghost has been seen and heard many times, walking under a nearby yew tree, knocking at the cottage door or sitting by the garden gate. Dogs have been known to growl and bristle when they go near the yew tree.

▶ *On minor roads between A3057 and A3090, 3 miles N of Romsey.*

THE KING'S GHOST FOLLOWS

⑭ Chilbolton

At Chilbolton Rectory, the window where an apparition of a nun used to appear was bricked up to discourage her, but some years ago her ghost was seen again, as reported by two guests at the rectory. One said that he had seen a beautiful nurse gazing out of a window. The other awoke in the night and saw a nurse standing by his bed. The rector confirmed that there was no such person in the house on either occasion. In 1393, a nun named Katherine Faukener broke her vows and ran away from the nearby Benedictine Abbey of St Cross at Wherwell. On her repentant return seven years later, she is believed to have been met with little forgiveness. As punishment she was walled up alive on the site of the rectory, which was then a nunnery.
▶ *Just E of A3057, 4 miles S of Andover.*

⑮ Wherwell

Some time before Wherwell Priory was dissolved in 1538, a fearful winged monster was hatched in the cellars, by a toad incubating a cock's egg, or so legend tells. When fully grown, the cockatrice – a kind of dragon with the head and feet of a rooster – was given to flying around the priory in search of people to eat, and a reward of 1.6 hectares (4 acres) of land was offered to anyone who could kill it. Many died in the attempt. At last, a man named Green came up with a scheme. He lowered a mirror of polished steel into the cockatrice's lair and waited while it battled with its reflection until dropping exhausted to the floor. Then Green stepped in and ran it through with a spear. A plot of land in Harewood Forest, near Wherwell, is still known as 'Green's Acres'.

A weather vane in the form of a cockatrice once adorned the steeple of St Peter and Holy Cross at Wherwell. Today the extraordinary vane is exhibited in Andover Museum. A mat in the church tells the story of the fearsome beast and its brave conquerer.
▶ *On B3420, off A3057, 2 miles S of Andover.*

⑯ South Tidworth

In April 1661, the rattle of a phantom drum at Tidworth House signalled the beginning of a peculiar haunting. In the year that followed, the Mompessons, who lived in the house, were continually disturbed by drumbeats, their children were bruised and battered by an unseen force, furniture hurled itself about the house and floorboards moved of their own accord. It was thought that the haunting had something to do with William Drury, a vagrant musician demobilised from Cromwell's Model Army. Drury used the drum as a form of begging with menace – counting on the fact that if he made enough noise, people would pay him to go away. Exasperated, the magistrate John Mompesson had confiscated the drum, but although Drury admitted that he was involved, the extraordinary nature of the disturbances – and his hand in them – has never been properly explained. Several leading scientists of the day were called to investigate the manifestations. Charles II even sent a Royal Commission. 'The Drummer Of Tidworth', a contemporary illustration, portrayed the phantom as a winged devil surrounded by demons but, in fact, no one ever saw the ghost.
▶ *On A338 2 miles N of its junction with A303, 8 miles W of Andover.*

⑰ Vernham Dean

The rector of Vernham Dean, desperate to save his parish and himself from the Great Plague of 1665, persuaded all the villagers who had been in contact with the disease to go into voluntary isolation in a closed camp on top of the hill beside Chute Causeway, just outside the village. He promised to bring them regular supplies of food, but once they had shut themselves off, he became so terrified that he deserted them. Those who did not die of disease starved to death – and it was all in vain. Vernham Dean was ravaged by plague and the rector was one of the many who died. Since then, his guilt-stricken ghost has often been seen climbing towards the hilltop where his cowardice caused so many to die.
▶ *On minor roads 8 miles N of Andover.*

A BLOODY TRAIL INTO TOWN
MINSTEAD

HERTFORDSHIRE

Busy Watling Street was once a magnet for highwaymen – and at least one woman. Now the spectre of Catherine Ferrers, the Wicked Lady, is Hertfordshire's most famous – and most active – ghost.

❶ Anstey

A cave known as the Devil's Hole is rumoured to lead to a mound a mile away on which an 11th-century castle once stood.
The entrance has been sealed with rubble ever since Blind George, a fiddler from Anstey, met his untimely end there. During the 17th century, the fiddlers of Anstey were well known. Blind George, who was particularly popular, used to play at the Chequers Inn. He ridiculed the idea that the cave was full of demons and volunteered to explore its entire length accompanied only by his dog. The villagers watched as he tucked his fiddle under his chin and strode into the murky depths of the cave, playing as he went. They followed the muffled sounds of his music across the stubbled fields until, suddenly, the tune ended in a terrible screech and an equally awful silence. They rushed back to the entrance and there met George's dog, whose every hair was singed off. George was never seen again.

▶ *On minor road from B1368, 9 miles NW of Bishop's Stortford.*

② Brent Pelham

Piers Shonks, the squire of Pelham, was a legendary hunter, who was always accompanied on his expeditions by his groom and three faithful hounds. One day, they cornered a dragon in its lair beneath a yew tree in Great Pepsells field. During the fight, which was long and bloody, Shonks was badly wounded, but at last the dragon writhed in its death agony at the hero's feet. Just then, Satan appeared and demanded the squire's body and soul as payment for the death of his creature. Piers replied that his soul was God's, and his body would lie where his arrow fell. He strung an arrow to his bow and fired it towards Brent Pelham church. It entered through the south window, striking the north wall of the nave, and there Piers rests in his elaborately carved 11th-century tomb, beneath an inscription that concludes:

'… Shonks one serpent kills, t'other defies,
And in this wall, as in a fortress lies.'

▶ *7 miles NW of Bishop's Stortford on B1038.*

③ Sawbridgeworth

Hyde Hall, now a school, was once the home of Sir John Jocelyn. He was refused burial for himself and his favourite horse in the village churchyard, and was interred in his own land. Now, on November 1 each year, his ghost, mounted on a white horse, is said to ride furiously down the old carriage drive.
▶ *On A1184 4 miles N of Harlow.*

④ Burnham Green

Stories of phantom white horses galloping about the area may represent a memory of the white horse emblem on ancient Danish battle flags. The animals are usually described as being headless, which is probably an allegory for the slaughter inflicted upon the Danes when the local Saxons rose against them in 1002. A sunken lane leading to Welwyn Village is a particular haunt of these fearsome creatures. Many local people tend to avoid the lane after dark, while horses are said to be shy of it at any time.
▶ *On minor roads 3 miles N of Welwyn Garden City.*

⑤ St Albans

Ghost stories abound in St Albans. On moonlit nights a coach drawn by headless white horses toils up the steep slopes of Holywell Hill. Ghostly monks perform the ancient sung matins in the precincts of the abbey. On May 22, anniversary of the Battle of St Albans in 1455, old houses that stand on the supposed site of the battle resound with the clash of armies locked in combat.
▶ *3 miles N of Junctions 21A and 22 of M25.*

ST ALBANS ABBEY

⑥ Wigginton

During the Civil War, Wigginton Common was used by Cromwell's army to launch an artillery attack on nearby Berkhamsted Castle, which was destroyed by their cannon. According to local legend, a phantom Roundhead army is sometimes seen manoeuvring on the common at dusk.

▶ *Just S of A41, 1 mile S of Tring.*

⑦ Aldbury

The last inhabitant of the castle in Aldbury, which stood until the 14th century, was Sir Guy de Gravade. He used to raise the dead from their graves, with the help of the Devil, and from them learnt how to turn base metals into gold, by which skill he amassed a great fortune. Then his servant, John Bond, who had been spying on his employer, began experimenting on his own account, and the castle and all its occupants disappeared in a flash of lightning and a roll of thunder. Some said that the Devil came to claim his own. Apparently, on certain nights, the sinister building reappears, and through its windows can be seen the spectres of Sir Guy and John Bond, both condemned to slave in an everlasting quest for gold.

▶ *On minor road 2 miles E of Tring.*

⑧ Markyate

Hertfordshire's best authenticated spectre – that of 'The Wicked Lady', Catherine Ferrers – has haunted her old home of Markyate Cell since she died in the middle of the 17th century. The house, near Markyate, remains privately owned. It stands on the site of a Benedictine priory, and the fact that it was rebuilt 200 years after her death has not deterred Lady Ferrers in the least. Hoofbeats are often heard along the quiet lanes, and sometimes Catherine herself appears, leaping the hedgerows on a coal-black horse or galloping over the grass at the side of the drive, using the turf to muffle her horse's hoofbeats, exactly as she did in life.

She is suspected of being the instigator of a serious fire in the house in 1840 and, when repairs were being carried out, terrified the workmen by swinging from the branch of a tree in broad daylight. She was often seen in the kitchen, and appeared on the great staircase with such regularity that a previous owner used to bid her 'goodnight' as he went up to bed. Her most spectacular appearance – and one that may indicate that ghosts have a sense of humour – occurred at a parish tea early in the 20th century. Cakes and curates, children and sandwiches scattered in all directions as Lady Ferrers grinned horribly at the assembled company from her favourite perch in a tree.

It all began when Catherine was married in her teens to a man she disliked. From the start, she found life in the country tedious. To enliven her miserable state, she disguised herself as a highwayman and began robbing the coaches on nearby Watling Street. The mysterious highwayman who always rode a great black horse became the terror of the neighbourhood, and a byword for sheer audacity in a series of bold robberies. But Lady Ferrers pursued her career for excitement, and had little need of the valuables she stole. She hid them, together with her disguise, in a secret room above the kitchen at Markyate Cell. At last her luck ran out. She was wounded – some say by her lover – while robbing a coach near St Albans, and struggled home to die at the door of her chamber. Her horrified husband buried her quietly, and sealed her secret room, mistakenly believing that to be the last that anyone would hear of her.

▶ *On A5 2 miles NW of Junction 9 of M1.*

⑨ Preston

The mossy stones and crumbling arches of ruined Minsden Chapel, built in the 14th century and abandoned some 300 years later, are haunted by a ghostly monk who appears at Halloween. The long-lost chapel bells are first heard tolling, and sweet strains of music fill the air, before the cowled figure drifts into view under the derelict south arch. As the sounds die away, he walks, with head bowed as if in meditation, up steps that no longer exist, and fades away. The music then returns – but only a few sad, plaintive notes are heard before all is still and silent once again.

▶ *On minor roads 3 miles S of Hitchin.*

⑩ Hitchin

Moated Hitchin Priory was built in 1770–71 on the site of a 14th-century Carmelite house. It is reputedly visited by the ghost of a Cavalier named Goring, who was killed in front of his fiancée by a party of Roundheads at nearby High Down House. Each year, on June 15, his headless ghost is said to ride to the site of his hiding place in the grounds of the priory.

▶ *On A602 3 miles W of Junction 8 of A1(M).*

KENT

The Garden of England is a county of contrasts. A pastoral idyll of orchards, farms and woods shelters the most haunted village in the country. Ghostly events occur in busy towns, and even on main roads.

❶ Rainham

A strange legend about a phantom coach is still current in Rainham. The coach is believed to leave the church at midnight, drawn by headless horses and driven by a headless coachman. Inside sits a headless man, holding his head in his hands. The coach stops at Queen Court in Berengrave Lane (now absorbed in a housing estate) to water the headless horses, while an old woman sits spinning on top of a barn. Then the coach carries on to Bloor's Place, enters the grounds of the house, and disappears. The passenger in the coach is said to be the ghost of Christopher Bloor, who had a reputation as a ladies' man in Tudor times. The legend says that the town's irate husbands banded together and waylaid him at midnight. His head was cut off and placed on a spike, high on the church tower. However, the records show that Christopher Bloor actually died in bed, and there is no written reference to his allegedly lecherous habits. Until the mid 1960s the owners of Bloor's old house used to put out a full glass of brandy for the coach-travelling ghost every Christmas Eve, and the glass was always empty in the morning. The local policeman was once questioned about the mystery. 'It's a fact,' he said. 'But I blames the postman.'

▶ *5 miles E of Rochester on A2.*

❷ Aylesford

On Blue Bell Hill, remains of several Medway megaliths can be found. These mark a group of prehistoric burial chambers, and one, Kit's Coty House, is reputed to be where a British chieftain who was killed in personal combat with the Jutish leader, Horsa, in AD 455, was laid to rest. Phantom combatants are said to re-enact the battle occasionally 'in uncanny silence'.

But Blue Bell Hill – in particular a stretch of the A229 close to Maidstone – is notable as the location of some modern events that are widely considered to be ghost sightings. The first occurred in 1974, when a man from Rochester walked into Maidstone Police station to report an accident in the early hours of July 13. He claimed he had hit a young woman on the road – she had simply walked out in front of him. Passing cars had failed to stop, so he covered the injured girl with a blanket and left her by the side of the road. Returning to the scene, police and a sniffer dog failed to find any sign of her, nor was there any damage to the car. A press appeal was launched, in case the victim might have been dazed and wandered off, or even abducted, but no information was forthcoming. The incident was put down to the shaken driver's imagination.

In 1992, a driver heading along the southbound carriageway at around 11.50pm saw a young woman on the road close to the central reservation. Within seconds she had run in front of his car and the driver, who couldn't avoid hitting her, reported she was looking right at him all the time. He pulled over, but failed to find any sign of her, so he drove directly to Maidstone Police station to report the accident. Police returned with him, but the search for the body proved fruitless. A fortnight later, a woman wearing a red scarf ran out in front of a young man, again heading for Maidstone, and again the police failed to find the body.

Newspapers seeking a paranormal explanation linked the 'ghost' to one of four girls involved in a fatal car crash on Blue Bell Hill in 1965 – a tragedy made all the more poignant by the fact that one of the women was due to get married the following day. But no real link to the women involved has ever been established. Various drivers along that stretch of carriageway have reported seeing a 'girl' or 'young woman' on the roadside at night, and two an old, hag-like woman, exuding what they described as a strong sense of evil. All were shaken by their experience.

▶ *Close to Junction 6 of M20. Kit's Coty House 1 mile N of village.*

SOUTHERN ENGLAND

❸ Newington

A large boulder stands at the entrance to St Mary the Virgin church in Newington, near Rainham. This is the Devil's Stone and imprinted on it is his footprint, 38cm (15in) long. An old story tells that Satan, unable to endure the ringing of the church bells, collected them in a sack one night, and leapt down from the church tower. Overbalancing as he landed, he left his footprint on the stone near the church gate, and the bells rolled out of the sack to vanish for ever in a nearby stream.

▶ *On A2 7 miles E of Rochester.*

❹ Canterbury

The passage between the old infirmary cloister and the Green Court in Canterbury Cathedral is known as the Dark Entry and is reputedly haunted by Nell Cook, a servant of a canon of the cathedral in Tudor times. Nell discovered that her employer was having an affair with his so-called niece and, outraged, killed them both with a poisoned pie. The authorities buried her alive beneath the pavement of the Dark Entry, and her ghost has haunted the passageway ever since. According to R.H. Barham (1788-1845), author of the *Ingoldsby Legends*, the visitations occur on Friday nights, and anyone who sees the spirit will die.

▶ *16 miles NW of Dover on A2.*

➎ Reculver

Listen carefully and, on stormy nights, babies can be heard crying on the wind that blows around Reculver towers. These twin towers are all that are left of the Saxon church of St Mary's, which was built on the site of a Roman fort. The old local tale of whimpering children was given some substance in the 1960s when archaeologists excavating the Roman fort found a number of babies' skeletons. It has been suggested that that the children were buried alive as sacrifices, possibly to protect the occupants of the fort from harm.

The main part of the church was demolished in 1809 to prevent it from falling into the sea, but the towers were saved. The shoreline continues to recede, though, and sea defences were strengthened in the 1990s.

▶ *On minor road N of A299, 3 miles E of Herne Bay.*

BABIES CAN BE HEARD CRYING ON THE WIND
RECULVER TOWERS

ELIZABETHAN TOWER, SISSINGHURST

❻ Sissinghurst

A staircase in Sissinghurst Castle, owned by the National Trust, is believed to be haunted. A few years ago, the late Lady Nicolson (Vita Sackville-West), who restored the castle and its gardens, was walking towards the stairs with her dog when it suddenly raised its hackles and refused to go on. She sensed nothing strange but was sure that the dog had been frightened by something supernatural. More than three centuries earlier, two Protestant women had hidden under this staircase to avoid the owner, Sir John Baker, who sent so many Protestants to the stake during Queen Mary's reign that he was known as 'Bloody Baker'. On this occasion, he was followed by a servant carrying the body of a woman, believed to have been murdered. As the servant climbed the stairs one of the dead woman's hands got caught in the banisters and Sir John hacked it off. The hand fell into the lap of one of the women crouched below. Just whose unquiet spirit returns to the scene is not clear.
▶ *14 miles W of Ashford on A262.*

❼ Otford

Becket's Well, which was excavated some years ago, is said to have miraculous origins. Archbishop Thomas Becket, visiting Otford, was unhappy about the quality of the local water. So he struck the ground with his crozier and two springs of clear water bubbled up from that spot. Becket is also held responsible for the absence of nightingales in the village. When the song of a nightingale disturbed his devotions, he commanded that none should sing there again – and, apparently, none has.
▶ *3 miles N of Sevenoaks on A225.*

❽ Pluckley

There seems to be no particular reason why the pretty village of Pluckley, just a couple of miles off the busy A20 between Maidstone and Ashford, should be a centre of paranormal activity. But with at least 12 ghosts to its name, the village has for many years laid claim to be the most haunted in Britain and is listed as such in the book of *Guinness World Records*. Among Pluckley's most famous ghostly residents is the highwayman of Fright Corner on the Smarden Road – a spectre who, legend has it, often appears pinned to a tree. The story goes that this unfortunate rascal used a hollow tree at the side of the road as a vantage point from which to surprise the unwary, but was caught out when one traveller took the precaution of running his sword through the trunk with the highwayman still inside it. The area is also said to be haunted by a drunken gypsy woman who fell asleep while smoking a pipe, setting her gin-sodden clothing alight.

Closer to the centre of the village, a ghostly horse and carriage can allegedly be seen in The Street, although its origins are unknown. Pluckley's two hostelries are both reputedly haunted, the Dering Arms by a Victorian woman who lurks beside the bar, and the Black Horse by a poltergeist that frequently hides items, only to put them back in places where they cannot have been overlooked.

No less than three ghostly women are said to haunt the parish church of St Nicholas, including that of a former lady of the manor who insisted on being buried inside three lead coffins in an effort to prevent her body from decaying. At Greystones House in Station Road, which was once the rectory, a phantom monk is among the disquieted spirits said to roam both house and grounds.

Several books have been written about the ghosts of Pluckley, although the village's paranormal credibility was shaken when the popular BBC Radio 2 presenter Desmond Carrington confessed to having 'made up' a number of stories for an article he wrote about them for *TV Times* back in the 1960s. It also seems likely that many of the ghostly screechings that have been reported in and around the nearby woods over the years are, in fact, the mating calls of foxes, which are known to reach a crescendo in the foggy months of midwinter. Yet in spite of the fact that no ghost has actually been seen in Pluckley since the late 1990s, the tales of the village's phantoms live on – just as they have for hundreds of years.
▶ *On minor roads 5 miles NW of Ashford.*

SOMETHING EERIE
ON THE STAIRS
SISSINGHURST CASTLE

OXFORDSHIRE

Inhabited long before the Celts held sway, Oxfordshire is steeped in ancient history. Traces remain among gently rolling hills and valleys, where age-old spirits are joined by the ghosts of later conflicts.

❶ Adderbury

Sir George Cobb's phantom in a ghostly coach-and-four, its horses breathing fire, was seen by several poachers, who reported the apparition crossing parkland near where Cobb House once stood. Sir George was the last occupant of Cobb House, which faced Adderbury Green and was demolished in the early 19th century. He gave orders that four particular oak trees in the park were never to be felled. However, shortly after his death in 1762, the trees were cut down, whereupon Sir George returned to the spot to show his displeasure.

  The Devil must have been in a particularly good mood when he directed his attention to the churches in Adderbury and Bloxham, lending a willing hand in their construction and asking for nothing in return – not even a soul or two. The churches' 14th-century spires are credited as being partly the work of the Evil One. The story goes that the two brothers who built the churches employed an itinerant mason who, without payment, worked many times faster than his colleagues. The buildings were completed in record time and the mason disappeared, leaving behind him a faint whiff of sulphur and an uneasy recollection of his curiously shaped feet.
▶ *4 miles S of Banbury on A4260.*

❷ Ambrosden

When the foundations of the church of St Mary were being laid in Church Leys field at Ambrosden, the Devil for some reason disapproved of the site. Each morning the builders found that the materials they had placed in the field on the previous day had been mysteriously moved to another spot. Finally, the workers gave in and built the church on the site chosen by the Devil. A similar tale is told of the church of St Peter and St Paul at Checkendon. There, the intended site of the building is still known as the Devil's Churchyard.
▶ *2 miles SE of Bicester.*

❸ Woodstock

North of the bridge that spans the lake in Blenheim Palace Park is an inscribed stone, marking the site where Woodstock Manor once stood. The Black Prince was born there in 1331, and the manor was a royal house until its destruction during the Civil War. From October 13 to November 2, 1649, Cromwell's Parliamentary Commissioners stayed in the manor, and were plagued by a spirit that became known as the 'Royalist Devil of Woodstock'. Night after night, beds moved up and down, candles were blown out, broken glass was hurled about the rooms and servants were drenched in 'stinking ditch-water'. The Commissioners finally left, never to return, and the Royalist Devil was never heard of again.
▶ *8 miles NW of Oxford on A44.*

❹ Oxford

Surprisingly for a town so steeped in history, Oxford has remarkably few ghosts. One, however, is that of Archbishop Laud, who was beheaded as 'an enemy to Parliament' on Tower Hill in 1645. Allegedly, his mutilated spectre rolls its head around the library floor of St John's College, where he once studied and where he was elected chancellor of the university in 1630.
▶ *8 miles W of Junction 8 of M40.*

❺ Cumnor

Until its demolition in 1810, Cumnor Hall was said to be haunted by the ghost of 28-year-old Amy Robsart, wife of Robert Dudley, one of the favourite courtiers of Elizabeth I. On September 8, 1560, Amy was found at the bottom of the staircase, her neck broken. Her husband was suspected of plotting her death so that he could marry Elizabeth, but nothing was proved and Dudley, later Earl of Leicester, remained the Queen's favourite. But in 1588, while staying at Cornbury Park, Oxfordshire, he reputedly met his wife's ghost in nearby Wychwood Forest, and she warned him that he would soon join her. A few days later he died of a sudden illness. Her phantom is still said to roam Cornbury Park, and to see this ghost is a certain warning that death is imminent.
▶ *4 miles SW of Oxford on A420.*

DEVILISH TALES OF OXFORDSHIRE

SATAN SEEMS TO HAVE devoted much of his time to Oxfordshire where, contrary to his usual practice, he has on occasions assisted humankind. As well as helping to build two churches (see page 74), he sometimes concerned himself with Sabbath breakers. At North Leigh, a group of neighbours decided to go badger-hunting one Sunday instead of attending church. After a long struggle, they dragged a large badger from its sett and pushed it into a sack, but by the time they reached home, the creature had vanished, and all that remained was an 'awful smell of brimstone'. On another Sunday, also in North Leigh, a stranger joined in a cricket match and proved to be an outstanding player, but as he bowled out the last batsman, he suddenly disappeared in a cloud of smoke.

However, at Oxford University in 1834, the Devil resumed one of his nastier guises when summoned by a group of undergraduates, allegedly members of Brasenose College Hellfire Club. A Fellow of the college was walking back home down Brasenose Lane one evening when he saw a figure in a long black cloak at the window of the room occupied by Edward Trafford, president of the club. While he watched, he saw the figure pulling Trafford through the wire security mesh on the window, face first, and heard the young man's screams of agony. On investigation, Trafford was found dead on the floor of his room, covered in blood from a burst blood vessel. That Edward Trafford died that night is a matter of record – whether the Devil came to claim his own remains a matter of conjecture.

❻ Clifton Hampden

Much neglected by her husband, the beautiful Sarah Fletcher lived a sad and lonely life at Courtiers House in Clifton Hampden. Finally, in despair over his infidelity, she hanged herself in her bedroom there in 1799. Although her tomb is in Dorchester Abbey, her ghost has often appeared in the house. Those who have reported seeing it claim that the purple ribbon she always wore in her curly auburn hair is distinctly visible, as well as the expression of anguish on her face.
▶ *On A415 7 miles S of Oxford.*

❼ Little Wittenham

Sinodun Hill, near Little Wittenham, is the site of a Roman fort, where some unspecified treasure is supposed to be buried in a hollow known as the 'Money Pit'. A story relates how one villager dug deep in search of it, and just as he found an iron chest, a raven alighted on it and cried, 'He is not born yet!' Taking this to mean that he was not the one fated to find the treasure, the man immediately filled in the hole and left.
▶ *On minor roads 2 miles S of A415, 8 miles S of Oxford.*

SOUTHERN ENGLAND

❽ Uffington Castle

In reality, this castle is a large Iron Age hillfort, and its imposing chalk ramparts still loom protectively over Berkshire's Vale of the White Horse. It may have been a spiritual centre at one time, but even more important to the Celtic tribe who carved its battlements out of the hillside shortly before the Roman invasion was the fact that it commanded the Ridgeway, the prehistoric track that runs across England from the coast near Dover to Ilchester in Somerset. So obvious is this dominance that some people believe Uffington was Mount Badon, where King Arthur finally defeated the Saxons, in about AD 518. There is little doubt that in the days when the valleys were thickly forested, whoever held the high Ridgeway route would control the West of England.

The 114m (374ft) long White Horse that gave the Vale its name is cut into the turf close to the castle, and may well date from the same period. It is the oldest chalk-cut figure in Britain, and probably represents a Celtic god or is a tribal symbol, yet for centuries local people maintained that it was a portrait of the dragon killed by St George on nearby Dragon's Hill.

▶ *S of B4507, 6 miles W of Wantage.*

❾ Faringdon

The churchyard in Faringdon was once haunted by the spirit of Hampden Pye, an officer in the Royal Navy. His stepmother, desperate for her son rather than Hampden to inherit the family fortune, bribed his captain to arrange his demise, which was easily done. During a naval battle in the Spanish War, with the connivance of a gunner, Hampden was pushed in front of a canon and his head was blown off. Returning from the memorial service at the local church, his stepmother found Hampden's headless ghost sitting beside her in the coach. His spectre also haunted the gunner and the captain, a story recorded in an engraving by John Leech.

▶ *Junction of A420 and A417, 17 miles SW of Oxford.*

❿ North Leigh

In drought conditions, a particular pattern of parched grass appears just beyond the excavations of a large Roman villa. Unearthed in 1813, the villa has a well-preserved mosaic floor and evidence of hot baths among its 60 rooms. The mysterious pattern is actually thought to indicate where service buildings once stood.

▶ *3 miles NE of Witney on A4095. Roman villa 2 miles N of North Leigh.*

⓫ Minster Lovell

Francis, the 1st Viscount Lovell, supported the impostor Lambert Simnel in his attempt to depose Henry VII, and when Simnel was defeated in 1487, Francis disappeared. It was said that he managed to make his way back to Minster Lovell Hall to hide, but the servant who was looking after him died suddenly. Francis, unable to unlock the door of his hiding place, starved to death. In 1708, a secret underground room was discovered with a skeleton inside it, sitting at a table. Whether this was Francis will never be known, because the bones crumbled to dust almost as soon as the room was opened. Minster Lovell Hall was systematically demolished in the 18th century, and remains a picturesque ruin.

▶ *2 miles W of Witney on B4047.*

⓬ The Rollright Stones

For more than 2,000 years, a king and his conquering army have waited in the Cotswolds for someone with powerful magic to break the spell that turned them all to stone. That, at least, is how legend explains the Rollright Stones – in reality a Bronze Age formation on the boundary between Oxfordshire and Warwickshire. The legend mentions an army of indeterminate size and, although there seem to be 72 stones, some people still believe that 'the man will never live who shall count the stones three times and find the number the same'. The cluster consists of a circle about 30m (100ft) in diameter, a separate group known as the Whispering Knights, and the King Stone, which stands apart from the others.

The story is that the army had conquered England as far north as Little Rollright before disaster struck. Marching up the hill on which the village stands, the victorious king met a witch, who said, 'Seven long strides thou shalt take! If Long Compton thou canst see, King of England thou shalt be!' Knowing that Long Compton was just over the brow of the hill, the king took seven strides forward. Unfortunately, a mound obscured his view, and the witch cackled, 'As Long Compton thou canst not see, thou and thy men hoar stones shalt be.' And stones they still remain.

The Rollright Stones are also said to be a favourite haunt of Oxfordshire fairies and Warwickshire witches. According to some fanciful accounts, the stones sometimes come alive at midnight to perform strange dances and even walk down to Little Rollright Spinney for a drink.

▶ *1 mile S of Long Compton on A3400, 21 miles NW of Oxford.*

CELTIC GOD OR TRIBAL SYMBOL?

WHITE HORSE HILL, UFFINGTON

RREY

as its quota of headless monks and other unsettled spirits,
as a puma – a mysterious big cat that stalks the heaths,
and leafy village lanes, and has been caught only on camera.

❶ Shepperton

During the 1940s, several people claimed to have seen the ghost of a headless monk in Shepperton. Rumour had it this was the spirit of a monk from Chertsey Abbey who broke his vows and left his order to live with a woman on a shepherd's farm. The monk was pursued and beheaded. His ghost, dressed in monastic robes, wanders through the houses of the town that grew up around the farm, still trying to escape from his pursuers.

▶ *3 miles E of Chertsey on B375.*

❷ Walton-on-Thames

The identity of the ghostly judge that is said to haunt Walton's 15th-century manor house is undecided because the manor was the home of two notorious judges – John Bradshaw, President of the Court that condemned Charles I to death, and Chief Justice Jeffreys, who conducted the Bloody Assizes after Monmouth's rebellion against James II.

▶ *Junction of A244 and A3050, 6 miles SW of Kingston upon Thames.*

❸ Weybridge

Brooklands, near Weybridge, is a famous name in both motor-racing and aviation history. Damaged during the Second World War, the place fell into disrepair until it was partly restored by the Brooklands Society and Museum. The clubhouse and some famous sections of the huge oval circuit have been preserved, including the Railway Straight, where Percy Lambert was killed in October 1913. Lambert, the first person to cover 100 miles in an hour, was trying to regain the speed record when his Talbot car crashed by some aircraft sheds. After that, and especially while the site was run-down, all sorts of seemingly supernatural incidents were reported. Often, at night, the roar of engines and the squeal of tyres were heard. On several occasions, night-workers challenged an overalled, helmeted figure, and even chased it until it disappeared through a solid wall. Perhaps this was the ghost of Lambert. Some people believe he haunts Brooklands still.

▶ *2 miles E of Junction 11 of M25 on A317. Brooklands is 2 miles S of town centre.*

❹ Epsom

Pitt Place, now demolished, once belonged to Lord Lyttelton, who died there on November 27, 1779. Just before his death, he was warned by an unidentified ghost that he had three days to live. He seemed perfectly healthy until an hour before the ultimatum was due to expire, when he had a sudden fatal seizure. At that moment, his friend Miles Andrews, asleep in his bed in Dartford, awoke to see Lyttelton wearing a dressing-gown that was kept for his use when he came to stay. Lyttelton said, 'It's all up with me, Andrews,' and walked into the dressing room. Andrews followed, but the room was empty and the gown hung on its usual hook. Thinking it was all a joke, he returned to bed, and was horrified to learn the next morning that Lyttelton was dead.

▶ *3 miles NE of Junction 9 of M25 on A24.*

❺ Buckland

Two explanations are given for the red staining on a rock beside the village stream. A long time ago, the lord of the manor attempted to seduce a local girl, who was so frightened that she dropped dead at his feet. Overcome by remorse, the man stabbed himself, and his blood ran over the stone. For years afterwards, villagers avoided it, because it was said to ooze the lord's guilty blood.

Alternatively, the stains could have been made by the victims of the Buckland Shag, a water horse that terrified wayfarers for generations. Eventually, the local vicar exorcised the creature with bell, book and candle and banished it to the Red Sea – a frequent place of exile for ghosts and goblins.

▶ *2 miles W of Reigate on A25.*

❻ Coldharbour

In a wood near Coldharbour is Mag's Well, long credited with healing properties. People still regard it as a wishing well, but it is important to drop a coin into its waters before wishing, in order to placate the spirit of the place. The spring is one of the sources of Pip Brook, which runs through Dorking to the River Mole.

▶ *On minor roads 1 mile W of A24, 4 miles S of Dorking.*

7 Abinger Common

This picturesque village has been inhabited since the Stone Age, but in April 2004 it joined the growing list of Surrey villages renowned for an altogether different kind of occupant – namely, some unknown species of big cat. Sightings of the so-called 'Surrey Puma' date back to 1955, when a woman out walking her dog in Abinger Hammer reported seeing a 'puma-like' animal slinking away from the mutilated body of a dead calf. After that, reports of both puma and panther-like cats cropped up all over the southwest of the county, culminating in a blurred photograph taken in 1966, which some experts identified as a puma. In 1968 a local farmer claimed to have shot a creature resembling a big cat, but no body was ever found. Reports of mysterious 'dark brown' and 'rabbit-coloured' cat-like creatures stalking the countryside continued to appear sporadically and the Abinger Common sightings became just the next in a list of more than 1,000 recorded incidents. A year later, a man named Harry Fowler recorded blurred video footage of what appeared to be a dark, cat-like creature prowling across a field near Winkworth Arboretum. It is impossible to establish the identity of the animal, but many Surrey residents need no further convincing.
▶ *On minor road 1 mile S of A25, 4 miles W of Dorking.*

8 Shere

A small lake surrounded by trees, a mile west of Shere, is known as the 'Silent Pool'. An uncanny hush seems to hang over it, caused, if the legend is true, by the lechery of a prince and two tragic deaths. One day, so the story goes, when all this area was dense forest, a woodman gave refreshment to a passing stranger, who turned out to be Prince John, Regent of Britain while his brother Richard was crusading in Palestine. The stranger followed the woodman's daughter to the pool, intending to seduce her, but in her efforts to escape, both she and her brother, who came to her rescue, drowned.

When their distraught father found them later, he spotted a feather caught in a tree, and recognised it as coming from the stranger's hat. With retribution on his mind, he attended an audience at Guildford Castle, told his story and denounced the Prince Regent. Legend does not say how the audience ended, but certainly the woodman had his revenge. By tradition, the tragic deaths of his children confirmed the barons in their hatred of John, and helped pave the way for their triumph over him at Runnymede in 1215.
▶ *Just S of A25, 5 miles E of Guildford.*

9 Cranleigh

Two miles from the town stands the great Tudor mansion of Baynards Park, which, for a time at least, sheltered the decapitated head of Thomas More. Sir (and later, Saint) Thomas was executed in 1535 for refusing to acknowledge Henry VIII's supremacy over the Pope in the Church in England. His head was impaled on Tower Bridge, and was afterwards ordered to be thrown into the Thames. More's daughter, Margaret Roper, bribed the executioner to give it to her, and she brought it to Baynards Park. The ghost of Thomas More has frequently been reported there. The mansion was destroyed by fire in 1979. Today only the original gatehouse and tower remain.
▶ *9 miles SE of Guildford on B2128.*

10 Hambledon

Treasure may have been buried in Tolt Hill, near Hambledon. The ground rang hollow if stamped on, and rattled when ploughed, but no one tried to excavate the site because, whatever it was, the treasure was thought to belong to the Devil. People avoided the place after dark.
▶ *Just E of A283, 5 miles S of Godalming.*

11 Godalming

The restless spirit of Bonnie Prince Charlie may roam the paths of Westbrook Place. He is alleged to have conferred with his supporters there before the rising of 1745 and, in the interests of secrecy, could take exercise only at night. A mysterious figure, closely wrapped in a brown cloak, has often been seen walking in the twilight.

An imperial phantom may reside at the King's Arms Royal Hotel in the High Street. Peter the Great, Czar of Russia, stayed there in 1698 with 20 companions, and their rowdy behaviour caused scandal in the town. Perhaps the party is still going on, for, apparently without human agency, glasses and other objects are sometimes thrown about the room they once occupied.
▶ *4 miles SW of Godalming on A3100.*

12 Farnham

Near Moor Park and Waverley Abbey lies the cave of Mother Ludlam, a medieval white witch who would lend her possessions to anyone who needed them. However, after a cauldron was not returned on time, Mother Ludlam never lent anything again. When the cauldron finally appeared, she ignored it, and it was taken to Frensham church for safekeeping.
▶ *9 miles W of Guildford on A31.*

SOUTHERN ENGLAND

SUSSEX

The ghostly presence of Viking, Roman and Norman settlers is evident all over Sussex, in eerie woods and haunted groves, in dragon tales and in stories of the Devil's work.

❶ Brede

In reality, Sir Goddard Oxenbridge of Brede Place, who died in 1537, seems to have been an amiable and pious man, yet for some reason he has gone down in history as a terrible child-eating ogre whom no steel weapon could hurt. One day, when this legendary Sir Goddard was drunk, a great band of children ambushed him on Groaning Bridge and sawed him in half with a two-handled wooden saw – the children of East Sussex taking one end, and those of West Sussex the other. The severed portions of his body are still said to haunt both Brede Place and the bridge.
▶ *6 miles N of Hastings on A28.*

❷ Battle

The abbey marks the site of the Battle of Hastings, which the Normans called Senlac – 'Lake of Blood'. An old belief that the ground still sweats blood after rain may be accounted for by the iron in the soil that occasionally tinges puddles red. At the Reformation, Battle Abbey was given to Sir Anthony Browne. At the first banquet he held there, a monk appeared and told him that his name would be wiped from the land by fire and water. This fate was long delayed, but in 1793, Cowdray Hall, near Midhurst, the home of Sir Anthony's descendant Lord Montague, was burnt down. A week later, the direct line of the family came to an end when the young viscount was drowned in the Rhine.
▶ *6 miles NW of Hastings on A2100.*

❸ Herstmonceux

Ghostly drumming is frequently heard on the battlements of Herstmonceux Castle and a 3m (9ft) tall phantom drummer has been seen there. The spectre is that of a previous lord of the manor. Apparently, he used to beat a drum in order to frighten away any young men who, in his jealous mind, might have been intent on seducing his young wife.
▶ *On minor road S of A271, 8 miles N of Eastbourne.*

❹ Alfriston

The 14th-century church of St Andrew is said to have been inspired by the miraculous appearance of four white oxen on the village green. The animals lay down with their rumps together, forming a cross, and the church was built on that spot and in that shape.
▶ *1 mile S of A27, 8 miles NW of Eastbourne.*

❺ Lewes

November 5 has long been celebrated in Lewes with great pageantry. During the reign of the Catholic Mary Tudor, Lewes folk were largely Protestant, and many of them were burnt as heretics on School Hill in the town centre. The ensuing anti-papist resentment found an outlet in Bonfire Night. A tradition that originated even longer ago involved hurling a blazing tar barrel into the River Ouse. Several processions used to converge on the bridge for the ceremony, which was a relic of pagan Celtic rites – fire doused by water represented winter overcoming summer. Today, seven Bonfire Societies are based in Lewes, and people from outside the area are urged not to go to watch the fireworks, because of traffic congestion.
▶ *8 miles NE of Brighton on A27.*

❻ Brighton

Ghosts are well represented in Brighton and its environs. A wailing child who died of neglect, and a murderer whose phantom hands still attempt to strangle anyone who sleeps in a particular bed, haunt houses in Shoreham. The ghost of a monk, who was walled up alive for running away with a local girl, favours Meeting House Lane, where he has often been seen disappearing through a bricked-up doorway next to the Friends' Meeting House. Many legends surround the ancient stone plinth in St Nicholas's churchyard. According to one version, a knight and his horse, both in armour, are buried beneath it, and on moonlit nights the horse emerges alone and gallops round the graves.
▶ *30 miles S of Junction 11 of M23 on A23.*

THE DRAGON FOREST

FOR THOUSANDS OF YEARS, the dragon has played a prominent part in western mythology, and for a time its fearsomeness was harnessed militarily. Roman soldiers inscribed dragon symbols on their battle standards, and Celts did the same. The flag of Wales still features a red dragon. Despite this, dragons were usually regarded as malignant and their slaughter symbolised the victory of good over evil. In St Leonard's Forest, about halfway between Horsham and Pease Pottage, the 6th-century hermit-saint fought and killed a dragon that had been terrorising the neighbourhood. Wherever the saint's blood fell, lilies-of-the-valley sprang up, and the wild lily beds are still there to prove it. As a reward for his courage, God decreed that adders in the forest would not sting, and nightingales, which had disturbed St Leonard's prayers, would never sing there again.

However, St Leonard did not manage to free the forest of dragons permanently, for three local villagers claimed to have come across a 'strange and monstrous serpent' in 1614, and rumours of hideous creatures lurking among the trees lingered on until well into the 19th century.

The villagers who saw the 1614 dragon described it in great detail. It was about 3m (9ft) long, thick in the middle and thin at the ends, with red scales on its belly, black ones on its back and a ring of white markings around its neck. It had large feet, could run as fast as a man and left tracks of 'glutinous and slimie matter which is very corrupt and offensive to the smell'. It was reputedly able to spit its deadly venom over a great distance and was held responsible for the deaths of two people. 'As by woeful experience it was proved on the bodies of a man and a woman coming that way, who afterwards were found dead, being poysoned and very much swelled, but not prayed upon.' It killed two dogs but did not eat them, either. Apparently, it lived mainly on a diet of rabbits. Neither history nor legend relate what eventually happened to the creature.

Dragons were not the only hazard in the forest. It was also said to be haunted by a certain Squire Paulett, whose headless ghost used to leap up behind any rider passing among the trees, grip him round the waist, and ride behind him to the forest's edge. Who he had been in life and how he lost his head, was – and still is – a matter of mystery.

❼ Devil's Dyke

This great winding cleft carved out of the South Downs near Brighton has supernatural origins, according to local tradition. The enthusiasm of Sussex people for religion made the Devil decide to drown them all by digging a ditch through to the sea. As he reached the halfway mark, an old woman rushed up the hill with a lighted candle and a sieve. The light woke a cock, which began to crow, whereupon the Devil, seeing the candle through the sieve, imagined that sunrise was upon him, and fled.

In fact, this huge dry valley, the largest in Britain, was probably formed during the last glaciation, but not much is known about its history. The walls of an ancient hillfort are evident, so it may have been occupied 2,000 years ago. A public footpath runs the whole length of the Dyke, more than 7 miles.

▶ *5 miles NW of Brighton on South Downs Way.*

❽ Worthing

A triangle of land in the middle of a road intersection by Broadwater Green may seem an inauspicious site for haunting. However, years ago, skeletons were said to rise on Midsummer Eve from beneath an old oak that grew there, and dance hand in hand around the tree until the first cock crowed, but there have been no recent sightings.

▶ *11 miles W of Brighton.*

❾ Chanctonbury Ring

Surrounded by ramparts of eroded turf, this Iron Age hillfort is an eerie place. The air within the clump of beech trees on its summit strikes chill by comparison with the downland outside, even on sunny days, and bird song is a rarity. One belief is that to count the trees accurately would raise the ghosts of Julius Caesar and his armies. The Devil, too, can be conjured up, by running seven times backwards around the clump at midnight on Midsummer Eve. When he appears, he proffers a bowl of porridge and takes the soul of anyone who accepts it. In another version, he grants his summoner's dearest wish. The thudding hooves of invisible horses have often been heard on the hilltop, and a mysterious, white-bearded man has been reported, said to be the ghost of an old Druid, searching for buried treasure.

▶ *On South Downs Way 3 miles W of Steyning, 11 miles NW of Brighton.*

❿ Lyminster

Knuckler Hole is a deep pool that lies about 140m (460ft) northwest of Lyminster churchyard wall. Tradition maintains that it was the lair of a dragon that gradually devoured all the young women in the region until just one was left, the King of Sussex's daughter. Desperately, her father offered her in marriage, together with half of his kingdom, to anyone who killed the beast. Fortunately, a knight took on the challenge, despatched the dragon and married the princess. Whether they lived happily ever after is not recorded, but in the north transept of the church stands an early Norman coffin slab known as 'The Slayer's Stone', and this is reputed to be the knight's tomb.

▶ *2 miles N of Littlehampton on A284.*

⓫ Bosham

In the waters of the creek in front of the church is a place known as the Bell Hole. There, according to legend, lies the church's tenor bell, which was stolen by Danish pirates in the 10th century. As the raiders sailed away, the monks on shore rang the remaining bells to tell the villagers, who had run to hide in the woods, that it was safe for them to return. When the last peal rang out, the tenor bell in the boat joined in. It rocked and swayed until it capsized the boat, taking the pirates with it to the bottom of the creek. It is said that the tenor bell still joins in whenever the bells are rung.

▶ *Just S of A259, 4 miles W of Chichester.*

⑫ Kingley Vale

An incident recorded in the Anglo-Saxon Chronicle describes how, in AD 874, a marauding band of Vikings ravaged the Chichester countryside, 'and the citizens put them to flight, and killed many hundreds of them'. Kingley Vale, 4 miles northwest of Chichester, is the suggested site of the battle, and the grove of ancient yews there is supposed to be descended from 60 trees planted on the graves of those who died in the fighting. At night, according to legend, the trees change their shapes and move stealthily about the valley, mingling with the ghosts of slaughtered Vikings and Saxon defenders.

▶ *On footpaths from B2141, 4 miles NW of Chichester.*

SHAPE-CHANGING TREES THAT MINGLE WITH GHOSTS
KINGLEY VALE YEWS

WILTSHIRE

Puzzling man-made landmarks thousands of years old are scattered across the undulating countryside, but Wiltshire is also the scene of modern phenomena in the shape of crop circles and UFOs.

❶ Purton

Halfway between Purton and Purton Stoke is a bend in the road known as Watkins' Corner. This is where a man of that name was hanged for a murder to which his father later confessed. As he swung from the gallows, a storm blew up, which so frightened the hangman's horse that it bolted and threw its rider, breaking the hangman's neck. Allegedly, Watkin's ghost haunts the spot.
▶ *5 miles NW of Swindon on minor roads.*

❷ Rodbourne Cheney

An underground tunnel, now bricked up, is supposed to run between the church of St Mary and the manor house in Cheney Road. In the 16th century, fearing for the safety of the church's treasures during the Dissolution, the villagers hid them in the tunnel. The story persists that one of the treasures, a solid gold altar, was never returned, and remains hidden somewhere in the tunnel.
▶ *3 miles NW of Swindon town centre.*

❸ Broad Hinton

In the church at Broad Hinton is a 16th-century monument dedicated to the Wroughton family, showing Sir Thomas Wroughton and his wife Anne kneeling in prayer, along with their four children. The odd thing about it is that Sir Thomas and the children have no hands. The story goes that Sir Thomas returned from hunting one day to find Anne reading the Bible instead of cooking his supper. He grabbed the book from her in anger, and threw it into the fire. She managed to rescue it, but badly burnt her hands in doing so. As punishment for this blasphemy, Sir Thomas's hands and those of his four children withered away. The monument includes a Bible with a corner missing, to show where it was burnt.
▶ *7 miles S of Swindon on A4361.*

SILBURY HILL

❹ Avebury Stone Circles

Most of Avebury village lies within the largest prehistoric monument in Europe. Built about 2500 BC, the huge size of the Avebury circles indicates the existence of a large, well-organised population controlled by priests. The place was once believed to have been dedicated to serpent worship, because its plan suggested a coiled snake, but now it seems more likely that this was an open temple where pagan rites were practised. Surrounded by a bank and ditch 427m (1,400ft) in diameter, the main circle is formed by nearly 100 upright sarsen stones, some of which weigh up to 60 tonnes. The Avenue, which runs between pairs of standing megaliths, connects Avebury with the Sanctuary, a smaller temple on Overton Down a mile away.

In the Middle Ages, the Church became alarmed by the revival of paganism at Avebury, and instructed the villagers to bury the stones. When the place was investigated in 1938, a man's skeleton was found under one of them, along with several coins and surgical tools that identified him as a surgeon-barber. He died in about 1320 and may have been killed by the boulder falling on him accidentally. The restored megalith is known as 'the Barber's Stone'.

In the 17th and 18th centuries, local people helped themselves to whatever they wanted from the site, and tales were told of other accidents and near misses involving the stones. In one such story, the parish clerk sheltered from a storm under one of the ancient stones, and had just moved when it was struck by lightning.

Massive restoration took place during the 20th century, and many of the original stones were recovered. Avebury is run by the National Trust, and is a popular tourist attraction, but it remains a place of mystery and a magnet for those of pagan persuasion. Rites and ceremonies still take place in the circles, and tales are whispered of ghostly figures drifting among the stones at night and singing being heard when no singers are present.
▶ *12 miles S of Swindon near junction of A4361 and A4.*

❺ Silbury Hill

Silbury Hill, near Avebury, is the site of the largest prehistoric man-made mound in Europe – a 40m (130ft) high cone of chalk that was constructed in three phases beginning in 2,600 BC, around the time when Stonehenge was built. Silbury's true purpose remains unknown, but during the 1980s it became an excellent vantage point from which to spot examples of that other most enigmatic of creations, the crop circle.

Although around 90 per cent of crop circle appearances have occurred in southern England, the majority in Wiltshire, the phenomenon is not unknown in other parts of the world in countries as far apart as China and Canada. The huge and relatively sudden proliferation of circles in the 1980s was later blamed on two hoaxers, Doug Bower and Dave Chorley, who in 1992 claimed personally to have created more than 250 such circles since 1978. The number of incidences has dramatically declined in this century, leading some researchers to conclude that all crop circles are man-made. Others, however, remain unconvinced, pointing out that 'genuine' circles are actually slightly elliptical, and therefore impossible to mark out using the rope-and-peg method employed by Doug and Dave. It also seems that the stalks of corn laid flat within a real crop circle show no signs of breakage, but instead appear to have been 'bent' by some mysterious force.

Among the more scientific theories put forward for the existence of crop circles is that they are the result of some as yet unknown atmospheric condition, perhaps related to the electrostatic effect known as 'ball lightning'. Another theory ascribes the phenomenon to the sudden radioactive decay of minerals in the soil. For the time being, though, the mystery of crop circles, and of Silbury Hill, continues to baffle.
▶ *Silbury Hill is just N of A4, 7 miles W of Marlborough.*

❻ Littlecote House

The landing in the house – now a hotel – and a stile in the park are both said to be haunted. One night in 1575, the local midwife assisted a masked woman to give birth to a son, whereupon the masked man who had brought her, blindfolded, to the house, snatched the baby and threw it into the blazing fire. The horrified midwife managed to cut a piece of material from the bed-curtain and, blindfolded again, counted the stairs on the way out. This led to the house being identified as Littlecote, and the murderer as its owner, 'Wild' Darrell. Despite the evidence, Darrell was acquitted. But in 1589, while hunting in Littlecote Park, he was thrown from his horse and killed. The place is still called 'Darrell's Stile', and is allegedly frequented by his ghost. The child's mother – some say she was Darrell's sister – is supposed to haunt the landing.

Guests in the hotel, which provides ghost tours, have reported feelings of intense cold, unexplained lights and shadows on their photographs and rapidly drained batteries.
▶ *On minor road off B4192, 2 miles W of Hungerford.*

SOUTHERN ENGLAND

Circle of life and death

Stonehenge is an iconic monument to an ancient time – a prehistoric enigma that remains one of Britain's great mysteries.

Few places on Earth have inspired such fervent debate as the stone circle at Stonehenge. Rising from Salisbury Plain like the stumps of some ancient, petrified forest, the stones' existence has been pondered ever since the amateur antiquary William Stukeley first made them the subject of serious study in the 18th century. The earliest of the stones dates back to around 3000 BC, with the circle in its present form erected some 900 years later; and although there are stone circles all over north-western Europe, Stonehenge is unquestionably the finest example.

Stonehenge fell into disuse around 1600 BC. During the Middle Ages, it was regarded with extreme suspicion: some tales said it was built by giants; others that it was the work of King Arthur's magician Merlin or the devil himself. After the monument's age was determined in the late 19th century, scholarly opinion settled on the Druids – the priestly cult that held sway over the Celtic Britons before the arrival of the Romans in 55 BC. People envisioned terrible deeds and ritual sacrifices amid the ancient stones and Stonehenge's already sinister reputation took a bloody turn.

In fact, Stonehenge was built in the Neolithic by the people who had pioneered farming in north-western Europe from about 5000 bc. With their growing reliance on agriculture, these farmers found themselves ever more at the mercy of natural forces. There was also more competition, and frequent violent disputes – very likely over land. Ritual and superstition became ways of coping with the stress of daily existence. And for deities, the Neolithic people looked no further than the great lights in the sky – the Sun and the Moon – which regulated the patterns and seasons by which they lived their lives.

Mighty observatory

The extraordinary alignment of the stones at Stonehenge supports the theory that it was built as an astronomical observatory – possibly to serve as an agricultural calendar, possibly to chart the timings of annual ceremonies. A line of sight taken from the separate heelstone to the giant inner ring of capped stones known as 'trilithons' and on to the outer circle marks sunrise at the summer and winter solstices – the longest and shortest days of the year. Beyond the outer circle are the remains of the

The stones stand at the hub of a vast prehistoric landscape, with links to the River Avon

STONEHENGE

'station stones' that are thought to mark stages in the 18.6 year cycle of the Moon through the heavens – a remarkable astronomical calculation. Meanwhile, the 56 small stones that encircle the site may mark the Moon's monthly cycle through the year.

Builders, burials and belief

A far greater mystery is why the Stonehenge builders chose the place they did to erect their monument. This mystery is compounded by the fact that the 5-tonne bluestones that form the inner horseshoe were brought over land and sea from southwest Wales, near what is now the town of Preseli, more than 200 miles away. The largest – the 45 tonne sarsen stones – were dragged uphill from nearby land without the aid of wheels or water. What – or who – could have prompted Stonehenge's builders to contemplate such a colossal feat of engineering? What could have compelled entire communities to devote months, even years, of labour to the task, forsaking all differences and rivalries in the meantime?

Clearly, the location of the circle was a place of quite exceptional religious, political or practical significance – or perhaps a combination of all three – long before the first stones were laid. There is evidence of human activity on the site by hunter-gatherers from around 7000 bc. The first construction was a simple ditch and bank built around 3000 bc and there are signs that it was used as a burial ground between 2700 and 2600 bc – before the present arrangement came into being.

One recent theory formulated by archaeologist Mike Parker Pearson, based on his work there since 2003, suggests that Stonehenge is just part of a huge complex, comprising neighbouring Durrington Walls – the world's largest-known ditch and bank monument that was once topped with concentric rings of huge timber posts. He suggests that Durrington Walls was a monument to the living, while Stonehenge was reserved for the ancestral dead. Burials have been found in all phases of its construction, and Parker Pearson believes they were the kings or the elite of society and that the stones embodied their spirits.

A place of healing

Another recent theory suggested by archaeologists Timothy Darvill and Geoff Wainright, following excavations inside the circle, holds that Stonehenge was a site blessed with healing powers. The skeletal remains they discovered had suffered a considerable level of disease and injury, suggesting the monument was a place of pilgrimage where people came to be healed. The Preseli bluestones were quarried near healing springs in Wales, and these archaeologists believe the stones were transported to Stonehenge and erected there to tap into the same mystical force.

What is certain, is that the circle was a place of great importance – probably around the time of the winter and summer solstices – and that people from miles around would be drawn there to witness the time when the Sun would reaffirm its promise to watch over them for another year.

❼ Wilcot

In the early 17th century, Wilcot Vicarage was plagued by the sound of a bell, which tolled incessantly every night in one of the bedrooms. A wizard of Devizes is said to have caused this at the request of a drunkard who was annoyed by the vicar's refusal to ring the church bells late at night. The phantom bell became so famous that people made nocturnal pilgrimages to Wilcot to hear it, and James I is reputed to have visited the vicarage to listen to it. The ringing could be heard inside the bedroom but not outside. It finally stopped when the wizard died and the spell's power was lost with him. Later, the vicarage was rebuilt.

▶ *On minor road 1 mile W of A345, 5 miles S of Marlborough.*

❽ Salisbury Plain

One terrifying night in 1786, as lightning flashes illuminated Salisbury Plain, a sailor named Gervase Matcharn saw a ghostly drummer boy gliding towards him while he and another sailor were making their way northwards. Unable to bear the phantom's presence, he confessed to his companion that he had murdered the boy some years previously. Matcharn was hanged, and was accompanied to the gallows by the ghost of his victim.

▶ *N of A303 and S of A342, 10 miles N of Salisbury.*

❾ Longleat House

A top-floor corridor in the house is known as 'the Green Lady's Walk'. This is where, in the 18th century, Thomas Thynne, the 2nd Viscount Weymouth, is said to have killed his wife's lover in a duel. The ghost of his grief-sticken wife, Lady Louisa Carteret, has often been reported walking up and down the passage. The viscount is supposed to have buried the body in the cellar and, as if in confirmation of the tale, early in the 20th century, a man's skeleton, wearing 18th-century boots, was found under the stone flags of the cellar floor.

▶ *4 miles W of Warminster.*

❿ Cley Hill

Legend attributes the building of Cley Hill, an earthworks near Warminster, to the Devil. Displeased with the people of Devizes, Satan was returning from Somerset with a huge sack of earth on his back to throw at the town. Passing another walker, he asked the distance to Devizes. The old man replied that he had been searching for the town for so long that his hair had turned grey, whereupon the Devil lost heart and emptied his load of soil on the ground where he was standing, so forming the hill.

▶ *2 miles W of Warminster.*

⑪ Warminster

Residents of Warminster on the edge of Salisbury Plain are more accustomed than most to unusual goings-on. As the location of one of the nation's most important military bases, the countryside around the town is used for dozens of land-based and airborne exercises each year, and the many soldiers stationed in the area are unlikely to concoct gratuitous stories of alien activity. Yet the fact remains that since one extraordinary Christmas morning in 1964, when both local residents and servicemen claimed to have been taken aback by deafening whistling and crashing sounds from outside, accompanied by jarring vibrations, the skies above Warminster have been the source of a steady stream of strange phenomena – enough to make the town one of England's premier UFO hot spots.

The mysterious sounds heard on Christmas Day were heard again at intervals over the following three months. Then, in the summer of 1965, came a flood of reported sightings of strange glowing cigar-shaped objects and bright red 'balls of fire' in the night sky, often moving at incredible speed. At the end of August, the sightings abruptly ceased. But by then, the story of the Warminster 'Thing' had taken root in the public's imagination.

Sceptics point out that with the town's military connections, the phenomena are most likely to have been associated with the testing of some new weapon. The Ministry of Defence, however, has never confirmed this, and it seems unlikely that the secret could have been so well kept for so long.

▶ *20 miles NW of Salisbury on A36.*

⑫ Langley Burrell

Reginald de Cobham, the young lord of the manor of Langley Burrell, was burnt at the stake in 1413 because he was a follower of John Wycliffe, whose anti-papist teachings were believed to be heretical. Reginald was taken to the top of Steinbrook Hill, stripped, and slowly roasted to death. Now, at midnight on moonlit nights, he is said to walk naked around the hill, and surprisingly, considering the manner of his death, carries his head under his arm.

▶ *1 mile NE of Chippenham town centre.*

⑬ Draycot Cerne

The manor house in Draycot Cerne had been in the Long family for generations, but in 1610 Sir Walter Long, urged by his second wife, hired a clerk to change his will so as to prevent his son John from inheriting it. It was not that simple. Each time the clerk tried to write the vital clause, a white hand appeared between parchment and candle. Long's first wife was said to be intervening on her son's behalf.

▶ *1 mile SE of Junction 17 of M4.*

A MOUND BUILT BY THE DEVIL
CLEY HILL

INNER
LONDON
90-97

Regent's Park

King's Cross

St Pancras

Euston

16

Marylebone

A41

A5205

A41

A400

A501

A1

A501

A10

A1202

M4

A4

1

A40

A5

Paddington

A4202

INNER
LONDON
90-97

6

20

Liverpool
Street

7

Blackfriars

2

3

15

Hyde Park

14

8

5

4

Cannon
Street

Fenchurch
Street

17

Charing
Cross

Thames

London
Bridge

Thames

12

13

11

Green
Park

10

St James's
Park

9

Waterloo

A100

A4

19

A302

18

Victoria

A3213

A202

A201

A3

A2

A308

A3212

A3204

A4180

London

This ancient river settlement throngs with the vibrant spirits of the living ... and the restless shadows of the dead. Kings, queens, aristocratic ladies and theatrical gentlemen haunt the city's drawing rooms, stairwells and streets, destined to remain Londoners for all eternity.

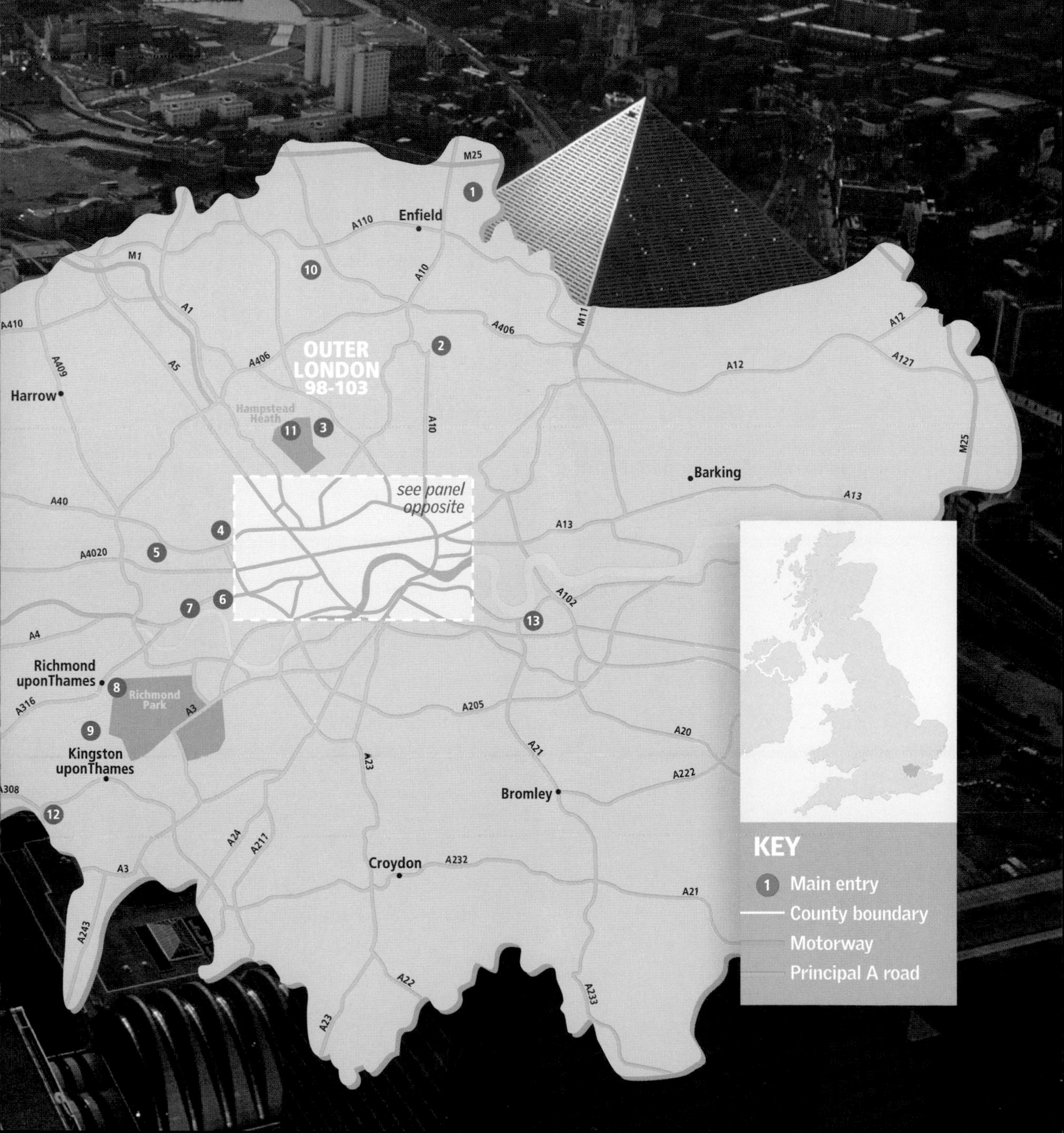

M25

① A110 **Enfield** M11

⑩ A10 A12

M1 A406 A12 A127

A1 ②

A410 A406 **OUTER LONDON 98–103** A10

A409 A5 A12

A40 **Harrow**• Hampstead Heath ⑪ ③ •**Barking** A13 M25

see panel opposite A13

④ A102

A4020 ⑤ ⑬

⑦ ⑥

A4

Richmond uponThames • ⑧ Richmond Park

A316 ⑨ A3 A205 A20

Kingston uponThames• A23 A21 A222

A308 **Bromley**•

⑫ A2A A211 A21

A3 **Croydon** A232

A243 A22

A23 A22 A233

INNER LONDON

Actors, politicians, regicides, royalty, prostitutes, felons and their relatives – not to mention doppelgangers – all prowl the city, that proved gold-paved for some but the downfall of others.

❶ Brick Lane

When the Truman Brewery was built in Brick Lane near Hanbury Street, a row of houses was demolished to make way for it, including number 29. That was where Annie Chapman met her untimely end in September 1888, the second victim of an unknown serial killer who quickly became known as Jack the Ripper. By July 1889, another six prostitutes had been murdered in London's East End. The similarity of the gruesome mutilations inflicted upon the victims led the police to assume the killings were the work of one man, but no one was ever caught, or charged with the crimes. Theories continue to be put forward about his identity, and cases have been made for a butcher, a surgeon, an artist and a member of the Royal Family, but no conclusive proof has ever been uncovered. Meanwhile, Annie Chapman's ghost continues to haunt the street where she endured such a violent death.
▶ *Hanbury St runs E from Commercial St near Old Spitalfields Market. Shoreditch tube.*

❷ Bank of England

The Bank's nickname, 'The Old Lady of Threadneedle Street', originated with a Gillray cartoon that was published in 1797, but later it was applied to a real person, Sarah Whitehead. Her brother Philip, a disgruntled former employee of the Bank, was found guilty of forgery in 1811 and executed. Sarah was unhinged by the shock, and every day for the next 25 years she appeared at the Bank, asking for her brother. When she died she was buried in the old churchyard that later became part of the Bank's gardens. Her ghost has been reported in the area on many occasions.
▶ *Threadneedle St. Bank tube.*

❸ Cornhill

While pealing the bells of St Michael's church during a violent storm, a team of early 16th-century bellringers were horrified to see 'an ugly shapen sight' come in at one window and float over to another. They fell unconscious, and later discovered deep scars in the stonework. The scars became known as the Devil's clawmarks, and for years the church had a sinister reputation.
▶ *St Michael's church is S of Cornhill close to junction with Bishopsgate. Bank tube.*

❹ London Stone

A remnant of this ancient block of limestone is set behind a grille in the wall of number 111 Cannon Street. It once stood in the roadway, opposite where it is now, but nobody knows who put it there, or why it was erected. One suggestion is that the Romans measured distances from it along their road network, but there is no evidence of this. The name crops up in written records for the first time in 1100, and the first mayor of London is recorded, in about 1190, as Henry, son of 'Ailwyn of London Stone'. It seems to have had some significance still in medieval times. When Jack Cade, the rebel leader, entered the town in 1450, he made a point of striking it with his sword while proclaiming himself 'Lord of London'.

By 1742 the stone was worn and had become a nuisance where it stood, so what was left of it was moved out of the roadway and propped up against St Swithin's church. Eventually, it was put into an alcove in the wall, where it remained until the church was demolished in 1962 and number 111 was built in its place. London Stone is listed Grade II, and should that building be demolished, the stone will still be accommodated on the site. If it has to be moved, it will be given a temporary home in the Museum of London. The legend that Brutus the Trojan, mythical founder of the city, laid the stone as a temple altar, and that 'so long as Brutus's stone is safe, so long shall London flourish' was, apparently, invented in 1862, but nevertheless the future of the stone appears to be secure.
▶ *Opposite entrance to Cannon St Station. Cannon St tube.*

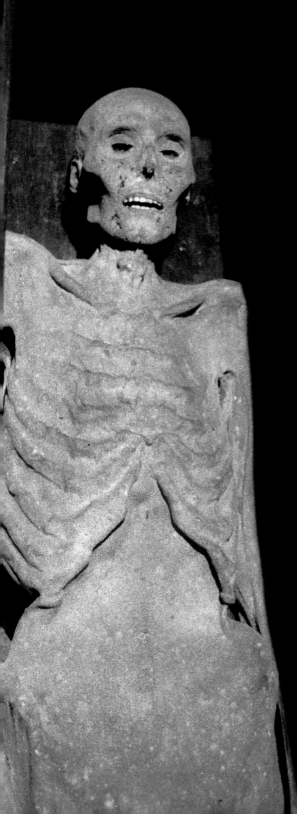

OLD JIMMY GARLICK

➎ Garlick Hill

In the 19th century, the embalmed body of a man was found under the floor of the church of St James Garlickhythe. No clues to his identity or how long he had been there have ever been discovered. The church itself was totally gutted in the Great Fire of London in 1666 and all records had been lost by the time it was completely rebuilt by Sir Christopher Wren. Theories about who he was are not lacking, though. Suggestions include a Roman general, Richard de Rothing, founder of the church in 1326, and Henry Fitzailwyn, who died in 1212, the first of six early mayors of London, who are known to have been buried in the church. He may even be Dick Whittington himself. Whoever he is, for years his mummified remains have been displayed in a glass case on the premises, but since the church was bombed during the Second World War, 'Old Jimmy Garlick', as the mummy is nicknamed, has apparently become restless. Several visitors to the church have reported seeing a shrouded ghost standing on the tower steps and in various other parts of the building.

▶ *St James Garlickhythe at foot of Garlick Hill, which runs S from Queen Victoria St at Mansion House. Mansion House tube.*

➏ Red Lion Square

Three cloaked figures have occasionally been reported in the Square. They are reputed to be the ghosts of Oliver Cromwell, John Bradshaw and Henry Ireton, all of whom signed Charles I's death warrant. Red Lion Square is one of the sites put forward as Cromwell's burial place.

▶ *S of Theobald's Rd and E of Drake St. Holborn tube.*

➐ Dean Street

The shadowy figure of a woman has been seen drifting through the Gargoyle Club, and she leaves behind her a powerful scent of gardenias. The ghost is thought to be that of Charles II's favourite mistress, the orange seller turned actress Nell Gwyn, who once lived there.

Fanny Kelly, the founder of Miss Kelly's Theatre and Dramatic School in 1840 – which became the Old Royalty Theatre in Dean Street – haunted the place for more than 50 years after her death in 1882. One of her last appearances was in 1934, when she was seen in a box, eagerly watching a rehearsal – she herself had been an actress, and excelled in melodrama. Property developers drove her out when they built offices on the site.

▶ *Runs N–S between Oxford St and Shaftesbury Ave. Tottenham Court Rd tube.*

London's bloody tower

The Tower of London was once synonymous with terror, torture and execution, as the ghosts that remain testify.

When William the Conqueror built the White Tower, the first of the great bastions that are collectively known as the Tower of London, it is said that he ordered bulls' blood to be mixed with the mortar, to symbolise strength and a royal power that would last forever. The Tower has stood for more than 900 years and to the modern visitor it evokes a sense of tradition and stability amid the ever-changing high-rises of the city. Yet for much of its history, this Norman castle was a place to be feared – a symbol of the king's power, the instrument of his vengeance, and, occasionally, the scene of his deadliest intrigues. The list of ghosts that have been seen in the building over the centuries reads like a *Who's Who* of medieval and Tudor English history. Almost all of these people met a grisly fate – the majority within the confines of the Tower's walls.

Early hauntings

Among the first of the famous historical ghosts to be spotted in the Tower was that of Thomas Becket, the pious Archbishop of Canterbury who was murdered in the nave of his cathedral on the orders of his former friend, King Henry II, in 1170. The sighting so alarmed Henry's grandson, Henry III, that he abandoned construction of the inner curtain wall that he was bulding there and ordered a chapel to be built in its place. Becket's ghost was never seen again – unlike those of the Two Princes, the 12-year-old King Edward V of England and his 10-year-old brother Richard, Duke of York, who haunt the Bloody Tower to this day. The apparitions, if seen, hold hands on the staircase, only to melt away into the walls.

Edward and his brother disappeared in 1483, having been imprisoned in the Tower by their uncle, Richard, Duke of Gloucester, who contested their legitimacy and wanted the throne of England for himself. Later, in 1502, a former supporter of Richard's, Sir James Tyrrell, confessed under torture to having suffocated the boys as they slept, although he was unable to state the whereabouts of the bodies. Tyrrell's 'confession' may have been unreliable, but there seems little doubt that Richard was behind the killings – a deed that earned him immortality as the villain of Shakespeare's *Richard the Third*. In 1674 a casket retrieved from the walls during alterations to the White Tower was found to contain two skeletons. The remains were buried in Westminster Abbey on the orders of King Charles II, but were disinterred in 1933 by an English archaeologist who determined that they were those of two children aged around 8 and 13.

Among the most turbulent spirits said to haunt the Tower are those of Henry VIII's second and fifth wives, Anne Boleyn and Catherine Howard, both of whom were imprisoned and beheaded there on the king's orders following their alleged adultery. Anne is to be seen in the White Tower, her head in her hands, and in the chapel of St Peter ad Vincula, while Catherine can be heard screaming as she pleads for her life. Another victim of Henry VIII's was the spirited 70-year-old Countess of Salisbury, who fled from the block during her bungled execution in 1541 and was hacked to death as she ran. The shadow of an axe is said to fall over the spot on the anniversary of her death. It was Henry's daughter and successor, Mary, who ordered the execution of the 17-year-old Lady Jane Grey for supposedly plotting against her, leaving the tragic teenager's ghost to haunt the Salts Tower – a place where no dog will go to this day, and where a Yeoman Warder once reported being squeezed around the throat by a pair of ghostly hands. Sir Walter Raleigh, one-time favourite of Henry's younger daughter, Elizabeth I, met a similar fate at the hands of James I, the first Stuart king: his ghost was reportedly seen several times in 1864 by members of the Tower Guard. James I's cousin, Arabella Stuart, died in 1615 in what today is the Queen's House on Tower Green. Guests staying there have frequently reported been awoken in the night by the feeling that they are being strangled.

Ghostly menagerie

During the 18th century the Tower was home to the royal menagerie. All kinds of exotic animals were housed there, including lions, leopards and an elephant. In 1815, a sentry is said to have died of fright after confronting a phantom bear that lunged at him from a doorway in the Martin Tower. In fact, the bear was probably real, since the menagerie kept a grizzly bear from 1811 to 1838 – a present from the Hudson's Bay Company to King George III.

The Tower's most famous animal occupants are the ravens which have roosted there almost continuously since the Norman Conquest. Legend has it that should the birds ever leave, it will signal the end of the monarchy – and indeed, during the Second World War, the Blitz saw their number dwindle to just one, a bird named 'Grip'. However, the Tower authorities took care to ensure that a new flock of ravens was installed, their wings suitably clipped, before the Tower was reopened to the public in 1946.

The countess refused to kneel at the block
and ran screaming round the scaffold until
she was cut down by the executioner's axe

TOWER OF LONDON

8 Covent Garden

Comedian Dan Leno is said to haunt the Theatre Royal, Drury Lane, which also has its 'Man in Grey'. Theatregoers have often reported seeing the ghost of an unknown man, either sitting in the upper circle or walking from one side of the theatre to the other – but only at matinées. He is tall, grey-haired and distinguished, and his clothes suggest that in life he was a mid 18th-century gentleman of fashion. Apparently, his judgment is faultless, and his appearance at a play is a sure sign that it will be a success.

The Adelphi, in the Strand, is visited by a phantom thought to be William Terriss, who was stabbed at the stage door in 1907. He also appears at Covent Garden tube station in Edwardian dress.
▶ *Covent Garden tube.*

9 Westminster Abbey

The abbey has several ghosts, including a murdered monk who walks the cloisters in the early evening and occasionally chats to visitors. John Bradshaw, who appears in Red Lion Square from time to time, haunts the deanery, apparently unable to find rest after signing the death warrant of Charles I. Wounded and muddy from the Flanders battlefields, an unknown soldier also puts in rare appearances.

In an old tale, when the abbey was built, about AD 816, St Peter appeared to a Thames fisherman and guaranteed large catches on the condition that one-tenth would be given to the abbey's clergy.
▶ *S of Parliament Sq. Westminster tube.*

10 St James's Palace

A phantom figure that has been seen at the palace, its throat slit from ear to ear, is thought to be the ghost of a valet who was murdered by the Duke of Cumberland, son of George III. The palace, which was built by Henry VIII on the site of a leper hospital, is still used by the royal family and is not open to the public.
▶ *N of The Mall. Green Park tube.*

11 Apsley House, Piccadilly

For some reason, Oliver Cromwell appeared to the Duke of Wellington at Apsley House in 1832, at the height of the Reform Bill crisis. An unruly mob were breaking the Duke's windows, and Cromwell was seen pointing sternly at the crowd.
▶ *Junction of Piccadilly and Park Lane. Hyde Park Corner tube.*

12 Holland House

During the 19th century, Holland House was renowned as a hotbed of political and social intrigue but the Jacobean mansion, once owned by Sir Henry Rich, 1st Earl of Holland, is now mostly ruins. One wing has been restored as a youth hostel and the summer ballroom has been turned into a restaurant. The park surrounding the house was opened to the public in 1952, and is allegedly haunted by the headless ghost of Sir Henry, who was executed during the Civil War. A more unusual spectre is the ghost of oneself – several people have reputedly met their 'doubles' in the park. Such a meeting is said to be a warning of imminent death.
▶ *S of Holland Park Ave and N of Kensington High St. Holland Park tube.*

13 Kensington Palace

The ghost of George II has often been reported gazing anxiously out of a window of Kensington Palace towards the weather-vane. During his last illness he was worried by the non-arrival of despatches from his beloved Hanover, and constantly asked the direction of the wind.
▶ *Kensington Gardens. High St Kensington tube.*

14 Berkeley Square

A bedroom of number 50 has reputedly been haunted for more than a century by a peculiarly repulsive ghost, described as a shapeless, slithering mass. Once, a young army officer volunteered to spend a night in the room. Only if he rang twice was anyone to come to his assistance. The family waited apprehensively and, on the stroke of midnight, the bell rang once. After a couple of minutes, the bell rang a second time so wildly that the family raced for the stairs, but before they could reach the bedroom, a shot rang out. The young man had killed himself from the horror of what he had seen.
▶ *Mayfair, N of Piccadilly. Green Park tube.*

15 Tyburn Gallows

A stone plaque on a traffic island near Marble Arch marks the site of Tyburn gallows, which took several forms over the centuries – executions took place there from 1196 to 1783. One edifice, the Triple Tree, was a three-branched affair that could accommodate up to 24 felons at the same time, although it probably did so once only. On one occasion, in 1661, the bodies of Cromwell, Bradshaw and Ireton were exhumed and hung at Tyburn from sunrise to sunset, on the orders of Charles II. These were the men who had signed his father's death warrant. The gallows fell down one night in 1678, 'up-rooted by its ghosts' according to popular gossip. So many people lost their lives on the gallows at Tyburn that it is hardly surprising the place is supposed to be haunted.
▶ *Junction of Oxford St, Park Lane, Bayswater Rd and Edgware Rd. Marble Arch tube.*

16 University College

The fully clothed, straw-upholstered skeleton of Jeremy Bentham, the law reformer who died in 1832, sits in a glass case in the cloister of University College, where his ghost has apparently been seen and heard. Bentham's preserved head, originally placed between his feet, was removed and stored separately when it became rank, and was stolen many times. Once it was found in a left-luggage locker in Aberdeen. Today it rests in a refrigerator in the college vaults but, despite the odd attack by beetles, his wax-headed body continues to live an active life. In 2002 it was taken to Essen's Ruhrlandmuseum.
▶ *Junction of Euston Rd and Gower St. Euston Sq tube.*

95

⑰ Haymarket

Former actor-manager J.B. Buckstone occasionally appears at the Haymarket Theatre, and his ghost is welcome because it is said to bring good luck. He seems to prefer the dressing rooms, but he was actually seen on stage by a stage manager in 1964. The figure, in 19th-century clothes, was not, however, visible to the audience.

▶ *S from Piccadilly Circus. Piccadilly Circus tube.*

⑱ Eaton Square

On June 22, 1893, Lady Tryon was giving a cocktail party in her house in Eaton Square when the drawing-room door opened and her husband, Admiral Sir George Tryon, strode in. He spoke to no one, but walked purposefully across the room and out of a door at the other end. Curiously, Lady Tryon did not see him, but those among her guests who did were astonished, because they knew, or thought they knew, that he could not be in London. In fact, at that precise moment, the Admiral was on his ship, HMS *Victoria*, the flagship of the Mediterranean Squadron, off the coast of Syria. He had given a misjudged order and the great battleship had collided with HMS *Camperdown*, keeled over and gone down with the loss of all hands. Sir George's body was never found. His wife and friends did not learn of his death until several days later.

▶ *Belgravia, NE along Clivedon Pl from Sloane Sq. Sloane Sq tube.*

⑲ Victoria & Albert Museum

The Great Bed of Ware, which is kept in the museum, is said to be haunted by its maker, Jonas Fosbrooke, a carpenter from Ware in Hertfordshire. He made the mammoth bed in 1463 for Edward IV. It measured approximately 3.4m (11ft) long and 3.3m (10ft 9in) wide. When the king's 13-year-old son and heir disappeared in 1483, probably murdered, the bed was sold and eventually came into the ownership of a succession of Ware innkeepers, who used it during local festivals when the town was crowded. Once, in the 17th century, 12 married couples are alleged to have slept in it together. From beyond the grave, Jonas Fosbrooke was not at all happy about his great bed's fall in status, and his ghost was reputed to pinch and scratch anyone who slept in it, because his gift was not being used by royalty.

▶ *Junction of Cromwell Rd and Exhibition Rd. South Kensington tube.*

⑳ Cock Lane

In 1762, the whole of London was held spellbound by the apparently unearthly events that were taking place in a small, terraced house in Cock Lane, behind St Sepulchre's church, near Smithfield. Each night, 11-year-old Elizabeth Parsons lay trembling and shivering in her bed, unable to sleep because of a constant scratching and knocking in the room. It was suggested that the room was haunted. Mary Frazer, a servant in the house, established contact with the ghost, and identified it as the spirit of Fanny Lynes, who used to rent a room there with her partner and brother-in-law, William Kent.

When William was away, Elizabeth had shared a bed with Fanny, and they had heard strange knockings and tappings. Fanny believed them to be the spirit of her dead sister, foretelling her own

imminent death. When William returned, they moved to other lodgings and soon afterwards Fanny died of smallpox. In the normal course of events, any unease felt at this uncanny coincidence would soon have faded, but that was when the poltergeist made a return appearance in Cock Lane, targeting Elizabeth. This time it was Fanny's spirit, claiming that William had poisoned her.

The whole story was sensational news at the time, and people flocked to the house. Seances were held, enterprising tradesmen sold food and drink to the onlookers and for a little while 'Scratching Fanny', as the ghost was known, became a popular source of entertainment.

Elizabeth went to stay in neighbours' houses and the poltergeist followed her, but when she was restrained, no noises were heard, and when a group of witnesses assembled in the vault in St John's church, Clerkenwell, where Fanny's coffin lay, as instructed by the spirit, nothing happened. Eventually, Elizabeth was caught hiding a small wooden board in her bed and the game was up, although she maintained that she had never cheated before. The whole thing was assumed to be an attempt by Elizabeth's father to discredit William in order to avoid paying back some money that William had lent him. The father was put in the pillory three times and spent two years in jail, and his wife, daughter and servant were convicted as accomplices.

So one of London's most famous ghost stories was exposed as a hoax, but as an interesting corollary, about 100 years later, when the loose lid of Fanny's coffin was removed, her face was found to be perfectly preserved, which is a well-known effect of arsenic poisoning.
▶ *Off Giltspur St, S of Smithfield Market. St Paul's tube.*

THEATRICAL GHOSTS BRING GOOD LUCK
THEATRE ROYAL, DRURY LANE

OUTER LONDON

London is encircled by a wealth of weird, unearthly sites. Victorian mausoleums, grand mansions, museums, and public parks throng with suburban spectres, from weeping mistresses to drunken cavaliers.

❶ Enfield

A phantom coach has often been seen in Bell Lane, usually on clear, moonless nights just before Christmas. Many eyewitness accounts agree that the coach is jet black, holds two or three passengers and careers along at full gallop some 2m (6ft) above the ground. In 1977, the Enfield poltergeist subjected a family of five to months of paranormal activity, which was thoroughly investigated and pronounced genuine.
▶ *N London. Bell Lane is S of Albany Park, E of A1010 Hertford Rd.*

❷ Tottenham

Bruce Castle, a 16th-century manor house that houses the Tottenham Museum, is haunted by Lady Constantia Coleraine. Her jealous husband was obsessed with the idea that some unprincipled rival would steal her from him, and so he imprisoned her in the clock-tower. On November 3, 1680, she threw herself to her death from a balcony, and every year on that date the castle is said to ring with her screams.
▶ *N London. Museum in Bruce Castle Park on Lordship Lane.*

HIGHGATE CEMETERY

By the 1960s, the place had more or less been abandoned. The neglected paths and monuments had fallen into disrepair and the cemetery had become very overgrown and decidedly eerie. Rumours of sinister cults and supernatural encounters circulated, often featuring a figure with glowing red eyes, and vampire stories were rife. Journalists and occultists swarmed around in pursuit of the undead. On March 13, 1970, following a spate of media publicity about an ongoing investigation into supposed vampire activity among the tombs, so many people turned up that police were unable to control the crowds. After that mass vampire hunt, thrill-seekers as well as those more seriously interested continued to invade the cemetery. A man who was arrested carrying a hammer, a stake and a spade told the magistrate later that he had come to settle the Highgate Vampire for good.

Since then, the charity Friends of Highgate Cemetery has undertaken the restoration and management of the site, and reports of ghostly activity are much reduced, although not unknown. A mad woman with long grey hair searches among the graves for her children, whom she murdered. A shrouded figure that disappears and then reappears a little farther away has also allegedly been seen, but nothing more has been heard of vampires.

▶ *N London. S of Highgate High St along Swains Lane.*

❹ North Kensington

St Mark's Road and Cambridge Gardens are said to be the route of a phantom bus that used to tear along with lights blazing at dead of night. A man and his wife reported seeing it in 1934, but when they went to board it, the mystery bus pulled away empty, speeded up and vanished.

▶ *W London. Cambridge Gardens and St Mark's Rd W of B450 Ladbroke Grove close to Ladbroke Grove tube.*

❺ East Acton

Many people have reported seeing strange, cowled figures trooping through St Dunstan's church – sometimes singly and sometimes in groups of as many as a dozen, walking in pairs. This otherworldly procession moves slowly down the aisle and into the chancel, and then fades from sight. In the Middle Ages, a chapter of monks from the church of St Bartholomew the Great, Smithfield, lived near the site.

▶ *W London. St Dunstan's church is on Friars Place Lane, S of A40 Western Ave.*

❸ Highgate Cemetery

In the early 19th century, the problem of where to bury the dead of the fast-expanding city of London was getting to crisis point and permission was granted for seven private cemeteries to be built. Highgate was one of these. The West Cemetery opened in 1839 and, across Swains Lane, the East Cemetery followed in 1854. This side is still used for burials and is open to the public, while the West Cemetery was closed in 1975 and the public can visit only by taking a guided tour.

When it opened, Highgate immediately became the most fashionable place to be buried, and Victorians vied to see who could provide the most spectacular of resting places. As well as elaborate headstones, the cemetery is full of expensive memorials, crypts and mausoleums, notably in Egyptian Avenue.

THE CAPITAL'S ONCE GREAT FOREST

A MAGNIFICENT SWATHE OF TREES and forest land once stretched from Bow in London almost to Cambridge and Colchester. Within its green miles lay numerous isolated villages and hamlets. Its dark glades of oak, elm and beech sheltered hermits, vagrants and gipsies, as well as outlaws and highwaymen – Dick Turpin among them. His ghost can still be seen, it's rumoured, with one of his victims clinging to him.

Gypsies of the Lee family made a living telling fortunes at forest fairs, and one famous inhabitant, Old Dido, prescribed secret remedies based on forest herbs.

Dido lived in a tent near Hainault towards the end of the 19th century. Another character who lived about the same time was a white witch known as Old Mother Jenkins, the Goose Charmer. She could often be seen waving her stick and muttering incantations over a flock of geese at the roadside. Many farmers paid her to do this when their flocks of goslings reached a certain age, because they believed that their geese would not fatten without her blessing. All that now remains of London's great wood is Epping Forest.

⑥ Hammersmith

Before the ardent Royalist, Sir Nicholas Crisp, died in 1666, he expressed a wish that his heart might be buried at the feet of Charles I. Instead, his heart was entombed in an urn, which stands underneath a bust of the king in St Paul's church in Hammersmith, and his body was buried in the churchyard outside. Crisp made provision in his will for his heart to be removed from the urn once a year and refreshed with a glass of wine. This ritual was carried out until the mid 18th century, when the urn was finally sealed for ever.

In January 1804, a churchyard in Hammersmith was terrorised by an immensely tall, white-shrouded apparition that flitted among the tombstones. The first person to see it was a pregnant woman. It chased and caught her, holding her fiercely, and two days later she died from the shock. Some local people surmised that the spectre was that of a man who had

A SPECTRAL MESSENGER

committed suicide a year earlier by cutting his throat, but some began to suspect a hoax. A few people decided to find out and, armed with guns, lay in wait for the ghost. Francis Smith thought he caught a glimpse of it in Black Lion Lane, and fired. Unfortunately, the target turned out to be a workman dressed in white overalls. Smith was convicted of murder and sentenced to death, which was later commuted to a year in jail. Two deaths, apparently, were enough to soothe the ghost's ill feelings because it was never seen again. The identity of the hoaxer, if such it was, has never been discovered.

▶ *W London. St Paul's Church is in the centre of Hammersmith on the Broadway.*

❼ Chiswick

The privately owned Walpole House in Chiswick is said to be haunted by the ghost of its former owner, Barbara, Duchess of Cleveland, mistress of Charles II. She appears at windows as a diseased old woman, wringing her hands in despair for her vanished beauty.

▶ *W London. Walpole House is on Chiswick Mall which runs alongside the River Thames.*

❽ Richmond

A red-brick gatehouse and a courtyard are all that remain of Richmond Palace, where Elizabeth I died in 1603. At the moment of her death, it is said that a ring was taken from her finger and thrown to a mounted messenger from a window of the gatehouse. The rider galloped the 400 miles to Edinburgh in 62 hours to announce to James VI of Scotland that he was now James I of England. Phantom hoofbeats believed to be those of the messenger's horse can sometimes be heard by the gatehouse of the palace.

▶ *SW London. Remains of Richmond Palace close to River Thames W of centre of Richmond.*

❾ Ham House

The drunken figure of a Cavalier, sometimes seen staggering along the towpath near Ham House in broad daylight, is thought to be that of a courtier of Charles II who, while staying there with the Duke of Lauderdale, became so drunk at a party that he fell into the Thames and drowned. Ham House itself, now

run by the National Trust, is said to be haunted by the Duchess of Lauderdale, and a phantom spaniel has allegedly been seen in the gardens.

▶ *SW London. Close to S bank of River Thames at end of Ham St, off A307 Upper Ham Rd.*

❿ Barnet

Oak Hill Park is all that remains of a vast expanse of woodland that once covered the area, and is a centre of supernatural activity, if reports in a local newspaper, the *Barnet Press*, are to be believed. Among alleged sightings of 'headless hounds, decapitated bodies, spectres in the trees', the ghost of Geoffrey de Mandeville is worth mention. The medieval knight appears in armour on horseback, galloping across the park. In life, his single-minded and ruthless quest for power and social standing brought him many powerful enemies, who denied him a Christian burial after a violent death around 1144. This terrible slight is thought to be why his spirit remains restless.

The old Finchley Manor, now the Sternberg Centre, in East End Road, is believed to be the most haunted house in the borough. It is visited by various apparitions including that of William Hastings, who can be seen walking the grounds of the house carrying his severed head. The ghost of William Brereton is another spiritual visitor. He was one of the five men accused by Henry VIII of adultery with Anne Boleyn. This led to his execution on May 17, 1536.

▶ *N London. Oak Hill Park lies W of A111 and E of Oakleigh Park Station in East Barnet. The Sternberg Centre is on A504 East End Rd, Church End, 0.5 mile SE of Finchley Central tube.*

⓫ Hampstead

Spaniards Inn, situated on the edge of Hampstead Heath, is one of London's most famous pubs – not least because of its ghostly reputation. Two former landlords, Juan and Francesco Porero, from whom the inn may have derived its name, fought a duel there over a woman. The body of Juan, the loser, was buried in the garden and his ghost is said to haunt the area. Dick Turpin's father is believed to have been the landlord at one time, and his highwayman son's much-travelled, cloaked apparition has been seen inside the pub and on the road outside.

▶ *N London. Spaniards Inn is on B519 Spaniards Road, 1 mile N of Hampstead tube.*

RIDES FROM THE PALACE
RICHMOND

⑫ Hampton Court

Many people believe that the passion and pain unleashed by two of Henry VIII's unfortunate wives have left a mark on Hampton Court Palace that time will never eradicate, and the ghost of Henry himself is said to revisit the place. Jane Seymour became his third queen in 1536, and died the following year shortly after giving birth to Henry's only son, Edward. Her ghost, dressed in white, has been seen in the palace, carrying a lighted candle as it glides from the State Apartments to the Silver Stick Gallery and Clock Court.

When Henry's fifth wife, Catherine Howard, was charged with adultery in 1541, she broke away from her guards in the long gallery, and ran to the chapel door, hidden between the tapestries, in an attempt to make a last-ditch appeal to the king. But the door was locked, and Henry ignored her frantic pleas. Some say that her shrieks as she was dragged away echo along the gallery to this day.

Not all the ghosts that frequent the palace are royal. Sybil Penn, the Grey Lady, was nurse to Edward VI and served four Tudor monarchs. She is still supposed to work at her spinning wheel in one of the old courtier's houses. Then in October 2003, a phantom that became known as 'Skeletor' put in an appearance. A fire door near Clock Court opened with great force on three consecutive days, apparently of its own volition, but on the second occasion, a ghostly figure in period dress closed the door before security staff could get there. All three incidents were caught on CCTV camera and Skeletor made international news.

▶ *SW London. On N bank of River Thames at junction of A308 Hampton Court Rd and A309 Hampton Court Way.*

⑬ Greenwich

In 1966, two Canadian tourists – Mr R.W. Hardy, a retired clergyman, and his wife – visited the 17th-century Queen's House at Greenwich, which now forms part of the National Maritime Museum. One of the photographs they took was of the Tulip Staircase, which seemed at the time to be empty, but when the picture was developed, it showed what looks like one or perhaps two cowled and ghostly figures. The film was closely examined, and displayed no signs of technical interference. The Hardys themselves were sceptical about ghosts. There is no tradition of the Queen's House being haunted, but after the photograph was taken, members of staff remembered seeing strange figures near the staircase, and hearing what may have been the footsteps of the mysterious cowled visitors.

In May 2002, the figure of a woman, wearing a pale, crinoline-style dress, was seen to glide across a balcony in the Queen's House and through a solid wall. The gallery assistant who witnessed this phenomenon, and his two colleagues, reported feeling very cold.

Charlton House, a beautiful Jacobean mansion built between 1607 and 1612, has been the location of much paranormal activity. In particular, there have been visitations from one of its former owners, Sir William Langhorne, said to be endlessly searching for a fertile bride. He was a successful and wealthy East India merchant who had married twice, but he died childless at the age of 85. The lack of an heir is thought to be the cause of his distress.

▶ *SE London. National Maritime Museum is on A206 Romney Rd close to centre of Greenwich. Cutty Sark DLR station. Charlton House is on B210 Charlton Road, 2 miles E of centre of Greenwich.*

THE PHOTOGRAPH SHOWED ONE, OR PERHAPS TWO, COWLED, GHOSTLY FIGURES

GREENWICH

TULIP STAIRCASE, QUEEN'S HOUSE

Hunstanton

A149

Cromer ⑥

⑤

A148

Fakenham
④ ⑦

③

A149

A140

The Broads

⑧

⑨

King's Lynn
②

①

A47

East Dereham

⑩

⑪

Wisbech

A47

A1122

Downham Market

Swaffham

A47

NORFOLK
116–121

⑭

Norwich

A146

A47

Great Yarmouth

⑫

A1 6

Peterborough

A1

⑯

A47

A10

A1101

A134

A1065

⑮

A11

⑯

A140

Lowestof

⑥

A11(M)

A141

⑮

A1101

A142

A11

⑰

Thetford

A1066

A143

A143

⑤

④

Southwold

⑦

Ely

CAMBRIDGESHIRE
106–111

A10

A142

③

SUFFOLK
124–127

⑧

A12

Huntingdon

A14

⑫

②

⑭

Bury St Edmunds

A14

A12

Aldeburgh

⑨

St Neots

A1

A14

⑬

⑧

⑬

A428

Cambridge

⑩ ⑨

Newmarket

A14

A134

Stowmarket

①

②

⑩

A14

⑪

A11

③

Ipswich

⑪

⑥ ⑦

⑤

A10

A505

Sudbury

①

⑫

⑪

Felixstowe

④

Saffron Walden

⑫

Harwich

A120

A14

M11

ESSEX
112–115

A131

Colchester

A133

Harlow

A120

Braintree

A120

②

A12

Clacton-on-Sea

③

Chelmsford

⑪

⑤

Maldon

④

A414

A12

A130

⑩

M25

Brentwood

⑥

A127

Southend-on-Sea

⑨

Basildon

⑦

⑧

A13

KEY
① Main entry
County boundary
Motorway
Principal A road

East Anglia

The low lying landscape of the watery Fens is home to many tall tales of death and terror, filled with strange lights and pale, drifting wraiths, while to the south and west, old Saxon legends of unearthly creatures still strike a chill.

CAMBRIDGESHIRE

An enormous black dog roams the lanes, riverbanks and marshes of the county, foretelling death, while the shadows of those long passed haunt the living near the scenes of their untimely ends.

❶ Waterbeach

Denny Abbey, built on an ancient island in the marshes, was wrested from its original Benedictine incumbents by the Templars, before it was granted to the Poor Clares in 1336. When the marsh was drained the abbey became a farmhouse and today forms part of a farm museum. Rumours of tunnels leading from the building to the old island's edge were borne out when underground workings were discovered, together with two previously unknown wells. Visitors had long told of hearing the sound of water being drawn from a well, despite there being none in the building. More mysterious are reports of animals near the farmhouse acting in a disturbed manner at 8.20 in the evenings, as if somebody — or something unsettling — had passed.
▶ *6 miles NE of Cambridge on A10. Denny Abbey and the Farmland Museum are 1 mile N of Waterbeach.*

❷ Wicken

Between Wicken and the marshes of Spinney Abbey, a large shaggy dog may sometimes be seen. This is Black Shuck, who appears all over East Anglia in various guises. In Cambridgeshire, he is diabolical and sinister and those who encounter him should look the other way, since his appearance is said to warn of a death in the family. However, Black Shuck is not the only apparition to add to the ghostly reputation of Wicken Fen, which is one of Britain's oldest nature reserves. A priory once stood on the site of Spinney Abbey Farm and, on still nights, spectral monks have been seen and heard chanting across the fen, and strange lights bob towards Spinney Bank.
▶ *On A1123, 7 miles NW of Newmarket.*

❸ West Wratting

A folk-myth inherited from Viking settlers may account for the tradition that the countryside between West Wratting and Balsham is haunted by the Shug Monkey. The creature, either ghost or demon, is said to be jet-black and shaggy-haired, with a monkey's face and staring eyes.
▶ *8 miles SW of Newmarket on B1052.*

❹ Heydon

Heydon Ditch, an ancient earthwork rampart, about 1.5m (5ft) high at its tallest point, runs for nearly 3 miles from Heydon to Fowlmere. Probably built by the Saxons as a defence against the British, who were attempting to drive them out of East Anglia, the ditch and the nearby fields have long been said to be haunted by the spectres of giant warriors. The story was given some credence in the 1950s when a number of burial pits, containing the decapitated skeletons of tall Saxon soldiers, were discovered during archaeological excavations.
▶ *On minor road 2 miles S of A505, 10 miles S of Cambridge.*

❺ Steeple Morden

A restless spirit lies in the village churchyard at Steeple Morden. Elizabeth Pateman, who worked at Moco Farm, now demolished, on Cheyney Water, was murdered in 1734 with a billhook, a knife and a ploughblade. No one was ever charged with the crime but, according to local gossip, her employer and his wife were the culprits. It all began when a peddlar visited Steeple Morden on one of his regular trips to sell ribbons and laces. He lodged, as he always did, at Moco Farm. Villagers saw him arrive but next morning he did not appear, and he was never seen again. Dark stories began to circulate that the farmer had murdered him. It was noticed, too, that the farmer stopped using his well, and a few weeks later filled it in. Then, one night, so the gossips surmised, the farmer and his wife overheard Elizabeth tell her sweetheart that she had a secret to tell him the next time he visited her. So, thinking they were about to be betrayed, the couple silenced her. The stone marking Elizabeth's grave was carved with the implements of her demise, and her ghost, wringing its hands and sobbing plaintively, has been reported in the vicinity of the cottages that once formed part of Moco Farm.
▶ *On minor road 3 miles N of A505, 5 miles W of Royston.*

❻ Whittlesford

In 1826, the local landowner attempted to level the Chronical Hills near Whittlesford and, in the process, some Roman remains were uncovered, including several skeletons. A labourer named Matthews reputedly took home a skull and placed it on the mantelpiece in his bedroom. That night, he was woken by knocking on his front door, and he got up and looked out of the window to see who it was. In front of the house stood a headless skeleton, which, in a rasping voice, demanded the return of its head. Terrified, Matthews grabbed the skull and threw it out.

An old Whittlesford tradition claims that on St Mark's Eve (April 25) the wraiths of those destined to be buried in the churchyard in the next twelve months come out to inspect their graves. When they find the plots where they are to be buried, they lie down and vanish underground. At the same time, the figures of those destined to be married walk arm in arm around the church.

▶ *6 miles S of Cambridge, on minor roads N of A505.*

SPECTRAL MONKS CHANT ACROSS THE FEN
WICKEN

❼ Sawston

The present Sawston Hall was built by Mary Tudor as a reward for the loyalty of the Huddleston family, who sheltered her from the followers of Lady Jane Grey in 1553, and enabled her to escape dressed as a milkmaid. The Duke of Northumberland's men burnt down the original house. Mary is still occasionally seen flitting at great speed through the gardens, or gliding serenely along the long gallery – perhaps because Sawston is one of the few places in which she found true friends in her entire unhappy life.

The tradition that Mary slept in the Tapestry Room is probably untrue, but the four-poster bed may have survived the fire. What is certain, though, according to those who have stayed there, is that it is impossible to spend a night in 'Mary's Room' without being disturbed by phantoms. A Lady in Grey is said to knock three times at the door and then float across the room. An undergraduate and a clairvoyant are among the people who have stayed overnight in the room and declared next morning that their sleep had been disturbed by repeated rapping at the door and the sound of someone fiddling with the latch.

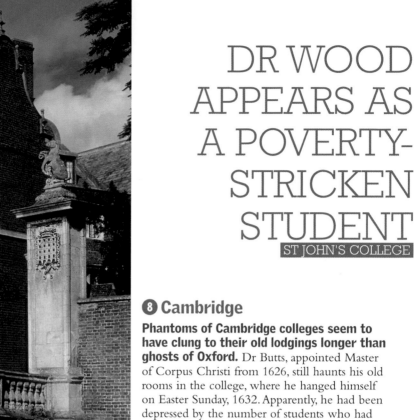

DR WOOD APPEARS AS A POVERTY-STRICKEN STUDENT
ST JOHN'S COLLEGE

ST JOHN'S COLLEGE, CAMBRIDGE

8 Cambridge

Phantoms of Cambridge colleges seem to have clung to their old lodgings longer than ghosts of Oxford. Dr Butts, appointed Master of Corpus Christi from 1626, still haunts his old rooms in the college, where he hanged himself on Easter Sunday, 1632. Apparently, he had been depressed by the number of students who had died of the plague that year, and wrote to a friend that there was not an undergraduate to be seen in college or the town. Another Corpus Christi ghost is that of a 17th-century student who fell in love with a Master's daughter. When one of their secret liaisons was interrupted, he hid in a kitchen cupboard and was suffocated.

Dr Wood, Master of St John's, died in 1839 and, since then, has often been seen on Staircase O of the college. He is said to appear not as the grand figure of his later years, but as the poverty-stricken student he once was. Unable to afford either fire or light, he used to wrap his feet in straw each evening and study by the feeble light of the rush candle that lit the staircase.

Merton Hall, which belongs to St John's, is reputedly haunted by a large, furry, penguin-like creature. Whatever it is, it seems to have wandered from Abbey House in the Newmarket Road, where it has also been reported. The house is built on the site of an Augustinian priory, and is said to be linked by a secret passage to Jesus College, once St Radegund's Nunnery.

In town, the stone lions that flank the entrance to the Fitzwilliam Museum come to life when the clock of the Catholic church strikes midnight. According to different versions of the tale, the lions either roar, come down to drink from the Trumpington Street gutters, or leave their plinths and go inside the museum.
▶ *2 miles E of Junction 12 of M11.*

The Huddlestons, who lived at the Hall until 1970, have always been Catholic. There is a priest's hole beneath the staircase of the tower, cunningly constructed by Nicholas Owen, a Jesuit carpenter, who built similar hiding places all over England during the reign of Elizabeth I. He died under torture rather than betray his friends, and was canonised in 1970. A strange tapping has been heard in one of the nearby bedrooms, and other inexplicable sounds that have been heard in the house include the distant music of a spinet, and the trill of a girl's laughter.
▶ *6 miles S of Cambridge, just E of A1301.*

EAST ANGLIA

❾ The Gog Magog Hills

The Iron Age hillfort of Wandlebury Ring, the remains of which can still be seen on the summit of these low-lying chalk hills, was once a stronghold of Boudicca and the Iceni, and later a Roman encampment. On a clear day, from its grass-covered ramparts, you can see as far as Ely, which is a distance of some 20 miles. No one, native or invader, could fail to recognise the strategic importance of this site, which rises from the surrounding flat fenland – for if you hold Wandlebury, Cambridgeshire becomes your kingdom.

In legend, Wandlebury was once ruled by a mysterious night-rider whom no mortal could defeat. Anyone brave enough to try had only to ride into the camp on a moonlit night, shout, 'Knight to knight, come forth!' and the warrior would appear. Sir Osbert, a Norman knight who was quartered in Cambridge, issued the challenge and managed to unseat the dark rider with a lance. He seized his opponent's black horse and began to lead it away but, as he went, the fallen warrior hurled his own lance and pierced the knight's thigh. The Norman brought the black horse to Cambridge, but by dawn it had disappeared and was never seen again. On every anniversary of the fight, the wound in Sir Osbert's thigh bled again, as if it had been freshly inflicted.

This is not the only legend to feature in the area. Somewhere under the chalk slopes lie the last two of an ancient race of giants, Gog and Magog, after whom the hills are named. In 1954, excavations were undertaken in the place where the outline of a giant was said to have been visible until the 18th century. The archaeologists revealed a strange pattern cut into the turf. One theory suggests the pattern represents Gog and Magog in the form of ancient pagan gods. A giant horse is also said to be buried nearby, and beneath Mutlow Hill lies a golden chariot.
▶ *4 miles SE of Cambridge, just off A1307.*

❿ Grantchester

The entrance to a passageway, long disused and blocked by rubble, is supposed to be located in the cellars under the old Manor House. The story goes that long ago a fiddler entered the tunnel, playing as he went, to try to find where it ended. The music grew fainter until it could be heard no more, and the fiddler never returned.

The ghosts of two famous literary figures have been seen in the area. Byron's Pool lies among managed woodland and was declared a local nature reserve in January 2005. Lord Byron is still supposed to enjoy a spectral swim there, near the weir on the River Cam, while Rupert Brooke revisits the Old Vicarage. His ghost is said to walk through the garden towards the sitting-room of the house, where he lived during his undergraduate days at Cambridge University, and for which he was so famously homesick.
▶ *2 miles SW of Cambridge.*

⓫ Great Gransden

The antiquated wooden postmill that stands less than half a mile east of the village stopped working in 1867 for a period of three years. William Webb, the owner, had come across a book of black magic, entitled *An Infidel's Bible*, among his dead brother's effects, and had taken it to the mill to keep it out of harm's way. The mill sails remained motionless until the book was burnt, three years later.
▶ *12 miles W of Cambridge on B1046.*

⓬ Holywell

In the days of Hereward the Wake, a girl called Juliet hanged herself, for unrequited love, from a willow tree on the banks of the Ouse. She could not be laid to rest in the sanctified ground of the churchyard, since she had taken her own life, so she was buried on the riverbank, and her grave was marked by a simple slab of grey stone. Later, the Ferry Boat Inn was built on the site and Juliet's gravestone is still to be seen there, in the floor of the bar. On the anniversary of her suicide, March 17, people gather at the inn, hoping to see her ghost rise from the grave and drift towards the riverbank where she met her death.
▶ *On minor roads S of A1123, 1 mile SE of St Ives.*

⓭ Caxton Gibbet

Near the junction of the A1198 and A428 stands a wooden gibbet, marking the spot where, according to legend, a murderer was suspended in an iron cage. Having killed a man named Partridge, he rashly boasted of having taken a nest of partridges without being caught by the gamekeeper. He was sentenced to remain in the cage until he starved to death, but a passing baker took pity on him and gave him a loaf. For this kind act, so the story goes, the baker was also suspended from the same gibbet. In fact, the original gibbet was probably erected to display the body of a Royston highwayman named Gatwood, executed in 1753 for robbing mail coaches on the Great North Road.
▶ *10 miles W of Cambridge.*

⓮ Kimbolton

Catherine of Aragon, Henry VIII's divorced first wife, died a prisoner in Kimbolton Castle in 1536. For many years, the ghost of the unhappy queen was said to haunt the castle, undeterred by the several phases of renovation that have gone into the present building.
▶ *7 miles NW of St Neots at junction of B645 and B660.*

⓯ Upwood

Thomas Hursey, owner of Upwood Manor in the 1750s, had refused his daughter Maria permission to marry a penniless naval captain. One night, when her father was in London, Maria woke to find him smiling down at her. The next morning a messenger brought news of Hursey's death. With his dying words he had given his blessing to the match.
▶ *On minor roads 8 miles N of Huntingdon.*

⓰ Helpston

During the Civil War, Dr Michael Hudson, a chaplain to Charles I, organised a band of yeomen to harass Oliver Cromwell's troops in the district of Helpston. From his home base, Woodcroft Castle, which was built in the 13th century as a fortified manor house, Hudson led his men in forays against the Roundheads, but one night the castle was stormed by the soldiers and all Hudson's men were killed. The chaplain was driven over the edge of the roof and, as he clung there, a Roundhead officer cut off his fingers and Hudson fell, landing in the moat, from which he was dragged and disembowelled. Every year his ghost returns to the scene of his gruesome death (now a private house) and sometimes the castle reverberates to the sound of clashing swords, cries of 'Mercy!' and 'Give quarter!' and the unfortunate chaplain's chilling screams.
▶ *On B1443 1 mile W of A15, 6 miles NW of Peterborough.*

WITCHFINDER GENERAL

THE FRENZY THAT GRIPPED East Anglia for 14 terrible months in 1645–46 was a symptom of a nation at war with itself. Long before the struggle between King and Parliament led to open war in 1642, the people of the eastern counties had taken sides. Solidly Puritan, they were swayed by preachers bent on seeking out the slightest whiff of heresy, and local hysteria produced a figurehead – an unsuccessful lawyer from Manningtree named Matthew Hopkins. Through questioning Elizabeth Clarke, he discovered a talent for terrorising old women, and she implicated 32 other people, many of whom were hanged with her at Chelmsford.

Detection was based on the notion that witches kept and suckled imps or familiars at a supernumerary nipple. Once the witch's mark had been discovered, a confession was obtained, often by torture – starvation, solitary confinement and being tied cross-legged for days at a time were all effective, as was being walked up and down a cell for five days and nights without rest. Although the number of supposed witches he put to death will never be known for certain, it was probably around 400 – more than a third of the total number executed in two centuries of English

witch-hunting. Hopkins had 68 people put to death in Bury St Edmunds alone, and 19 hanged at Chelmsford in a single day. Such fearful excesses have ensured that the name of the self-styled Witchfinder General is still remembered with horror.

ESSEX

The lonesome Essex marshes, once the haunt of smugglers, retain an eerie atmosphere, as the tales of their freebooting inhabitants echo down the years, while the Devil makes mischief where he can.

➊ Borley

A tumble of red bricks breaking through the grassy floor of an orchard and an overgrown path still called the Nun's Walk are all that remain of the building that was once considered 'The most haunted house in England'. However, whether the destruction of Borley Rectory has brought peace to the Essex village, no one is yet prepared to say. The sad-faced nun who was apparently at the root of the trouble, wandered around the site long before the rectory was built, and some people believe that she walks there still.

Marie Lairre was a fairly conventional phantom. One story was that she had been walled up alive for an illicit affair with a monk, another that she was strangled in the 16th century. Whatever the reason for her restlessness, she walked the village roads, often accompanied by a spectral coach drawn by headless horses, but when, in 1863, the rectory was built more or less across her route, she seems to have objected from the start. A phantom coach would tear across the rectory's dining-room, through the wall and disappear on the lawn. She would gaze into the house through the windows, and often appeared in daylight – both the gardener and the postman mistook her for a visiting Sister of Mercy.

A succession of incumbents reported the phenomena and one, Eric Smith, contacted the *Daily Mirror*. In 1929, the newspaper sent a well-known writer on psychic matters, Harry Price, to investigate. The spirits could not have been more cooperative. Ghostly fingers tapped out messages on a looking glass, vases shattered against walls, keys hurled themselves out of key holes and an invisible hand flung a candlestick at Price's head. Borley Rectory became front-page news. In 1937, Harry Price leased the rectory for a year, enlisting the help of some 40 investigators. Rooms were sealed, movable objects ringed with chalk, and thermometers, to record the drop in temperature that traditionally announces a ghostly arrival, were placed in every corridor. Once again, candlesticks hurled themselves about and bricks poised in mid air to be photographed.

Seances were held at which Marie Lairre identified herself, saying she had been strangled on May 17, 1667, and had been buried in the garden. Nothing was found, and at a further seance, on March 27, 1938, another spirit interrupted to announce that the rectory would burn down that very night. The evening passed without incident and, in May, Price relinquished his lease to the new owner, a Captain Gregson. The Captain did not enjoy his tenancy for long. The ghost was as active as ever, his dogs disappeared, and then on February 27, 1939, exactly eleven months later than scheduled, a lamp toppled over – apparently of its own volition – and Borley Rectory burst into flames. While the old house burnt furiously, several onlookers saw strange figures in the smoke and, silhouetted against a flame-lit window, the form of a nun.

▶ *On minor roads 2 miles NW of Sudbury.*

❷ Coggeshall

The ghost of a 16th-century woodcutter named Robin has been reported near a tributary of the Blackwater river, known locally as Robin's Brook, and the blows of his ghostly axe have been heard at a distance. Robin is said to have carved a beautiful statue, 'the Angel of the Christmas Mysteries', which was hidden during the Reformation and never found afterwards.

▶ *Off A120, 6 miles E of Braintree.*

❸ Tolleshunt Knights

Many years ago, Satanic rites were practised on the banks of a bottomless pool in the wood at Tolleshunt Knight, which is still sometimes known as the Devil's Wood. When the site was earmarked for a house, the rituals had to stop and, allegedly, the arch-fiend himself came to see what could be done to stop the building going ahead. However, a watchman had stayed behind on the site with his three dogs. When Satan asked who was there, the watchman replied, 'God and myself and my three spey bitches,' and the Devil could do nothing because the man had put God's name first. On the following night he asked the same question and received the same reply, but on the third night, the reply was slightly different – 'Myself and my three spey bitches and God.' By setting himself before God, the watchman had lost his invulnerability. Satan sprang on him, clawed open his body and tore out his heart, screaming in the dying man's ear that he was lost whether his heart was buried in a churchyard, field or road. But the watchman's friends buried his heart in the wall of Tolleshunt Knights church and so saved his soul.

▶ *On B1023 3 miles S of A12, 12 miles NE of Chelmsford.*

BORLEY RECTORY AFTER THE FIRE

OLD LEGENDS AND LONELY CREEKS
MERSEA

4 Virley

An upturned boat in Virley churchyard marked the burial place of a gang of Excise men, who had been found on Sunken Island near Mersea in the early 1800s with their throats cut. The lonely creeks of the Essex marshes were the scene of many bloody and desperate fights, with no mercy shown on either side, and memories of those wild days of smuggling are kept alive by old legends and chance discoveries. Local ghost stories were cleverly exploited by the smugglers to cloak their operations. Brandy smugglers on the River Crouch, for example, used a 'ghost cart' – luminously painted and with muffled wheels – to keep unwanted visitors away. At Hadleigh Castle, a pair of phantoms known as the White Lady and the Black Man made dramatic appearances, but always before the arrival of an illicit shipment of liquor. Virley church itself is the survivor of the Essex earthquake of 1884, the most destructive in Britain for 400 years.
▶ *Just off B1026, 8 miles SW of Colchester.*

5 Danbury

According to a chronicle of 1653, the Walsingham *Historia Anglicana*, the Devil appeared at the church of St John the Baptist in 1402 'in the likeness of a Grey Fryer and Thunder'. He broke down the top of the steeple and scattered the chancel, then mounted the altar and sprang from side to side. As he left, he passed between the legs of a parishioner 'who soon fell in mortal disease, his feet and part of his legs becoming black'.
▶ *5 miles E of Chelmsford on A414.*

6 Canewdon

This area of Essex was once a hotbed of witchcraft, and legend says that as long as the tower of St Nicholas's church stands, there will be seven witches in Canewdon. The tower is still standing but the last known master-witch, George Pickingill, died in 1909. He used to extort beer from farmers by threatening to stop their machinery by magic. A headless ghost,

thought to be a witch, occasionally materialises near the church and drifts down to the river. Anyone who meets her is whirled into the air and deposited in the nearest ditch.
▶ *On minor roads 6 miles N of Southend-on-Sea.*

❼ Rochford

Rochford Hall, now privately owned, was where Anne Boleyn spent much of her youth and where she met Henry VIII. It is also one of the many houses that her overworked phantom is supposed to haunt. In this instance, she appears at Christmas as a white apparition that flits through the grounds.
▶ *4 miles N of Southend-on-Sea.*

❽ Canvey Island

On moonlit nights, a patch of mist drifts over the lonely mudflats at Canvey Point, shortly resolving itself, to some eyes, into a ghostly Viking. Legend says he is one of the old Norse raiders, and is still seeking a ship to take him home.
▶ *On A130, 5 miles S of Basildon.*

❾ Basildon

The 16th-century church of the Holy Cross, near Basildon, is said to be haunted by a red-robed figure. No one knows the ghost's identity, but there is a local tradition that he might be one of the two rectors of the church who were expelled at the Reformation. Residents claim to have seen the phantom walk through solid objects near the building.
▶ *Reached by A127 or A13, 25 miles E of London.*

❿ Theydon Bois

Hill Hall was built in the 16th century. Apparently, a young girl who once lived there was courted by seven brothers but could not make up her mind which one to marry. To simplify the decision, the brothers fought a seven-cornered duel in the terrified girl's presence, and every one of them was killed. Bloodstains that were impossible to remove marked the walls and floor for years afterwards.

Shortly before the First World War, a phantom black dog was sometimes seen lying on one of the beds at Hill Hall, but no one ever discovered why. The house was badly damaged by fire in the 1960s, but this does not seem to have spoilt its reputation for being haunted. The ghost of an unknown grey-haired woman flits among the ruins of the house, and a phantom, mustard-coloured coach is reputed

to trundle down the drive on the stroke of midnight every May 31. It is thought that the coachman may be the 'Duke de Morrow', an eccentric who awarded the title to himself and lived at the Hall from 1900 to 1908.
▶ *On B172, 1 mile SW of Junction 27 of M25.*

⓫ Chelmsford

Essex has the melancholy distinction of having hanged more witches than any other English county. Assizes were usually held at Chelmsford, and between 1566 and 1645 some 90 supposed witches were sent to the scaffold. These poor, and generally elderly, women were convicted on evidence that would have been thrown out by many other courts in the country. The main reason for the peculiar vindictiveness of Essex witchhunts, and the fear that lay behind them, was that most people in this part of East Anglia belonged to Protestant sects and believed that witches were Satan's prime agents in his efforts to drag mankind to damnation.

The first major English trial for witchcraft – although sorcery had often been a secondary charge in treason trials – featured Agnes Waterhouse, her daughter Joan, and Elizabeth Francis, all from Hatfield Peverell. The three were linked by the possession of a cat named Satan – a resourceful creature that spoke in a strange, hollow voice and occasionally assumed the shapes of a toad and a black dog. According to the prosecution, Satan killed a man who refused to respond to Elizabeth's advances, and later procured her a husband and child. She then gave the cat to the Waterhouses for whom it spoilt butter and cheese, drowned a neighbour's cows and bewitched a man to death. Despite this damning indictment, Elizabeth Francis received only a year's imprisonment and survived until she was hanged for witchcraft in 1579. Joan Waterhouse was released, but her mother, confessing to all the charges, was hanged.
▶ *Off A12, 13 miles NE of Junction 28 of M25.*

⓬ Chrishall

The old village, which stood about a mile away from the present one, was completely destroyed by fire some 500 years ago. The fire may have been started deliberately to cleanse the village after an outbreak of plague. The victims of the disease were buried in a single grave, the site of which is marked by a yew tree, and on no account must that part of the churchyard be visited. Shadowy figures have occasionally been reported dancing around the burial pit.
▶ *On B1039, 6 miles W of Saffron Walden.*

EAST ANGLIA

NORFOLK

The tranquil Broads offer spiritual peace for the living, but not the dead. The county's ghosts lament their corporeal misfortunes and the misdeeds of their wicked, aristocratic tormentors.

❶ Walpole St Peter

In the grand old church at Walpole St Peter, a crumbling effigy is thought to represent Tom Hickathrift, a local hero who supposedly fought with the Devil in the churchyard. His main claim to fame, however, was as a giant killer. Tom, who was born in the time of William the Conqueror, grew to be very tall and incredibly strong, and he won local admiration by killing an even bigger man who had terrorised the fenlands near Wisbech for years. Other memorials to Tom include Hickathrift House, Farm and Corner, all near Wisbech, and Hickathrift's Candlesticks, three old stone crosses. One stands in the vicarage garden of Terrington St John's, and the other two are in the churchyard of Tilney All Saints, where Tom was buried.
▶ *On minor roads 2 miles S of A17, 8 miles W of King's Lynn.*

❷ King's Lynn

A diamond-shaped brick, with a heart carved in its centre, is set in the wall of a house on the northwest corner of the ancient Tuesday Market in King's Lynn. Local tradition asserts that it marks the spot where a witch's heart, bursting from her body as she burnt at the stake, and hurtling across the market place, smashed against the wall. Margaret Read was burnt in 1590, and was one of the few witches in England to suffer death by fire. Her death inspired another story, which relates how her evil heart, refusing to submit, had bounded down one of the nearby lanes and jumped into the River Ouse.
▶ *A17 from W, A10 from S (Ely), A47 from E (Norwich).*

❸ Castle Rising

Edward III imprisoned his mother, Queen Isabella, in the Norman keep – which still stands – for having consented to the torture and murder of her husband, Edward II, at Berkeley Castle (see page 133). Legend says she went mad with loneliness, and her insane screams are still said to ring over the countryside. In fact, she was pardoned and simply retired.
▶ *Just W of A149, 4 miles NE of King's Lynn.*

❹ East Raynham

The Brown Lady, a stately figure wearing a dress of brown brocade and often carrying a lamp, her terrifying aspect heightened by empty eye sockets, has haunted the corridors and staircase of 17th-century Raynham Hall for more than 250 years. She is thought to be the ghost of Dorothy Walpole, Sir Robert Walpole's sister, who married the widowed owner of the Hall, Viscount Charles Townshend, in 1713. Unfortunately for Dorothy Townshend later discovered that, before their marriage, she had once had an affair with a known rake. He was so angry he kept Dorothy at Raynham Hall for the rest of her life, not even allowing any of her five children to visit her. She reputedly died in 1726, aged 40, some say of smallpox, others say of a broken neck after she was pushed down the main staircase. Another story says the funeral was a sham and she lived to reach an old age, a prisoner in the house.

However she died, she seems unwilling to leave the scene of her distressing life, and her appearances have been well documented. She so scared George IV when he was staying there that he left immediately, saying, 'I will not spend another hour in this accursed house.' Colonel Loftus saw her twice at Christmas 1835, setting off a major investigation that involved the local police. When Captain Marryat, the 19th-century author of sea stories, saw her, he fired a pistol at her. The bullets went straight through and lodged in the door behind her.

She next appeared in 1926, when a son of the house met her on the stairs. Ten years later, two photographers, who were taking pictures for *Country Life* magazine, not only saw an apparition but took a photograph of it, although there is some dispute about its authenticity, and the ghost is not of a woman with no eyes, wearing a brown dress, but of a 'misty form' descending the staircase.

Sightings of the Brown Lady, or any other apparition, have been rare since then, but some reports suggest that she has moved. A spectral lady in brown, and with the same ghastly disfigurement, has been reported on the road between South and West Raynham.
▶ *1 mile W of A1065, 4 miles SW of Fakenham.*

CASTLE RISING

THE SPIRIT OF ANNE HAUNTS THE HOUSE

BLICKLING HALL

⑤ Walsingham

The Christian shrine of Our Lady of Walsingham is advertised as 'a place of pilgrimage, healing and renewal' and 'England's Nazareth'. It all started when Lady Richeldis, wife of a Norman lord, had a vision there in 1061 in which the Virgin Mary appeared to her, took her in spirit to Christ's home in Nazareth and commanded her to build an exact replica of it in Walsingham. With heavenly aid, she built the Walsingham shrine, which soon became so famous that pilgrims made their way there from all over Europe – Edward the Confessor, Richard the Lionheart and Erasmus among them. Miraculous healing powers were attributed to Our Lady's Well, and even the Milky Way became known as the Walsingham Way, because it pointed across the heavens to England's Nazareth. At the Reformation, however, the shrine and all the buildings that clustered around it were destroyed, and it was not until 1931 that sufficient funds were found to rebuild it. Today, Walsingham reflects some of its former glory. On spring bank holiday each year, the statue of Our Lady of Walsingham is carried in colourful procession from the priory ruins through the village to the modern shrine, water from the ancient well is used in church services, and throughout the year believers flock to the village as they did centuries ago in medieval England.

▶ *On minor roads 6 miles N of Fakenham.*

7 Blickling

Before the current magnificent Jacobean mansion replaced it, Blickling Hall was a medieval moated manor house, which came into the possession of the Boleyn family in 1437. Since the date of birth of the family's most famous daughter, Anne, has never been confirmed, it's not known for certain whether she was born at Blickling Hall or at Hever Castle in Kent. However, what is known is that the spirits of Anne and her father return to haunt the Hall each year on the anniversary of her death.

Anne, Henry VIII's second wife, forfeited the king's favour when she gave birth to a stillborn son, and she was executed on May 19, 1536 for alleged adultery and treason. Her brother, George, was implicated and he, too, was executed. At midnight on that date, a phantom coach drawn by four headless horses and driven by a headless coachman is said to convey Anne's ghost, holding its severed head on its lap, up to the Hall door. Another phantom coach carries Sir Thomas Boleyn, who was cursed by the king. Pursued by shrieking demons, Sir Thomas's coach careers wildly around the surrounding countryside, in a desperate race to drive over a number of Norfolk bridges between midnight and cockcrow. That is his yearly penance for his children's executions.
▶ *1 mile W of A140, 8 miles S of Cromer.*

6 Aylmerton

On the wooded slopes behind the village, near to an enclosure called Roman Camp, a number of circular depressions are to be seen. These are all that remain of nearly 2,000 such hollows, which may have been the work of a Stone Age tribe. They are known as the Shrieking Pits because the tall, white figure of a woman has sometimes been seen there, peering into them, wringing her hands and uttering piercing cries. Some say the ghost is of someone from the original tribe, others of someone murdered nearby. Whatever her origins may be, her shrieks have terrified local residents on many occasions.
▶ *Just S of A148, 3 miles SW of Cromer.*

8 Happisburgh

This lonely coastline is haunted by the hideous ghost of a legless smuggler, whose head hangs backwards between his shoulders, suspended on a strip of skin from his neck. The spectre glides inland from the sea, carrying a sack in its arms, and disappears into the ground at Well Corner. The phantom was first seen in about 1800 by several local farmers, who watched it drop the sack into the well, which is no longer there, and then jump in after it. Later, a man's torso was found with a sack containing his severed head and legs. He may have been a smuggler, murdered in an argument over booty.
▶ *On minor roads 7 miles E of North Walsham.*

❾ Waxham

Six members of the Brograve family reputedly haunt Waxham Hall. They all died violently in battle. Sir Ralph was killed in the Crusades, Sir Edmund in the Barons' Wars, Sir John at Agincourt, Sir Francis in the Wars of the Roses, Sir Thomas in the Civil War and Sir Charles at Ramillies. A late 18th-century owner of the house, Sir Berney, once invited them all to dinner, and drank with them until midnight, when they vanished. Sir Berney is accused of having sold his soul to the Devil.
▶ *On the coast, along minor roads 10 miles E of North Walsham.*

❿ Potter Heigham

Sometimes, at about 7pm on misty February evenings, the roll of a drum can be heard across Hickling Broad, and the phantom of a drummer boy appears through the gloom, beating a tattoo as he tries to summon his long lost love. The story goes that in the winter before the battle of Waterloo, the drummer boy, home on leave, fell in love with a girl from Potter Heigham. Although she returned his love, her father refused to accept a soldier as a son-in-law, and the two were compelled to meet secretly at a place called Swim Coots, on the Heigham side of Hickling Broad. Each evening, the young drummer would skate across the ice-covered Broad to meet her. One night, the ice gave way and the boy drowned, but his ghost skates on to keep his tryst with his sweetheart.

Another Potter Heigham ghost is that of the beautiful Lady Carew, who was married on May 31, 1742. It was said that she had sold her soul to the Devil, and on her wedding night, a coach drawn by four black horses and driven by two skeletons was sent to collect her. Despite her screams and struggles, the terrible coachmen threw her into the vehicle, and set off towards Potter Heigham. When the coach reached the old bridge over the River Thurne, it suddenly swerved, tore through the parapet and disappeared beneath the dark river in a hiss of steam. According to local people, each year at midnight on May 31, the scene is re-enacted.
▶ *12 miles NW of Great Yarmouth on A149 at its junction with A1062.*

⓫ Horning

Originally a mead storehouse for nearby St Benet's Abbey, the 15th-century Old Ferry Inn on the River Bure at Horning is haunted by the ghost of a girl in a green cloak that glides through the bar and disappears into the water outside. A girl is supposed to have been raped and murdered there by drunken monks from the abbey, and they threw her body into the river in an attempt to conceal their crime. Sometimes she is seen wandering distractedly along the riverbank near the abbey itself.
▶ *On A1062, 8 miles SE of North Walsham.*

⓬ Tunstall

From the depths of a boggy pool near the small, quiet village of Tunstall, the muffled sound of bells has occasionally been reported. The old church is now a ruin but, centuries ago, it was allegedly visited by the Devil. The church tower had been badly damaged by fire and an argument broke out between the churchwarden and the parson over who should take possession of the church bells until they could be rehoused. Suddenly, the Devil materialised from nowhere and settled the matter by taking the bells himself. The parson, chanting Latin prayers, rushed after him, but the Devil escaped by plunging into the boggy pool, which was said locally to lead directly to Hell.
▶ *On minor roads S of A47, 8 miles W of Great Yarmouth.*

⓭ Great Yarmouth

Inclement weather is a fact of life for those living by the seaside, but on August 7, 2000 the residents of Great Yarmouth found they had something altogether different to complain about. The popular east coast resort was suddenly inundated with showers of small, silvery fish. One local man reported that the sky turned dark and he heard the sound of thunder, after which he found his garden strewn with the tiny creatures. Just a handful of terraced houses were affected, all about half a mile from the sea.

In fact, sudden falls of fish, baby frogs and other objects are nothing new, nor are they exclusive to East Anglia. In Britain, there are records of fish

HIS GHOST SKATES ON TO
POTTER HEIGHAM

falls dating back to the 3rd century AD, and references to fish raining from the sky occur in Izaak Walton's *The Compleat Angler* (1653) and Samuel Pepys' *Diaries* (1661). Similar events may even have been the origin of some of the biblical 'Plagues of Egypt'. Meteorologists think that the phenomenon is caused by waterspouts – vortices of hot and cold air that develop out at sea and can whisk shoals of small fish feeding near the surface into the clouds. The moist, fish-laden air may then be carried for many miles by inshore breezes before it meets a warm front and falls to the earth as rain. A similar process taking place over fresh water could account for the tales of young frogs that have fallen from the skies and may even explain the phenomenon of 'raining blood', in which red dust particles coagulate in the atmosphere. Other items reported to have rained from the skies include tomatoes and pieces of coal.

▶ *10 miles N of Lowestoft on A12.*

⑭ Great Melton

Four headless bridesmaids in a phantom coach driven by a headless coachman are reported to haunt the old Norwich Road at Great Melton. The hapless young ladies are said to have been murdered by a highwayman several centuries ago while on their way home from the wedding. The coach was found immersed in a deep pond by the roadside, and until frequent appearances of the spectres aroused local suspicion, it was assumed their deaths were the result of an accident. As usual with Norfolk's many headless ghosts, those who see the spectres are doomed to misfortune.

▶ *Just W of A47, 4 miles W of Norwich.*

⑮ Griston

Two small ghosts reportedly wander among the trees in Wayland Wood, near Griston. In life, these two Babes in the Wood were a 16th-century brother and sister who were left in the care of an uncle by their dying father, Arthur Truelove. In order to steal their inheritance, the uncle hired two ruffians to kill them. One villain could not do the deed so killed the other and left the children to starve instead. Legend says that a robin covered their dead bodies with moss and leaves.

▶ *12 miles N of Thetford on A1075.*

⑯ Breckles

The listed Grade I Elizabethan manor house in the tiny village of Breckles, near Watton, is privately owned, and the old spelling has been retained. Breccles Hall provides the scene for a chilling ghost story. Several variations of the tale exist but, in essence, it is always the same. On occasions, when the house is empty, a phantom coach appears on the stroke of midnight, the house lights up and, through the windows, a ball can be seen in progress with dancers and music. When the coach draws up, the door of the Hall swings open and a woman steps down from the carriage. If she raises her head and looks someone in the eyes, as she inevitably does, that person is doomed and drops dead on the spot. It happened one night to George Mace, a local poacher. Towards the end of the 19th century, Mace and some of his cronies were going about their unlawful business in the grounds of the Hall, which was not occupied at the time, and rather foolishly – or perhaps through bravado – approached the building at the fateful hour. All was dark and quiet, and when Mace tried the main door it was locked. Then, on the stroke of midnight, up the drive swept a coach and four, glowing eerily, and every window in the house lit up. All happened as predicted and the poachers fled in terror, leaving Mace collapsed on the ground. Next morning he was found dead at the Hall's front door, with not a mark on him.

▶ *5 miles S of Watton on A1075.*

⑰ Thetford

Plenty of ghostly incidents have been reported in and around Thetford. The Elizabethan Bell Inn is reputedly haunted by the ghost of Betty Radcliffe, who was landlady of the pub in the early 19th century and was murdered on the premises by her lover, the stableman. The remains of a medieval lazar house, or leper hospital, in Thetford Warren were inhabited by a particularly gruesome ghost – a phantom leper with burning eyes and a white, curiously two-dimensional face. Since the ruins were demolished, the ghost has occasionally been reported wandering about the countryside nearby, gibbering horribly.

▶ *On A11, 20 miles NE of Newmarket and 28 miles SW of Norwich.*

EAST ANGLIA

KEEP HIS LOVER'S TRYST

Legends of the Fens

Once a mist-bound marsh of waterways and islands, the East Anglian landscape is alive with supernatural stories.

At the time of the Roman invasion of AD 43, wetlands of what would later be known as East Anglia were an eerie, sparcely populated stretch of pasture and marsh that made an ideal refuge for fugitive Britons. After Queen Boudicca's death in AD 62, the Romans grazed their horses on the lush grass of the Fenlands, but local dissidents constantly ambushed the guards until a general from Italy's Pontine Marshes trained a legion in the use of stilts when fighting in boggy country. At first, the local people or Fenmen as they were known, were helpless against the new guards, but they soon learnt how to knock the Romans off their stilts and stab them as they fell to the ground. Tradition holds that the stilts left behind by the Romans inspired the Fenmen to use them for crossing the marshes.

Holy refuge

Later as Christianity took hold in Saxon England, the Fenlands became a spiritual refuge for many, including the hermit-saint Guthlac, his sister Pega, and Etheldreda, the first abbess of Ely, who founded a monastery on an island there in 673. Five hundred years later, magnificent Ely Cathedral was built on the same spot, rising above the flat, featureless landscape like some magical fairy palace.

The cathedral's inaccessibility left it largely unscathed by the ravages of the Reformation, although the shrine to St Etheldreda was destroyed and her remains removed. Amazingly, her left hand turned up almost 300 years later in a reliquary discovered bricked up in the wall behind a priest's hole in Arundel Castle in Sussex. The hand was retuned to Ely, where it now resides in a shrine dedicated to the saint in St Etheldreda's Catholic church. Its ghostly likeness has been seen many times over the years, particularly in the former monastic buildings that now comprise King's School. Meanwhile, along the nearby waterfront, the ghost of a lady dressed in black is said to haunt the banks of the River Great Ouse to utter plaintive screams at night.

Marshes and monks

The Fenland city of Ely is still officially known as an island, although it has not been encircled by water since the Fens were drained in the 18th century. It was given its name – 'The Place of Eels' – by St Dunstan in the 10th century. He was scandalised to discover that most of the monks belonging to the abbey on the island were either married to or living with women. In fury, the holy man changed them into eels, and the descendants of those eels live in the rivers and creeks of East Anglia to this day.

St Dunstan may have been above reproach, but other men of the church plotted and schemed. In AD 974, the Abbot of Ely sent his monks to steal the body of St Withburga from East Dereham, where she had founded a nunnery in AD 654. They were to bring it to Ely in the hope that the saint would attract pilgrims who might contribute to the abbey's income. When the monks dug up the coffin, a spring of healing water bubbled up from her empty grave, resulting in so many miraculous cures that pilgrims continued to flock to Dereham. A phantom barge has often been reported drifting along the Little Ouse towards Ely on misty evenings, its spectral crew chanting over the saint's shrouded corpse.

Marsh-dwelling monks did not fare much better in the 11th century. The Fenland is one of several places where King Canute (1016–35) is said to have

rebuked his fawning courtiers by illustrating his inability to turn back the tide. In this story, having done so, the king went fishing and was still in his boat when darkness fell. He asked for shelter at a nearby monastery, but the drunken monks refused him, and he found refuge in the hut of a poor fisherman named Legres. This man told the king how, years before, monks from the same monastery had raped his wife and when he had gone to rescue her, he had been brutally flogged. His wife later died in childbirth, and each year for 18 years, on the anniversary of his wife's death, Legres killed a monk. The next day Canute summoned his fleet and ordered it to attack the monastery. Many of the dissolute monks were killed, and the remainder forced to build a village, which today is known as Lillleport. In return for his kindness to the king, Legres was made its first mayor.

Whistling up the fairies

Until the draining of the swamplands was completed at the beginning of the 20th century, lurid tales were told of terrifying Jack o' Lanterns, fairies that used to seek out lonely travellers crossing the marshes at night. Glowing eerily, their flames were said to flicker above the water in a ghostly dance, weaving an hypnotic spell on whoever encountered them and inviting the wayfarer to follow them to certain death in the deep bogs. Fen dwellers thought that whistling attracted the Jack o' Lanterns, also known as Lantern Men and Will-o'-the-Wisps, and that the safest thing to do if you saw them coming was to lie face downwards on the path until they danced away. Probably most of the lights were the result of marsh gas given off by rotting vegetation – occasionally such gas ignites by spontaneous combustion and glows for a while before burning out.

Devil-worship has also been laid as a charge against the many witches who have been accused of inhabiting the Fenlands over the centuries, doubtless taking advantage of the region's unique geography in order to avoid the unwelcome attentions of its witch-hunters. A number of the Fens' present inhabitants claim to follow the spiritual traditions of their predecessors but, like the Fens themselves, their presence seems altogether more benign than the dark, brooding and mysterious Fenlands of old.

The medieval cathedral
rises from the misty Fens,
dominating an ancient
landscape of Jack o' Lanterns
and Will-o'-the-Wisps

ELY

SUFFOLK

The Devil frolicks the flatlands of Suffolk, where demons and fairies come to Earth, ghostly figures defy the encroaching sea and an old jockey re-rides the races of his life.

❶ Woolpit

In Saxon times, when wolves roamed the forests of East Anglia, any that were captured were thrown into a pit where this village now stands, and left to die. This explains both the name of the village, derived from wolf pit, and the tradition that a local farmer once saw a phantom wolf emerge from the ground and vanish before his eyes.

It was in Woolpit that the Green Children were found – two fairies who came to Suffolk by accident some time in the 12th century. At harvest time, a young boy and girl with green skin were found near the old wolf pits, dressed in a material that no one had ever seen before. They were adopted by the villagers and given food, but at first would eat nothing but beans. The boy soon died, but the girl settled down. She took to eating the same food as everyone else and her skin gradually lost its green colour.

When she had mastered the English language, she told the villagers that her people lived in a twilight land where the sun never shone, on the other side of a broad river. She and her brother had followed an enchanting sound of bells, which led them into a cavern, and eventually brought them out by the wolf pits, where they had been found, dazzled by the sun and unable to return home. The girl is said to have married a man from King's Lynn and lived a long and happy life.
▶ *Just S of A14, 8 miles E of Bury St Edmunds.*

❷ Stowmarket

At the beginning of the 19th century, the 'good people' were occasionally seen dancing in a ring in the meadows that bordered the road between Stowmarket and Bury St Edmunds. They were described as being about 1m (3ft) tall, and sparkling from head to foot.
▶ *On A14, 14 miles E of Bury St Edmunds.*

CLAWMARKS WERE DISCOVERED ON THE DOOR
BLYTHBURGH CHURCH

❸ Hoxne

Goldbrook Bridge carried a curse from King Edmund of East Anglia. After his defeat by the Danes at the Battle of Hoxne in AD 870, Edmund hid under the bridge. A newly married couple who were crossing it saw the glint of his golden spurs reflected in the water of the River Dove, and betrayed him to the Danish troops who were searching for him. As he was dragged away to be beheaded, Edmund shouted out an angry curse on all bridal couples who should ever cross the bridge, and until well into the 19th century wedding parties avoided passing that way. The gleam of his spurs, it is said, can be seen from the bridge on moonlit nights.
▶ *Just S of B1118, 4 miles E of Diss.*

❹ Bungay

During a great storm in 1577, a black demon dog caused havoc in the local church. An old pamphlet states that he left in his wake two worshippers strangled, and another 'as shrunken as a piece of leather scorched in a hot fire'.

Demon dogs have haunted East Anglia for more than 1,000 years, always known as Black Shuck or Old Shuck, the term coming from 'scucca', Anglo-Saxon for demon. In Suffolk, Black Shuck is fairly harmless if left alone, but when challenged he has been known to strike his aggressor senseless, and death usually follows. Often, he can be detected only by the touch of his rough coat as he passes.
▶ *On A143, 14 miles SE of Norwich.*

❺ Beccles

Roos Hall is one of the most haunted houses in England. The Devil's footprint adorns an inside wall of this Tudor mansion. A headless coachman is said to drive a phantom coach and horses up to the door on Christmas Eve, another ghost haunts a guest room and a third walks in the garden, while in the grounds an old oak known as Nelson's Tree is revisited by the souls of those who were once hanged there.
▶ *9 miles W of Lowestoft on A146.*

❻ Oulton Broad

Although no one has seen them for a few years, a phantom horseman with his pack of hounds, and a white-robed lady carrying a cup of poison, reputedly haunt 16th-century Oulton High House. Several legends have grown up around them, all of which agree that the phantoms were connected with a murder, or possibly two murders, that took place in the house some time in the 18th century.

In one version, the owner of the house (the spectral rider) poisoned his wife (the phantom woman). In another, the woman stood by while her lover ran his sword through her husband's heart, and then the two of them fled to Belgium with most of the family's gold and jewels. Years later, for what reason the legend does not say, the murdered man's daughter, who was still living in the house, was kidnapped on her wedding eve and taken to her mother. In the struggle, her husband-to-be was killed. Later still, the mother poisoned her daughter, although again her motive is a mystery.
▶ *2 miles W of Lowestoft town centre on A146.*

❼ Blythburgh

The Devil, in the form of a black dog, once disrupted a service in the 15th-century Blythburgh Church of the Holy Trinity. On Sunday, August 4, 1577, according to an old pamphlet, 'a strange and terrible tempest' struck the church, toppled the spire through the roof so that it shattered the font, killed three people and badly scorched others in the congregation. Proof that this was a visitation from the Devil were the clawmarks discovered on the door through which he rushed out towards Bungay.

The church contains some fine carved bench-ends representing the seven deadly sins. They include greed with swollen stomach, slander with protruding tongue, and avarice sitting on a money chest.
▶ *On A12, 5 miles W of Southwold.*

GREYFRIARS PRIORY

❽ Dunwich

Once East Anglia's major seaport, Dunwich was undermined by the sea in January 1328, when a great storm washed in sand and shingle to block the harbour, the basis of the city's prosperity, and afterwards houses started to crumble into the water. The present small village and a few ruins are all that remain after 700 years of coastal erosion, but local people claim that the submerged town's church bells still ring, on occasions, to warn them of approaching storms.

Ashore, the shadowy figures sometimes seen on the cliff tops are thought to be the ghosts of Dunwich's former citizens. From the ruins of the 13th-century Greyfriars Priory, mysterious lights have been reported, and strange sounds like the chanting of monks are said to mingle with the tolling of spectral bells.

▶ *On minor roads 2 miles E of B1125, 4 miles S of Southwold.*

❾ Blaxhall

At Stone Farm, a sandstone boulder is constantly increasing in size. The Blaxhall Stone is supposed to have had the proportions of a small loaf when it was first noticed more than a century ago, and has since grown to its present weight of about 5 tonnes. The belief that pebbles actually grow in the soil and develop into large stones was once common in East Anglia.

▶ *On minor roads 2 miles E of A12, 4 miles S of Saxmundham.*

❿ Rendlesham Forest

One of the most celebrated and best-documented UFO sightings to be recorded in Britain took place in December 1980 amid the pine trees of Rendlesham forest, a vast expanse of open woodland that lies between two NATO air bases – RAF Bentwaters and RAF

Woodbridge – and the coastal spit of Orford Ness. On the night of December 26, Gorden Leavitt, a local man who lived on the edge of the forest, reported seeing a 'mushroom-shaped' object in the sky that emitted a greenish-white glow. Leavitt's dog began to act strangely and in fact died a few days later. Meanwhile the same incident was witnessed by two USAF security personnel at RAF Woodbridge – John Burroughs and Budd Parker. They chased what they reported to be a small, conical-shaped craft about the size of a small car into the woods, where it appeared to hover within a foot of the ground. As well as emitting a bright white light that lit up the surrounding trees, the object appeared to give off some kind of 'force field' that prevented the servicemen – who by this time had been joined by two colleagues – from getting near it and caused their hair to stand on end. The following night, the American deputy commander, Lt Col Charles Halt, took a party of men from the base into the forest, which had been cordoned off from the public, to investigate further. For some time, the only light in the sky was the familiar pulse of nearby Orford Ness lighthouse. Then, shortly before 2am, the airmen were taken aback by the appearance of a 'pyramid-shaped object', which emitted a bright white light that split into a prismatic rainbow of colours. The party chased the object through the forest for about an hour before it suddenly lofted skywards and vanished. The entire incident had been captured on audio tape, and Halt subsequently filed a report. Higher than normal radiation readings had been taken from three shallow depressions in the ground that appeared to have been made by the object. There is also a record of an unidentified object being tracked on the same evening by the radar base at nearby RAF Neatishead.

Controversy still rages about the Rendlesham Forest incident. According to British astronomer Ian Ridpath, the 'lights' reported by the US servicemen were simply the beam of Orford Ness lighthouse, which in the 1980s was equipped with a more powerful light than it is today. He has taken convincing photographs to back his claim, suggesting that the entire incident rested in the collective imagination of Halt and his men – a group of servicemen who were far from home, and who had only just finished celebrating Christmas. Yet UFO watchers remain unsure, citing the level-headedness of Halt's report as clear evidence that he and his men had indeed seen something eerily out of the ordinary. Today, visitors to the area are invited to make up their own minds by following the special UFO trail laid out for walkers by the Forestry Commission.
▶ *On both sides of B1084, 5 miles E of Woodbridge.*

⑪ Polstead

In 1827, Maria Martin was murdered by her lover William Corder in a barn at Polstead. Corder told her parents that he had married her in London, but three times her mother dreamt of murder. A search was made, Maria's body was found and Corder was hanged. His skin was used to bind a copy of the court's proceeding, which can be seen at Moyses Hall, Bury St Edmunds.
▶ *8 miles E of Sudbury on minor roads between A1071 and B1068.*

⑫ Little Cornard

A most unusual battle is alleged to have taken place near Little Cornard on the afternoon of Friday, September 26, 1449, according to a contemporary chronicle now in Canterbury Cathedral. Two fire-breathing dragons engaged in a fierce, hour-long struggle, 'to the admiration of many beholding them'. The site of the battle, a marshy field on the Suffolk-Essex border, is known as Sharpfight Meadow.
▶ *2 miles SE of Sudbury.*

⑬ Newmarket

On the evidence of both jockeys and punters, a phantom sometimes joins the field at Newmarket racecourse – a shapeless white apparition that floats around the track level with the jockeys, keeping well up with the leaders. Occasionally, too, horses swerve to avoid some object that is invisible to humans, and the fact that horses are notoriously clairvoyant lends some weight to the suggestion that it may be a ghost. According to one theory, the phantom is that of jockey Fred Archer, who won the Derby four times and died at the age of 29 in 1886.
▶ *Just off A14, 12 miles NE of Cambridge.*

⑭ Kentford

About 1½ miles beyond Kentford, at a crossroads on the main road to Bury St Edmunds, is 'The Gypsy Boy's Grave', marked with a simple wooden cross. This is the burial place of a young shepherd who hanged himself, date unknown, possibly after fearing he had lost a sheep, or being accused of sheep stealing. Suicides were customarily buried at crossroads, to prevent the unhappy spirit from wandering, but such graves were considered to have an uncanny atmosphere. Several cyclists have said they were forced to dismount when passing the shepherd's grave, due to a strange force emanating from it.
▶ *Just S of A14, 4 miles NE of Newmarket.*

EAST ANGLIA

LINCOLNSHIRE
142-143

DERBYSHIRE
130-131

NOTTINGHAMSHIRE
146-147

STAFFORDSHIRE
152-153

SHROPSHIRE
150-151

LEICESTERSHIRE
and RUTLAND
140-141

WARWICKSHIRE
and WEST MIDLANDS
154-155

NORTHAMPTONSHIRE
144-145

HEREFORDSHIRE
135-139

WORCESTERSHIRE
156-157

GLOUCESTERSHIRE
132-134

KEY

- **1** Main entry
- County boundary
- Motorway
- Principal A road

Scunthorpe
Worksop
Chesterfield
Lincoln
Buxton
Matlock
Newark-on-Trent
Mansfield
Leek
Stoke-on-Trent
Ashbourne
Nottingham
Grantham
Whitchurch
Stone
Derby
Oswestry
Stafford
Burton-upon-Trent
Loughborough
Melton Mowbray
Shrewsbury
Cannock
Lichfield
Leicester
Oakham
Stamford
Telford
Tamworth
Bridgnorth
Walsall
Wolverhampton
Nuneaton
Market Harborough
Corby
Ludlow
Birmingham
Coventry
Kettering
Kidderminster
Bromsgrove
Rugby
Northampton
Leominster
Redditch
Warwick
Daventry
Worcester
Great Malvern
Stratford-upon-Avon
Hereford
Evesham
Ross-on-Wye
Tewkesbury
Stow-on-the-Wold
Cheltenham
Gloucester
Forest of Dean
GLOUCESTERSHIRE
132-134
Cotswold Hills
Cirencester

Peak District National Park

Central England

From pretty Cotswold villages to the rugged Derbyshire peaks, the spirits of the dead still disturb the living, making their presence felt in a range of unusual ways. Deep underground, knights slumber, fairies hoard treasure and the Devil toys with mortal souls.

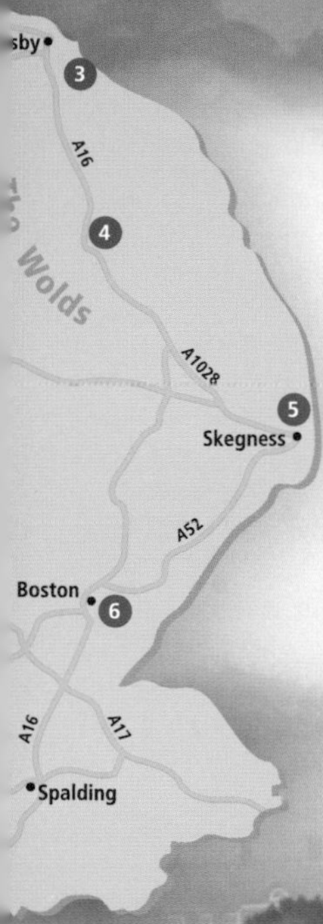

sby

3

A16

Wolds

4

A1028

5

Skegness

A52

Boston

6

A16

A17

Spalding

DERBYSHIRE

The remote hills, dark caves and thunderous waterfalls of the Peak District are home to goblins, elves and mermaids, while an ancient cleft is beset with legends of hell.

❶ Kinder Scout

Kinder Downfall is the highest waterfall in the county. From its lip, the Mermaid's Pool is visible far below, near Kinder reservoir. Apparently, staring intently into the dark waters of the pool at midnight, just as Easter Sunday begins, conjures up the sight of a mermaid swimming. Anyone who sees this sprite will either become immortal or be dragged down into the depths of the pool and drowned. An old legend suggests that a mystical connection exists between the pool and the Atlantic Ocean, making the water unsuitable for fish to live in and for animals to drink. The only creature able to survive in it is the mermaid.

▶ *Hayfield is on the A624, 5 miles S of Glossop. Kinder Scout lies 3 miles NE of Hayfield.*

❷ Hathersage

Robin Hood's henchman, Little John, may have been born in Hathersage. Certainly, he is buried there. In St Michael's churchyard, his grave – over 3m (10ft) long and surrounded by low railings – is marked by an inscribed headstone. His cap and great yew bow, 2m (6ft) long and tipped with horn, used to hang in the church, but were later moved to Cannon Hall, near Barnsley. When his grave was opened in the late 18th century, a huge thigh-bone was found. It was supposed to have been re-interred after the man who ordered the exhumation suffered a series of accidents, but, according to one story, the parish clerk took it home and eventually buried it in his back garden.

▶ *10 miles SW of Sheffield.*

❸ Beeley

Derbyshire is traditionally inhabited by goblins, especially those who prefer to live in lonely and remote places. Deepdale has one example of a goblin's home and on Harland Edge, outside the village of Beeley and near Chatsworth House, lies another – Hob Hurst's House. This is actually a Bronze Age round barrow burial mound. It is overgrown with heather and bracken in summer, but is not too difficult to find.

▶ *On B6012, 3 miles E of Bakewell.*

❹ Derby

The Jacobean House, built in 1611, was the first building in Derby to be constructed of brick. Two of its original five gables were lost when a road was driven through it in the 19th century but, with no less than 14 ghosts to its name, it is probably the most haunted building in Derby. Its most famous phantom resident is the Blue Lady – an apparently benign spirit in a blue dress who smiles at onlookers before vanishing into thin air. Another is the dark figure of a man who appears around the Wardwick entrance to the house. Numerous office workers over the years have reported 'seeing things' in the building, and items are repeatedly said to go missing, only to turn up again in the oddest places. A solicitor who once occupied an office there allegedly left because he could no longer bear to work in the Jacobean House alone at night.

▶ *7 miles W of Junction 25 of M1.*

❺ Deepdale

A cave below Topley Pike is known as Thirst House, which is an abbreviation of Hob o' the Hurst's House – 'hurst' meaning a wooded place. This cave was the home of a tiny elf, or hob, the fairy guardian of a nearby spring. A farmer walking home to Chelmorten caught the hob one day, and put it in his bag, but it shrieked so piteously that he let it go again, and it raced back to the dark security of its cave. The water from this spring was once thought to cure every disease, if it was drunk on Good Friday.

▶ *Access Deepdale on footpaths from A6, 4 miles W of Bakewell.*

❻ Tunstead

An ancient skull, known as Dickie, is kept at a farm in Tunstead, which is nearly 3 miles northeast of Buxton. The skull is said to be that of Ned Dixon, whose cousin murdered him in the house. All kinds of disasters are supposed to follow if the skull is moved. When someone had it buried, things soon began to go wrong on the farm – pigs died, cows became ill and crops failed – but when the skull was retrieved, all went well again.

▶ *On minor roads E of A6, 3 miles NE of Buxton.*

❼ Eldon Hole

This pothole, about 1 mile north of Peak Forest village, was once thought to be the Devil's bolt-hole to hell. In the 16th century, the Earl of Leicester arranged for a local man to be lowered down the hole on a rope, but when he was hauled out he was unconscious and died without speaking another word. Local folk took this as conclusive evidence that he had come face to face with Satan.

Other stories about the hole include the claim that a man named Charles Cotton was dropped down the shaft at the end of a rope that was over a mile long and didn't reach the bottom. On another occasion, two highwaymen forced a victim to walk over the edge so that 'he stept at once into eternity'. Charles Leigh, an early 18th-century writer, felt sure that it had something to do with Noah's Flood. At about the same time, a Fellow of the Royal Society decided to investigate the pothole for himself, and discovered that, in fact, it was just over 55m (180ft) deep.

▶ *Peak Forest village is on the A623, 3 miles E of Chapel-en-le-Frith.*

LEGENDARY ENTRANCE TO HELL
ELDON HOLE

GLOUCESTERSHIRE

Investigators of the paranormal are kept busy in the county's big towns, but in the countryside the urban spectacles are put in the shade by the echoing, agonised screams of a murdered king.

❶ Gloucester

As befits such an ancient and historic city, Gloucester has more than its fair share of ghosts. Among the most famous is that of Bishop John Hooper, who was publicly burned in 1555 before the cathedral in Westgate for his Protestant beliefs on the orders of the Roman Catholic Queen Mary. Yet in recent years, paranormal investigators have flocked to a more prosaic location, the Poundstretcher shop in Eastgate Street, where the ghostly figure of what might be taken for a Victorian woman has been captured on the store's CCTV security cameras, knocking over a stack of pallets in the cellar. According to staff, this incident was one of many strange goings-on in the building, where shelves are frequently found to be in disarray in the morning, and people report feeling suddenly icy cold, or as if they are about to choke. The haunting is thought to date back to the late 19th century, when the building housed Gloucester's Theatre Royal — a favourite venue for the celebrated acting partnership of Sir Henry Irving and Ellen Terry. In 1880, a young woman named Eliza Johnson joined the theatre's company but hanged herself from the rafters after a doomed love affair. She is said to have been roaming the aisles ever since, and once allegedly inscribed a ghostly letter 'E' on the cellar walls.
▶ *4 miles W of Junction 11 of M5.*

❷ Cheltenham

Between 1882 and 1889 a tall, weeping woman in black was seen by at least ten people in a house in Cheltenham, and heard by 20. The large family house, which has now been split into flats and is called St Anne's, was occupied by the Despard family, and the primary witness was Rosina Despard, a 19-year-old medical student. Rosina tried to communicate with the ghost and to photograph it. On several occasions she set fine strings across the stairs at various heights and at least twice saw the figure pass through them. Rosina would follow the figure into a corner and even try to touch it, but it always eluded her. Her two young sisters were equally unsuccessful. The spectre's most probable identity is Imogen Swinhoe, the unhappily married second wife of the house's first owner.

Imogen died at the age of 41 in 1878, two years after her husband. When Rosina looked at an old album and picked a photograph resembling the apparition, it was a portrait of Imogen's sister, who was said to be very like her.

The house is not haunted now — although in 1970 a Mrs Jackson was passing the house while taking a driving lesson and a tall woman in black stepped in front of the car. Mrs Jackson braked sharply, but her instructor saw nothing.
▶ *3 miles E of Junction 11 of M5.*

❸ Deerhurst

Long ago, the people of Deerhurst lived in terror of a monstrous serpent, which poisoned men and cattle. Eventually, the king promised a piece of land on Walton Hill to any man who could slay the beast, and a labourer named Smith came forward. He placed a trough of milk outside the dragon's lair, the creature drank it and fell asleep in the sun. Smith took his axe and struck a mighty blow between the ruffled-up scales of the dragon's neck, completely severing its head. The Smiths held the land until the 16th century, and in the 18th century, a Mr Lane, who had married the widow of one of Smith's descendants, was reported to possess the axe that was supposed to have killed the dragon. No one knows who owns the supposed dragon slaying axe today, or even if it exists.
▶ *On minor road N of B4213, 3 miles S of Tewkesbury.*

❹ Whittington

An unfortified Elizabethan manor house, Whittington Court belonged to Sir Lawrence and Lady Tanfield in the early 17th century. Their greed and overbearing attitude made them highly unpopular in the neighbourhood, and also in the districts of their other two properties, Burford Priory and Great Tew Manor, both in Oxfordshire. They are buried together in an elaborate tomb in Burford church, and Lady Tanfield is said to have haunted their two Oxfordshire houses. The spectre of Sir Lawrence, however, occasionally rode around Whittington in a phantom coach drawn by four black horses. Anyone who saw the coach died soon afterwards.
▶ *On A40, 4 miles E of Cheltenham.*

❺ Poulton

The crossroads at Poulton are also known as Betty's Grave. Betty, a local girl, poisoned herself and, like many suicides, was buried at the crossroads as a means of confusing her restless, earthbound spirit. The crossroads are also supposed to be haunted by some witches from Fairford. Out of sheer malice, they used their magic to imprison market-bound pedlars at that spot and released them when it was too late for them to sell their goods.
▶ *5 miles E of Cirencester on A417.*

❻ Torbarrow Hill

This hill is the focus of an old legend. In 1685, two men discovered a chamber where a knight was feebly trying to extinguish a candle. Near him lay two embalmed bodies. On the third attempt, the knight managed his task. As the men fled, terrified, they heard a long low moan, the cave collapsed behind them and the knight and mummies were buried for ever. A memory of old wars may be the basis of this eerie tale. In AD 879, Gurmund the Dane is said to have captured Cirencester from the Saxons by trapping a huge flock of sparrows, tying flaming twigs to them and releasing them to fly over the city. The walls burnt down, and Gurmund's Vikings marched in.
▶ *W of junction of A417 and A429, NE of Cirencester town centre.*

❼ Wotton-under-Edge

From the outside, it looks the epitome of a pretty English country pub, but step inside the Ancient Ram Inn and even hardened sceptics are forced to agree that there is a chilling, oppressive – even evil – atmosphere about the place. Reputedly built on the site of a megalithic burial mound, parts of the present building date back to the early 12th century. Masons employed to build the nearby church of St Mary the Virgin were housed there, and two tunnels (now blocked) lead from the inn to the church and to what was once a neighbouring abbey. By the 17th century, the inn had acquired a reputation as a true den of iniquity, the haunt of highwaymen and other villains, and a place of devil worship in which children were sacrificed during the course of unspeakable satanic rituals.

Today, the inn, which is in private hands and no longer serves alcohol, has become a favourite venue for paranormal investigators and overnight guests keen to be scared out of their wits amid the bric a brac that clutters the dark, gloomy interior. Countless ghosts have been seen there over the years, including a priest/monk, a cavalier, a witch, a highwayman and two phantom cats. Much of the ghostly activity centres on the Bishop's Room, the name implying a link with former illicit visits by ecclesiastical brethren, perhaps through the tunnels. More recently, paranormal investigators who have visited the site report the widespread presence of light anomalies (orbs) in their video footage, along with the cold spots and mysterious noises that are often encountered in haunted premises. In 2005, one researcher who participated in a ouija session there reported that he felt a sudden cold, dull pain in his back as the board spelt out the words 'stab' and 'die'.
▶ *10 miles SW of Stroud, at junction of B4058 and B4060.*

❽ Berkeley

In the Norman keep of Berkeley Castle, a deep well is concealed in the thickness of the wall. It was once said to contain a toad that would slowly devour any prisoners flung down to it. A more reliable tradition, perhaps, asserts that the well was a refuse pit, into which the carcasses of animals and men were thrown and left to rot. The frightful stench rose upwards to a tiny cell built over the pit, and it was in this room that one of the most famous and brutal murders in English history took place. The victim was Edward II, the weak son of a strong father, whose disastrous efforts as a soldier resulted in the Scottish victory at Bannockburn in 1314. His fondness for Piers Gaveston and other young men, and the honours he bestowed upon them, alienated and disgusted both his council and his French queen, Isabella (see page 116). With the queen's connivance, he was deposed in 1327 and imprisoned in the cell at Berkeley Castle, where it was hoped that the disease and foul odours emanating from the well would shortly make an end of him.

However, the king's constitution was proof against both, and after five months more direct action was deemed necessary. Lord Berkeley, finding business to occupy him elsewhere, left Edward with his gaolers. On September 21, they burst into the cell and pinned him between two mattresses. Some accounts say they suffocated him, others that they murdered him hideously with a red-hot iron spit. The king's agonised screams are said to echo round the countryside to this day.

The 12th-century castle replaced a fortress that was probably built by the 11th-century Earl of Wessex, Godwin, on the site of a convent. Godwin is supposed to have slaughtered the nuns to obtain the land. A Saxon chalice on display in the castle is believed to have belonged to him.
▶ *1 mile W of A38, 16 miles SW of Gloucester.*

CENTRAL ENGLAND

9 Nympsfield

Ghostly goings-on are not normally associated with unfinished buildings, but the remarkable neo-Gothic Cotswold stone mansion of Woodchester near Stroud is something of an exception. Construction of the house, which was designed by the Victorian architect Benjamin Bucknall, began in the 1850s at the behest of a devoutly religious local businessman, William Leigh, whose family had acquired their fortune from the slave trade. After Leigh's death in 1873, his family abandoned the project and the half-finished building eventually passed into the hands of the Woodchester Mansion Trust. The stated intention of this organisation is to repair and preserve the existing parts so that it may remain 'an unfinished masterpiece'.

Several groups of paranormal investigators who have visited the site in recent years have recorded light anomalies (orbs), object displacement and cold spots. They point to the fact that the site was once an ancient burial ground as significant. On a more rational level, Woodchester Mansion sits in a deep valley that is prone to 'cold ponding', in which pockets of cold, damp air become trapped and account for sudden dramatic falls in temperature. Could this be what sends such a chill down visitors' spines?

▶ *On B4066, 5 miles SW of Stroud.*

WOODCHESTER MANSION

HEREFORDSHIRE

Old healing wells and saintly miracle workers reassure the living,
but the troubled spirits of those long gone seek release from
the lingering memory of brutality and heartbreak.

❶ Marden

**Ethelbert, the king of East Anglia, was
murdered in Marden on the instructions of
Offa, king of Mercia.** Later, Offa negotiated
absolution with the pope and, as part of his
penance, built a church over the place of
Ethelbert's burial, and paid for the young man's
canonisation (see page 139). Offa also built a
stone church at Hereford, which was to be
St Ethelbert's permanent resting place. When
the body was exhumed in preparation for the
journey, a well bubbled up by the empty grave.
Offa's church at Marden was burnt down in 1055,
but St Ethelbert's Well remains, and can be seen
at the west end of the present church, which
was built in the 14th century.

A tale featuring a previous church at Marden
tells of a bell falling into the River Lugg and
being seized by a mermaid. Since she would not
return it, the parishioners tried to retrieve it while
she was asleep. But their plan failed when one
man spoke too loudly and awoke the mermaid,
who promptly hid it in a pool. The bell was never
recovered, although sometimes it has been heard
tolling beneath the water, echoing the other
church bells.
▶ *On minor road 1 mile E of A49, 5 miles N
of Hereford.*

❷ Kington

**Thomas Vaughan and his wife Gethin lived at
Hergest Court, which was much grander in
those days** than the current stone and timbered
farmhouse. Now they both lie buried in Kington
church, and are remembered in local legend as
Gethin the Terrible and Black Vaughan, a wicked
tyrant while he lived and an evil spirit after death.
The ghost of Black Vaughan, who died at the

Battle of Banbury in 1469, turned over farm carts,
changed into a fly to torment horses, rampaged
through the market place in the form of a bull
and devastated the church. Twelve parsons, called
in to exorcise the spirit by prayer, combined their
skills to shrink it until it could be imprisoned in
a snuff box. Eleven failed, but the twelfth, whose
courage may have been related to his reputation
as a drinker, persevered until the spirit shrank into
the box. This was immediately thrown into nearby
Hergest Pool, after which Black Vaughan's spirit
ceased to trouble the district. However, both in
life and afterwards Black Vaughan was
accompanied by his faithful bloodhound, and
Hergest Court continued to be haunted by a
great black dog. It tended to appear whenever a
member of the Vaughan family was about to die.
Many local people are still wary of Hergest Court
and refuse to pass the house at night.
▶ *14 miles W of Leominster on A44.*

❸ Brampton Bryan

**During the Civil War, Sir Robert Harley of
Brampton Bryan Castle sided with Cromwell
against the king, with the result that**
Herefordshire Royalists twice besieged his castle
while he was away in London. On the second
occasion, in 1644, they captured and destroyed it.
Harley and Cromwell later quarrelled, and their
relationship remained turbulent until Cromwell
died on September 3, 1658. On this day, a great
storm raged through Brampton Bryan Park,
destroying so many trees that Harley swore that
the Devil had dragged Cromwell across the
parkland as he took him down to Hell. Tradition
maintains that every year, on September 3, the
Devil returns to rampage through the park with
Cromwell's soul.
▶ *5 miles E of Knighton on A4113.*

CENTRAL ENGLAND

12 PARSONS PRAYED
TO SHRINK THE SPIRIT
HERGEST COURT

❹ Colwall

The reason why a block of limestone was erected in Colwall has been lost in the mists of time. In one legend, the Devil left it there. In another, it was a giant from the Malvern Hills, who suspected his wife of infidelity and stoned her to death in the village. The stone is supposed to have been replaced in the late 19th century by another, dragged there by a team of horses, but the motive for this also remains a mystery.

▶ *Just W of B4218, 3 miles SW of Great Malvern.*

❺ Ledbury

Hellens Manor, a magnificent medieval manor house, dates back to 1096, when the land it was built on was granted to the de Balun family. Later it passed through the hands of the powerful Mortimer family and the Earls of Gloucester before being leased by them to the family of Walter de Helyon, from whom the house derives its name. In the late 14th century ownership passed to the Walwyn family, who continued to extend the building for nearly two centuries despite its being severely damaged by an earthquake in 1571. Following the Reformation, the Walwyns stuck stubbornly to their Catholic faith and were so confident of the patronage of Henry VIII's eldest daughter, the devoutly Catholic Mary Tudor, that they prepared a room for her – now known as 'Bloody Mary's Room' – in expectation of a royal visit. In fact, Mary's visit never came, but the Walwyns went on to take the Catholic King Charles I's side during the English Civil War and it was during this conflict that the brutal murder of a Catholic priest took place in the manor at the hands of Roundhead soldiers. His ghost is said to haunt the house today, as is that of Hetty Walwyn, a member of the family who was incarcerated in the building for 30 years following her elopement with a lowly farmhand. During this time, she slowly went mad. The present curator of the building maintains that he once found poor Hetty standing beside him, 'a dark, semi-solid figure' – only for her to vanish when he turned away. Carved into the window surround of the bedroom in which Hetty spent most of her tragic life are the words: 'It is a part of virtue to abstain from what we love if it should prove our bain'.

▶ *Ledbury is 4 miles NW of Junction 2 of M50. Hellens Manor is near Much Marcle off the A449, 5 miles SW of Ledbury.*

❻ Weston under Penyard

According to local tradition, a farmer once found two massive iron doors beneath the ruins of Penyard Castle, and collected a team of 20 oxen to tear them open. He urged on the cattle using a whip made of rowan, which he knew would protect him against evil spirits. As an additional safeguard, he carried in his pocket a splinter from a yew tree. Eventually, the doors groaned open, and inside were two great casks full of treasure, with a jackdaw perched on top of them. Just as the farmer was about to go in, the doors clanged shut again, and a sepulchral voice said, 'Had it not been for your quicken-tree goad and your yew-tree pin, you and your cattle had all been drawn in.' Terrified, the farmer fled. If the story has a grain of truth in it, the treasure is still there to be recovered.

▶ *2 miles E of Ross-on-Wye on A40.*

❼ Ross-on-Wye

Until the beginning of the 20th century at least, a phantom woman in a small boat was said to appear every evening at 8 o'clock, sailing down the river from Hereford towards Ross-on-Wye. Her vessel travelled fast, even when it was moving against the wind or in a flat calm. She always went ashore at a spot about 7 miles from the town, at the site of a long-vanished village, where she wept and wailed hysterically. Then she would return to her boat and sail back towards Hereford, disappearing when she was about half a mile from the city. The stretch of river on which she was seen was called the 'Spectre's Voyage', and local boatmen believed that anyone who met the phantom on the water would die shortly afterwards.
▶ *1 mile from Junction 4 of M50.*

THEY NAMED THE SPOT 'SPECTRE'S VOYAGE'
ROSS-ON-WYE

❽ Goodrich

The ruins of 12th-century Goodrich Castle are haunted by two lovers who died during the Civil War. In 1646, Alice Birch eloped with Charles Clifford, and the couple were given refuge in the castle by their Royalist friends. While they were there, the stronghold was besieged by Roundhead troops under Colonel Birch, Alice's uncle, and the two lovers drowned in the River Wye while attempting to escape. Their ghosts have been seen trying to cross the river on a phantom horse.

▶ *Just E of A40, 4 miles S of Ross-on-Wye.*

❾ Kentchurch

Mythical trickster Jack o' Kent reputedly lived in this neighbourhood, and, as if to give the claim credence, a tombstone to the memory of one John à Kent is to be found in nearby Grosmont churchyard. Jack had an ongoing, if somewhat foolhardy, rivalry with the Devil but he always seemed to win. One day, he persuaded the Devil to help him to build a bridge across the River Monnow, between Kentchurch and Grosmont, by agreeing that the Evil One could have the first living creature to cross it. As soon as the bridge was finished, Jack threw a bone across for a hungry dog to chase, and the Devil was thwarted in his plan to claim a human soul.

Jack knew that, having tricked the Devil so often, when he died he would have to struggle to avoid eternal damnation. On his deathbed, he told his friends to impale some liver on Kentchurch (or perhaps Grosmont) church steeple. He said that a dove and a raven would come to fight over it, and they would know if his soul was saved because the dove would win. Some claim that no one ever knew how the battle ended, but others affirm that the dove triumphed.

At Kentchurch Court, a private house that dates, in part, from the 14th century, there is a cellar where Jack is supposed to have stabled his magic horses, and a bedroom where his ghost still walks on stormy nights.

▶ *On B4347 1 mile SE of A465, 11 miles SW of Hereford.*

GOODRICH CASTLE CHAPEL

⑩ Aconbury

As midnight chimes on Twelfth Night, so it is said, the water in St Anne's Well bubbles furiously and gives off blue smoke. Until the First World War at least, there used to be fierce competition to draw the first bucket after Twelfth Night because the water was held to be of great medicinal value, especially in curing eye trouble.

St Anne's Well and Pool are found just below Aconbury Hill, where the remains of an Iron Age hillfort are now covered by trees. The fort was still occupied in Roman times and is often referred to as the Roman camp. Pottery finds are in the Hereford Museum.

Lady Well, in a coppice just beyond St Anne's, is haunted by a pair of lovers whose names have long been forgotten. The girl murdered the boy, believing him to be unfaithful, and on discovering his innocence, she died of a broken heart. At one time Lady Well may have been dedicated to St Catherine, as was a 12th-century priory, built by Margaret de Lacy. All that remains is the church, now dedicated to St John the Baptist and supposedly haunted. A cowled figure has occasionally been reported near the tomb of Roger de Clifford. It may be the last manifestation of a troublesome spirit that was exorcised and driven into a bottle by the clergy and buried beneath the church wall about 250 years ago.
▶ *Just E of A49, 5 miles S of Hereford.*

⑪ Callow

In the early part of the 19th century, several coach passengers mysteriously disappeared from a coaching inn near Callow Hill, where they were lodging overnight. Eventually their bodies were discovered inside an old house at the top of the hill. The murderers were caught, tried and executed. The house fell into disrepair and gradually crumbled away until nothing was left of it. However, a ghost house has occasionally been seen on the same site, and one woman, who claimed to have seen the apparition many times, reported that she had felt an almost overwhelming sense of fear each time she saw it.
▶ *Just W of A49, 3 miles S of Hereford.*

⑫ Hereford

The cathedral stands on the site of a stone church that was erected in memory of St Ethelbert by Offa, king of Mercia, in AD 795 (see page 135). Ethelbert, who ruled East Anglia, was to marry Offa's daughter, Alfrida, to cement an uneasy truce between the two kingdoms, but while negotiations were taking place at Offa's palace, Offa had Ethelbert murdered – he was allegedly beheaded with his own sword. The disposal of the head and body proved troublesome, however, because wherever they were buried miraculous lights appeared above the spot. Eventually, Offa approached the pope to expiate his crime. First, he built the church at Marden to serve as a temporary sanctuary, and when the shrine in Hereford was ready, the saint's remains were dug up and taken there for re-burial. A well formed in the first grave at Marden, and at a place on the journey where the body briefly touched the ground, near the entrance to Castle Green, a spring appeared. Both are known as St Ethelbert's Well.

Another saint, Thomas Cantilupe, was buried in the north transept of the cathedral and the base of his medieval tomb may still be seen there. Thomas was Bishop of Hereford from 1275-82. He died on his way back from Rome, where he had gone to seek the pope's support in a quarrel he was having with the Archbishop of Canterbury. Thomas's bones were brought to Hereford and his shrine at once became the focus of a whole series of miracles and a place of pilgrimage. During the next 25 years, 420 miracles were attributed to him, including 66 cases of bringing the dead back to life. In 1320, Thomas was canonised by the pope.

In 1960, a doll was found buried in the town, with a written curse tucked into its skirt – 'I act this spell upon you from my whole heart, wishing you to never rest nor eat nor sleep the restern part of your life. I hope your flesh will waste away and I hope you will never spend another penny I ought to have.' Nothing is known of its history and the doll is now in the Hereford Museum & Art Gallery.
▶ *A49 from N (Leominster), A438 from E (Ledbury), A49 from S (Ross-on-Wye).*

CENTRAL ENGLAND

A GHOST HOUSE CAN BE SEEN ON THE SITE
CALLOW

LEICESTERSHIRE & RUTLAND

Remnants of paganism survive in an old stone statue of the mother goddess, and in traditional games to welcome the annual rebirth of spring, despite fearful congregations seeing witchcraft at every turn.

❶ Griffydam

A roadside well, lined with stone, is said to have been guarded by a griffin – a beast that was half-eagle and half-lion. Villagers had to fetch their water from a priory over 2 miles away until one day a knight rode by. In exchange for a cup of water he shot the monster with bow and arrow before riding away.
▶ *Just N of A512, 3 miles E of Ashby-de-la-Zouch.*

❷ Bottesford

Francis Manners, the 6th Earl of Rutland, died in 1632 and lies buried in the village church. On his tomb are effigies of his two sons who, it says in the inscription, 'dyed in their infancy by wicked practice and sorcerye'. In 1618, the witches of Belvoir were hanged at Lincoln for having murdered them by witchcraft.
▶ *Just N of A52, 7 miles W of Grantham.*

BOTTESFORD CHURCH

❸ Vale of Belvoir

The most notorious witches who ever terrorised the Midlands lived in the Vale of Belvoir, in the 17th century. Their leader was Joan Flower, whose daughters, Margaret and Philippa, worked for the Earl and Countess of Rutland at Belvoir Castle. Joan openly boasted about weaving magic with the aid of the Devil and her favourite cat, Rutterkin. She publicly cursed the earl when Margaret was dismissed for pilfering, and with her daughters and three other women – Anne Baker, Joan Willimott and Ellen Green – she planned her revenge. Within a year, the earl's two infant sons had died. Five years later, in 1618, Joan and her fellow witches were arrested, and tried at Lincoln. They confessed to killing the children with enchantments, and to making the earl and his wife sterile. Joan admitted that they had brewed spells to make the infants ill and then die. Little Henry, Lord Roos, lived just a week after the witches' ceremony, when they pricked one of his gloves with pins and boiled it in hot water. His brother, Francis, suffered a short illness, recovered and died later.

The witches went on to admit even more dreadful sorceries, and sensational evidence was given about their coven meetings on nearby Blackberry Hill. Then Joan Flower recanted and denied murdering the two boys. She asked for bread and butter, and ate it, saying, 'May this choke me if I'm guilty.' It did, and she collapsed in the courtroom. The other witches were all found guilty and were hanged at Lincoln on March 11, 1618.

▶ *Crossed by A52, 8 miles W of Grantham.*

❹ Braunston

A 2,000-year-old stone carving of a Celtic earth mother stands outside Braunston church, close to the north wall. It is thought to represent a goddess who was worshipped with primitive fertility rites that took place on the site of the church in pre-Christian times.

▶ *On minor roads 2 miles SW of Oakham.*

❺ Wistow

This small village, set in quiet countryside near the Grand Union Canal, between Arnesby on the A5199 and Great Glen on the A6, has a modern maze, a rural centre and, if such things are to be believed, a supernatural happening on June 1 each year. Wistow Hall and St Wistan's church are all there is left of the old village, which stood to the southeast of the Hall and was abandoned in the 17th century. The name is a shortened form of Wistanstowe, holy place of Wistan, and he is the one responsible for the annual 'miracle'.

Wistan was a Saxon prince, heir to the throne of Mercia. His mother, Elfleda, was appointed regent on the death of the king. Wistan's cousin and godfather, Britfardus, proposed marriage to the queen in order to strengthen his own claim to the throne, but the prince opposed the match, on the grounds that it was incestuous in the eyes of the Church. On the pretext of discussing the matter, Britfardus lured the boy to a lonely spot and there split his skull in two. His crime was discovered when a column of light appeared over the boy's burial place, and where his blood had been spilt, human hair sprouted from the ground. Vilified by the Church and people, and tortured by his own conscience, Britfardus went insane. Wistan was re-interred at Repton, where fragments of his bones attracted pilgrims until the Reformation, when they disappeared. Now, on the anniversary of the murder, for one hour during the day hair supposedly springs from the ground once more.

▶ *On minor roads 6 miles SE of Leicester.*

❻ Husbands Bosworth

A floor stain at Husbands Bosworth Hall, said to be still damp after more than 300 years, was made by a priest trying to escape Cromwell's men. The stain is either consecrated wine – or his blood. The ghost of 19th-century Protestant Lady Lisgar, who refused to allow a priest to enter the house to administer the last rites to a dying Catholic servant, also haunts the house.

▶ *Junction of A4304 and A5199, 6 miles W of Market Harborough.*

❼ Hinckley

In 1727, 20-year-old saddler Richard Smith joined a crowd surrounding a recruiting sergeant. As the soldier harangued and cajoled the men of the village to join his troop, the young man replied with quips and jokes, until the exasperated sergeant lost his temper and ran him through with his pike. The youth's tombstone is said to sweat blood on April 12, the anniversary of his death.

▶ *2 miles N of Junction 1 of M69.*

CENTRAL ENGLAND

LINCOLNSHIRE

All kinds of ghouls and ghosts – from the vengeful, spear-wielding 10th century martyr St Edmund, to a Canadian pilot of the Second World War – haunt Lincolnshire's fens, wolds and castles.

❶ Gainsborough

A castle once occupied the site where medieval Gainsborough Old Hall stands today. On February 2, 1014, King Sweyn of Denmark, ruthless leader of the second great Danish invasion of England, died in torment there after he had threatened to destroy Bury St Edmunds. It was rumoured that he met his death at the hands of the vengeful, spear-wielding ghost of St Edmund, who had been martyred by the Danes 140 years earlier.

Soon afterwards, in the same castle, Sweyn's son Canute was proclaimed king, and Gainsborough is one of several places in England where the best-known legend of Canute is supposed to have taken place. The River Trent, flowing close by the castle, is famous for the Aegir, a 2m (6ft) high wall of water that rushes upstream with the spring tides. Bored by his courtiers' flattery, Canute decided on a practical way to bring an end to it. He sat by the river bank, ordered the tide not to touch him and, of course, got drenched. 'Let all the world know that the power of monarchs is vain,' Canute lectured his entourage, '… no one deserves the name of King but He whose Will the Heavens, Earth and Sea do obey.'
▶ *Junction of A156 and A631, 15 miles NW of Lincoln.*

❷ Epworth

For two months, from December 1715 to January 1716, Epworth Rectory was the scene of a terrifying and still unexplained haunting. The victims were the Reverend Samuel Wesley, his wife, his servants and some of his 19 children, although not his famous son John, who was then 13 years old and away at school.

Mournful groans and strange howls echoed round the old house, and upstairs in the attic there was an almost incessant banging. One night, Reverend Samuel was woken by the sound of coins being tipped on to the floor. Another night he heard heavy footsteps on the stairs and bottles being smashed. No one could trace the source of these noises, or of any of the other many disturbances. Often freak winds howled around the house while Old Jeffrey, as the ghost was known, wrought havoc inside. A few members of the household claimed to have caught fleeting glimpses of it. Hetty, one of the daughters, said that it looked like someone in a long, white gown, while Mrs Wesley considered it to be more like a headless badger.
▶ *10 miles N of Gainsborough on A161.*

❸ Cleethorpes

On September 22, 1956, hundreds of strollers along the promenade at Cleethorpes saw a silent gleaming object in the sky, which they described as resembling a glass sphere. The UFO was also observed through telescopes and by radar from the nearby RAF station then in operation at Manby, where the craft was estimated to be 24m (80ft) in diameter, and to be hovering at a height of 16,500m (54,000ft). It remained in the same position for about an hour, then vanished as two jet fighters closed in to investigate. The event has never been satisfactorily explained.
▶ *2 miles S of Grimsby.*

❹ Louth

Thorpe Hall and its vicinity are reputedly haunted by a lady in green, who is believed to be the ghost of Donna Leonora Oviedo. Sir John Bolle of Thorpe Hall commanded one of the ships in the Earl of Essex's fleet, and fought in the Battle of Cadiz in 1596. One story says that Donna Leonora was among the captives after the battle, others that Sir John was himself a captive whom the beautiful Spanish noblewoman helped to release. Either way, she fell in love with him and wanted to accompany him back to England. Sir John, however, was happily married and refused her offer. Broken-hearted, Donna Leonora pledged her undying love to Sir John, and gave him jewels for his wife and a portrait of herself in a green dress. On his return, Sir John hung the portrait in the Hall, while Donna Leonora entered a convent, where she spent the rest of her life.
▶ *15 miles S of Grimsby on A16.*

❺ Skegness

Now in the care of the National Trust, Gunby Hall, 7 miles west of Skegness, was built in 1700 by Sir William Massingberd. Some years earlier, when his family lived at nearby Bratoft Castle, his daughter Margaret tried to elope with one of his postilion-riders, but her father shot the man dead as they were crossing the castle moat. Sir William was accused of murder and sentenced to appear in London once a year, when his family coat-of-arms was ceremonially smeared with blood. Overcome by remorse, he demolished Bratoft Castle in 1698 and then built Gunby Hall. It is said that the spectres of his daughter and the postilion-rider have been seen on a path that runs near the Hall, called the Ghost Walk.

▶ *A52 from N, A158 from W, A52 from S. Gunby Hall 7 miles W on A158.*

❻ Boston

The breezes that blow round the exposed church tower known as Boston Stump are said to be the result of a struggle between St Botolph and the Devil. The saint so berated Satan that he huffed and puffed, raising a wind that has not yet died down. The Stump is, in fact, the tall, octagonal tower of St Botolph's church, which has stood as a landmark for sailors and the people of the surrounding flat fenlands for 700 years. Nearby is the site where the Saxon saint founded his monastery in AD 654, which grew into the modern town of Boston.

▶ *14 miles N of Spalding on A16.*

❼ Anwick

Two rocks that lie outside the entrance to Anwick churchyard are known as the Drake Stones. According to legend, when a local farmer was ploughing a nearby field, he lost his horses in a bog, and as they were sucked down, a drake flew out of the hole in the swampy land. Next day he found a huge drake-shaped stone near the spot.

In 1832, attempts were made to move the stone. Chains lashed to it snapped, and a drake – some said its guardian spirit – flew from underneath. It was hauled to its present position in 1913, but broke into two pieces, the largest about 2m (6ft) long and 1m (3ft) wide, and the other half the size. Residents say they often see two drakes sheltering under the stones, and believe the original was a Druids' memorial.

▶ *5 miles NE of Sleaford on A153.*

❽ RAF Coleby Grange, Metheringham, Lincolnshire

Many former wartime RAF bases in the East of England are reputed to echo with the spirits of airmen who lost their lives during the Allied bombing of Germany. Among the most famous is RAF Coleby Grange, just south of Lincoln, which served as a nightfighter station between 1941 and 1945, and was briefly reinstated in 1959 as an operational base for American Thor nuclear missiles. Today, little remains of the former airfield apart from the crumbling control tower, but both this and the surrounding area are said to have been the site of many strange happenings over the years – notably the appearance of a ghostly airman who paces anxiously between the tower and the runway. A BBC television crew who visited the airfield in August 2005 recorded a series of light anomalies and ghostly mists, which convinced them that they were witnessing some kind of paranormal activity, and several of the crew reported being pelted by small stones. The ghost may be that of the commander of 409 squadron of the Royal Canadian Air Force, whose Beaufighter aircraft crashed on landing shortly after the squadron took up a posting there in July 1941.

▶ *5 miles S of Lincoln.*

❾ Lincoln

The imposing fortress of Lincoln Castle is one of the oldest and finest medieval castles in England. Built in stone in 1136, the stronghold replaced an earlier wooden structure, built by William the Conqueror in 1068. The castle houses one of only four surviving versions of Magna Carta, as well as a section of the cross erected there by the grieving Edward I in memory of his beloved Queen Eleanor. The building's fine state of repair is partly explained by the fact that it was a working prison until 1878, with public executions taking place on the roof of the tower known as Cobb Hall up until that date. Unsurprisingly, the tower and the dungeons below are said to be home to the spirits of countless tortured souls, one of whom was once blamed for flinging a small child down the staircase. According to local legend, the nearby Great Hall is haunted by the ghost of a woman whose presence is connected with a skull that was once on display there. When attempts were made to remove the skull, the story goes, the spectre began screaming hideously. The skull was bricked up in the castle walls to prevent any accidental recurrence of the incident.

▶ *A46 from SW, A15 from N and S.*

CENTRAL ENGLAND

NORTHAMPTONSHIRE

Among the rebuilt castles, restored churches and oddly shaped houses, the ghosts of those who suffered at the hands of miscreants mingle with those of wrong-doers, and one fiddler effects a glorious hoax.

❶ Rockingham

The present castle is the result of much rebuilding, renovation and restoration of the stronghold that was built on the site for William the Conqueror. Long ago, the castle was used mainly as a hunting lodge, and was the scene of a tragedy. When young Lord Zouch and his friend Lord Neville were out hunting, Neville mentioned that Lady Zouch had a lover. Lord Zouch rode straight back home and found his wife with a monk. In blind fury, he plunged his sword into the figure, only to discover that it was his sister Clara, who had left her nunnery in disguise to meet her own lover. Neville's spiteful warning sprang from jealousy and hurt pride, because Zouch's wife had rejected his advances. Bent on revenge, Lord Zouch was about to ride in pursuit of Neville when Clara's monk arrived and stopped him. Just as Zouch was about to strike him down, an apparition appeared. It told them that Neville was already dead, Lord Zouch, his wife and son would die in seven days, and for seven years, at the September feast of Holyrood, his ghost must re-enact the tragedy – but with ringing footsteps to warn everyone of his coming. Clara's monk was to keep a vow of silence until the haunting ended.

According to the legend, that's exactly what happened. Within a week Lord Zouch and his family were dead. The castle rang to his ghostly footsteps every September for seven years, after which the monk told the story, and died.

▶ *1 mile N of Corby just W of A6003.*

❷ Woodford

One of the reasons St Mary's church attracts visitors is to see the remains of a human heart through a small glass panel in a pillar in the north aisle. It was probably discovered during restoration in 1867, and its origins are not known for certain. However, a story sprung up that it belonged to a former vicar of the parish, John Styles. In about 1550, the Catholic Styles lost the parish and fled to a monastery in Belgium, taking with him a valuable chalice from the church. Soon afterwards he died there. The new vicar, Andrew Powlet, brought the chalice, together with John's heart, back to Woodford several years later, but with the passage of time, both relics were mislaid and forgotten. In 1862, Powlet's ghost was seen in

SKULKING DUDLEY

THE TRUTH OF THIS TALE is lost in the mists of time but the legend lives on in several versions. In one, Skulking Dudley is the bullying owner of Clapton Manor, who feigned illness to avoid settling a dispute over land. His daughter rode to the joust in his stead, lost the fight but married her opponent. Dudley later murdered – or was murdered by – one of his own workmen, and his ghost continued to torment the villagers of Clapton long after his death, until laid by the combined skills of 12 clergymen.

In another version, possibly nearer the truth, heiress Agnes Hotot took her father's place because he had the gout. Agnes won the contest and, taking off her helmet, shook her hair loose and exposed her breasts to prove a woman had been the victor. Agnes later married a Dudley and the image of a woman with dishevelled hair and bared breast adorned their coat of arms for many years.

the hallway of Woodford Rectory by the young man who was living there at the time. It appeared twice, each time hovering near a certain panel in the wall. Examination revealed a secret cavity, which contained the missing chalice and a faded letter that led to the discovery of the heart, entombed in a pillar in the church.

St Mary's also has a ghost. It came to light in 1964 when the image of a figure kneeling at the altar appeared on a photograph, when nobody had been there. The camera and film showed no signs of interference and the phenomenon remains a mystery, although some say the figure was the spectre of John Styles.
▶ *Just S of A14, 7 miles E of Kettering.*

❸ Ringstead

Lydia Atley, a young girl rejected by her lover, disappeared in 1850 after going to meet him at his orchard. For the next 20 years, her ghost haunted the area. It would walk from the orchard to the church – and to a spot where the skeleton of a girl was found in a ditch in 1865.
▶ *On minor road just W of A45, 8 miles NE of Wellingborough.*

❹ Passenham

A monument in St Guthlac's church marks the place where Sir Robert Banastre lies buried. He is recorded as being a man of piety and a benefactor of the church. Yet, according to local tradition, he was an evil, grasping landlord who expelled tenants in order to avoid payment of Poor Law dues. For this, apparently, he was condemned to an uneasy death and a restless, miserable existence in the hereafter.

The villagers rejoiced when they heard of his death in 1649, but their elation was short-lived. Within a few hours, his armour-clad figure was seen in the lanes and by the bedsides of his former tenants. The sexton was startled into fits when Sir Robert appeared beside his half-dug grave. To him, as to the others, the ghost said, 'I am not yet ready.' With some trepidation, the priest began the burial service. In muffled tones from the coffin came the familiar refrain: 'I am not yet ready.' On inspection, the corpse exhibited the usual symptoms of mortality, but after burial his ghost continued to terrify the district, although the words changed to 'Beware! Be ready!' A service of exorcism was held, in the middle of which Sir Robert appeared and begged the assembled clerics to stop, promising to desist from further hauntings. So far, the ghost has kept its promise.
▶ *Just S of Stony Stratford off A5, 5 miles W of Milton Keynes.*

❺ Boughton

The ghost that reputedly haunts the church ruins at Christmas time is, some say, that of George Catherall, also known as Captain Slash. He was the leader of a gang that plagued the district in the early 1800s and was hanged at Northampton in 1826. His mother had predicted that he would die with his boots on, but he proved her wrong by kicking them off just before the hanging. Captain Slash was the most notorious inmate of a lock-up that used to stand on the village green. For 500 years, until the end of the 19th century, one of the largest Midland horse fairs was held annually on the green, and anyone who was drunk or disorderly was held in the lock-up. Captain Slash was gaoled for demanding protection money from stall-holders.
▶ *4 miles N of Northampton on A508.*

❻ Rushton

The Triangular Lodge was built in the grounds of 15th-century Rushton Hall in about 1590. The Hall is now a country estate hotel and spa, and the Lodge is owned by English Heritage. It is a curious, three-sided building with triangular rooms, windows and chimneys, dedicated to the Holy Trinity by its owner and designer, Sir Thomas Tresham. He died in 1605, and later that year, his son and heir Francis was executed for his part in the Gunpowder Plot. It's possible that the conspirators may have schemed together in the Lodge, but the tale linked to it has a less sombre aspect and stems from the late 18th century, when the estate was in the hands of Lord Robert Cullen.

An underground passage was discovered, leading from the Lodge, but no one was brave enough to explore it. Lord Cullen offered £50 to any man who would venture in, and the offer was taken up by a local fiddler. He gave the money to his wife and scrambled into the darkness with a candle in his hatband and playing his favourite tune – 'Moll in the Wad'. The music faded, and the fiddler failed to return. Later, fearful searchers reported finding hat and candle beside an apparently bottomless pit. His distraught wife wailed in despair, but promises of more money calmed her. Two years later she produced a remarkable letter from her husband, who, she said, had fallen all the way through the world, tumbling out in newly discovered Australia. People were so impressed that they gave her the fare to go to find him, and she left the village. The fiddler, of course, had eventually found a way out of the passage, dodged his rescuers and gone into hiding to wait for his wife to join him.
▶ *4 miles NW of Kettering on minor roads.*

CENTRAL ENGLAND

NOTTINGHAMSHIRE

The fretful spirits that roam this old shire county are overshadowed by the mystical symbol of the ancient forests that lived on in the legend of Robin Hood – the mysterious and powerful Green Man.

❶ Ollerton

Rufford Abbey and country park are located about 2 miles from the village of Ollerton. The abbey is in a state of disrepair, but is now in the care of English Heritage. The site is apparently haunted by the ghost of a giant monk, his cowl pulled over his skull. The parish register for Edwinstowe records the death of a man 'from fright after seeing the Rufford ghost'.
▶ *Close to junction of A614, A616 and A6075, 18 miles N of Nottingham.*

❷ Harlow Wood

The ghost of Elizabeth Sheppard, a 17-year-old girl brutally murdered on her way to seek work in Mansfield, is said to haunt the spot where she died on July 7, 1817. It appears whenever her memorial stone, near the junction of the A60 and B6020 roads, is moved. Her murderer was a scissors grinder named Charles Rotherham, who, thinking she had money, attacked her with a stake ripped from the hedge. But all she had of value were her shoes and an umbrella. He was caught in Mansfield, after he had tried to sell the items at the Three Crowns Inn, at Redhill, and later hanged on Gallows Hill in Nottingham.
▶ *Along A60, 3 miles S of Mansfield.*

❸ Arnold

Bestwood Lodge, once the residence of a royal hunting park, was demolished in 1860 and rebuilt as a Gothic mansion. In the mid 1970s it was converted into a hotel and members of staff have reported strange occurrences since then. A chambermaid claimed there was a strong smell of oranges in certain rooms whenever children had stayed – it is perhaps a coincidence that the lodge was once the retreat of Charles II and his mistress Nell Gwyn. Children were allegedly heard crying in various parts of the hotel, and strange footsteps echoed where no one was supposed to be present. Bar staff reported ghostly voices in the cellar, and lights that flickered and went out for no reason. The hotel was the venue of Ghostcon 2003, a public conference on ghosts, hauntings and the spirit world.
▶ *Bestwood Lodge is just W of the A60 at Arnold, 6 miles N of Nottingham.*

❹ Newstead

Built in 1170 and later the home of the Byron family, Newstead Abbey is famous for its ghosts. Lord Byron himself is said to have seen the Black Friar, whose appearances always herald disaster, just before his luckless marriage to Annabella Milbanke in 1815. There is also a White Lady, said to be the spirit of Sophia Hyett, a bookseller's daughter, who was so obsessed by the poet that she still haunts his old home, especially the grounds, crying, 'Alas, my Lord Byron!' Another ghost is that of an earlier Byron, 16th-century Little Sir John with the Great Beard, which was seen sitting in a chair by the fireplace, reading.
▶ *1 mile W of A60, 12 miles N of Nottingham.*

❺ Nottingham

The Trip to Jerusalem, which is reputed to be the oldest pub in England, is built on the site of a brewhouse. This would have served the castle on the rock above, and travellers to the Holy Land bought ale there. The pub's cellars are hewn out of solid rock and include a cave and passage leading up to the castle. The cave is known as Mortimer's Hole, because Roger Mortimer, 1st Earl of March, is said to have hidden there, trying to evade capture by Edward III. It did him no good, because the king's men crept down the passageway and cornered him. He was later executed and his ghost is said to haunt the cave.
▶ *6 miles E of Junctions 25 and 26 of M1.*

❻ Clifton

The imposing Clifton Hall stands on the edge of Clifton village with fine views of Clifton Grove and the River Trent. It was purchased in 2006 by Anwar Rashid, a 32-year-old businessman with a property portfolio in Dubai. From the first evening, Mr Rashid and his family were troubled by knockings on the walls, and a man's voice asking 'Is anyone there?' For the next eight months they were tormented by screams in the corridors, strange manifestations and ghostly figures. One night, Mrs Rashid went to prepare milk for her baby son and found their young daughter downstairs watching TV. When she went back upstairs, she found her daughter in bed, sleeping.

Paranormal investigators were equally spooked, and when unexplained spots of blood were found on the baby's quilt, the family moved out, handing the keys to the bank. Subsequently, Darren Brookes, owner of a security firm that had supplied staff to guard the house, said that some of his staff refused to work there.

The hall, which has a 600-year history, had been a grand family home, the Clifton Girls Grammar School from 1958 and an administrative building for Nottingham Trent University from 1976. It had not previously had a reputation for being haunted.
▶ *On A453, 4 miles S of Nottingham.*

THE BLACK FRIAR'S GHOST HERALDS DISASTER
NEWSTEAD ABBEY

The medieval forest was
both a place of refuge
and a place of danger —
depending on which side
of the law you stood

SHERWOOD FOREST

Tales from the greenwood

Britain's wilder woods have inspired many myths and legends, from ancient tree spirits to the mischievous Green Man.

In the heart of England, 17 miles north of Nottingham, lies Sherwood Forest – the home of one of the country's most enduring legendary figures: Robin Hood. Sherwood itself is a remnant of a wide expanse of broad-leafed woodland that covered much of central and southern England from the end of the Ice Age until the Middle Ages. Its ancient trees – one of which, the Major Oak, is thought to have been growing since the time of the Norman Conquest – have borne witness to much of the nation's recorded history. According to some, those same trees are the repository of ancient spirits whose activities pre-date the coming of Christianity and whose restless slumbers still occasionally intrude in the affairs of humankind.

Gods and shades

The concept of woodland spirits is common to all the forested areas of the world. In the rainforests of central Africa, the forest inhabitants believe that every tree possesses its own unique spirit; to the Native Americans, each tree had a 'shade' that watched over those who passed it by. In ancient Greece, which was once much more thickly forested than it is today, the god Pan roamed among the ilex trees, rustling branches, twitching leaves and mischievously causing unwary travellers to lose their way. Indeed, the modern word 'panic' is derived from Pan, and originally described the strange, irrational fear that occasionally seizes hold of those who find themselves alone and seemingly lost in the forest.

Farther north, among the tribes of what was once Germania and in pre-Roman Celtic Britain, the spirits of the forest were regarded with a mixture of veneration and fear. Ceremonies among woodland glades were commonplace, and the forest became a place of refuge for those cast out from society – both living and dead. In medieval Lithuania, whose heavily forested borders once extended far to the south into what is now present-day Ukraine, the pagan worship of woodland spirits continued to be the official religion until the 14th century and remained prevalent well into the 20th.

The Green Man

It was around the same time that ballads began to be sung of Sherwood Forest's most famous occupant, although in those days his persona was very different from the warrior-hero who led his band of merry men in a quest to restore to the poor people of England what had been robbed from them by rapacious Norman barons and their duplicitous allies, the Church. The original Robin Hood was indeed a fearless fighter, yet he appears to have been none too discriminating as to whom he fought against. Little John, the one member of Robin's mythical band to figure significantly in the original ballads, appears to have embodied the common man – doughty, strong and unyielding in the face of Robin's impudent challenge to give way after John had trespassed into 'his' forest. Meanwhile, Robin himself, clad from head to foot in green, has much in common with an altogether older figure in English mythology – that of the Green Man, a mischievous and restless Pan-like woodland spirit whose pagan origins had not been effaced entirely by the country's conversion to Christianity. Commonly portrayed as the face of an old man surrounded by leaves, the Green Man can be found carved in stone and wood in medieval churches throughout central and southern England – an indication that he still occupied a position of importance in the hearts and minds of ordinary people, and harked back to the beliefs of an otherwise forgotten time.

Mortal danger

Commoners and nobility alike had more practical reasons to fear the forest in those days. Around the time of King John (1199-1216) England faced an economic crisis in which the population began to outstrip the availability of land and work. Those who owned the land found themselves with a glut of labour and wages fell accordingly. In response, many people stole or otherwise transgressed the law in order to feed their families and then fled to the forest to form bands of 'out-laws' that would prey on any unwary traveller who came their way – rich or poor.

But then, in the mid 14th century, came the Black Death. Over a period of some 70 years, following recurrent outbreaks of the plague, the population of England fell by around two-thirds to a level from which it would not recover until the middle of the 17th century. With work now plentiful, the outlaws began to move out of the forest and resume normal lives. They brought with them the stories of the greenwood that would inspire future generations to view their desperate struggle for survival in an altogether more heroic light. Only the ancient trees of the forest – and their watchful shades – remained to bear witness to what really happened during those dark days in 'merrie Sherwode'.

SHROPSHIRE

Country houses and parks are the domain of unhappy souls, but legends of giants and guarded treasure tell of a wilder time, when a local hero was doomed to a sleepless afterlife for making peace with the enemy.

❶ Child's Ercall

Centuries ago, two local farmworkers were on their way to work one morning when they saw a strange creature rising dripping from a pond. Assuming it to be the Devil, they turned and ran, but the creature called after them and they realised that their Devil was a mermaid. She told them that treasure lay at the bottom of the pond, and they could have as much of it as they liked if they were prepared to come into the pond and take it from her hands. So while she dived beneath the surface, they waded in until the water came almost up to their chins. When the mermaid reappeared cradling a lump of gold as large as a man's head, one of them was so amazed that he swore he had never had such luck in his life. It was a mistake he probably regretted for ever after. When the mermaid heard his oath, she screamed and dived back down to the depths, taking the gold with her. Neither the mermaid nor the treasure has been seen again.
▶ *7 miles S of Market Drayton, on minor roads S from A41.*

❷ Newport

Chetwynd Park lies about a mile north of the town of Newport, and during the mid 18th century the mansion was the home of the Pigott family. Shortly before the birth of Madam Pigott's first child, a doctor warned her husband that he must choose between saving the baby or the mother. Pigott callously replied, 'One should lop the root to save the branch,' but in the event both mother and child died. For many years afterwards their ghosts appeared on moonlit nights, haunting the park and nearby roads. Cheney Hill, within the park, is known as Madam Pigott's Hill because she was so often seen combing her baby's hair there. In 1850, 12 parsons combined to exorcise the phantoms, which have not been seen since.
▶ *8 miles NE of Telford on A518.*

❸ The Wrekin

This distinctive 400m (1,300ft) hill, which dominates the surrounding countryside, has been a place of human activity since at least the Bronze Age, when it was populated by a tribe of Celts. A folk tale about its origins suggests that two giants built it out of earth dug from the bed of the River Severn. When it was finished, they quarrelled. One struck at the other with a spade, missed and split the rock, leaving a scar now called the Needle's Eye. A raven prevented the next blow from falling by pecking at the giant's eye. The tear he shed formed the

ACCORDING TO LEGEND, TWO GIANTS BUILT THE HILL
THE WREKIN

pool known as Raven's Bowl, which has never run dry since. With the third blow, one giant knocked the other unconscious, and immediately imprisoned him in Ercall Hill. To this day, the giant can sometimes be heard groaning at dead of night from beneath the earth there.
▶ *On minor roads 5 miles W of Telford.*

❹ Much Wenlock

South of the highest point on Wenlock Edge – a limestone escarpment that lies southwest of Much Wenlock – stands Ippikin's Rock. This bluff is named after a robber who once lived in a cave in the cliffside, where he also died, buried by a landslide together with his ill-gotten gains. In the unlikely event that anyone should stand on the rock and shout, 'Ippikin! Ippikin! Keep away with your long chin!', that person will be pushed over the cliff by Ippikin's ghost.
▶ *9 miles NW of Bridgnorth on A458.*

❺ Kinlet

Before his death in 1581, the squire of Kinlet, Sir George Blount, swore that he would haunt his daughter Dorothy and her descendants because she had married beneath her. Apparently, he kept his word. On several occasions he returned from the grave in a spectral coach drawn by four white horses, and drove straight across the dining-room table at the Hall as Dorothy and her family sat down to dinner. His spectre is also supposed to have frightened the women of the village away from the pool where they washed clothes. Eventually, a party of clergymen exorcised his vengeful spirit and imprisoned it in a bottle. By one account this was thrown into the sea, by another it was left under Sir George's monument in Kinlet church, with a warning that anyone who broke the bottle would release the ghost. The bottle is said to have remained there until the 1890s, when the church was restored. Today, the effigy of Sir George can still be seen in the church, kneeling alongside his wife, son and daughter, whose marriage so angered him in life and death.
▶ *10 miles S of Bridgnorth on B4363.*

❻ Minsterley

Wild Edric, the hero of Welsh border rebellions against William the Conqueror, is said to appear when war threatens Britain. Just before the Crimean War, a man and his daughter declared they saw him galloping past Minsterley. The date of Edric's death and his burial place are both unknown. Some say he did not die at all but, as punishment for making peace with the Conqueror in 1070, he and his men are condemned to haunt the lead mines beneath Stiperstones, an impressive rocky ridge in the Shropshire hills. Miners who heard them believed the knocking to be an omen of a good mineral lode nearby. A recognised walking route in the region is still known as Wild Edric's Path.
▶ *10 miles SW of Shrewsbury on A488.*

❼ Shrewsbury

St Alkmond's church in the town was largely rebuilt in 1795, although the spire is much older. One day in 1553, a terrible storm blew up during mass. According to local records, the Devil appeared and shot up the steeple, where he tore out the wires of the clock and clawed the fourth bell. The claw marks are still visible, and the pinnacle, which the Devil knocked off in passing, is still missing.
▶ *15 miles W of Telford on A5.*

CENTRAL ENGLAND

151

STAFFORDSHIRE

Ancient wraiths cling fast to Staffordshire's historic monuments, while the modern mysteries of this old manufacturing county continue to baffle witnesses – and challenge modern science.

❶ Dilhorne

On March 21, 1983, the little village of Dilhorne between Cheadle and Stoke-on-Trent bore witness to one of the most extraordinary events in English meteorological history when it was bombarded with unusual, tiny seashells during a freak thunderstorm. Residents, who at first thought that the shells were hailstones, were amazed when the storm subsided to find their gardens sprinkled with the mysterious shells that had fallen from the skies. The plot thickened when subsquent examination showed them to be Dove shells of the *Columbellidae* family – a species found only in tropical seas. Meteorologists suggest that the shells were swept up by a cyclone somewhere in the vicinity of the Philippines and were carried by jetstreams in the upper atmosphere all the way to their final resting place in rural Staffordshire.

▶ *3 miles W of Cheadle on minor roads.*

❷ Croxden

Ghostly figures of both monks and nuns are said to glide silently across the grounds surrounding the ruins of the former Cistercian Abbey of Croxden, which was established by monks from France in 1176. Very little is known about the history of the abbey, other than that it was the permanent residence of exactly 12 monks up until 1538, when they were expelled in accordance with Henry VIII's edict for the Dissolution of the Monasteries. The fact that the ghostly sightings reach their peak in July may be connected in some way with the anniversary of the monks' expulsion, although sceptics have pointed out that that ghost-watchers are far more likely to take an evening stroll at this time of year.

▶ *On minor roads 5 miles N of Uttoxeter.*

❸ Tamworth

Staff at Tamworth Castle have experienced all manner of bizarre happenings, from hearing footsteps and furniture being dragged around to feeling strange presences. On one occasion, an engineer summoned to reset the alarms saw someone looking out of a window when there was no one known to be present in that area, and another time two members of staff saw a swirl of blue mist in one room.

The castle, which was given to Robert de Marmion by William the Conqueror, has long been haunted by a Saxon nun named Editha, otherwise known as the Black Lady. Apparently, when de Marmion took possession of the estate, he expelled the nuns from a nearby convent. Editha, who had founded the order in the 9th century, was summoned from her grave by the prayers of her followers and, in 1139, attacked the 3rd Baron Marmion in his bedroom with her crozier. The pain from the wound stopped only when he had made restoration and the nuns had returned to the convent. Editha still walks the castle, and has been reported in de Marmion's room and on the staircase, both of which are open to the public.

The other known ghost at Tamworth is the White Lady, who paces the terrace and battlements, crying for her murdered lover. The story goes that she was captured and imprisoned in the castle by Sir Tarquin, with whom she fell in love. While she watched, unable to intervene, he was killed in the Lady Meadows by her would-be rescuer, Sir Lancelot.

▶ *3 miles W of Junction 10 of M42.*

❹ Cannock

Located at the southwestern tip of Cannock Chase, Hatherton Hall stands amid parkland that includes some of central England's finest mature trees. The Gothic mansion was built in 1817 on the site of a former manor house that dated back to the reign of James I. The house is said to be haunted by the ghost of a former lord of the manor from those days, Sir Hugh Hatherton. He appears as a dark figure in a cloak to all except, for some reason, members of his own family.

Sir Hugh's suit of armour used to be kept at the Hall and during a party there a group of revellers thought it would be a good idea to use his helmet as a beer mug. This must have outraged the old knight because the armour-desecrators soon found themselves confronted by his headless ghost.

▶ *3 miles NE of Junction 11 of M6 and Junction T8 of M6 Toll.*

❺ Cannock Chase

The 26sq miles of gently wooded lowland heath between Stafford and Rugely known as Cannock Chase is a beauty spot much beloved by those seeking a breather from the urban sprawl of the West Midlands. Whether or not the area also attracts visitors from much farther afield is matter of continuing speculation, but the fact remains that for more than 20 years it has acquired a steadily growing reputation as a UFO hotspot. One famous incident that occurred in December 1987 and was reported by hundreds of local residents subsequently turned out to be a NATO in-flight refuelling exercise involving an F-111 strike aircraft and a pair of giant KC-135 airborne tankers. But since then, the sightings have continued more or less unabated, and several mysterious glowing lights and saucer-shaped objects have been captured on video footage. Many of the reports bear a remarkable similarity to those emanating from the 'Falkirk Triangle' in Scotland (see page 217), leading those in search of a rational explanation for the sightings to suggest that the same sort of – as yet unexplained – atmospheric phenomena might be responsible. Meanwhile, the area's UFO watchers keep their eyes trained on the heavens, comforted by the knowledge that another sighting is only a matter of time.

▶ *Between A34, A460 and A513, 6 miles N of Cannock.*

CENTRAL ENGLAND

WARWICKSHIRE & WEST MIDLANDS

A ghostly battle plays out on the site of a Civil War massacre, a gruesome mummified arm is blamed for paranormal activity, and a bottled ghost creates havoc in an old ancestral home.

❶ Bilston

A ghostly tale features one Bilston coal mine. In the late 18th century, an evil spirit haunted the workings, upsetting the miners so much that they called in an exorcist. He made magic signs over them, and told them to visit the pit at midnight. Their leader should carry a Bible in his right hand and a key in his left, and as the miners walked through the galleries they should repeat the spell: 'Matthew, Mark, Luke and John, God bless the errand we're come on.' They were also told to recite the Lord's Prayer backwards.

On the chime of midnight, the men marched into the mine. As they drew near the coalface, the evil spirit appeared and began creeping menacingly towards them, seemingly unaffected by their spells. Suddenly, one of the miners noticed that Caggie, their leader, was holding the Bible in the wrong hand. Once he'd put that right, the apparition vanished, and all that was left was the acrid smell of brimstone.

▶ *3 miles SE of centre of Wolverhampton.*

❷ Walsall

The restored White Hart Inn at Caldmore Green is now part of a joint heritage centre and housing association complex. The original 17th-century manor house was converted into a pub in 1817 and, when it was renovated in 1870, the mummified arm of an infant and a Cromwellian sword were discovered in the attic. The arm, which had been surgically removed, was at one time thought to be a relic of witchcraft and became known in the district, incorrectly, as a 'Hand of Glory'. In folklore, a Hand of Glory was the hand of a hanged criminal pickled in various salts and dried in the sunlight. It was used as a holder for a candle made from a hanged man's fat, virgin wax and sesame – a form of illumination much esteemed by burglars, because it lulled householders to sleep. The arm is in the safekeeping of the Walsall Museum.

Both the arm and the sword became associated in popular belief with various hauntings at the inn, thought to be the work of a young girl who had killed herself there about a century earlier. Other unexplained occurrences in the building include a handprint that appeared in the dust on a table in the attic, although it was impossible for anyone to have been there, and phantom footsteps thumping across the attic floor.

▶ *1 mile E of Junctions 9 and 10 of M6.*

❸ Long Lawford

Lawford Hall, Little Lawford, was originally the home of the Boughton family, and it seems that when the Elizabethan house burnt down in 1790 and the family moved to Brownsover Hall, a few miles away, the spectre of one of their long-dead relatives followed them. The ghost of Squire Boughton – known as One-handed Boughton after he lost a hand in an accident – for some unknown reason terrorised the neighbourhoods of both Halls in a spectral coach and horses. At one time 12 clergymen were enlisted to exorcise the ghost, and they claimed to have achieved the feat by capturing him in a bottle and throwing it in a pond. But the wild squire's spirit was not so easily contained and the hauntings continued, albeit less often. When the bottle was inadvertently retrieved by an angler and returned to the family, they increased once again. The bottle has, apparently, been buried and Brownsover Hall is now a hotel, but some say the squire's spirit has not been laid to rest and his phantom continues to haunt the place.

▶ *2 miles W of Rugby on A428.*

❹ Kineton

On October 23, 1642, Charles I's army fought the Parliamentarian forces at Edgehill, about 2 miles southeast of Kineton, in the first major action of the Civil War. The result was inconclusive, and by Christmas Eve, sheep were grazing on the battlefield. The shepherds looking after them were startled to hear the sound of fighting men, together with the crash of cannon and the ring of steel on steel. Terrified out of their wits by these continuing noises, they were about to run when they were transfixed by the sight of the phantom armies. Unable to move, they watched the Battle of Edgehill refought by spectres.

When dawn brought an end to the performance, the shepherds hurried to Kineton, and told their story to the local magistrate and the parson. Both men visited the spot on the following night and saw the same spectral conflict. This amazing sight was seen several times, and when the king heard the story, he sent six of his officers from Oxford. They, too, saw the unearthly combatants, and claimed to recognise friends who had been killed in the fighting.

▶ *10 miles NW of Banbury on B4100.*

⑤ Alcock's Arbour

Just off the road between Stratford and Alcester, near the Haselor–Temple Grafton crossroads, is a curious conical hill, which has been known for centuries as Alcock's Arbour. An indentation at the foot of the hill is said to be all that remains of the cave that was once the home of a famous robber named Alcock. Before he died, Alcock put his stolen hoard into an iron-bound chest and secured it with three locks. He buried the chest at the back of the cave and set a large cockerel to guard it. One day, an Oxford scholar found the chest, and managed to open two of the locks, but as he tried to open the third, the cockerel seized him and tore him to pieces. According to the legend, if one of Alcock's bones could be found and shown to the bird, it would allow the chest to be opened.

The hill is also known as the Devil's Bag of Nuts, from a story that tells how Satan went nutting on September 21 – Devil's Nutting Day – and had filled an enormous sack when he was interrupted by the Virgin. She told him to drop the sack, which he did, thus forming the hill.

▶ *Close to A46, 5 miles W of Stratford-upon-Avon.*

SPECTRES BATTLE IT OUT IN THE FIELD
EDGEHILL

WORCESTERSHIRE

Shadows of misfortune, a gruesome find on a church door and a guilt-ridden spectre that once roamed the countryside number among the county's extraordinary repertoire of mysteries.

❶ Lickey Hills

Designated a country park in 1971, the Lickey Hills are the location of a Devil story or two. In one, the Devil and his chief huntsman, Harry-ca-nab, both mounted on white bulls, used to chase wild boars through the hills at night, accompanied by a pack of hounds that the Devil kept at Halesowen. In another, the night sky over the hills was haunted by the Seven Whistlers, which some people claimed were seven of the Devil's hounds. Others said that they were six birds of fate in search of a seventh. If ever they found it, the world would end.
▶ *Close to village of Lickey on B4096, 4 miles N of Bromsgrove.*

❷ Worcester

The library at Worcester Cathedral was founded in Saxon times and today holds a fine collection of medieval manuscripts, post-medieval books and archive documents. It is also houses a curious artefact. During the Danish raids of the 10th and 11th centuries, Worcester was terrorised by waves of marauding Norsemen. According to a story passed down for generations, a Dane was caught hiding in the cathedral after a raid and, as retribution for the destruction wrought by his countrymen, was flayed alive. His skin was tanned and nailed to the inner side of the main doors as a warning to other invaders.

Similar legends exist throughout southeast England, particularly in Essex. The cladding of many Saxon doors was supposed to have come from a thieving Dane. Antiquarians of the 17th and 18th century popularised the story and souvenir hunters subsequently attempted to pick the remaining doors (many of which were of Norman or later date) clean. Fragments were saved, including examples from Copford church and East Thurrock in Essex. There is even a preserved fragment from a door in Wesminster Abbey. While 19th-century examination upheld the tales, 20th-century analysis revealed most of the skin to be nothing more sinister than cow hide.

Worcester cathedral's covered doors were removed during restoration and thought lost, but they were rediscovered in the 1850s in much the same state as they were in upon removal, with a wafery parchment-like material still attached. A small piece of the material was analysed by Birmingham University in the 1980s and was verified as human skin. The remaining portion of skin can be viewed by appointment.
▶ *3 miles W of Junctions 6 and 7 of M5.*

❸ St John's

Farmers across Worcestershire have, for many years, complained of savage attacks on their livestock. Reports of cat-like creatures in the vicinity prompted the British Big Cats Society to undertake a survey, which was published in 2006. It listed a total of 48 sightings in Herefordshire and Worcestershire between April 2004 and July 2005.

Cats may still be present in the region. In March 2009, two men walking their dogs in St John's saw what they described as a black cat, but about the size of an Alsatian dog, lurking in the undergrowth. The 'cat' disappeared as the men approached.
▶ *1 mile SW of Worcester city centre.*

❹ Leigh

The listed Grade I tithe barn at Leigh Court is a huge timber-framed construction, built in the 1300s, and now under the joint guardianship of Leigh Court and English Heritage. This is where the ghost of Edmund Colles used to come in a coach drawn by four horses that breathed fire. At the foot of the steep hill by St Edburga's church, the phantom coach would take a flying leap over the barn and plunge into the River Teme beyond.

In real life, Colles was conscience-stricken by an attempt he had made one night to rob a friend whom he knew to be bringing money from Worcester. In the dark, his friend slashed out at Colles with his sword as Colles grabbed his horse's reins. When the friend returned home, he was horrified to discover that a severed hand wearing Colles's signet ring was still grasping the bridle. Next day, he found Colles at his home in Leigh, bearing the marks of the dreadful wound. Colles confessed to the crime and begged his friend's forgiveness, which was freely given. Colles died from his wounds soon afterwards, and his guilty spirit roamed the countryside until 12 clergymen exorcised it in a midnight service. They laid the spirit in a local pond, which they filled in afterwards.

Edmund is buried in St Edburga's church, and the tomb of his father, William Colles, and mother, Mary Palmer, is found there, too, surrounded by effigies of all their 12 children, including the unfortunate Edmund.

▶ *On minor road 1 mile W of A4103, 4 miles SW of Worcester.*

❺ Malvern Hills

The shadow of Raggedstone Hill, one of the Malvern Hills, is said to bring misfortune to anyone upon whom it falls. This superstition began in the Middle Ages with the death of a monk from a nearby priory – probably the 12th-century Little Malvern Priory, one of two local priory churches. As penance for a misdeed, the monk had to crawl up Raggedstone Hill daily on his hands and knees. The punishment continued until his limbs were raw and festered, and he became so weak he was barely able to drag himself up the hill. In torment, he cursed his persecutors – 'May all upon whom the shadow of this stone falls die untimely as I do.' Then he fell dead.

▶ *S and W of Great Malvern, 8 miles S of Worcester.*

❻ Besford

At one time, a member of the well-known Worcestershire family of Seabright used to kennel his foxhounds at Church Farm, where part of the land is still known as Dog Kennel Piece. One night, the owner heard a disturbance among the hounds and sent his kennelman to find out the cause of it. The man did not reappear, but next morning his hunting boots were discovered, still spurred and containing the lower part of his legs and feet. Ever since, it is said, the kennelman's boots march across Dog Kennel Piece on dark nights, accompanied by the sound of jingling spurs and the baying of hounds.

▶ *On minor roads 2 miles W of Pershore.*

❼ Beckford

The tower arch of the nave in the 12th-century parish church at Beckford features three carvings – two demonic faces and an alien-headed centaur. The centaur may be a representation of Sagittarius, or may simply be a mythical beast from pagan times.

▶ *On A46, 8 miles SW of Evesham.*

❽ Broadway

The ghost of a kennelman is supposed to haunt the village, wearing a nightshirt. Apparently, he was roused from his bed by the noise of his dogs barking, but when he rushed out in his night clothes to see what was wrong, the dogs failed to recognise him and tore him to pieces.

▶ *Just S of A44, 5 miles SE of Evesham.*

CENTRAL ENGLAND

A BLACK CAT ABOUT THE SIZE OF AN ALSATIAN DOG WAS SEEN LURKING IN THE UNDERGROWTH
ST JOHN'S

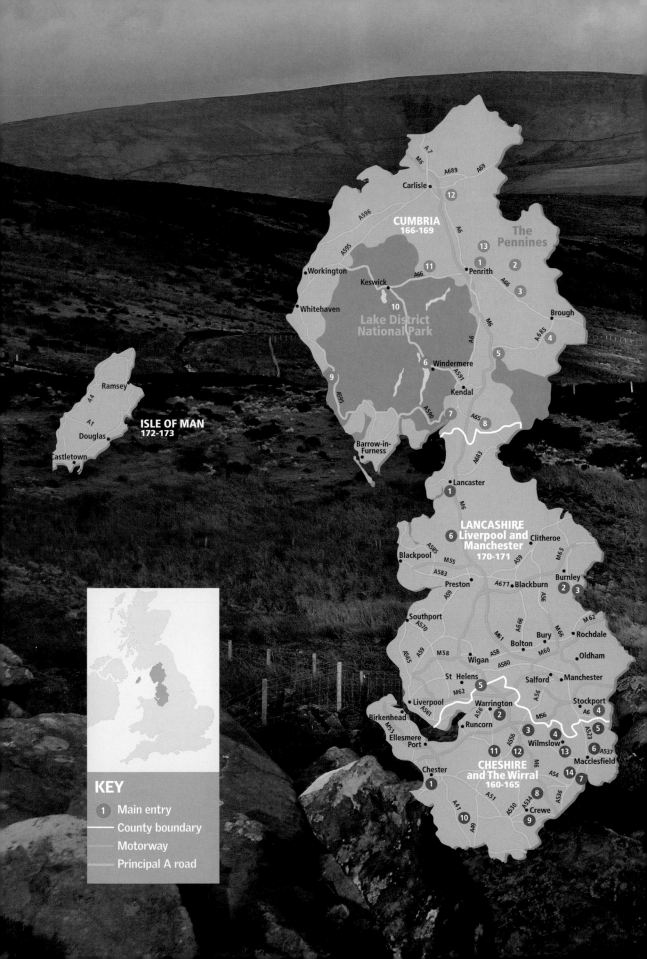

ISLE OF MAN
172-173

Ramsey
A4
A1
Douglas
Castletown

CUMBRIA
166-169

Carlisle
A7
M6
A689
A69
12
13
The Pennines
A596
A595
A66
11
1
2
Workington
Penrith
Keswick
A66
3
Whitehaven
10
Brough
Lake District
National Park
M6
A685
4
A6
9
5
A595
6
Windermere
A59
Kendal
7
A65
8
Barrow-in-
Furness
A683

LANCASHIRE
Liverpool and
Manchester
170-171

Lancaster
1
M6

Clitheroe
6
A585
M65
Blackpool
M55
Burnley
A583
2
3
Preston
A677
Blackburn
A59
A56
Southport
A666
M62
A570
M61
Bury
M66
Rochdale
A565
A59
Bolton
M60
Oldham
M58
Wigan
A58
Salford
Manchester
A580
A56
St Helens
5
Stockport
M62
Warrington
A56
4
Liverpool
A561
2
M56
A6
5
Birkenhead
Runcorn
3
4
A523
M53
Ellesmere
Wilmslow
13
6
A537
Port
11
12
Macclesfield
CHESHIRE
14
7
and The Wirral
M6
A4
Chester
160-165
1
A51
8
A536
A41
A530
A534
Crewe
10
A49
9

KEY
1 Main entry
   County boundary
   Motorway
   Principal A road

Northwest England

Demons were once believed to haunt the fells of the Northwest, a landscape whose dark beauty and brooding skies inspired fear in lonely travellers. In villages and towns, wicked deeds live on in the lamenting spirits of the wronged.

CHESHIRE & THE WIRRAL

A city has graced the banks of the River Dee for centuries, and from Chester's Roman founding to the present day, the sad spirits of its woe-begone citizens are unable to relinquish their tenure.

❶ Chester

The ancient Roman settlement of Chester has a strong claim to being one of the most haunted places in Britain with more than 80 instances of ghostly or poltergeist activity recorded throughout the city. The George and Dragon Hotel, near the town centre, is built on the site of a 1,600-year-old Roman cemetery, and is said to echo to the measured tread of a Roman legionary on eternal sentry duty. Footsteps have been heard pacing the upper floor, from one end to the other, in the early morning. Twenty minutes later, they are heard coming back, and pass through solid brick walls on the way.

Spectres of monks and nuns have been seen at various places around the town. A ghostly monk makes his way to and from St John's church, speaking in a guttural Saxon tongue, while a beautiful nun in a blue habit wafts around the churchyard. Another monk wakes sleepers at the Victorian mansion at Dee Hills Park, and in a furniture store in Pepper Street, two cowled phantoms have been spotted.

Besieged by Roundhead troops for 18 months during the Civil War in the 17th century, Chester still has links to that turbulent period. At Brown Heath crossroads, two figures in buff overcoats and broad-brimmed hats are occasionally seen, and Cavalier soldiers appear on the city walls at Morgan's Mount. Farther along the walls, Cavaliers and their ladies are said to promenade while at St Werburgh's Street, Civil War horsemen carry on the fight. At the Tudor House in Upper Bridge Street, a headless phantom is said to be a Cavalier who was beheaded by a random cannonball.

Several of those who lived and died wretchedly continue to haunt Chester's public houses. At the Deva pub, a boy who fell to his death in a fire in Victorian times returns to the spot, while the ghost of a mistreated maid throws glasses and beermats around the Falcon Inn. In the cellar at the Marborough Arms, the dying gurgles of a Victorian landlord who cut his throat can still be heard.

Several ghosts of more recent origin have been reported by terrified staff on the West Cheshire hospital campus. Some old buildings once housed the Cheshire County Asylum and office staff working there have seen a woman dressed in black and experienced a range of eerie phenomena, such as hearing footsteps in empty corridors and feeling the sensation of someone sitting next to them.

One of Chester's favourite ghosts has been affectionately named Sarah by staff at a chocolate shop in Eastgate Street. Jilted on her wedding day, she is particularly active around Valentine's Day when she throws boxes of chocolates around the store. The site has two other ghosts, a jolly aproned man and an almost invisible spirit.

The city even has a herd of phantom cattle, heard lowing plaintively early in the mornings at the foot of St Mary's Hill.

▶ *2 miles SW of Junction 12 of M53.*

ROSTHERNE MERE

❷ Warrington

Walton Hall, a red-brick Gothic hall in Warrington built in the 1830s, has been the site of many paranormal experiences and hauntings. Once inside, several visitors have reported feeling a sensation of being stabbed. Others, particularly on one of the staircases, have felt as though they were being pushed. Reported sightings include a slim military man with a limp, a woman in white and a maid in Victorian dress, who has brushed past visitors. The figure of an old lady who may — according to stories — have died in the bath has been seen in Lady Daresbury's bedroom, and another woman has been seen outside the door. In the banqueting room, a sinister man has disconcerted a number of visitors, while there have been frequent reports of orbs of light, children's laughter and poltergeist activity.
▶ *4 miles W of Junction 21 of M6.*

❸ Rostherne

The mere at Rostherne, one of the largest and deepest in Cheshire, is said to be visited by a mermaid. On Easter Sunday she may be heard singing and ringing a sunken bell that lies on the bed of the lake. Allegedly, the bell rolled into the water by accident, either when it was being transported to St Mary's church, or while workmen were trying to install it. The mermaid, however, arrives in the mere by swimming up a subterranean channel that supposedly connects the lake to the Irish Sea, possibly via the River Mersey. In fact, a particular saltwater fish that breeds in freshwater, the smelt, used to live in the mere, so the one-time existence of an underground stream may not be so far-fetched.

Rostherne Mere is a National Nature Reserve and visitors must have a permit.
▶ *Just S of Junctions 7 and 8 of M56.*

❹ Styal

The ghost of a woman haunts the upper floors of Quarry Bank Mill, part of an 18th century industrial heritage site run by the National Trust. The imposing cotton mill looms large on the banks of the River Bolin on the Styal Estate, a purpose-built complex comprising a workers' village, gardens and farmland. The mill ghost reportedly wears Victorian-style clothing and has frequently been witnessed watching people from a window. Guides have named her 'Annie', but who she is, and why she haunts the mill is a mystery.

The estate also has a three-storey Apprentice House, where pauper children were lodged, fed and schooled, in exchange for their labour in the mill. The detatched house was large enough to house 60 children; clearly none felt sufficiently attached to the place to take up residence as a spirit, for the two ghosts, like the spirit in the mill, are women. Builders carrying out renovation work in the 1980s saw a 'white lady' in the medical room and visitors to the attic have also seen a woman while on the tour. The lane close to the Apprentice House is known for its eerie atmosphere.

▶ *On B5166, 2 miles N of Wilmslow.*

❺ Disley

A phantom funeral procession has often been reported in Lyme Park, followed by the white-draped spectre of a weeping woman. The deceased is said to be Sir Piers Legh, who died in 1422 of wounds received at the Battle of Agincourt. The woman is his sweetheart Blanche, who died of grief when she heard the news. Blanche may also haunt Lyme Hall – a woman in white has often been seen there, sometimes together with the sound of distant bells.

▶ *6 miles SE of Stockport on A6. Lyme Park is S of Disley.*

❻ Rainow

An inscribed stone at Saltersford, near Rainow, records and marks the spot of a mysterious and tragic death. On Christmas Eve, 1735, John Turner, who ran a string of packhorses between Chester and Derby, was returning to his home at Saltersford through a snowstorm. Anxious to be with his family in time for Christmas Day, he ignored advice and pressed on through the blizzard. When he failed to appear, a search party was sent out and found his string of packhorses safe but Turner frozen to death less than a mile from home. In the snow beside him was a footprint, which seemed to be that of a woman. This mystery has never been explained.

▶ *3 miles NE of Macclesfield on B5470.*

❼ Bosley

Until the 1880s, a gallows on Gun Hill stood as a grim memorial to John Naden, whose decomposing body hung there in chains after his execution in 1731. Naden murdered his employer, Robert Brough, apparently at the instigation of the victim's wife. When the drunken Naden returned home and told her what he had done, she at once went out and rifled the dead man's pockets to make it appear that he had been waylaid by thieves, but she failed to notice Naden's knife lying beside the corpse. This was sufficient to secure the murderer's conviction.

Tradition does not record whether the wife was tried, but ironically it was ordered that Naden should be executed outside her door. His body was afterwards gibbeted on Gun Hill, and when the gallows was at last removed, the timbers were used in local field stiles. Some people believe that these stiles are still haunted by Naden's ghost.

▶ *4 miles NE of Congleton.*

THE FOOTPRINT BESIDE HIM
RAINOW

❽ Sandbach

The Old Hall Hotel at Sandbach, which dates back to 1656, has a plethora of colourful ghosts. One of the most distinctive is an old lady referred to as the Bee Keeper, who walks nonchalantly around the hall dressed in old-fashioned beekeeping garb. Another female spirit, the Grey Lady, appeared when panelling from neighbouring Haslington Hall was moved to the Old Hall. In the process, the skeleton of a baby had been discovered, and it seems that the woman may have followed the removal men to search for her child behind the panelling in its new location.

Behind the fireplace, a priest hole made a hazardous hiding place for fugitive clerics, some of whom burned to death. The strange orbs of light that sometimes appear in the lounge are possibly remnants of their presence. Sir John Radcliffe, the Hall's first owner, has been known to disconcert hotel guests by shaking door latches and pushing pint glasses, but the Old Hall's most haunted room is a bedroom – number 11. Guests have reported waking with a feeling that the covers were in flames, and have seen the ghost of an elderly woman sitting by the bed. Other ghostly inhabitants of number 11 are two children, who have also been seen running through the hotel and are thought to terrorise chefs and kitchen staff by rearranging knives and other implements.
▶ *1 mile SW of Junction 17 of M6.*

❾ Crewe

The Lyceum Theatre, which was built in 1882 on the site of a Catholic church and its graveyard, is the stamping ground of a number of ghosts. The first is a monk with a guilty conscience, who has been seen in the shadowy recesses below the auditorium. In recent times, he has seemingly abandoned the bowels of the building to appear in the Three Lamps pub behind the theatre. Two of the other ghosts are performers. One, an elderly actor, is usually seen in the vicinity of the stage door. The other, a ballet dancer, hanged herself in the dressing room, where she has frequently been seen. A fourth ghost is an old lady whose presence is marked by the scent of lavender. Despite an exorcism in 1969, all the spirits still remain – in the mid 1970s the actor and dancer both attended a play, and were seen by the whole cast, apparently enthralled by the production.
▶ *5 miles W of Junction 16 of M6.*

❿ Bickerton

A cave on Bickerton Hill is known locally as Mad Allen's Hole. In the 18th and early 19th century it was said to be occupied by a man who shunned society after he was prevented from marrying the woman he loved. The story relates that Allen, who came from Handley, lost his reason when both sets of parents objected to the marriage. He sold all the property that he had inherited and retired to the cave, where he lived until he died, aged 99.

The story of Mad Allen may have become entangled with that of John Harris, known as the English hermit, whose almost identical tale of jilted love was published in a pamphlet of 1809. Harris lived a solitary life in a rock shelter at Carden (today part of a golf course on the Carden Park estate). Later, he moved to nearby Allenscombe Cave, but not to Mad Allen's Hole.

Harris's story seems equally improbable, but archaeological excavations in 1999 revealed that the shelter had been shaped and enlarged by chiselling, and niches had been cut into the walls. Slots in the stone suggest that the shelter once had a wooden frontage, and pottery finds date the construction to the mid 18th century. Someone is believed to have made a home in the shelter – quite possibly Harris the hermit.
▶ *On minor roads, 2 miles SE of junction of A41 and A534, 10 miles S of Chester.*

HAS NEVER BEEN EXPLAINED

NORTHWEST ENGLAND

ALDERLEY EDGE

⑪ Northwich

Eight hundred years ago, a Cistercian monastery stood in the grounds of what is now the Vale Royal Abbey golf course. Following Henry VIII's Dissolution of the Monasteries in the 16th century, much of the abbey was demolished but some of the cloisters were incorporated into a manor house. A monument known as the 'Nun's Grave' survives, built as a memorial to a 14th-century nun, Ida Godman, who cared for the abbey's ailing abbot. A figure believed to be Ida's ghost has been photographed inside the clubhouse. Taken in the library, the picture shows a face surrounded by either a cowl or a mass of dark hair. People entering the library have reported a chill, and a woman in a nun's habit has been seen amid the ruined abbey buildings.

▶ *17 miles E of Chester, at junction of A533 and A559.*

⑫ Plumley

Before 14th-century Tabley Old Hall fell down and was abandoned in 1927, the ghosts of a man and a woman had sometimes been reported leaning over the house's balustrade. The spectral pair were a jealous husband, killed in a duel, and his wife, who committed suicide. To avoid scandal, their bodies were reputedly walled up inside the house.

▶ *On minor road E of A556, 2 miles S of Junction 19 of M6.*

⑬ Alderley Edge

Among the trees that cover this steep, red sandstone cliff, a natural spring has formed a well, which is inscribed: 'Drink of this and take thy fill, For the water falls by the wizard's will.' The wizard in question is Merlin. The story goes that he stopped a farmer on the way to Macclesfield market with a fine white mare to sell. The bearded old man made an offer that the farmer refused, because he was hoping to get a better price in Macclesfield, but although the animal was greatly admired, no one would buy it. On his way home, the farmer met the wizard again. The old man led horse and rider through the wood to a rock, which he touched, and a pair of massive gates appeared, flying open with a noise like thunder. In the cavern beyond, said the wizard, lay King Arthur and his knights, sleeping with their horses until England needed them again – but they were one white horse short. The terrified farmer accepted a purse of gold for his horse and ran out. The gates clashed behind him as he hurtled into the daylight, and no one has seen the cavern since.

▶ *Just N of B5087, 2 miles S of Wilmslow.*

⑭ Gawsworth

Elizabeth I's maid of honour, Mary Fitton, is said to haunt her family home, the Old Hall at Gawsworth. Mary, who may have been the 'dark lady' of Shakespeare's sonnets, was banished after a scandalous affair with the Earl of Pembroke. She was subsequently married twice and never saw her home again, although she is buried in the local church.

An eccentric 18th-century playwright and dancing master, who was the last professional jester in the country, is also buried in Gawsworth, but not in the churchyard. Samuel 'Maggotty' Johnson's final jest was to elect to become a ghost by being buried in unconsecrated ground – a spinney known as Maggotty's Wood. He justified his unusual choice in verse on his tombstone. In 1851, another gravestone was placed beside the original, inscribed with a more sombre verse, which was thought to be more in keeping with the circumstances than the humour of the first.

▶ *Just E of A536, 3 miles SW of Macclesfield.*

'THE WATER FALLS BY THE WIZARD'S WILL'
ALDERLEY EDGE

LEFT TO FALL INTO RUINS ONCE AGAIN

PENDRAGON CASTLE

CUMBRIA

Wordsworth's gentle lakes and valleys seem like a different country when storm clouds roll in and a fierce wind roars across the fells. Then, tales of wailing fiends and prophetic visions are all too believable.

❶ Edenhall

A 13th-century Syrian drinking glass with flared rim, decorated with painted enamels and gilding and now on display in the Victoria and Albert Museum was, by tradition, found at Edenhall. Known as 'The Luck of Edenhall', the glass is supposed to be enchanted. The story behind the legend is that a group of fairies were surprised with the glass near a well and, as they scattered, the Fairy Queen called out that if ever it was broken, 'Farewell the Luck of Edenhall'. Inevitably, the glass was treated with special care and reverence by succeeding generations until, in 1926, the Museum took it on loan and finally acquired it in 1958.

▶ *3 miles NE of Penrith, just S of A86.*

❷ Cross Fell

The rolling moorland of Cross Fell, the highest point on the Pennine Way, was once surmounted by an early Christian cross, erected to protect wandering travellers from demons that were supposed to haunt the moors. These spirits were probably barguests – fiends that wailed across the fells, waiting to seize the unwary. Cross Fell was once called 'Fiends' Fell', and the reason may well be a weather phenomenon known as the helm wind. This roaring gale can blow up without warning and go on for days. Helm means hilltop and the wind is accompanied by a bank of cloud that sometimes obscures the summit of the fell.

▶ *10 miles E of Penrith.*

❸ Crackenthorpe

On the other side of the main road from the village, secluded among trees, stands Crackenthorpe Hall. It was once the home of the Machell family, and is said to be haunted by the ghost of Elizabeth Sleddall, known locally as 'Peg Sneddle'. During Cromwell's time, Peg was married to the owner of the Hall. When he died she felt cheated out of her share in the estate by the terms of his will, and subsequently haunted the area. She was sometimes seen in a coach drawn by four black horses, and became so troublesome that her remains were exhumed and reburied under a large boulder on the riverbed after a service of exorcism. Despite this, she is still said to revisit the Hall from time to time.
▶ *2 miles N of Appleby-in-Westmorland on minor roads.*

❹ Nateby

The ruins of Pendragon Castle stand on privately owned land, near Nateby. In legend, the castle was built by Uther Pendragon, father of King Arthur, who tried to divert the River Eden to form a moat – a local rhyme goes: 'Let Uther Pendragon do what he can, Eden will run where Eden ran.' In fact, the original castle was probably built by Hugh de Morville, one of Thomas Becket's murderers, in the 12th century. It was destroyed by fire twice but eventually restored in the 17th century by Lady Anne Clifford. After her death it was left to fall into ruins once again.
▶ *1 mile S of Kirkby Stephen on B6259.*

❺ Tebay

Mary Baynes, the famous 'Witch of Tebay' who died in 1811 at the age of 90, is reputed to have prophesied that 'fiery horseless carriages' would speed over nearby Loups Fell, which is now the route of the London–Glasgow railway. She was greatly feared by her neighbours, who blamed her for everything that went wrong in the community. Local people claimed that she withered and died at the same moment that a number of eggs she had bewitched were fried in boiling fat. Her cat once strayed into the gardens of the Cross Keys Inn and was killed by the inn's dog. Now she is said to haunt the place, some say searching for her cat. She has apparently been seen there, wearing a blue dress.
▶ *Just E of Junction 38 of M6.*

❻ Troutbeck Bridge

During the 17th century, Calgarth Hall in Troutbeck Bridge was the home of Myles Phillipson and his family, but it was haunted by two grinning and screaming skulls. He built the house on land that, together with a small farm, had previously belonged to Kraster and Dorothy Cook, who refused to sell it. Phillipson devised a plan whereby he wrongly accused them of stealing a silver bowl, or cup. Since he was the local magistrate, he presided at their trial, sentenced the couple to death and appropriated their farm. As she was led away, Dorothy cursed him and his heirs, saying that he could not get rid of her and her husband so easily. They would never leave him, and his entire family would perish in poverty and distress. Two skulls soon appeared at Calgarth. In his attempts to destroy them, Phillipson had them buried, burnt, smashed to pieces and thrown into Lake Windermere, but the skulls always returned to the Hall. True to the prophecy, the Phillipsons grew poorer and poorer and, in 1705, the family line died out. The Bishop of Llandaff, who later lived at Calgarth, finally performed a service of exorcism over the skulls and they were never seen again.

▶ *1 mile N of Windermere on A591.*

❼ Levens

Some time during the 18th century, a gipsy woman died of starvation after being turned away from Levens Hall, and her ghost – the Grey Lady – still haunts the house. Before she died, she cursed the family, saying that no male heir would be born until the River Kent ran dry and a white stag was born in the park. After years without a direct heir, a boy was finally born in 1896 – the river had frozen solid in 1895 and a pale-coloured stag had been born to a black fallow deer in the herd that lived in the park. The birth of a white fawn is still said to herald a change in the family's luck.

As well as the Grey Lady, a woman in pink, whose origins appear to be unknown, roams the house and grounds, and on the stairs of the hall, a spectral black dog sometimes rushes playfully in front of visitors, tripping them up before vanishing into thin air. In 1973 a phantom figure often appeared on the narrow bridge by the house, once nearly causing an accident.

In 1950, a visiting priest saw the owner of the house playing the harpsichord under a bright electric light – only to discover that the owner was away and there was a power cut at the time.

▶ *5 miles S of Kendal. Levens Hall is S of the village.*

❽ Kirkby Lonsdale

The Devil's Bridge across the River Lune was supposedly built by Satan himself. The story is essentially the same as is told about the trickster Jack o' Kent, from Kentchurch in Herefordshire, although in this version, the Devil appears to an old woman whose cow has strayed across the river. He promises to build her a bridge on condition that he can have the first living soul to cross it. She agrees and the bridge is completed. A mark in the masonry is said to represent the Devil's footprint. Then the old woman cheats her adversary by hurling a bun across the bridge for her dog to retrieve. Also in this Cumbrian version, in his haste to build the bridge, Satan drops many of the stones he carries in his apron, explaining why so many are scattered around the area – the Devil's Neck-collar, Castleton Fell and the Apron-full-of-Stones at the head of Kingsdale are all said to have been formed in this way.

▶ *12 miles SE of Kendal on A65.*

❾ Ravenglass

Muncaster Castle, near Ravenglass, is reputedly haunted by several ghosts, including Henry VI. Sir John Pennington sheltered the king there after his defeat by the Yorkists at Towton in 1461, and for this service Henry presented Sir John with a gold-and-white glass bowl, blessing it by saying that as long as it remained unbroken, the Penningtons would flourish. The bowl, known as the 'Luck of Muncaster', remains in the possession of the Penningtons, and the family still owns the castle, which is open to the public.

The Tapestry Room is allegedly the most haunted room in the building, full of ghostly presences and sounds, including babies crying. Mary Bragg, a local woman who was murdered in the area in 1805, occasionally appears in the grounds, but another ghost, that of Thomas Skelton, is held responsible for many of the castle's supernatural occurrences. Tom, who died in about 1600, was the Penningtons' jester, although he seems to have had a macabre sense of humour. He was said to loiter under a chestnut tree outside the castle and direct travellers to the quicksands rather than the London road. Even more gruesomely, he is supposed to have cut off the head of a local carpenter – who was the lover of his employer's daughter, Helwise – apparently at the behest of either her father or her fiancée. Thomas Skelton's portrait hangs in the castle.

▶ *16 miles S of Whitehaven on A595.*

LONG MEG

⑩ Armboth Fell

Below Helvellyn, Thirlmere reservoir was created in 1894 by joining two of the fell's smaller lakes. In the process, some low-lying cottages and farms, an inn and the small village of Armboth were drowned. One of the inundated buildings, Armboth House, was once notorious for being haunted. According to the story, the daughter of the house was murdered by being deliberately pushed into Thirlmere Lake at Halloween on her wedding eve. Every year, on the anniversary, bells were said to ring, a ghostly dog swam in the lake, and unseen hands would lay dishes for the wedding feast.
▶ *W of Thirlmere, 6 miles S of Keswick.*

⑪ Souther Fell

On several occasions during the early part of the 18th century, a phantom army was seen marching and riding across the summit of Souther Fell, near Mungrisdale. No trace of its passage was ever found, and those who saw it didn't believe that real soldiers could have moved so quickly on the steep slopes. Later, when Bonnie Prince Charlie's troops passed that way, it was said that the apparitions had been a prophetic vision of the Jacobite army on the march.
▶ *2 miles N of A66, 7 miles E of Keswick.*

⑫ Great Corby

The Radiant Boy, a luminous apparition that haunts Corby Castle, seat of the Howard family, was said to foretell great power but a violent death for any member of the family who saw it. The Reverend Henry Redburgh, rector of Greystoke, saw the spectre when he visited the house in 1803. He and his wife left the next morning rather than staying for the arranged few days, but nothing untoward happened to him, perhaps because he was not a Howard.
▶ *5 miles E of Carlisle on minor roads S of A69.*

⑬ Little Salkeld

According to legend, Michael Scot, the 13th-century wizard, came across a coven of witches holding their sabbat outside Little Salkeld, and turned them all to stone. The stone circle, known as Long Meg and her Daughters, still stands. By tradition, if anyone can count the stones twice and arrive at the same number, the enchantment will be broken. Apparently, no one has yet succeeded. Also, if Long Meg herself is ever broken, the stone will run with blood.
▶ *5 miles NE of Penrith on minor roads N of A686.*

NORTHWEST ENGLAND

LANCASHIRE, LIVERPOOL & MANCHESTER

Long before Lancashire became synonymous with the cotton industry, it was famous for its witches, and the rivalry that eventually lead two families along a trail from Pendle to Lancaster – and the gallows.

❶ Lancaster

On Thursday, August 20, 1612, three generations of women were marched through the streets of Lancaster to the gallows, about a mile out of town, and hanged before large crowds. All but one of the ten came from Pendle Forest, and the group included a crazy, decrepit, half-blind beggar known as Old Chattox. Her rival, Mother Demdike, also in her 80s, would have gone to the gallows, too, beside her daughter Bessie and two of her teenaged grandchildren, had she not cheated the hangman by dying in jail. These were the witches of Pendle.

The incident that started the witch hunt occurred six months earlier, on March 18. John Law, a pedlar, refused to give Alizon, one of Mother Demdike's granddaughters, some pins, so she cursed him. A few minutes later he had a stroke, and both he and Alizon believed that her curse had caused it. He lived just long enough to testify against her at her trial.

A fortnight after John Law's stroke, Alizon, her mother Bessie and her brother James were questioned by the local magistrate Roger Nowell, and Alizon readily confessed her responsibility. In chilling detail, she described her close acquaintance with witchcraft, as well as that of her family and friends. By the end of the day, Mother Demdike and Old Chattox stood accused as witches and murderers, and Bessie had been stripped, searched and shown to have a supernumerary nipple for suckling the Devil.

One of the mysteries of the hunt is the ease with which Nowell secured confessions. By August, without using torture, he had enough evidence to convict all ten of desecration of graves, communing with imps and the Devil, plotting to blow up Lancaster Castle by magic, and at least 16 murders. It may be that he phrased his questions to encourage incriminating answers, a suggestion borne out by the fact that another of Demdike's granddaughters, nine-year-old Jennet, was one of his chief witnesses. The two old women may have been bent on settling a feud that had begun more than ten years earlier, and in trying to destroy one another, they destroyed themselves and their children. It is also possible that the two families did practise a form of black magic, and believed – as Alizon did – that it worked. Being slow-witted, they may not have realised until the ropes snapped tight around their necks how cruelly they could be punished under James I's new laws against witchcraft.

▶ *2 miles SW of Junction 34 of M6.*

❷ Walk Mill

Barcroft Hall, a Grade II listed manor house, has been converted into private dwellings, but its early history includes a particularly unpleasant event. In 1641, so the story goes, Thomas Barcroft chained his mentally deficient elder brother William to the wall of the cellar and starved him to death so that he might inherit the family estate. As the unhappy William lay dying in his secret prison, he is said to have put a curse upon the Barcrofts, and this seems to have been fulfilled in 1688, when the family line died out at Thomas's death. At one time, confused scribbles could be seen on the walls of the cellar, which were alleged to have been made by William.

▶ *2 miles S of Burnley on A646.*

❸ Cliviger Gorge

As darkness falls on Halloween, Eagle's Crag, near Burnley, is supposed to be haunted by the spectres of a doe, a hound and a huntsman. This is where Lord William Towneley is said to have buried his wife, Lady Sybil, who was known to dabble in the Black Arts. Initially, she rejected Lord William's advances, so he asked another witch for help and was advised to hunt a white doe – a form that was favoured by Lady Sybil – on the crag at All Hallows (November 1). A magical dog helped him trap the doe, and when he tied up the deer, using an enchanted silken rope, the creature changed back into Lady Sybil. She agreed to reject sorcery and marry him, but she would not mend her ways, and wasted away after having a hand chopped off at Cliviger mill, while causing mischief in the shape of a cat.

▶ *The A646 from Burnley to Todmorden runs through the Cliviger Gorge. Eagle's Crag is close to the village of Cornholme, 5 miles SE of Burnley.*

WATER SPRITES AND RIVER NYMPHS

BRITAIN'S RIVERS, STREAMS AND POOLS are the source of many legends, some featuring alluring nymphs who rise from the waters to waylay travellers, others more gruesome characters. One particular story centres on the stepping stones that span the river Ribble near Brungerley, Clitheroe. Here, the river is said to be the haunt of an evil spirit who claims one life every seven years by dragging some unwary traveller to a watery grave.

The tale is probably a warning to children not to go near the water, or Jenny Greenteeth the water witch will pull them in and devour them, although Jenny's Irish equivalent, the Bean-Fionn, drowns adults rather than children. In Lancashire, Cheshire and Shropshire, Jenny Greenteeth is possibly just another name for green water plants, such as duckweed, that can ensnare bathers by wrapping its fronds around their limbs and dragging them down.

❹ Winwick

The site of Winwick church was chosen by a mysterious pig, the effigy of which is carved on the church tower. The construction of the building originally began nearby, but when darkness fell, the pig suddenly appeared and carried off the masonry in its mouth to the present site, said to be the place where St Oswald died in AD 642. As the pig ran to and fro, it squealed 'We-ee-wick, we-ee-wick', and this apparently inspired the name of the parish.
▶ *Just N of Junction 9 of M62.*

❺ Garstang

Boggarts are troublesome supernatural spirits that are particularly common in the northwest of England. The Boggart of the Brook, the caretaker of a bridge near Garstang, is allegedly the ghost of a murdered woman, and takes the form of a skeleton closely wrapped in a cloak and hood. She used to hitch lifts from

horsemen at night, and only reveal her true identity when mounted behind them. With a diabolical cackle, she would whip the horse into a gallop and cling with bony hands to the rider's back until, fainting with terror, he was thrown from the horse and injured or killed.
▶ *11 miles S of Lancaster on A6.*

❻ Marple

All that is left to indicate where Marple Hall once stood is a lintel stone dated 1658. During the Civil War, the hall was owned by Henry Bradshawe, a stern Parliamentarian whose daughter fell in love with a Royalist officer, who came to visit her one day when he was carrying dispatches for the king. His presence was discovered, and a servant, under the pretext of helping him to escape, drowned him in the River Goyt. The girl died of a broken heart and is said to haunt the spot where her lover was killed.
▶ *3 miles E of Stockport on A626. The site of Marple Hall is W of Marple.*

171

Fables, phantoms and fairy folk

The Isle of Man is a rich bastion of Celtic legend. It is also, according to many, home to an ancient and invisible race.

There are no more enduring figures in folklore than the 'Little People' – the elusive, mischievous and occasionally spiteful creatures who occupy a hidden, secret world and whose somewhat capricious involvement in human affairs has given rise to countless legends and fables over the centuries. Of all the places in Britain where the work of 'fairy-folk' is still spoken of in hushed, half-believing whispers, none can quite compare with the Isle of Man.

Rising defiantly out of the storm-swept Irish Sea, almost equidistant from Scotland, Ireland and Wales, the island has clung to its Celtic traditions as stubbornly as its people have maintained their own unique sense of identity. Legend recounts how the

island was formed when the Irish giant Fionn Mac Cumhaill, also known as Finn McCool, scooped up a mighty handful of earth (the present-day Lough Neagh) to fling at his Scots rival, Fingal. Missing his mark, Finn's missile landed in the midst of the sea, while a smaller chunk flew off to form the isle of Rockall to the south. Later in its history, during the 9th century, the Isle of Man became a bloody battleground for the Celts and the Vikings, who eventually emerged victorious and gave the world its oldest surviving parliament – the Tynwald. The island passed into English hands after the 1703 Act of Settlement with Scotland, laying the foundations for its present-day semi-independent status as a Dependency of the Crown.

People visit the bridge with flowers, wishes, thanks and dedications to the fairies

THE FAIRY BRIDGE,
ISLE OF MAN

The Manx people have for centuries borne these comings and goings with fortitude, falling back on their ancient beliefs and traditions to help them to endure the vicissitudes of a pastoral existence compromised both by invasion and by the unpredictable weather. They have also maintained a widespread and persistent belief that they are accompanied on their journey through this earthly realm by a race of fairy folk whose presence – by turns benevolent and malign – has a material bearing on their daily lives.

Kindred spirits

The Bugganes (shape-shifting goblins) and Fenoderees (hairy, brown-skinned dwarves) of the Isle of Man have many counterparts throughout the Celtic world, from the Leprechauns of Ireland and Boggarts of Scotland to the mine-spirits of Cornwall known as Knockers. None resemble the diaphanous winged fairies beloved of Victorian picture books: though similarly small in stature, the Little People possess a much more earthy nature, being given to stealing both material goods and children, playing mischievous pranks on their duller-witted human neighbours, and occasionally dispensing curses or afflictions on those who displease them.

By tradition these creatures inhabit the wilder parts of the island – wooded glens, remote hilltops and gloomy caves – and shun human society while nevertheless keeping a watchful eye upon it. They also have a strong association with animals – particularly domestic animals and pets – and are known to shape-shift into animal form whenever there is a risk of their activities being discovered by some hapless Manx farmer.

A persistent myth on the Isle of Man is that of the changeling – the new-born child that is 'stolen' or otherwise possessed by the fairy folk in recompense for some perceived debt. To guard against such an occurrence, midwives on the island suspended a pair of open scissors above the birthing table, the blades poised as if to cut the invisible threads by which the child would be spirited away. The cross shape made by the hanging scissors provided a double measure of protection.

Shreds of superstition

With the coming of the industrial age in the 19th century and an influx of residents from the mainland – who to this day are regarded with suspicion by the islanders – overt belief in the Little People began to decline. Yet charming reminders of the old superstitions remain, especially at the 'Fairy Bridge' over the Santon Burn on the road from Douglas to the southern port of Castletown, itself long regarded as the main residence of fairies on the island. There, on a nearby tree, local people still tie paper notes containing wishes, thanks and dedications and prayers to the fairies. It is the custom to bid the Little People 'good day' or to greet them with the words 'hello fairies' whenever crossing the bridge on foot or by car.

One story goes that during the Second World War, airmen stationed on the island were forbidden from indulging in this practice by their commanding officer, on the grounds that it was superstitious nonsense. Over the following months, the stormy skies over the Irish Sea claimed an unusually high number of aircraft lost; yet when the airmen were allowed to resume their courteous greeting, the losses abruptly ceased.

Superstition or not, such tales still carry a very real meaning on the Isle of Man – a place where the Celtic traditions and beliefs of Britain's colourful ancient inhabitants refuse to die. Surrounded by sea and guarded by a people who are fiercely protective of their heritage, perhaps they never will.

Northeast England

Witches, werewolves and gruesome-looking ghosts once terrified the populace of England's far north. Today, the old town of Whitby, with its magnificent abbey, embraces its connection with vampires and Cottingley village draws those in search of fairies.

Berwick-
upon-Tweed

A1

1

2

Bamburgh

3

A697

Alnwick

4

5

Northumberland
National
Park

6

A68

7

Otterburn

A1068

Morpeth

A696

A189

NORTHUMBERLAND
and Tyneside
178–183

8

Newcastle-
upon-Tyne

15

A69

Hexham

Gateshead

13

16

12

9

14

10

Sunderland

11

6

A692

1

Consett

2

A167

3

Durham

4

A1(M)

DURHAM
and Teesside
176–177

Bishop
Auckland

5

Hartlepool

A689

Barnard
Castle

A688

A66

Middlesbrough

7

Darlington

A66

A172

Whitby

3

Richmond

A66

2

Hawes

A1

A79

North York Moors
National Park

A171

1

Yorkshire Dales
National Park

A65

Thirsk

A170

Scarborough

Pickering

A64

A165

10

22

Settle

21

20

19

Ripon

A61

A168

11

YORKSHIRE
184–191

A166

4

9

8

7

5

6

A59

12

A1237

14

York

13

Harrogate

A1(M)

A64

18

A629

A658

A614

A1079

A1035

Leeds

Selby

A63

Kingston-
upon-Hull

Bradford

M621

17

Halifax

A646

16

M62

A63

A58

Wakefield

A638

A79

M62

M18

M62

Huddersfield

15

A629

A635

A1(M)

Doncaster

A628

M1

Rotherham

A631

Sheffield

A57

KEY

1 Main entry

County boundary

Motorway

Principal A road

DURHAM & TEESSIDE

The county is full of reminders of mining and railway history, but the spectral appearance of a murdered boy, shivering with cold, and the antics of troublesome sprites ensure a darker past is not forgotten.

❶ Ebchester

An argument caused a local 18th-century landowner named Robert Johnson to disinherit his son. He said, 'I hope my right arm will burn away before I give him sixpence.' On his deathbed, however, he relented and reinstated the youth as his heir. At the funeral, an investigation of the coffin revealed that the right arm of the corpse had shrivelled as though burnt away.
▶ *2 miles N of Consett on A694.*

❷ Pelton

The village of Picktree, near Pelton, was once the domain of a mischievous spirit known as the Picktree Brag. Since it was able to change its shape, it appeared in many different forms but was most often seen as a donkey or a horse, which would throw anyone who attempted to ride it.
▶ *On A693 2 miles NW of Chester-le-Street.*

❸ Great Lumley

One night in 1631, the ghost of a young girl confronted the local miller, John Grahame. She said she had been murdered by his neighbour, John Walker, who had made her pregnant, and that she would haunt the miller until she was avenged. The terrified miller told the authorities, who found the girl's body and arrested Walker and another man. Their trial lasted just a day. It was hurried over after a witness said he saw the image of a girl standing on Walker's shoulders. Both Walker and his accomplice were hanged.
▶ *On minor roads 2 miles SE of Chester-le-Street.*

❹ Durham

Some years after he died in AD 687, St Cuthbert's body was moved from Lindisfarne to Durham – then called Dunholme – out of the way of marauding Danes. The corpse was remarkably preserved, and was still uncorrupted when examined in 1104 and again in 1537, but only bones were found when the tomb was opened in 1827. A story persists that these are the bones of a monk, and the saint's body lies elsewhere.

Paradoxically, St Cuthbert's resting place in the cathedral was found through the agency of two women – his dislike of women was as well known as his love for birds and beasts. The saint's coffin became rooted to the ground at a place called Ward-lawe, at which point it was revealed to the monks who were transporting it that it must be taken to Dunholme. They did not know where this was until they heard one woman tell another that she had lost her cow at nearby Dunholme. So when she set off to look for it, the monks followed her to the town.

Cuthbert's prejudice against women is said to stem from the time when he was living as a hermit in the Northumbrian hills, and a Pictish king's daughter falsely accused him of fathering her child. Appalled by the very idea, Cuthbert prayed aloud for a sign to prove his innocence, and the ground opened and swallowed up the princess. Cuthbert restored her on the condition that women must never approach him or enter churches dedicated to him.

The legend was kept alive long after St Cuthbert's body had been moved to Durham. A woman taking a short cut home through the cathedral's graveyard collapsed and later died. Another woman, who angered the saint by exploring the cathedral, was said to have been found next day with her throat cut, the fatal knife still clutched in her hand. In the 12th century, when Bishop Pudsey tried to build a Lady Chapel near the saint's tomb, the ground shook and pillars cracked, and the chapel had to be built farther away, at the west end of the cathedral.

Curfew is still rung in the city every night, except on Saturdays, because a bellringer mysteriously vanished on that day.
▶ *2 miles SW of Junction 62 of A1(M).*

❺ Sedgefield

In 1747, the church's rector died a few days before the tithes were due to be paid. His wife was reluctant to forfeit the money, so she hit upon the brilliant idea of preserving her husband's body in salt and keeping the news of his death secret. The rectory burnt down in 1792, but until then it was haunted by the vexed rector, known locally as 'The Pickled Parson'.
▶ *2 miles E of Junction 60 of A1(M).*

➏ Hilton (Hylton)

One room of Hilton Castle, in the valley of the Wear, was never used because it was said to be haunted by the Cauld Lad, the shivering ghost of stable boy Roger Skelton. He was killed in 1609 by the castle's owner, Robert Hilton, for which crime Hilton was pardoned. What actually happened that day may never be known. In one story, Hilton struck the boy with a scythe by accident while cutting grass, but in another version, he lost his temper at finding his horse not ready as instructed and the lad asleep in the stable. He lunged at the boy with a pitchfork, or sword, killing him instantly. Since then, anyone who sees the ghost is said to be permanently afflicted with damp, deathly cold.

This ghost has been confused in local tradition with a brownie, a domestic spirit who liked tidying things up at the castle. If they were tidied already, he crossly threw them into confusion. Growing tired of this, the servants laid a green cloak and hood out for him, the traditional method of encouraging a brownie to leave. The brownie put them on and disappeared, never to return.

▶ *Just N of A1231 on N bank of river Wear, 2 miles W of Sunderland city centre.*

➐ Darlington

Close to the River Tees, in the suburbs of Darlington, are four deep pools called Hell's Kettles. 'Spirits have oft been heard to cry out of them,' according to local tales, and a farmer who took hay waggons out on St Barnabas' Day (June 11), when pious folk should not work, was swallowed up in them – carts, horses and all. Some say they can still be seen there.

▶ *3 miles E of Junctions 58 and 59 of A1(M).*

DURHAM CATHEDRAL

NORTHUMBERLAND & TYNESIDE

The ferocity of the North Sea, whipped up by icy winds, is matched by the savage deaths suffered by the spirits that haunt this rugged county, from a slaughtered wedding party to a rebellious lord.

❶ Buckton

Grizzy's Clump, a group of trees by the road near Buckton, is said to be haunted by the ghost of Grizzel Cochrane. In July 1685, Sir John Cochrane of Ochiltree, Ayrshire, languished in an Edinburgh prison under sentence of death for his part in the Duke of Argyll's rising against James II in May of that year. As the execution warrant was being carried north on the mail coach, Cochrane's daughter Grizzel, disguised as a man, staged a hold-up and seized the postbag. This delayed the execution for several days, during which her father's friends managed to arrange a pardon.
▶ *10 miles SE of Berwick-upon-Tweed on A1.*

❷ Farne Islands

Cuthbert, Bishop of Lindisfarne, came to live on Farne Island in the 7th century, and had to evict the spirits that frequented the place. They retreated only as far as the outlying islands, where their screams could still be heard. Hideously deformed, dark-featured wraiths have been reported on the islands, usually riding on goats – a beast favoured by the Devil. Some people believe they are the ghosts of drowned sailors.
▶ *Off coast at Bamburgh. Visit by boat from Seahouses on B1340.*

❸ Bamburgh

Founded in AD 547, Bamburgh Castle was the ancient residence of Northumbrian kings. Oswald, the 7th-century king, was the first Christian ruler to live there, and his deeds of charity to the poor prompted St Aidan, Bishop of Lindisfarne, to bless his hand with the words, 'Never let this hand consume or wither.' When Oswald was killed in battle, his hand was severed and enclosed in a silver casket, which was kept in Bamburgh church. The casket was stolen in the 11th century, and at that time the hand inside was still uncorrupted.

Another tale of St Aidan is told in Bamburgh. In AD 651 the village was set on fire by Penda, the pagan king of Mercia, and St Aidan, seeing the flames from the neighbouring Farne Islands, prayed earnestly. In response to the holy man, the wind changed and the flames swept back on the besiegers, who fled.

Near the town, a whinstone pillar known as the Spindlestone is where the Childe of Wynde, son of the king of Northumbria, tethered his horse before going to fight the Laidley Worm in the old legend. People in the vicinity of Bamburgh were terrified by this fearsome creature, although it was really the king's daughter, who had been turned into a dragon by her stepmother. The queen was a witch, although the king didn't know that when he married her in his old age. The Childe volunteered to fight the monster, unaware that the creature was his sister, but the Worm refused to fight him. Revealing its true identity proved to be the antidote to the spell. The princess resumed her former shape, and the evil queen was changed into a toad.

The toad-queen is still said to live beneath Bamburgh Castle in a cave, the doors of which are opened every seventh Christmas Eve. She will retain her toad shape until some hero arrives, unsheathes the Childe of Wynde's sword three times, blows on the Childe's horn three times, and finally kisses the toad.
▶ *4 miles E from A1, 14 miles SE of Berwick-upon-Tweed.*

❹ Alnwick

Close by the historic town of Alnwick is the now disused Shilbottle Pit where one miner, working alone, had a terrifying experience. It was the man's job to check the mine's ventilation points. Working one day in a far corner of the mine, he went past a spot where, decades earlier, men had died when part of the roof collapsed. Suddenly his lamp went out. As he stood alone in the dark, he heard a man's voice say clearly, 'Have you got a light, mate?' and just as quickly, the lamp came on again – but no one was there. Terrified, he raced back to the pit-head, white with shock and exhaustion. So marked was he by the experience that, to the end of his working life, he would only venture into the mine when others were with him.

DUNSTANBURGH CASTLE

The imposing ruin of Dunstanburgh Castle, northeast of Alnwick, is haunted by its first lord, Thomas, Earl of Lancaster, who led a rebellion against his uncle, Edward II. The revolt failed and Thomas was imprisoned at Pontefract Castle in West Yorkshire and sentenced to death for treason. His end was horrific – it took an inexperienced executioner 11 blows to sever his head from his body and his ghost, carrying the mutilated head, has been seen walking amid the ruins of the great castle he built.

Another Dunstanburgh ghost is that of Sir Guy, a knight who sought shelter there one night. His ghost is said to be searching for a sleeping girl whom he believed he had encountered, and then lost, in a secret room in the castle.

Chillingham Castle's modern masters live alongside a host of spirits, particularly that of John Sage, who was renowned for his brutal torture of prisoners in Edward I's wars against the Scots. When the tide turned against him, Sage was hanged in the grounds of Chillingham and the crowd took souvenirs from his body, cutting off

his toes, fingers, testicles and nose while he was still alive. He has been seen wandering the castle many times since then. Some rooms in the castle bear witness to his methods – the Edward room is where Sage hacked a number of Scottish children to death, and it still has a foul smell and a strange atmosphere.

In the Pink Room a boy – known as the Blue Boy or the Radiant Boy – was walled up alive for apparently trying to aid the Spanish at the time of the Armada. When his body was found, the fingers had been worn away from trying to scrabble his way out. His cries of pain and fear have sometimes been heard around midnight and the figure of a boy has been seen.

The ghost of Lady Mary Berkeley roams the castle in search of her husband, Lord Grey, who ran off with her sister. Even Chillingham's lake is said to be cursed. The bodies of Scots' prisoners were thrown there and it is rumoured that if you dip a hand in, the dead will pull you under.
▶ *1 mile W of A1, 34 miles N of Newcastle upon Tyne.*

A SINISTER HEAD HANGS FROM THE GIBBET

ELSDON

❺ Alnmouth

The Schooner Hotel in Alnmouth's Northumberland Street has been twice voted Britain's most haunted hotel by the Poltergeist Society, and it's not hard to see why. Sixty individual supernatural entities have been glimpsed there over the years, with around 3,000 sightings in total. These include glowing orbs, a young boy on a tricycle, a uniformed man and a phantom chicken. Ghostly whispering and screams have been heard, and visitors have reported sensations of being watched in certain rooms, accompanied by feelings of dread, dizziness and even sickness.
▶ *5 miles E of Alnwick.*

❻ Rothbury

Although prehistoric carvings on stone are common in Northumberland, with about 950 examples of rock art in interwoven cup and ring shapes recorded on stone outcrops, a more recent find near Rothbury has baffled experts. It comprises a heart shape and the stylised carving of a face, along with a more complex pattern of lines and circles. The carvings seem to be much younger than the usual cup and ring designs – perhaps only 100 to 300 years old. It has been noted that the face looks like some early 20th-century works by Picasso – but any external influences have yet to be discovered.
▶ *12 miles SW of Alnwick on B6341.*

❼ Elsdon

Just outside the village of Elsdon is a gibbet from which hangs a sinister head. It has a curious history. On August 10 1792, a notorious criminal, William Winter, and two sisters, Jane and Eleanor Clark, were executed at the Westgate in Newcastle. They were alleged to have murdered an elderly woman, Margaret Crozier, at Raw Pele near Elsdon. The women's bodies were sent for dissection but Winter's was hung in chains on Whiskershields Common. When the remains were eventually cut down, Winter's bones were scattered and his skull dispatched to a Mr Darnell in Newcastle (it is not reported why). Some 75 years later, in 1867, the story was resurrected when, for some reason, Sir Walter Trevelyan had a replica of the gibbet put up on his land with a wooden body swinging from its arm. The current gibbet is a replica of the replica, following the first one's disappearance in 1998 after constant vandalism, and the head hanging there is made of glass fibre.
▶ *24 miles SW of Alnwick on B6341.*

❽ Stamfordham

Black Heddon, near Stamfordham, used to be haunted by a ghost known as Silky, because of the rustling made by her dress. Silky's most alarming habit was to jump up behind passing horsemen. Her favourite haunt, referred to as Silky's Chair, was in an old tree overlooking the waterfall at nearby Belsay. Silky was seen no more after the ceiling of a house in Black Heddon collapsed to reveal a bag of gold. From this it was deduced that she was a former owner of the house and wanted the money to be discovered.

In another version, Silky was a boggart, or mischievous spirit, who cleaned dirty houses by night but wreaked havoc in tidy ones. Once, she transfixed a waggoner's team of horses at a bridge south of Black Heddon. The horses would not move until a sprig of rowan, the traditional antidote to magic, was tied to the cart.
▶ *On B6309, 8 miles NE of Corbridge.*

❾ Dilston

The restored remains of the towerhouse and chapel are all that is left of Dilston Hall. When James Radcliffe, last Earl of Derwentwater, was beheaded on Tower Hill in 1716 for his part in the Jacobite rebellion, people said the corn ground on his estate was tinged red, and the Hall's gutters ran with blood. As his head rolled, the River Derwent became filled with adders where previously there had been none. Ever since then, the ghost of his unhappy wife, who taunted him and forced him into joining the rebels by demanding that he gave her his sword, has haunted the house, wringing her hands. The spectral earl himself is said to gallop over the countryside at night with his men.
▶ *1 mile SW of Corbridge.*

❿ Hedley on the Hill

The Hedley Kow used to plague the district by putting spinning wheels out of action, knocking over cooking pots and unravelling knitting. This troublesome fairy seems to have been a practical joker rather than malicious. He could assume strange shapes – one of his favourites was a truss of straw. When someone bent to pick up the bundle, it would become too heavy to carry, move off by itself and vanish with a loud laugh. Once, disguised as two girls, he led their boyfriends into a bog and then chased them into the river. The Kow has not been seen since the middle of the 19th century.
▶ *On minor roads 5 miles N of Consett.*

NORTHEAST ENGLAND

⑪ Blanchland

During the early 18th century, the Lord Crewe Arms Hotel was the home of General Tom Forster, who led the unsuccessful Jacobite rebellion of 1715. Captured and taken to London, he escaped from Newgate prison with the help of his sister Dorothy. For a time he is thought to have hidden in the medieval priest's hole, which is still preserved behind a fireplace in the hotel. After that, he went into exile in France and his sister never saw him again. The belief persists that Dorothy's ghost haunts the Lord Crewe Arms, in the vain hope of contacting her brother through the hotel's guests.

▶ *10 miles S of Hexham on B6306.*

⑫ Hexham

In the winter of 1904–5, a series of savage attacks were inflicted on livestock around the thriving town of Hexham, most notably in the village of Allendale. One farmer found a sheep disembowelled, and all that was left of another was its head and horns. Most of the animals had bites on their necks and legs. The most likely culprit was a young wolf cub, owned by a local man, Captain Bain, which had escaped three months before. Panic and hysteria grew and stories of the 'Wolf of Allendale' circulated. When a large wolf was reported behind Allenheads school, a crowd of 150 gathered there, many bearing guns. On December 9, a wolf apparently committed a 'great slaughter of a flock of sheep'. More than 100 people tracked it and it was shot at but escaped. The next day 200 or more armed villagers collected to search for it. Later, Mr W. Biddick, an 'Indian Game Hunter', was drafted in – but with no success. Hunts became social occasions and people wore fancy dress and sang specially composed songs.

In early January 1905, the body of a wolf was found 30 miles from the village on a railway track at Cumwinton in Cumbria. Captain Bain was called to the scene, but denied that it was his, stating that the beast was too mature to be his lost cub – perhaps he was motivated by a desire to avoid costly compensation claims. Despite the find, wolf sightings continued for a few weeks but petered out with a last report of a wolf seen with a snare on its leg.

Little had been heard of the so-called Allendale Wolf, or wolves, for nearly 70 years, when the young Robson brothers dug up two small carved heads with rough features in the woods near Hexham, a few minutes walk from where the wolf was said to have prowled. The heads were identified as Celtic, and seemed to be the catalyst for a strange and alarming presence that appeared to a number of people who came close to them. Half man and half wolf, the presence was seen by several people, but while frightening, it caused no actual harm. The heads were dispatched to various museum collections, including the British Museum. Their current whereabouts are not known – and it has been suggested that they were not ancient Celtic artefacts but toys, made in the 1950s by the former owners of the Robsons' house and then lost in the woods.

▶ *1 mile S of A69, 22 miles W of Newcastle upon Tyne*

⑬ Haltwhistle

Bellister Castle comprises a series of fortifications on the south bank of the Tyne. It dates from the late 11th century and was added to several times over the centuries to produce the current structure. Bellister is haunted by a gruesome spirit, known as the Grey Man of Bellister. He was a minstrel who had played for Lord Blenkinsopp, a 16th-century owner of the castle. On his way home along the Tyne, the man was set upon by a pack of dogs, belonging to Blenkinsopp and torn apart. His maimed ghost still visits the castle in search of shelter.

A large old sycamore at Bellister is known as the Hanging Tree – and is the place where Roundhead troops executed a number of Cavalier prisoners during the Civil War.

In the 14th century, the Blenkinsopp family owned another castle in the neighbourhood, which was named after them, and this ruin is haunted by the White Lady, wife of an early Lord Blenkinsopp. She died broken hearted at his desertion of her. Apparently, they met while he was fighting in the Crusades, and she, a wealthy

THE CATALYST FOR A STRANGE

THE HEXHAM HEADS

woman, brought a heavy chest of gold with her to England as a dowry. However, she soon became worried that he had married her for her money, and had the treasure chest hidden. When she refused to tell her husband where it was, he left her in the castle and, despite her strenuous efforts to find him, he never came back. She died full of regret and now her unhappy ghost cannot leave the castle until the treasure is found. From time to time, she tries to reveal the location of the secret vault but succeeds merely in terrifying people. In the 1970s the remains of a tunnel were found beneath the ruins but several attempts to explore it have met with failure because of the extreme bad air and gases it contains.

In unrelated sightings, another ghostly woman, this one said to be wearing Elizabethan dress, has been seen in a pub on the site of one of the castle's outbuildings. The privately owned ruins of Blenkinsopp Castle are undergoing joint conservation with English Heritage.
▶ *Bellister Castle 16 miles W of Hexham on A69. Blenkinsopp Castle off A69 3 miles W of Haltwhistle.*

⑭ Featherstone

The ghosts of members of a wedding party, including the bride and groom, are reputed to haunt the grounds of Featherstone Castle near Haltwhistle. They were waylaid in the woods of Pinkingscleugh Glen and murdered by the bride's rejected lover. During the terrible massacre, the victims' blood flowed into a hollow rock that became known as the Raven's stone. Legend does not record the date, but the bride was the daughter of a former Baron Featherstonehaugh, who never recovered from the loss of his child. The wedding party is said to ride again on the anniversary of the ambush.
▶ *On minor roads 3 miles SW of Haltwhistle.*

⑮ Housesteads

Some unknown form of treasure is said to lie at the bottom of Broomlee Lough, a lonely lake near Housesteads. Centuries ago the wealthy owner of the castle that once stood on Sewingshields Crags was forced to leave the fortress in a hurry. Determined not to forfeit his valuables, he stowed them in a box, had himself rowed away from the shore of the lough and threw it overboard. He put a spell on the chest so that it could be recovered only by the cooperation of twin horses, twin oxen, twin youths and a chain forged by a smith of kind, which is a seventh-generation smith.

Years later an attempt was made to raise the box, using the stipulated twins and chain. It was easy enough to find the spot – when the wind agitated the surface of the lake, the water above the chest remained calm and unruffled. However, the chain snapped during the recovery operation and the treasure has remained at the bottom of the lake ever since. One reason advanced for the chain breaking was that while the grandfather of the man who made it had been away for two or three days in another town, a handsome traveller had lodged in his house and slept with his wife. This traveller was the real grandfather of the chain-maker, who was, therefore, not a true smith of kind.

The view of Hadrian's Wall from Sewingshields Crags is spectacular, but according to legend, the real magic of the place lies deep underground, where the old castle's vaults are said to be the last resting place of King Arthur and his knights. A horn, sheathed sword and garter await anyone brave enough to use them. One story tells of a shepherd, passing the time while watching his sheep by knitting. He dropped his ball of wool in a rocky cleft, and in trying to retrieve it, found himself in the vast cavern. He drew the sword and cut the garter but quailed at blowing the horn, so Arthur and his men sleep on. The king allegedly lived in the castle, and his sword Excalibur is supposed to lie in Broomlee Lough, hurled there as the king lay dying.
▶ *On B6318 10 miles NW of Hexham.*

⑯ Bardon Mill

Hardriding farm, towards Haltwhistle, is haunted by the ghost of a robber who was killed there in the 14th century. The ghost's last reported visit was in 1933, when mysterious shouts and banging doors during the night awoke the people living at the farm.
▶ *On A69 10 miles W of Hexham.*

AND ALARMING PRESENCE

YORKSHIRE

Craggy moors and dales peppered with historic towns and cities, ruined castles and crumbling medieval abbeys, are ripe territory for the county's eerie legends and unquiet graves.

❶ Semer Water

A long-held belief about this large natural lake in the Yorkshire Dales, just south of Askrigg, is that the remains of a town can still sometimes be seen beneath the surface of the water. The reason is that a traveller who asked for shelter in the town was turned away by everyone except a poor couple, living in a hillside cottage. Next morning, the couple found that the traveller had gone, and the town had disappeared beneath the lake.
▶ *2 miles S of A684, 3 miles S of Askrigg.*

❷ Richmond

The market town of Richmond is dominated by its stone-built Norman castle, beneath which King Arthur and his knights are supposed to lie sleeping. A local story goes that a potter named Thompson discovered the secret tunnel and found Arthur and his entourage in their cavern. A horn and sword lay near them, but as Thompson picked up the horn, the knights began to stir. Terrified, he ran back up the tunnel and a voice echoed after him: 'Potter Thompson, Potter Thompson, If thou hadst drawn the sword or blown the horn, Thou hadst been the luckiest man e'er born.'

Another story tells of a drummer boy being sent along the underground passage from the castle to discover if it led to Easby Abbey, a mile away. His drumbeat was followed from above ground by his fellow soldiers, but it stopped halfway to the abbey and he was never seen again. Some say his drumming may still be heard.
▶ *On A6108, 4 miles SW of Scotch Corner on A1.*

❸ Whitby

Shipbuilding and whaling once thrived in Whitby – Captain Cook was apprenticed to a ship owner there in 1746, and later his four expeditionary ships were built in the town's shipyards. However, eclipsing all else is Whitby's association with vampires. Bram Stoker visited the town in the 1890s, and was inspired to write his classic Gothic horror novel, *Dracula*, which features the ruined abbey and the churchyard of St Mary's.

The fame of Whitby Abbey long precedes Bram Stoker, though, going back to Anglo-Saxon times. A monastery was founded on the site in AD 657 by St Hilda. One story relates how the abbess rid Eskdale of snakes by driving them to the edge of the cliffs and cutting off their heads with her whip. The ammonites – fossilised shellfish – found on the rocks below are said to be their remains. Stories also relate to Caedmon, who was, perhaps, England's first poet. In the late 7th century, he was a cowherd at the abbey and was teased because he could not sing. One night he had a vision of an angel who asked him to sing of the creation of the world, which he did and discovered his hidden creative talent. One of his manuscripts is kept in Cambridge University Library.
▶ *20 miles N of Scarborough on A171.*

❹ Flamborough

The ghost of a headless woman has been reported in the neighbourhood, and a spectral White Lady is said to haunt Danes' Dyke, which is an earthwork, probably Iron Age, to the west of the village. Local children were once kept in order by the threat of what would happen if they disturbed the ghost of Jenny Gallows. It was supposed to say:

'Ah'll put on mi bonnet
An tee on mi shoe,
An if thoo's not off
Ah'll be after thoo.'

▶ *4 miles NE of Bridlington on B1255.*

❺ Bridlington

Bringing five dead people back to life, restoring sight to a blind woman and healing a lame man are some of the miracles attributed to St John of Bridlington, 14th-century prior of the town's Augustinian monastery. The most spectacular of his good deeds was performed on behalf of some Hartlepool sailors, who had been caught in a storm off Flamborough Head. They saw the tower of Bridlington Priory and prayed to John for help. To their astonishment, a monk walked towards them across the mountainous waves, and when he reached their boat, he put his hand on the prow and pulled it safely to shore.
▶ *15 miles S of Scarborough on A165.*

THE ASSOCIATION WITH
VAMPIRES ECLIPSES ALL ELSE
WHITBY ABBEY

Carriages without horses shall go
And accidents fill the world with woe
Around the world thoughts shall fly
In the twinkling of an eye

PROPHESY ATTRIBUTED TO MOTHER SHIPTON
BORN IN 1488 AT THE PETRIFYING WELL
KNARESBOROUGH

The witches of Yorkshire

The power of prophesy brought posthumous fame to one northern seer, but nothing but shame and infamy to another.

Yorkshire's folk tales embrace an extraordinary cast of saints, shapeshifters and spellweaving crones, but the county's most celebrated character came not from these colourful legends, but from the town of Knaresborough.

The great prophetess of these parts known as Mother Shipton was born Ursula Sontheil in 1488 to a 15-year-old mother in a cave on the nearby River Nidd. A woman who attended Ursula's birth claimed that a smell of sulphur that was present indicated the presence of the devil, and that the new-born child was unusually large and ugly. Despite the strange circumstances surrounding her entry into the world, Ursula was brought up in Knaresborough and acquired a reputation for possessing psychic powers while still a child. In 1512, she married a carpenter, Toby Shipton, and began writing prophecies in the form of rhyming couplets, similar to the 'quatrains' of her French contemporary, the prophet Nostradamus. Her insistence on only using her powers for good seems to have saved her from any accusation of witchcraft and she died in peace at the age of 73.

Publishing sensation

After her death, the story of Mother Shipton and her prophetic poems were passed on through oral tradition. But from the 1640s, her quatrains, some allegedly recorded when Shipton was old by a woman named Joanne Waller, were widely published – and, it seems, greatly exaggerated. Although Samuel Pepys made mention of them in his Diaries in connection with a discussion he had with the king concerning Mother Shipton's prediction of the Great Fire of London, an edition of her writings from 1684 credited her with foretelling almost every significant event in English history of the preceding 200 years and may have employed her name to help to sell a random collection of prophecies accumulated by the publishers. Another collection of Mother Shipton's predictions published in the mid 19th century made such bold claims for her predictive powers that it led some modern scholars to question whether she existed at all and wasn't some elaborate concoction of the townsfolk of Knaresborough to put their town on the map. Either way, her prophecies, especially those concerning the technological age, still make fascinating reading.

The cave where Mother Shipton was born is a major tourist attraction today, and lays claim to be one of the oldest visitor sites in Britain. In Ursula's time, the cave was shunned as a place of magic, for the well there had strange properties. The spring was later discovered to have exceptionally high mineral content, particularly sulphur, accounting for the reported odour at the prophetess' birth. The minerals cause any object placed in the waters' flow to turn to rock within days, and a whole collection of bizarre objects now hang, awaiting petrification, at the well.

Confidence trickster

Mary Bateman, Yorkshire's other famous witch, was of far more questionable character than her benign predecessor and was one of the last women to be convicted and hanged for witchcraft in Yorkshire. Born Mary Harker in or around 1768 near the North Yorkshire town of Thirsk, she allegedly spent much of her youth in the company of gypsies, who, she later claimed, instructed her in the arts of soothsaying and preparing herbal medicines. By the age of 20 she was living in Leeds, ostensibly as a dressmaker, but in reality telling fortunes and selling quack remedies. In 1793 she married a simple-minded wheelwright named John Bateman. Mary's husband soon discovered that whatever mystical powers his wife possessed were more than matched by her criminal tendencies. Her favourite tricks included producing eggs from a hen inscribed with the words 'Jesus is Coming' and then charging her audience a penny to see them.

In 1803, Mary became involved with a wealthy Leeds cloth merchant, William Perigo, who believed that his wife, Rebecca, was possessed by an evil spirit. Having relieved Perigo of four golden guineas, Mary then fed the couple with puddings that were later found to be laced with arsenic. When Perigo's wife died in agony, her husband initially believed Mary's brazen explanation that the death had simply been the unfortunate result of the couple not following her instructions to the letter. But when William Perigo subsequently discovered that the four 'guinea notes' which Mary claimed to have sewn into his late wife's bedlinen to ward off evil spirits were, in fact, cabbage leaves, he pressed charges.

At her trial in York in March 1809, Mary once again attempted to talk her way out of trouble by claiming that she was pregnant. No one believed her and she was executed the following day in York Castle, after which her body was given to Leeds Infirmary for dissection. The hospital authorities, seizing the opportunity, placed it on public display and sold pieces of the skin as souvenirs.

❻ Atwick

A headless horseman, thought to be a highwayman, has been seen in the area occasionally, although no one knows his identity. At the foot of the hill on which the church stands, a spring used to be haunted by a hobgoblin called the Haliwell Boggle. The nearby old village of Attenwick has been submerged, due to coastal erosion.

▶ *On B1242, 5 miles S of A165 at Lissett, 6 miles S of Bridlington.*

❼ Harpham

The St Quintons used to be lords of the manor in Harpham, and whenever the head of the family was about to die, a ghostly drumming could be heard coming from a well near the church, known as the Drumming Well. Legend has it that a drummer boy was accidentally knocked into the well by one St Quinton, and the boy's mother prophesied the fatal omen. An alternative tale is that, having fought a battle in the neighbourhood, William the Conqueror promised to give Harpham and the surrounding lands to the first person to reach the village. This was the drummer boy, but a knight named St Quinton knocked him into the well and claimed the prize.

On the outskirts of the village, another well is dedicated to St John of Beverley, whose traditional birthplace is Harpham. Its waters reputedly delivered many miracles and could also subdue the fiercest animals. The well is decorated on the nearest Tuesday to May 7 each year.

▶ *Just S of A614, 6 miles SW of Bridlington.*

❽ Burton Agnes

The village's Elizabethan manor house, Burton Agnes Hall, was built by Sir Henry Griffith in the early 17th century – and the skull of one of his daughters, Anne, the youngest of three sisters, is said to be there still, bricked up in the entrance hall. One day, Anne was attacked by thieves and mortally wounded. Before she died, she begged that her head should be kept in the house she loved. Despite this, her whole body was buried in the churchyard, but such was the wailing and banging in the house that she was disinterred and her head brought home. Eventually, the skull was walled up so it could never be removed, and since then the house has been quiet, although Anne's ghost is said to drift through her old home occasionally. The house is still owned by descendants of Sir Henry and is open to the public.

▶ *On A614, 5 miles SW of Bridlington.*

❾ Rudston

A 8m (25ft) high late Stone Age monolith, thought to be the tallest in Britain, stands in the churchyard at Rudston, and is reputed to extend another 8m (25ft) below ground. One legend holds that it simply fell from the sky, 'killing certain desecrators of the churchyard'. Another states that it was thrown at the church by the Devil and landed in its present position because of his bad aim. The area is full of the remains of ancient burial mounds, notably at Willy Howe, Duggleby Howe and Ba'l Hill, and it may be that the stone had some religious significance, but nobody seems to know for sure.

▶ *5 miles W of Bridlington on B1253.*

❿ Wold Newton

An irregular chalk stream, the Gypsey Race, begins near the ancient burial mound at Duggleby Howe and winds it way through the Wolds valley to the sea at Bridlington. According to local tradition, it comes into full spate in Wold Newton only before some great disaster. Apparently, it flowed copiously before the Great Plague of 1666 and before both world wars.

▶ *On minor roads 9 miles NW of Bridlington.*

⓫ Aldborough

A little way from the village, towards Boroughbridge, the mysterious Devil's Arrows are to be found, three massive standing stones, each weighing about 40 tonnes. The local explanation for them is that they are crossbow-bolts that the Devil shot at Aldborough, an early Christian missionary settlement.

▶ *1 mile E of Junction 48 of A1(M).*

⓬ Beningbrough

The present Beningbrough Hall, a red-brick mansion, replaced a modest Elizabethan house that was at the hub of a murder in 1670. Local poacher William Vasey drowned the housekeeper at the instigation of estate steward, Philip Laurie – possibly Laurie was jealous of her attachment to the gamekeeper, Martin Giles. Vasey was caught by Giles breaking into the gamekeeper's cottage and later confessed to the murder. He was hanged at York, and Laurie committed suicide. The housekeeper's ghost was said to haunt the banks of the Ouse near the spot where she had died, but for some reason stopped doing so at the end of the 19th century.

▶ *On minor roads 2 miles W of Shipton on A19, 5 miles NW of York.*

⑬ York

Three 15th-century ghosts – father, mother and child – haunted Holy Trinity churchyard during the 1800s. The parents were buried there, but the child had died of plague and was interred outside the city. The mother's ghost would bring the child to the father, then take it back outside the city walls.

St George's churchyard is the resting place of Dick Turpin, who was hanged at York in 1739. Turpin's famous ride to York was almost certainly not made by him at all, but by another, equally celebrated robber, John Nevison, during the reign of Charles II. The king, amused by the exploit, is said to have granted Nevison a free pardon and christened him 'Swift Nicks'. In spite of this, Nevison had ended up on the gallows at York, in 1685. The leg-irons that held these two notorious highwaymen before their executions may be seen in York Castle Museum.

In the north transept of York Minster, St William's window commemorates the 36 miracles attributed to William Fitzherbert, who became Archbishop of York in 1141 and was canonised in the following century. On one occasion, in 1154, William was returning to York when the old wooden bridge that spanned the River Ouse collapsed beneath the weight of onlookers. Hundreds of people plunged into the deep river. William made the sign of the cross and prayed, and the waters formed themselves into a bridge, so that everyone could reach dry land.

During the Middle Ages, St William's fame rivalled that of St John of Beverley, his 8th-century predecessor at York, and another of the miracles depicted in the window is attributed to both saints. The Devil had caused a young student to fall so much in love with a local girl that he lost all taste for his books. To make a young man fall out of love took all the powers of a saint. One of them intervened, and the student was restored to his right mind.
▶ *12 miles E of Junction 47 of A1(M).*

⑭ Long Marston

In 1644, Oliver Cromwell defeated a Royalist army at the Battle of Marston Moor, about a mile north of Long Marston village. The ghosts of Royalist soldiers have often been seen in the area. Three phantoms in Cavalier costume were reported in the second part of the 20th century by two motorists travelling on the A59 York–Harrogate road. The Old Hall in the village, which was used by Cromwell during the battle, is said to be haunted by his ghost.
▶ *6 miles W of York on B1224.*

LINDISFARNE

JUST OFF THE NORTHEAST COAST, between Bamburgh and Berwick-upon-Tweed, lies Holy Island – Lindisfarne – famed as an important centre of early English Christianity. The religious connection is the basis of most of the mysterious tales about the island. Its air of remote seclusion encouraged St Aidan to found a monastery there in AD 635, and later St Cuthbert became its bishop, making it his base until his death in AD 684. Twice a day, the ebbing tide leaves a causeway of firm sand to the mainland, and this 'miraculous gift' is said to have been provided by Cuthbert, to enable people to attend his church on Sundays without getting their feet wet.

St Cuthbert is also allegedly responsible for 'Cuddy's beads', which he collected from the shore and made into a rosary. In fact, the beads are the fossilised remains of tiny prehistoric sea creatures.

Increasingly threatened by the Vikings, the island was sacked by Danish raiders in AD 875, an event that was said to be preceded by storms and 'fiery serpents' flying through the sky. The monks fled, taking St Cuthbert's still preserved body with them, eventually finding their way, with divine guidance, to Durham.

The island never regained its previous status, but thousands still flock there, hoping perhaps, like the 11th-century labourers building the priory, to feed on bread made from air and drink wine from a bottomless cup.

⓲ Wakefield

Old Heath Hall, which was demolished in the 1960s, was haunted by the ghost of Mary Bolles, who lived there in the 17th century.
In her will, Mary left instructions that the room in which she died was to be permanently sealed and, accordingly, after her death in 1661, the room was closed off. Fifty years later, however, it was opened, and after that her ghost never ceased to disturb the peace of the Hall, despite stone effigies being laid on her tomb in Ledsham church to quieten her restless spirit. Troops stationed at the Hall in 1943 claimed to have seen the ghost, and a caretaker reported that his German Shepherd guard dog would never walk through the death room. The door of the haunted bedroom has been preserved in Wakefield Museum.
▶ *8 miles S of Leeds.*

⓰ Bradford

Hundreds of stone heads have come to light in the west of Yorkshire, and while some of these are of Celtic origin, others are more recent. The Celts who lived in the area 2,300 years ago, when it was part of the kingdom of Brigantia, revered the human head as a fertility symbol and charm against evil. The severed heads of enemies, or their replicas in stone, were set as guardians at the entrances of cattle-byres and houses. Large numbers of these Celtic masks have been dug from the ground in Scotland, Ireland and across Europe, but in Bradford they were found in drystone walls, above cottage doors and in churches. The more recent examples – some are probably no more than 100 years old – are thought to be either a resurgence of folk art, or possibly evidence that an Iron Age cult may have survived in some form into the reign of Queen Victoria.
▶ *8 miles W of Leeds.*

⓱ Cottingley

When Elsie Wright and her cousin Frances Griffiths chattered about the fairies they met by the beck at the back of the Wrights' home, no one took any notice, so they borrowed a camera and took some photographs of them. Still the family remained sceptical until the pictures were seen by Edward Gardner, a psychic researcher, and Sir Arthur Conan Doyle, author of the Sherlock Holmes books and well known for his interest in spiritualism. Gardner and Conan Doyle published the pictures in the 1920 Christmas edition of *Strand Magazine*, and the controversy began. Were they fake or genuine?

In 1975, when the cousins were interviewed for the BBC, Elsie described them as 'photographs of figments of our imagination'. Then, in 1982, when they were interviewed separately for a magazine entitled *The Unexplained*, they finally admitted the photographs were faked with paper cut-outs – but they insisted that the fairies themselves were genuine, and they really did see them on the banks of the stream in Cottingley.
▶ *Just S of Junction 1 of M621, 2 miles SW of Leeds city centre.*

⓲ Ilkley Moor

On December 1 1987, retired police officer Phillip Spencer took a camera with him on a walk across windswept Ilkley Moor in the early hours of the morning in the hope of photographing the 'strange lights' that had recently been reported in the area. As well as being dark, the moor was swirling with mist, and Spencer doubted that he would get any pictures

TROLLERS GILL

19 Appletreewick

Trollers Gill, a gorge near Appletreewick, was once said to be haunted by a barguest, a fearsome ghost dog with huge saucer eyes and shaggy hair that drags a clanking chain. A story of 1881 records how a man went to the gorge at midnight and his body was found the next day. According to a contemporary ballad, 'Marks were imprest on the dead man's breast, but they seemed not by mortal hand.'
▶ *On minor roads E of B6160, 7 miles NE of Skipton.*

20 Burnsall

Elbolton Hill was famed as a haunt of fairies. One story is that a local man surprised a crowd of little folk in their moonlight revels. For a while he kept silent, but in his excitement he forgot himself and called out, 'Na' then, Ah'll sing a song if tha loikes.' The fairies were furious at his well-intentioned interruption, and beat him so soundly that he was bruised for days afterwards.
▶ *On B6160, 6 miles N of Skipton.*

21 Threshfield

The Well of Our Lady is renowned as a sanctuary from the powers of darkness. On his way home from the inn, a man was chased by a band of imps and fled to the well for refuge. Although the demons dared not approach, they surrounded him and kept him there all night, until they were forced to leave at cockcrow.
▶ *8 miles N of Skipton at junction of B6265 and B6160.*

22 Giggleswick

Near Giggleswick Scar, the Ebbing and Flowing Well is an oddity of nature. One explanation for it is that, when a nymph who was being chased by a satyr prayed to the gods for help, they turned her into a spring, which ebbed and flowed with her panting breaths.

The 17th-century highwayman John Nevison is said to have evaded capture by letting his horse drink at the well. The water gave the horse strength and Nevison escaped by leaping from the top of a cliff, which is still known as Nevison's Leap.
▶ *1 mile W of Settle, just N of A65.*

at all, despite having loaded his camera with ultra light-sensitive film. Suddenly, to his immense surprise, he spotted a small, human-like creature ahead of him in the gloom. Spencer clicked his camera and duly produced one of the most talked-about photographs in the history of unexplained phenomena. Although very blurred, the photograph appears to show a humanoid figure over 1m (4ft) high that bears an uncanny resemblance to the 'Greys' of UFO-watching legend. Spencer claimed he ran after the creature, which entered a 'dome-shaped' craft that rose rapidly into the sky before he could get a shot of it. Spencer remained adamant that what he had seen was an alien, and donated the photograph to UFO watchers. Analysis carried out at the Kodak laboratories in Hemel Hempstead suggested that the picture had not been interfered with in any way, but a later computer analysis of the photograph by US Navy expert Dr Bruce Maccabee proved inconclusive.
▶ *S of Ilkley on A65, 8 miles N of Bradford.*

NORTHEAST ENGLAND

Wales

The songs of the bards and the unfettered imagination of the poets have, for centuries, kept the old Welsh legends alive. These sites of myth and magic remain a special draw, from holy springs to weeping trees, wishing wells to castle ruins.

KEY

1 Main entry
   County boundary
   Motorway
   Principal A road

Anglesey

28 Holyhead
29 Bangor
    Caernarfon

Llandudno Rhyl
1   3
2   6   4
           Mold
           5
           Wrexham

Betws-y-coed
A5   A494
9
A499
8   A487   Porthmadog
10   12   Llangollen
11   Snowdonia   15   16
7   National   13 Bala
               Park
                    A494
               Dolgellau
                          14
                                A458   Welshpool
                              17   18
               Machynlleth
                          NORTH and MID WALES   A483
                          194-201   19

                                              Newtown
               A44
Aberystwyth   LLangurig
20   22
               A470
                              Llandrindod   A44
21   23   Wells
          Cambrian
          Mountains   24   Builth
                                             Wells
                         A485   A483   A470   A438
Cardigan
4   Llandovery
          A487   A40   Brecon
Fishguard   8   Black
                                                     Mountains
3 Pembrokeshire Coast   Llandeilo   Brecon   26   A479
   National Park   7   Beacons   27
        Carmarthen   National Park
Haverfordwest   A40   5   Abergavenny
                                                       Monmouth
Milford   A4076   A477   A48   25   10
Haven   9   A465   Merthyr
   Tenby   1   6   Tydfil   17   A4042
2   Llanelli   A470   12   Chepstow
              Swansea   Neath   M48
              19   18   Newport
              20   Port   M4   11
                              Talbot   13
                         Bridgend   14   Cardiff
                         16
                         15

NORTH & MID WALES

The lonely ruins of a 12th-century abbey, once a place of refuge, are visited by the phantom of a monk trying to rebuild its past, while shadowy cowled figures on a wildlife island warn of impending doom.

❶ Llanelian-yn-Rhôs, Conwy

Well into the 19th century, this village near Colwyn Bay was famous for its cursing well. Anyone who wanted to ill-wish an enemy would pay the keeper of the well to write the victim's name on a piece of paper, wrap it round a pebble and drop it into the water. The curse was believed to last for as long as the paper remained in the well, so people paid the keeper to remove their names. One keeper was imprisoned in 1854 for accepting money under false pretences, but the well was not finally covered over until 1929.
▶ *On minor roads 2 miles S of Colwyn Bay.*

❷ Llannefydd, Conwy

Katheryn Tudor of Berain, an ancient estate at Llannefydd, died in 1591 aged 57, leaving so many descendants that she is still known as Mam Cymru, the Mother of Wales. Legend says that she married seven times, and murdered all her husbands by pouring molten lead in their ears, burying them afterwards in an orchard. In fact, she married four times and never murdered anyone.
▶ *On minor roads, 6 miles NW of Denbigh.*

❸ Greenfield, Flintshire

A monk from 12th-century Basingwerk Abbey once heard a nightingale singing in a nearby wood, and its voice held him spellbound for what seemed like hours. When he returned to the abbey, he found it in ruins, and all the people around him were strangers. He asked what had happened, but no one seemed to understand him. One bystander remarked that his sudden appearance reminded him of the story of another monk, who had disappeared just as suddenly centuries before. The villagers offered the monk some food, but the moment he touched it he crumbled to dust.
▶ *10 miles SE of Prestatyn on A548.*

❹ Holywell, Flintshire

In the 7th century, a chieftain named Caradoc cut off St Winifred's head because she rebutted his advances. Water sprang from the ground where her head fell, and to this day St Winifred's Well at Holywell is said to have miraculous healing properties, especially for nervous disorders. Remarkably, Winifred's uncle, St Beuno, restored her head to her body, and she went on to become Abbess of Gwytherin in Conwy. St Beuno put a curse on Caradoc's descendants so that they barked like dogs and could be cured only by being immersed in the water from St Winifred's Well.
▶ *11 miles SE of Prestatyn on A548.*

❺ Mold, Flintshire

This atmospheric corner of northeast Wales, the site of a 4,000-year-old Bronze Age burial mound has a long history of being haunted by the spirits of those laid to rest there. It is known locally as the Hill of Goblins, and the most popular local legend told of the phantom of a man on horseback, who would appear wearing a golden suit of armour. It was therefore with some amazement that workmen quarrying for stone on the mound in 1833 came across a skeleton encased in what appeared to be fragments of thin decorated gold. It was not until 1954 that Professor Terence Powell, an archaeologist at Liverpool University, proved conclusively that the fragments were in fact the upper section of a cape that must once have enshrouded the upper body of its prehistoric wearer. From the grave goods that accompanied the cape, which included more than 300 amber beads, it seems likely that the wearer was not a man but a woman. Experts estimate that she and her precious apparel had lain undisturbed for some 3,000 years. The cape, now pieced together, is unique in its design, and is on display at the British Museum.
▶ *12 miles W of Chester.*

BASINGWERK ABBEY

6 Tremeirchion, Denbighshire

In 1567 Sir Richard Clough, a wealthy merchant and second husband of Katheryn Tudor of Berain, built Bachegraig house, near Tremeirchion. The unusual architectural style, possibly of Dutch origins, so shocked local people that they decided the Devil himself had been involved in the design, and it was rumoured that the Evil One had baked the bricks in the fires of hell, near a stream known as Nant y Cythraul, the Devil's brook. Eventually, the house came into the possession of Mrs Thrale, friend of Dr Johnson, who visited there in 1774. The main hall that had so upset the villagers was demolished in 1817, but the large gatehouse and the farm buildings were left standing. The gatehouse has been restored and is now run as Bach y Graig, a bed and breakfast hotel.
▶ *3 miles E of St Asaph on B5429.*

7 Bardsey Island, Gwynedd

The charitable trust that runs Bardsey Island, which is located 2 miles off the Llyn peninsula, aims not only to protect its wildlife and delicate ecosystem but also to present it as a place of natural beauty and peace. For many centuries, the island was an important centre for pilgrimage, and as many as 20,000 monks may be buried there. Mainlanders sometimes report seeing shadowy, cowled figures wandering along the island's shore, and these ghosts are regarded as omens of disease, drownings and storms. In Welsh, the island's name is Ynys Enlli, 'Isle of the Currents'. The wizard Merlin is said to be sleeping in a cave on the island, surrounded by a mound of ancient treasures, including the throne of Britain. He will wake from his sleep only when King Arthur returns from the dead.
▶ *Day trips from Porth Meudwy and Pwllheli.*

wales

195

❽ Nefyn, Gwynedd

A thornbush in Nefyn is known as Y Goeden Bechod, the tree of sin. A woman allegedly saw a phantom coach coming towards her there and in a few days she was dead. The ghostly carriage proved to be a fatal omen.

▶ *7 miles NW of Pwllheli on A497.*

❾ Clynnog-fawr, Gwynedd

The 15th-century church of St Beuno stands on the site of a much earlier building, which is thought to be the original chapel founded by St Beuno in the 7th century. A nearby well that bears his name is supposed to have healing powers. St Beuno's church developed into an important ecclesiastical institution, a combination of monastery and college, and became a stopover for pilgrims on the way to Bardsey Island (see page 195), which may explain its large size. Artefacts in the church include an old strong-box made from a single piece of wood, in which alms were once kept. It was customary for calves born with misshapen ears to be sold annually in the churchyard; the proceeds being given to the church and joining other donations locked in the chest.

▶ *12 miles N of Pwllheli on A499.*

❿ Criccieth, Gwynedd

An old tale relates how Die, a piper, and two fiddlers named Twm and Ned were enticed by fairies into Yr Ogof Ddu, the black cave, near Criccieth. They were never seen again, but the three traditional Welsh tunes they were playing when they disappeared may still occasionally be heard coming from the cave.

▶ *5 miles W of Porthmadog on A497.*

⓫ Borth-y-gest, Gwynedd

David Owen, harpist and composer, was born at Y Garreg Wen, a farm in the neighbourhood, around 1711. He wrote 'The Rising of the Lark' and is also thought to have composed 'David of the White Rock' (Dafydd Y Garreg Wen), which is a well-known folk song. The story goes that he wrote the melody on his deathbed – having dreamt he heard it being played in an evergreen country to an audience of two doves – and asked that it be played at his funeral. On that day, in 1741, two doves followed his coffin from Y Garreg Wen to Ynyscynhaearn church, where his grave can still be seen. The words to the song were added some years after his death.

▶ *On minor road 1 mile S of Porthmadog.*

⓬ Ffestiniog, Gwynedd

Near Ffestiniog is Llyn y Morwynion, the maidens' lake. The legend that inspired its name tells how the men of Ardudwy went to the Vale of Clwyd to find wives, and abducted several local girls. On the return journey, they were overtaken near the lake by the girls' menfolk, and in the ensuing fight were all killed. By this time, though, the girls had managed to fall in love with their captors and, in their grief, they threw themselves into the lake and drowned. It is said that their ghosts emerge from the water in the mornings to comb their hair.

▶ *Llyn y Morwynion is just N of the B4391, 2 miles E of Llan Ffestiniog.*

⓭ Llanuwchllyn, Gwynedd

A legendary giant named Rhita used to frequent the mountain roads of the district around Llanuwchllyn, where he killed and robbed travellers and cut off their beards to make himself a cloak. Rhita was eventually killed by King Arthur, and a huge cairn on the top of Snowdon marks the place where he was buried. Another version claims that his body lies under a great stone in the grounds of Tan y Bwlch, a 19th-century mansion now run by the Snowdonia National Park and used as a centre for residential courses.

▶ *5 miles SW of Bala on A494.*

⓮ Llanymawddwy, Gwynedd

In the 1840s Bryn Hall was haunted by a headless horseman that plagued one of the servants until he followed it into the orchard, where a grave was found. An illegitimate child of the owner of the Hall had been murdered and buried under the trees. This, it was assumed, had been the phantom's message, because after the discovery, the haunting ceased.

▶ *On minor road 4 miles NE from A470 at Dinas Mawddwy, 8 miles E of Dolgellau.*

⓯ Bala, Gwynedd

By tradition, the old town lies drowned beneath the lake, and one day Llyn Tegid, Bala Lake, will swallow up the new town as well. The lake also holds the body of an 18th-century harpist who is said to have given himself to the Devil by feeding communion bread to the dogs. He drowned one night on his way home from Fach Ddeiliog, now a hotel, and a cloud of smoke hung over the spot where he sank.

▶ *18 miles NE of Dolgellau on A494.*

A UNIVERSAL TALE CELEBRATED IN WALES

THE STORY OF A FAITHFUL HOUND being killed by its owner in the mistaken belief that the dog had killed his child is an ancient one, well known all over the world. David Pritchard, who took over as landlord of the local hostelry in Beth Kellarth in 1793, certainly heard it, as he adapted the tale to fit the village in an effort to boost trade. It was a masterstroke to introduce national hero Prince Llywelyn into the story, and another to incorporate a grave as tangible evidence of its truth. In his version of the story, Llywelyn returns from a hunting trip to be greeted by his favourite hound, Gelert, jaws dripping with blood. When the prince can't find his baby son, he naturally thinks that Gelert has savaged the child and plunges his sword into the dog's heart. As the dog howls in its death agony, a child's cry comes from under the cradle and there Llywelyn finds his son unharmed, next to the body of a huge wolf, killed by his own brave hound. Stricken with remorse, Llywelyn buries Gelert outside the castle walls, marking the place with a stone cairn so all will know of the dog's bravery. In a tribute to the success of Pritchard's plan, the name of the village was changed to Beddgelert, meaning 'Gelert's grave'. People still visit the cairn.

16 Chirk, Wrexham

Near Chirk Castle, 2 miles west of the village, at Castle Mill Bridge, a plaque marks the site of the Battle of Crogen. In 1165, the forces of Henry II of England were defeated by the princes of Wales under Owain Gwynedd. A gap in Offa's Dyke – the rampart built in the 8th century by Offa, King of Mercia – is known as Adwy'r Beddau, the pass of the graves, and a local belief claims that fields nearby should not be ploughed because this would disturb the bones of the soldiers and horses resting beneath.

▶ *8 miles S of Wrexham on A5.*

17 Llanfair Caereinion, Powys

Many years ago, a district near this market town on the River Banw was plagued by the ghost of an old squire. When a magician arrived to exorcise the phantom, it changed into a raging bull, but was eventually turned into a fly. The spirit agreed to take up residence in the conjurer's bottle, on condition that the bottle remained on the squire's estate. Legend says that the bottle was carefully kept in a local farmhouse, and remains there, permanently sealed for fear that the evil spirit will be released once more.

▶ *8 miles W of Welshpool on A458.*

Wales

18 Welshpool, Powys

Said to have been a stronghold of the Welsh Prince Llywelyn ap Gruyffydd, who led a rebellion against Edward I, 13th-century Powis Castle stands on a rocky promontory, commanding panoramic views of the surrounding countryside. It was a bastion of Royalist forces during the English Civil War, and the walls were extensively rebuilt in the 1660s during the Restoration. Now, within those walls, ghostly occurrences are reputed to be in evidence. Sightings of spectral figures, mysterious knockings at windows and doors and a host of other paranormal phenomena have been experienced over the years by the staff who work there. Perhaps the most charming haunting concerns a devoutly religious seamstress, who spent a night in the castle some time around 1780. She had been invited to stay while she did some spinning work for the master of the castle, the Earl of Powys. During the night, the woman was visited no less than three times by a ghostly gentleman, dressed from head to foot in gold lace. On the third occasion, the phantom asked her to follow him to another part of the castle, where he revealed a locked casket under a loose floorboard. He instructed her to send the box and its key immediately to the Earl of Powys in London, which she duly did the following day. Although the contents of the box are not known, the Earl was evidently so delighted by what it held that he made provision for the seamstress to live in comfort for the rest of her days.

▶ *20 miles W of Shrewsbury on A458.*

SPECTRAL FIGURES HAUNT THE GROUNDS
POWIS CASTLE

⑲ Montgomery, Powys

The 'Robber's Grave' in St Nicholas's churchyard is marked with a simple wooden cross, and recalls the story of John Davies, who was hanged in the early years of the 19th century for assault and robbery. Davies had taken a job as steward on a rundown farm belonging to Mrs Morris, a widow, and her daughter, Jane. In making the farm a success and becoming romantically involved with Jane, Davies unwittingly incurred the enmity of two men. One, Robert Parker, had wanted to buy the farm at a bargain price while it was not doing well, and the other, Thomas Pearce, was Jane's jilted fiancé. The pair carried out a robbery and made it appear as though Davies was the culprit. He

was tried and condemned to death, but from the scaffold he cursed his accusers, and swore that his innocence would be proved by the fact that no grass would grow on his grave, which it didn't for at least 100 years. Shortly after the trial, Parker was killed in a quarry explosion, and Pearce died of a wasting disease.
▶ *8 miles S of Welshpool on B4388.*

⑳ Rhydyfelin, Ceredigion

Nanteos, a Grade I listed 18th-century mansion just outside Aberystwyth, was once famed for a holy relic that was kept there – a wooden cup thought by some to be the original Holy Grail. When a group of monks fled from Glastonbury to the remote Strata Florida Abbey at the time of the Dissolution of the Monasteries, they took the cup with them. Eventually, it was given into the safekeeping of local landowners and passed into the hands of the Powell family, who owned Nanteos. The Nanteos cup, as it became known, was supposed to have miraculous healing powers and attracted many people in the hope of a cure. After the house was sold, the relic was kept in a bank vault but its present whereabouts are unknown.

The cup may be gone from Nanteos but the ghosts remain. Elizabeth Powell, wife of William Powell, who built the house, is known as the 'Jewell Lady'. She hid her valuable collection of gems shortly before her death and wanders the corridors in search of them. The Pink Room is haunted by a mysterious female figure, a woman who walks down the staircase carrying a candlestick is a forewarning of death in the family and a phantom horse and carriage pull up to the front entrance. Gruffydd Evans played the harp at Nanteos every Christmas for 69 years, and the sound of harp music may still be heard in the gardens and woods around the house.
▶ *2 miles S of Aberystwyth on A487.*

㉑ Pennant, Ceredigion

The magical powers of 19th-century recluse Mari Berllan Bitter were legendary in Pennant. When the miller refused to grind her corn, she made his mill wheel turn in the wrong direction. A young girl who stole an apple from Mari's orchard was forced to walk home backwards. Sometimes, Mari turned herself into a hare – a typical witch's trick – and not even the best shots could hit her. The overgrown ruins of her cottage, known as 'The Witch's Cottage', can still be seen.
▶ *4 miles E of Aberaeron on B4577.*

wales

22 Devil's Bridge, Ceredigion

Three bridges cross the River Mynach at a place where it cuts through a deep gorge. The legend attached to the lowest one is the same tale that is told about a bridge across the River Lune at Kirkby Lonsdale in Cumbria, and similar to the one about Jack o' Kent, from Kentchurch in Herefordshire. The bridge was built by the Devil when an old woman's cow became stranded on the other side of the gorge. Satan promised to build the bridge in return for the first living creature to use it. The woman agreed, but when the bridge was finished, she threw a piece of bread across it, her dog ran after the bread and Satan, outwitted, became the dog's new owner.

▶ *10 miles E of Aberystwyth on A4120.*

23 Strata Florida Abbey, Ceredigion

Among the ruins of this isolated 12th-century abbey stands a slate memorial to Dafydd ap Gwilym, a 14th-century poet who has been described as the greatest poet in the Welsh language. In its day, the abbey was an important place of pilgrimage and sanctuary, and although it was destroyed during the Reformation, tradition asserts that candles still sometimes blaze among the ruins and, on Christmas Eve, a ghostly monk has been seen trying to rebuild the altar.

▶ *On minor road 1 mile E of B4343, 6 miles NE of Tregaron.*

24 Cilmery, Powys

On the bank of the River Irfon at Cilmery, a rough-hewn stone monument marks the place where Llywelyn ap Gruffydd, the last of the Welsh princes, was killed by an English man-at-arms on December 11, 1282. Each year, on that date, a ceremony is held to commemorate his life. According to tradition, the spot where Llywelyn died was covered with broom, and the shrub has never grown there since because it still mourns the Welsh prince. Certainly, no broom grows about the obelisk now. Instead, it is surrounded by trees planted there to represent the counties of Wales.

▶ *3 miles W of Builth Wells on A483.*

SATAN WAS OUTWITTED
DEVIL'S BRIDGE

㉕ Ystradgynlais, Powys

Three cauldrons full of gold are said to lie buried beneath Y Garn Goch, the red cairn, on the summit of Mynydd y Drum, or Drum Mountain, just east of Ystradgynlais. One day a young girl will come to claim the treasure but, until then, fierce demons protect it from all booty hunters. A wizard once asked for a volunteer to help him to overpower the demons with magic, and a young man came forward, but their efforts were in vain. While the elements raged about them, a spirit on a wheel of fire swept the young man out of a protective circle the wizard had made on the ground, and the wizard was able to save his companion's life only for as long as a candle given to him by the demons lasted. The candle soon wasted away and the young man died.
▶ *14 miles NE of Swansea on A4067.*

㉖ Llangorse Lake, Powys

Llangorse Lake (Llyn Syfaddan) is one of the largest natural lakes in Wales and has been designated a Special Area of Conservation. According to legend, the land beneath it once belonged to a princess who agreed to marry her lover provided he could make her rich. He had no money of his own, so he robbed and murdered a wealthy merchant, and gave the proceeds to his beloved. The couple were duly married, but the merchant's ghost returned to warn them that their crime would be avenged upon the ninth generation of their family. They ignored the warning and both lived long lives until one night, when nine generations of the family were gathered together, a terrible flood burst from the hills and drowned the land and all its inhabitants. It is said that the city can still be seen beneath the lake's waters and the sound of its church bells can sometimes be heard.

The legend of the submerged city is told by Gerald of Wales, a medieval churchman descended from Marcher barons and Welsh princes, who travelled tirelessly and recorded all he saw. Since the lake was a source of both food and water, settlements would have sprung up around it, probably from prehistoric times.
▶ *6 miles E of Brecon.*

㉗ Llyn Cwm Llwch, Powys

This small lake occupies a rocky hollow at the foot of Pen y Fan, the highest peak in the Brecon Beacons National Park, and is the focus of folk tale. A secret door in the lakeside used to open every May 1 to admit mortals through a tunnel to a fairy island, which was invisible from the shore. The fairies entertained their visitors well but stipulated that nothing must be removed from the island, because it was sacred. Then one year a visitor stole a flower, and the next year no door was to be found. Years later, when the inhabitants of Brecon tried to drain the lake in search of its reputed treasures, a giant rose from the water and threatened to drown their town and all the land around the River Usk if they did not stop. The townsfolk sensibly abandoned their plan, and the lake remains undisturbed.
▶ *5 miles S of Brecon, access by footpaths.*

㉘ Llanddeusant, Anglesey

A Bronze Age burial mound and an older standing stone near the River Alaw are known as Bedd Branwen and, traditionally, mark the grave of a heroine of the 14th-century Welsh epic, the *Mabinogion*. The mound was opened in 1813 and found to hold a rough-baked clay urn containing fragments of burnt bone and ashes. Since the discovery of more funerary urns in 1967, the site has become more significant and is a scheduled ancient monument.
▶ *On minor roads 2 miles E of A5025, 8 miles NE of Holyhead.*

㉙ Llanddona, Anglesey

For centuries, Anglesey was troubled by the Llanddona witches, a group of sorcerers who passed their magical powers down through the generations. The women lived by extortion, cursing anyone who did not give them money or food. The men were smugglers who protected themselves from the excisemen by keeping a number of flies in their scarves. If the smugglers were ambushed, they would release the insects to fly into their attackers' eyes and blind them. So far as is known, the last Llanddona witch died more than a 100 years ago.
▶ *On minor road, 3 miles NW of Beaumaris.*

wales

Healing powers

A medieval tale of a lady, a lake, a broken promise – a supernatural prophesy with lasting consequences.

Situated just south of Llandovery in Carmarthenshire, near to the village of Myddfai on the north-western fringes of the Brecon Beacons National Park, lies the small lake of Llyn y Fan Fach – a stretch of water containing a secret that dates back to the 12th century. According to Welsh legend, around the time of the birth of Llewellyn the Great (1174-1240), a widow's son found himself wandering by the shores of the lake when suddenly, to his great astonishment, a beautiful woman arose from the waters. The woman told the young man that if he would agree to marry her, he would become the richest and most respected farmer in all of Wales – a prospect to which he readily agreed. However, the mysterious Lady of the Lake also warned him that should he speak of her supernatural origins, or dare to strike her three times, his new-found prosperity would desert him.

The couple were duly married and for a time the young man – now a farmer – could do no wrong: his cattle flourished, his horses were the strongest in the region and his sheep multiplied across the hillsides, while his wife bore him three sons and acted as a loyal, loving companion.

Yet in time the farmer grew complacent and after an argument with his increasingly neglected wife, was moved to strike her. Though he immediately begged her forgiveness, the incident happened a second time and then a third. On this last occasion, the wife reminded her husband of his original promise. She then gathered her possessions, called all of the farm's animals to her side, and strode with them back into the lake whence she had emerged, leaving the distraught farmer completely ruined. The farmer was not left entirely empty-handed, for it transpired that his wife had left their eldest son a bag containing instructions for making a multiplicity of remedies for healing the sick – her legacy to the people of Myddfai. Armed with the gift, her three sons went on to become the Physicians of Myddfai – renowned healers who tended, among others, Prince Llewellyn and who established a tradition in mid-Wales for the practice of herbal lore that was handed down from generation to generation.

Herbal tradition

While it might be tempting to dismiss the story of the Lady of the Lake as no more than a lesson in medieval morality, the sheer persistence of the Welsh reputation for concocting herbal remedies suggests that there is more to it. In 1861 an English translation appeared of the *Red Book of Hergest* – a work that was allegedly compiled by a herbalist named Hywel who claimed to have known the descendents of the Physicians of Myddfai; the last of the line, it seemed, was a man named John Jones, who had died in the village as late as 1739.

In the book, Hywel described much of the lore that had been passed on to him, including poultices to inhibit the growth of tumours and a recommendation that teeth should be cleaned with hazel bark in order to prevent them from decaying. Moreover, records show that a certain Doctor Rice (or Rhys) Williams of Aberystwyth claimed to have practised herbalism in the tradition of the Myddfai physicians right up until his death in 1842 at the age of 85. And a study of medical practices in South Wales just before the First World War observed that local people seemed to place an uncommon reliance on what they called 'Water-casters' or 'Water-doctors', who diagnosed and treated their patients with herbal remedies after first studying the colour and nature of their urine.

Water-borne wisdom

There may be a perfectly rational explanation for the apparent pre-eminence of herbalism in Wales – one that dates back to the seagoing Celts' ancient trading links with the Middle East. At that time the Persians led the world in their understanding of medicine, largely due to the work of the healer and polymath Avicenna (980–1037), who was the first to understand the transmission of infectious disease and had a working knowledge of the herbal remedies of the Far East, as well as a firm belief in the powers of aromatherapy.

Until the 18th century, medicine in most of Britain remained hidebound by the teachings of scholars within the universities, which set great store by physical intervention of one kind or another and paid little heed to the herbal remedies that country people had been concocting for centuries. Yet in Wales, which maintained a healthy disdain for the dictums of England, it is possible that the herb-lore and learning passed on to their Celtic ancestors through foreign trade took fertile root among the hills of Carmarthenshire – and that a healing tradition was established whose efficacy became the stuff of reality, as well as legend.

High in the Brecon
Beacons nestles a
remote lake from which
a mythical fairy lady is
said to have arisen. Her
herbal knowledge was
passed on by her sons

LLYN Y FAN FACH

A HEALING WELL LIES JUST BELOW THE TINY CHAPEL

ST GOVAN'S HEAD

SOUTH WALES

Arthurian legend features prominently in this Celtic land. The stories vie with myths of healing wells and traditional tales of saints and magicians, who perform miracles with unearthly panache.

❶ Tenby, Pembrokeshire

Carew Castle has a history stretching back to the Norman Conquest, and a collection of ghosts both traditional and exotic. They include a white lady, a Celtic warrior, a kitchen boy who creates a cacophony with pots and pans and a Barbary Ape – a small monkey with no tail. Various paranormal investigators claim to have experienced strange manifestations in the castle. Balls of light, or orbs, believed to be spirit entities, have been captured on digital film.
▶ *30 miles SW of Carmarthen. Carew Castle is 6 miles NW of Tenby.*

❷ St Govan's Head, Pembrokeshire

Snuggled against the cliffs, overlooking the sea at St Govan's Head – the southernmost point in Pembrokeshire – is a tiny chapel which is reached by around 70 steps cut into the cliff. The number is said to vary, depending on whether the person counting them is climbing up or down. Although the building is mostly 13th century, parts of it may date from the 5th century and, inside, a vertical cleft in the rock is reputedly where St Govan hid from his enemies. The fissure closed behind him in his hour of need, opening again when the danger had passed. The tradition now is that a wish made while standing in the cleft and facing the wall will be granted, providing supplicants don't change their minds before turning round. A healing well is situated just below the chapel, and the red clay in the cliffs has been credited with the power of healing sore eyes.

Despite the many miracles credited to him, no one is quite sure who St Govan was. Some authorities claim that he was a disciple of St David; others, that he was a thief, who in gratitude for the miraculous hiding place, became a convert. 'He' is also said to be a woman named Cofen, the wife of a 5th-century chief, who became a recluse.
▶ *6 miles S of Pembroke on B4319 then minor road.*

❸ St Davids, Pembrokeshire

The remains of St Non's Chapel are situated in a spectacular clifftop location, overlooking St Non's Bay. To the east of the chapel is the holy well, an old site of pilgrimage for people coming to give thanks and pray to the holy mother of St David. The well is said to have gushed up during a thunderstorm at the moment the saint gave birth. Pins and pebbles were reportedly offered to the well on St Non's day, March 2.
▶ *16 miles NW of Haverfordwest on A487. St Non's Chapel is 0.5 mile S of the city centre.*

❹ Nevern, Pembrokeshire

One of the finest Celtic crosses in Wales can be seen in St Brynach's churchyard in the small village of Nevern. It probably dates from the 10th or 11th century, and according to tradition, the first cuckoo to be heard in Pembrokeshire each year sings from the top of the cross on St Brynach's Day (April 7). More mysterious is a yew tree in the churchyard, part of an avenue of ancient trees, that exudes a bloody coloured sap. Old myths cite various reasons for the tree's constant weeping, proclaiming the tree will stop bleeding when Nevern Castle is returned to the Welsh, when an innocent man hanged for a crime is pardoned or when the world finds peace.
▶ *Just N of A487, 10 miles E of Fishguard.*

❺ Carmarthen Carmarthenshire

'When Myrddin's (Merlin's) tree shall tumble down, then shall fall Carmarthen town.' No doubt this prophecy was taken seriously as the town went to great lengths to preserve the famous oak that stood at the corner of Oak Lane and Priory Street. It was probably planted in 1659 to mark Charles II's accession and, some say, poisoned in the 19th century by someone fed up with townspeople using it as a meeting place. The tree died but was left where it was for years. In 1951, a branch was displayed at Carmarthenshire Museum, and when in 1978 the tree was too decayed, the stump was dug up and taken to be preserved at the Civic Hall.

According to another tradition, the great magician is still alive in a cave in Bryn Myrddin, Merlin's Hill, about 2 miles east of Carmarthen, kept there for ever in bonds of enchantment by his beloved Vivien. People once claimed that it was possible to hear his groans as he lamented his folly in letting a woman learn his secret spells. The hill is topped by an Iron Age hillfort.
▶ *A40 from E and W, A48 from SE (Swansea).*

wales

⑥ Kidwelly, Carmarthenshire

For centuries the ghost of Gwenllian, the wife of Gruffydd ap Rhys ap Tewder, prince of South Wales, haunted the countryside near Kidwelly Castle. She was decapitated in 1136 as she led an attack on the Norman stronghold, and legend says that her headless phantom could not find rest until her skull was unearthed on the ancient battlefield – known as Gwenllian's field, Maes Gwenllian – and returned to her.

Near Kidwelly, Spudder's Bridge over the River Gwendraeth Fawr is also known as the Bridge of the White Spirit. Nest, the daughter of the owner of the castle, kept a secret tryst there with her Norman lover, but a hidden assassin killed the knight and threw him in the river. Nest jumped in after him and was drowned. For years, her spirit returned to the scene of the tragedy.

▶ *9 miles S of Carmarthen on A484. Spudder's Bridge, on B4308 between Kidwelly and Trimsaran.*

⑦ Llandeilo, Carmarthenshire

Carreg Cennen Castle stands in ruins on the western fringes of the Brecon Beacons, about 4 miles from Llandeilo, and is open daily. A narrow underground tunnel, 46m (150ft) long, leads to a famous wishing well. Visitors once threw corks and pins into the dark water to make their wishes come true, and the water was reputed to have the power to heal eye and ear complaints.

The four neo-Gothic pinnacled towers of Newton House, a magnificent mansion set amid the tranquil surroundings of Dinefwr Park near Llandeilo, belie the building's origins, which actually date back to the 1660s. The house stands in the grounds of the ruined Dinefwr Castle. The grounds were completed in 1775 by the celebrated landscape architect Capability Brown and later additions to the structure were made during its heyday in the 19th century. Newton

House was sold by the Dinefwr family in 1974, after which it fell into disrepair. For a time it was occupied by squatters and, during the 1980s, housed a TV editing facilities company. It was while the TV company was there that Newton House's most famous ghost, the White Lady, put in several appearances. The phantom was thought to be that of Elinir Cavendish, a cousin of the owner's wife, who fled there in the 1720s to escape her betrothal to a man she hated. Sadly for Elinir, her would-be husband pursued her to the house and brutally murdered her. During the TV company's tenure, a number of editors fell ill, one after the other, for no apparent reason. Today, Newton House is open to the public under the auspices of the National Trust.

▶ *15 miles E of Carmarthen on A40. Carreg Cennen Castle is 4 miles SE of Llandeilo on minor roads. Newton House is 1 mile W of Llandeilo and is part of the National Trust's property, Dinefwr Park.*

❽ Cwrt-y-cadno, Carmarthenshire

The most famous of Welsh wizards, Dr John Harries, lived in the lonely hamlet of Cwrt-y-cadno. He was well educated, and until his death in 1839, people from all over the country came to consult him, because he was known as a healer as well as a magician and fortune-teller. It was believed that he could charm away pain and disease, cast out evil spirits, overcome witchcraft and find missing objects. A stone circle near the ruins of his home, Pantcoy, is said to be the scene of many of his magical rites. He refused to allow anyone to look in his *Book of Magic,* which was inherited by his son Henry, who followed in his father's footsteps. No one knows what happened to the book after Henry died in 1849.

▶ *On minor road 3 miles NE of A482 at Pumsaint, 8 miles SE of Lampeter.*

RUINS SHADOW THE FRINGES OF THE BRECON BEACONS

CARREG CENNEN CASTLE

9 Glyn-neath, Neath Port Talbot

The Craig-y-Ddinas cave near Glyn-neath (Glynnedd) is reputed to shelter the sleeping King Arthur and his knights. Legend tells of a wizard who met a Welsh drover, miles from home, who was carrying a hazelwood staff. He asked the Welshmen to take him to the tree from which the staff had been cut, because there they would find a great treasure. When they dug up the tree, they found a secret passage leading to a cave. At the entrance was a bell, and inside they saw King Arthur and his warriors sleeping beside a mound of silver and one of gold. The wizard told the drover to take as much silver and gold as he wanted but warned him not to touch the bell because, if he did, the warriors would wake. They would ask 'Is it day?' and he was to answer, 'No, sleep on.' Twice the drover became too greedy, overloaded himself with riches and touched the bell accidentally, but he remembered to give the correct answer. The third time it happened, however, he forgot the answer, and was beaten so badly by the knights that he was crippled for life, and could never find the cave again.

▶ *10 miles NE of Neath on A465. Craig-y-Ddinas cave is just N of A465, 1 mile NE of Glyn-neath.*

10 Abergavenny, Monmouthshire

The Skirrid Mountain Inn dates back to the Norman Conquest, and its bloody past has given rise to some spinechilling occurrences. Following the Duke of Monmouth's rebellion against Catholic James II, the inn served as a court for the notorious Judge Jeffreys, and 180 rebels were hanged there in 1685. The wear marks on the beam below the staircase, which carried the noose, can be seen to this day, adding to the already unsettling atmosphere. Numerous investigators have experienced paranormal activity in the building, including the crew of TV's *Most Haunted*, who conducted a recce there in January 2003 and detected the presence of a number of restless spirits, most of which dated back to the time of Judge Jeffreys.

Back in the 1990s a local medium sensed the spirit of a young woman who had died of consumption, and it was later discovered that, in the mid 18th century, Fanny Price, the landlord's wife, had died of that disease. Meanwhile, visitors report a variety of strange goings-on, including cold spots, glasses that appear to fly abruptly from the shelves behind the bar, and sudden feelings of constriction around the neck.

▶ *18 miles SE of Brecon on A40. Skirrid Mountain Inn is in Llanfihangel Crucorney, 5 miles N of Abergavenny on A465.*

11 Newport

The cathedral church of St Woolos on Stow Hill was founded by St Gwynllyw (Woolos is the Anglicised version). Before his conversion in the 5th century, Gwynllyw's wife and son struggled to turn his mind to God. One night, he was told in a dream to go to a certain hill where he would find a white ox with a black spot on its forehead. Next morning, he found the ox and, interpreting this as a message from God, he became a devout Christian. Disaster is supposed to befall anyone who desecrates the church. Once, when a band of pirates stole valuable items from the building, their ship ran into a terrible storm. St Gwynllyw pursued them, riding on the wind, and recovered the church plate before the pirates and their vessel vanished beneath the waves.

▶ *Access from Junctions 24, 26 or 28 of M4.*

CASTELL COCH

⑫ Mynyddislwyn, Caerphilly

Certain rocks found in Mynyddislwyn were referred to as hydrophobia stones. Until the end of the 19th century, if anyone in the neighbourhood was bitten by a mad dog, a piece of one of these stones was ground into fine powder, mixed with milk, and given to the wounded person. Alternatively, the sufferer was made to lick the stones. Apparently, these treatments were successful.

Beside the parish church of St Tudor, which stands on an old road across the mountain, is a tumulus known as Twyn Tudur, Tudor's mound. Many years ago, some thieves tried to dig into the mound, believing it to contain treasure, but a violent storm blew up frightening them away.

▶ *On minor roads 1 mile S of Pontllanfraith, 5 miles NE of Caerphilly.*

⑬ Tongwynlais, Cardiff

Castell Coch, the Red Castle, was built in the 1870s on the foundations of a much earlier fortress dating from the 12th century. The old castle was the stronghold of Ifor Bach, Lord of Senghennydd, who used to boast that his 1,200 men could beat 12,000 of any army sent against him. Tradition says that Ifor's treasure still lies beneath Castell Coch, concealed in a deep vault at the head of a tunnel leading to Cardiff Castle. The vault is guarded by three huge eagles who will tear to shreds anyone who approaches them. The eagles will continue to watch over the treasure in its great iron chest until Ifor Bach returns to claim it in the company of his 1,200 brave men of Glamorgan. The castle is open to the public.

▶ *1 mile N of Junction 32 of M4, 6 miles NW of Cardiff city centre.*

wales

⑭ St Nicholas, Vale of Glamorgan

The large standing stones on the Dyffryn estate were believed to have been cursed by the Druids. It is said that if you sleep among them on May Day Eve, St John's Eve (June 23) or Midwinter Eve, you will die, go mad or become a poet.
▶ *7 miles W of Cardiff on A48.*

⑮ St Donats, Vale of Glamorgan

An arts centre operates in the grounds of St Donat's, a large castle near Llantwit Major, the origins of which go back to medieval times. The castle houses a sixth-form college and has visitor days when it is open to the public. It is also haunted. Ghostly moans are said to echo through the rooms. One theory is that the ghost is mourning the passing of Thomas Stradling, whose family lost possession of the castle when he died in 1738. Other sightings include a panther that pads silently down the corridors, a woman in the gallery and bright lights resembling eyes in one of the bedrooms.
▶ *6 miles S of A48 at Cowbridge on B4270 and minor roads.*

⑯ Ogmore Castle, Vale of Glamorgan

The ruins of 12th-century Ogmore Castle are said to contain buried treasure, guarded by Y Ladi Wen, the White Lady. Near the castle, the River Ogmore is haunted by the tormented spirits of misers who died without disclosing their hidden wealth. They can be released from their penance only when somebody finds their valuables and throws them into the river, downstream of the castle.
▶ *3 miles SW of Bridgend on B4524.*

⑰ Gilfach, Caerphilly

A local legend relates how coal was discovered in the Rhymney Valley. The fairies of the valley were being harassed by a giant who came to live at Gilfach Fargoed. A fairy lad, whose parents had been eaten by the giant, decided to kill the monster, and an owl from nearby Pencoed Fawr farm agreed to help him. One night, when the giant was courting a witch under an apple tree, the owl shot an arrow into his heart and he died. Meanwhile, the witch was killed by a flock of the owl's companions. When the fairies burnt the giant's body in a huge pit, the ground caught fire and exposed the coal lying underneath. It is said that, on moonlit nights, the owl's descendants still come to Gilfach Fargoed and celebrate the giant's death in song.
▶ *Just S of Bargoed, 8 miles N of Caerphilly on A469.*

⑱ Port Talbot, Neath Port Talbot

Margam Castle, a Victorian mansion built in the Tudor Gothic style, stands in Margam Country Park, at the foot of a wooded hill and within sight of an 18th-century orangery and the ruins of a Cistercian abbey. However, no ecclesiastical spirits appear to haunt the house. Instead, it is plagued by the very angry ghost of gamekeeper Robert Scott. He has been seen climbing the steps to the house and on the Gothic staircase inside, and is reported to have slammed doors and thrown various objects. Apparently, he is finding it hard to come to terms with his death at the hands of a poacher.

A large figure that stalks the grounds may be the phantom of a blacksmith, while inside the building laughing children, footsteps, moving objects and orbs have all been reported, both by staff and psychic investigators.
▶ *Port Talbot can be reached from Junction 41 of the M4. Margam Country Park is 4 miles SE of Port Talbot.*

THE RIVER IS HAUNTED BY THE TORMENTED SPIRITS OF MISERS

OGMORE CASTLE

⑲ Reynoldston, Swansea

Arthur's Stone, Maen Ceti, stands on Cefn Bryn Common near Reynoldston. It actually marks a Neolithic burial chamber, dating back to 2500 BC, and was probably deposited there by glaciers in the last Ice Age. A fabled version is more imaginative, though. The stone is said to be the 'pebble' that King Arthur removed from his boot on his way to the Battle of Camlann in AD 539. He threw it over his shoulder and it landed on Cefn Bryn Common 7 miles away. Until the end of the 19th century, local girls would place a honey-cake soaked in milk on the stone at midnight, when the moon was full, and then crawl around it three times on their hands and knees. If a girl's lover was true, he would join her before the end of the last circuit.

▶ *1 mile N of A4118, 13 miles W of Swansea.*

⑳ Paviland

In 1823 the Reverend William Buckland, professor of geology at Oxford University, discovered a headless skeleton while excavating for animal bones in Goat's Hole Cave at Paviland. The body had been buried with periwinkle-shell and ivory jewellery and a mammoth head (now lost), and covered with a red ochre substance described as 'ruddle'. Buckland initially suggested the body was that of a customs officer, killed and buried by smugglers, but later thought it to be a Roman woman, possibly a prostitute working with Roman legionaries. According to the biblical account of creation, the age of the earth is 4,004 years, and so the reverend, according to his beliefs and those of the time, was not able to appreciate the significance of his find.

By the early 20th century, the red ochre-coloured bones were declared to be that of a young man of the Palaeolithic, ceremonially buried at least 21,000 years before. More recent studies, including analysis of flint tools found in the cave and radiocarbon dating of the bones, suggested the cave was occupied from around 40,000 years ago. A date of around 26,000 years was assigned to the burial, although this is still under debate and believed by some archaeologist to be 4,000 years older. The ochre stain is thought to be from the man's iron-oxide dyed tunic and trousers. Ochre is commonly associated with burials the world over. One theory is that the colour was used as a protection against evil spirits, or against the spirits of the dead. The site marks the oldest known ceremonial burial in Western Europe. The remains are on display at the National Museum Cardiff.

▶ *On minor roads 1 mile W of Port Eynon on A4118, 16 miles W of Swansea.*

OMENS AND SUPERSTITIONS OF THE WELSH MINERS

UNDERGROUND COAL MINING BEGAN in Wales more than 400 years ago. Generations of miners faced a daily struggle against darkness and danger, and belief in the supernatural came easily. Superstition was rife in coal-mining communities. It was unlucky to be late for work, or to forget something and return home for it. If, on his way to work, the miner met someone with a squint, or a rabbit or bird crossed his path, he would go home for the day. Whenever anyone in his family dreamt of death, an accident or broken shoes, a miner was often forced to stay at home by his frightened relatives on the day after the dream.

In South Wales, many colliers refused to start new work on a Friday – miners in Monmouthshire would complain of having 'the old black dog' on their backs, an evil spirit that caused illness and accidents. Throughout Wales, pitmen stayed away on Good Friday.

The sight of a robin, pigeon or dove flying around the pithead was thought to foretell disaster, and many miners refused to work if such birds were seen near the mines. They were called 'corpse birds' and are said to have been seen before the explosion at the Senghennydd Colliery in Glamorganshire in 1913, when more than 400 pitworkers died in the worst mining disaster in Welsh history.

Down in the mineshafts, whistling and the word 'cat' were strictly taboo, but on the positive side, lead miners believed in 'knockers', invisible spirits who made tapping noises to point the way to rich veins of ore.

In 1890, miners at the Morfa Colliery near Port Talbot reported many eerie manifestations that occurred both in the neighbourhood and in the mine itself. Fierce hounds, known locally as 'the Red Dogs of Morfa', were seen running through the district at night. The colliery was filled with a sweet, rose-like perfume emanating from invisible 'death flowers'. Cries for help and sounds of falling earth were heard, and flickering lights, called 'corpse candles', appeared in the tunnels. The ghosts of dead miners and coal trams drawn by phantom white horses were seen, and rats swarmed out of the mine. On March 10, nearly half of the workers on the morning shift stayed at home. Later that day there was an explosion at the colliery, and 87 miners were buried alive and died in the disaster.

wales

Scotland

Scotland's old cities play host to a whole spectrum of ghosts, haunted inns, sinister houses and stately homes. In the Highlands and Islands, wraiths re-enact their final hours of combat, and legends surround the monuments of the prehistoric past.

SOUTHWEST SCOTLAND

The old city of Glasgow has some modern theatrical ghosts to keep its culture-loving citizens company, while a rich collection of legends imbue the countryside with an air of eerie disquiet.

❶ Culzean, South Ayrshire

Built in the 18th century on the site of an earlier stronghold, Culzean Castle is linked with several versions of the Bluebeard story. Although the local version names the murderous husband as 'false Sir John', in an older ballad he is the supernatural Elf Knight, who abducts the heiress of Culzean and tells her he is going to kill her. She lulls him to sleep with a charm, steals his dirk and stabs him to death instead.

Near the castle, a tree-lined walk known as Piper's Brae sometimes rings to the skirl of bagpipes although there is never any sign of the musician. Tradition claims that the invisible piper always plays to herald the marriage of a future head of the Kennedy family, the former owners of the castle, but who the piper may be no one seems to know.

A tale from longer ago tells of the Laird of Culzean meeting a small boy by chance one morning. The boy begged for some ale for his sick mother and the laird sent the lad to his butler with orders to have the wooden bucket he was carrying filled. After a half-full barrel was emptied and the tiny bucket was still not full to the top, the mystified butler broached a new barrel and soon the little bucket was overflowing. Without a word of thanks, the boy took it off to his mother.

Some time later, in Flanders, the laird was taken prisoner. Suspected of spying by his captors, he was sentenced to be hanged, but the night before his execution, the cell door suddenly flew open and the same small boy magically appeared. Taking the laird on his shoulders, the fairy boy carried him with the speed of light back to Culzean, remarking, 'One guid turn deserves anither. Tak' ye that for bein' sae kind to ma auld mither.'

The castle and gardens at Culzean are run by the National Trust for Scotland and are open to the public.
▶ *On A719, 12 miles S of Ayr.*

CULZEAN CASTLE

② Electric Brae, South Ayrshire

Motorists driving along Croy Brae in South Ayrshire, sooner or later usually slow down, or stop, in confusion. The scenic road along the brae is one of the most disorienting places on Earth. Approaching from the north is an uncanny experience. The road appears to slope downwards and drivers assume that their cars will go faster, but if they apply the brakes, they are likely to grind to a complete halt. Despite every appearance to the contrary, the road runs uphill, not downhill. Unable to believe what has happened, many motorists not only come to a stop but find their cars sliding backwards, 'uphill'.

Travellers who are approaching from the south have the opposite experience. Thinking they are heading uphill they accelerate – only to discover that they are speeding along faster than they had intended, because the road actually goes down.

It was once believed that magnetic forces induced by surrounding iron-rich rocks exerted such a strong attraction that they could actually pull cars uphill. This explanation is now generally dismissed, and the cause attributed to an optical illusion caused by the surrounding topography. The phenomenon is not unique to Croy. There are similar places all over the world, including a spot on the road to Jerusalem near the village of Djabal Moukaber, Israel, and Magnetic Hill at Moncton, New Brunswick, Canada.

▶ *On A719, 9 miles S of Ayr.*

③ Glasgow

The ghost of a distinguished brain surgeon haunts Glasgow's Western Infirmary. Sir William MacEwen is said to walk the hospital in remorse for an operation that he failed to perform. Shortly before MacEwen died in 1924, he had refused to carry out a procedure that would have alleviated the crippling headaches suffered by a young artist. As the man left the surgeon's office, he was struck by one of the headaches and fell to his death down four flights of stairs. Sir William's ghost revisits the scene of the tragedy to reflect on the results of his decision.

Another hospital ghost is that of a ward sister at the Royal Infirmary who has been seen touring the wards at night. She appears normal – except that she is cut off at the knee. On Ward 27, Archie, the ghost of an elderly man has been seen talking to dying patients.

Strange events have occurred in a house in Duke Street. On one occasion, a shadow with a missing hand was seen with its arms held high in the air. Another time, children living in the house saw the ghost of a large dog – they said that the dog never wagged its tail and were frustrated because they could not get near enough to touch it. Someone else reported seeing a large dog-like shape on the stairs and feeling an overwhelming sense of evil in the house.

The Theatre Royal is haunted by the ghost of a failed actress, Nora, who was laughed off stage on her debut and committed suicide, but continues to revisit the scene of her humiliation.

At Craigmaddie Muir, the stones known as the Auld Wives Lifts were supposedly put there by three women competing to see who could carry the heaviest weight. Two stones bear a third and the legend is that if a female visitor does not climb through the gap, she will die before she is able to bear children.

▶ *The Western Infirmary is on Dumbarton Rd and the Royal Infirmary is on Castle St. Duke St runs E from the city centre. The Theatre Royal is N of the city centre in Hope St. Craigmaddie Muir is E of the A81, 9 miles N of Glasgow.*

④ Tynron, Dumfries & Galloway

Earthworks show that successive castles once stood on the steep hill of Tynron Doon, although no masonry remains. An old tale tells how one of these fortresses was the home of the Great McGachan. A MacMilligan of Balgarnock came courting his daughter but his sons considered the young man an unworthy suitor for their sister, and chased him, horse and all, over a crag. As he fell, his head was knocked off his shoulders and his decapitated ghost still haunts the district.

▶ *On minor road W of A702, 15 miles NE of New Galloway.*

⑤ Langholm, Dumfries & Galloway

This corner of Dumfries & Galloway was the domain of the Armstrong clan. These deeply feared outlaws raided cattle on both sides of the border when the moon was right. One of the most notorious, Johnnie Armstrong, lived in the Hallows Tower, on the road from Langholm to Canonbie, and his ghost is said to appear on the roof of his old home, swearing vengeance on his enemies.

For the Armstrongs, the phrase 'there will be moonlight again' had considerable significance, so perhaps it was appropriate that an Armstrong should have been the first man to set foot on the moon. Neil Armstrong, astronaut and descendant of the Armstrongs of Mangerton, was made a freeman of Langholm when he visited the town on March 11, 1972, during his world tour.

▶ *On A7, 20 miles N of Carlisle.*

FIFE & SOUTHEAST SCOTLAND

In a grim border fortress, among quiet abbey ruins and in historic city dwellings, old acts of vengeance has turned victims to ghouls. Meanwhile, otherworldly visitations light up the sky around Falkirk.

❶ Colinsburgh, Fife

At the end of the 17th century, trouble flared again between the Covenanters – militant Presbyterians – and Royalists of the Episcopalian faith. The most famous of the Royalist generals at this time was John Graham of Claverhouse, Viscount Dundee. 'Bonnie' Dundee raised the clans in 1689 to fight for James II against William of Orange, who was supported by the Covenanters, and many gentlemen from southern Scotland rode to join him. Lord Balcarres of Colinsburgh Castle, however, was prevented from doing so by being placed under house arrest by the Scottish Parliament. While he fretted in inactivity, his friend Dundee fought his last and greatest battle at Killiecrankie, and was killed in the moment of victory. At dawn the next morning, Balcarres awoke to see Dundee gazing sorrowfully at him from the bedside (see page 231). Not knowing he was dead, Balcarres cried out to him, whereupon the apparition vanished. Dundee's enemies believed him to be a warlock and said he had been shot with a silver bullet, which was thought to be the only means of killing supernatural creatures.
▶ *On B942, 2 miles N of Elie.*

❷ West Wemyss, Fife

The Castle of Wemyss was built in the 15th century and has often been visited by royalty. It was here that Mary, Queen of Scots first met her future husband, Lord Darnley, in 1565. Restored during the 1950s, it is still in residential use and is reputedly haunted by a tall, slim girl wearing a green dress, which rustles as though made of silk as she drifts by. 'Green Jean' has been seen and approached by members of the Wemyss family, but apparently some strange force prevents them from speaking to her. Below the castle, a series of caves have been hollowed out of the rock, and one of these is named after her. Jean's Cave is now bricked up.
▶ *Just E of A955, 4 miles N of Kirkcaldy.*

❸ Fordell

The ruined village mill is avoided by many people after dark, and even during the day there are those who are apprehensive about approaching it alone. The story runs that after the Battle of Pitreavie in 1651, Cromwell's victorious troops were quartered in the surrounding district, including at the mill. Despite the miller's remonstrations, the men billeted with him continually molested his wife and daughter, and in desperation he poisoned his unwelcome guests. A picket of soldiers was sent to avenge their comrades, but the miller had fled, so they hanged his assistant Jock instead, suspending the rope from a nearby tree. Now, on some moonlit nights, Jock's ghostly corpse, with agonised face and staring eyes, can be seen through the branches, and the hanging tree creaks dolefully as his body swings to and fro.
▶ *2 miles SW of Cowdenbeath.*

❹ Bonnybridge, Falkirk

Travellers in Scotland with a penchant for spotting UFOs could do worse than visit Bonnybridge, because in doing so they will at least have statistics on their side. Since 1989, this small town at the heart of the so-called 'Falkirk Triangle' between Edinburgh, Stirling and Fife has been the source of more UFO sightings than anywhere else in Britain, earning it the title of the nation's number one UFO hotspot. In fact, more unexplained phenomena have been spotted in Bonnybridge than almost anywhere else in the world. On average, the police and local press receive reports of around 300 sightings a year, mainly of mysterious white or red glowing lights in the sky.

One of the most convincing sightings took place in January 2009, when a resident of the nearby village of Banknock shot video footage of such an object after spotting it from his loft window. A cameraman for Scottish Television reported seeing an almost identical object while holidaying in Lerwick, Shetland, for the

New Year, although he did not have his camera with him at the time. Intriguingly, the Banknock sighting occurred in the same week that two blades were mysteriously torn from a wind turbine at a wind farm in Conisholme, Lincolnshire, leading to speculation that the two incidents were connected.

A Ministry of Defence report into UFOs released in 2000 under the Freedom of Information Act concluded that none of the Bonnybridge sightings to date had exhibited any form of outside control or threat to security, and that 95 per cent of them were likely to have been misinterpreted sightings of aircraft. In the meantime, however, the people of Bonnybridge have grown used to the idea of their home town becoming a worldwide mecca for UFO watchers, and to its popular nickname of the 'Scottish Roswell'.

▶ *4 miles W of Falkirk.*

❺ Linlithgow, West Lothian

The House of the Binns, just on the border with Falkirk, was once the home of Tam Dalyell, general of the Royalist forces during the wars that lacerated Scotland in the 17th century. Known as 'Bloody Tam' or the 'Muscovy brute' – he is supposed to have introduced the thumbscrews into Scotland from Russia – General Tam was feared and detested by the Covenanters, who swore he was in league with the Devil. The house's round towers were allegedly built by Dalyell to prevent the Devil from blowing the house away.

Apparently, the terrible pair played cards together, and one night, when Tam won, the Devil picked up a marble table and flung it at the general's head. Tam ducked and the table sailed through the window, landing in Sergeant's Pond at the foot of the hill. Sure enough, when the pond was being cleaned in 1878, the table was found there, and was restored to the house. As well as the table, the house contains other objects from Dalyell's time, including playing cards, a goblet and spoon, which all figured in Tam's carousing with Satan. His boots are said to disappear occasionally, when the general's ghost borrows them to ride round the district.

Sir Walter Scott's stories did much to promote the Dalyell legend. When Wandering Willie visits Hell in the story of Redgauntlet, he sees General Tam roistering with the Devil.

▶ *Linlithgow is 2 miles from Junctions 3 and 4 of M9. The House of the Binns is 4 miles E of Linlithgow.*

❻ Edinburgh

The tapping of a stick and the image of a woman's fire-blackened face occasionally disturb the normality of Edinburgh's Grassmarket. The stick belongs to Major Thomas Weir, one-time commander of the city's garrison, and the face is that of his elder sister, Grizel, both of whom were executed in 1670 for having dealings with the Devil. The pair lived in a house in West Bow in the mid 17th century. Major Weir's Presbyterian zeal was a byword, and he was a much-respected, if not much-loved, Edinburgh figure. Suddenly, at the age of 69, he confessed to the leading citizens that his whole life had been polluted by unspeakable crimes and he had indulged in revolting practices, with his sister as his criminal companion. On Weir's insistence, the two were arrested and brought to trial.

It seems clear that Grizel was demented. She advised the guards to seize Weir's staff, telling them that it was a gift from the Devil and the principal source of Thomas's power. This staff, she said, would go shopping for the major, answer the door to visitors and run before him to clear the way when he was walking in the streets. It appears likely that the old major, too, had been deeply disturbed by the hag-ridden beliefs of his time.

At their trial, neighbours recalled many strange occurrences having taken place at the house in West Bow, but the pair's conviction rested mainly on their confessing to necromancy, immorality and the use of a familiar spirit, and on Grizel's ability to spin abnormal quantities of yarn. They were both sentenced to be strangled and burnt. Major Weir's execution took place outside the city walls, and his staff was burnt with him. A witness stated that the stick 'gave rare turnings and was long a-burning as also himself'. Grizel was hanged on a gibbet in the Grassmarket. On the scaffold she tried to remove her clothes, whereupon the executioner turned her off the ladder prematurely.

For a century Major Weir's house remained empty, but his cloaked ghost, complete with magical staff, was reported to wander the streets at night. The empty house was said to glow with eerie lights, and music and laughter were heard within. Oddly enough, no one now remembers where in West Bow the Weirs' house stood.

The Last Drop Tavern in Grassmarket is home to more modern ghosts who lurk in the cellar. These spectres are thought responsible for the eerie atmosphere and are said to spook bar staff by calling out their names.

▶ *Grassmarket is just S of Edinburgh Castle.*

SCOTLAND

❼ The Palace of Holyroodhouse, Edinburgh

Famous for its connection with Mary, Queen of Scots, Holyroodhouse was the scene of the murder of David Rizzio, her secretary, by her wastrel husband Lord Darnley and his followers. A permanent bloodstain is said to mark the spot where Rizzio was stabbed 56 times. Mary herself is supposed to revisit the palace and it is also haunted by the ghost of a woman named Agnes Sampson, one of the North Berwick witches.

Agnes, a midwife of Keith, whose herbal and magical remedies were renowned in the district, was tried in Holyroodhouse in the presence of Mary's son, James VI, later James I of England. She stood alongside Dr John Fian, a young schoolmaster at Saltpans, Euphemia MacLean, daughter of Lord Cliftonhall, and Barbara Napier. An extraordinary plot to murder the king had come to light and

the prime mover was Francis Hepburn, Earl of Bothwell, James's cousin and heir-apparent should he die childless. Bothwell seems to have dressed as the Devil and persuaded local people to join a coven with the express purpose of getting rid of the monarch. Agnes Sampson told James of an unsuccessful plan to sink his ship as he returned from Norway with his bride, Anne of Denmark, and how the so-called witches had chanted curses over his wax image. Agnes and the other witches gave accounts of a great assembly at North Berwick church on All Hallows Eve, 1590, at which the Devil – probably Bothwell in costume – urged them to work evil upon his enemy, King James.

Eventually, James lost patience and declared the group to be 'extreme liars', but then Agnes did an astonishing thing. She said she would tell him something he could not doubt, and she whispered to him the words that had passed between Anne of Denmark and himself when they were alone

In 1901, the coffins passed from private ownership to the Museum of Scotland, and shortly afterwards, the museum received a letter. Its writer, who had lived in Edinburgh in 1836, recalled that her father's office was often visited by a deaf and dumb man, and when the little coffins were removed from the cave, he appeared there in a state of distress, with a drawing of three coffins, dated 1837, 1839 and 1840. This was the last time he was seen. In 1837, the father died, and in 1839 and 1840 two more of the woman's relatives also passed away. Were the coffins witches' charms, entombing the likeness of those they wished to destroy? Eight of the coffins and their figures are on display in the National Museum of Scotland. They found wider fame in 2001 when they featured in Ian Rankin's Inspector Rebus novel, *The Falls*.

▶ *The Palace of Holyroodhouse is at the foot of The Royal Mile, opposite the Scottish Parliament. The National Museum of Scotland is in the heart of the Old Town a short walk from the Royal Mile.*

❽ Dechmont Woods, West Lothian

Lying just outside the town of Livingston, Dechmont Woods was the site of an extraordinary experience of possible UFO activity. On the morning of November 9, 1979, Bob Taylor, a forestry worker, parked his truck at the foot of Dechmont Law. Accompanied by his dog, he walked up the slope and into a clearing, where he saw a dark, rough-textured, partly transparent metallic sphere about 6m (20ft) across set on a narrow flange. As Taylor came closer, two spiked spheres dropped from the structure and rolled towards him, attaching to his trousers and pulling him towards the larger sphere. Above the barking of the dog, he heard a hissing noise and smelled a choking, acrid odour.

He passed out, eventually coming round, face down in the grass. The objects were no longer there but his legs ached, his trousers were badly torn and he couldn't speak. Taylor crawled back to his truck but couldn't start it so was forced to walk home, where his wife, shocked at the state of him, called a doctor and the police. When the police checked the site, accompanied by Taylor, they found ladder-shaped marks and indentations that matched the paths of the spiky mine-like objects.

One explanation is that Taylor had witnessed a mirage of the planet Venus, which provoked an epileptic fit and accompanying hallucinations – although he had never had any such seizures before and has had none since. The police file on the case remains open.

▶ *Just N of Junction 3 of M8.*

HOLYROODHOUSE, EDINBURGH

together on their wedding night in Oslo. This convinced the king that Agnes was telling the truth, but it also sealed her fate, because she could not have learnt the words by mortal means. Agnes and Euphemia were executed on Castle Hill; Barbara was condemned but later released. Dr Fian, having admitted his part under torture, then retracted his confession and was finally strangled and burnt on Castle Hill in January 1591. As for Bothwell, he fled to Naples where he continued to practise sorcery until he died in poverty in 1624.

Almost 200 years later, Holyrood Park was the scene of a different kind of mystery. In 1836, a strange cache of 17 tiny wooden coffins, each no more than 10cm (4in) long, was discovered in a cave at Arthur's Seat. Each one contained a miniature carved figure, all of which were dressed differently. The coffins were arranged in three tiers, and had been put in the cave over a number of years – those at the bottom were more decayed.

❾ Rosslyn, Midlothian

Acknowledged for centuries as one of the finest examples of stonemasonry and carving in the whole of Europe, Rosslyn Chapel achieved worldwide fame in 2004, following the publication of Dan Brown's best-selling novel, *The Da Vinci Code*, which named it as the final resting place of the fabled Holy Grail. Brown chose the location on the basis that the chapel's builder, Sir William St Clair (or Sinclair), Prince of Orkney, had been a prominent member of the Order of the Knights Templar – a society formed in the 11th century to fight in the Crusades. The Templars were officially disbanded in 1312 by Pope Clement V after a quarrel with the French king, Philip IV, by which time their influence extended far and wide across northwestern Europe and they had acquired a reputation for 'heretical' practices and secret initiation ceremonies. The Templars were also rumoured to possess a number of important holy relics, the Grail among them, following their occupation of the Temple Mount in Jerusalem after the First Crusade. The Order continued in spite of the ban.

Construction of the chapel – properly called the Collegiate Church of St Matthew – began in 1456, and Sir William himself was buried there on his death in 1484. A century later, during the Reformation, the chapel's altars were smashed and the building ransacked. It was left to fall into disrepair for nearly 300 years until a later member of the St Clair family, James, ordered the floor to be relaid and the roof fixed. A full programme of restoration was initiated in 1861 by the 3rd Earl of Roslin, and the chapel was rededicated in 1862, although restoration work is ongoing.

Rosslyn Chapel's colourful history – Cromwell's troops were once billeted in it and the poet William Wordsworth wrote a sonnet there while sheltering from a storm – has merely encouraged the notion of paranormal activity. Its most famous ghost is said to be that of a young apprentice stonemason who completed many of the building's most famous carvings while his master was on a research trip to Rome. The apprentice was struck down by the mason in a fit of jealous rage, when he returned to Scotland to find his work done for him.

Two other famous Rosslyn phantoms – a black knight on horseback and a gigantic hound – predate the chapel, being the likenesses of an English commander and his dog who were killed by the Scots during a famous battle on the site in 1303. It is also said that the chapel glows, 'as if on fire', whenever a prominent member of the Sinclair family is about to die.

▶ *Just E of A701, 8 miles S of Edinburgh.*

THE CHAPEL GLOWS, AS IF ON FIRE
ROSSLYN CHAPEL

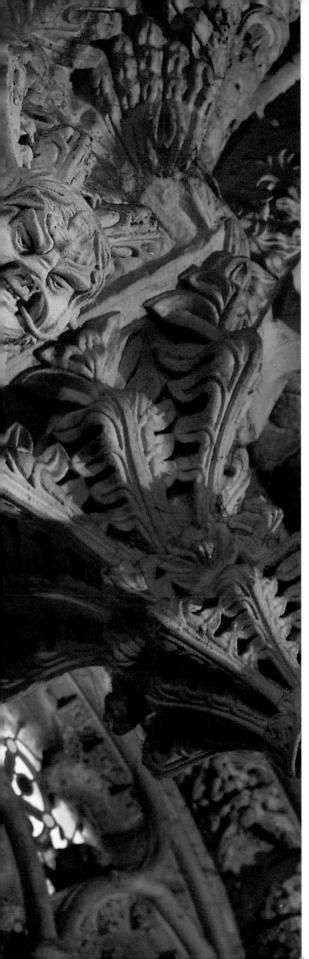

⑩ Stenton, East Lothian

Until the 19th century, Whittingehame, near Stenton, was haunted by the ghost of an unbaptised child, who, since it had no name, could not identify itself in the next world. No one dared speak to the unhappy creature, until a drunkard, reeling home late one night, cried to it, 'Hows a' this morning, Short-Hoggers?' The spirit rushed off joyfully, shouting, 'They ca' me Short-Hoggers o' Whittingehame' – and was never seen again. Short-hoggers are socks without feet, which people thought to be an apt name when they considered how long the spirit had wandered the district.

▶ *On B6370, 6 miles SW of Dunbar.*

⑪ Preston, East Lothian

A fortress known as Etin's or Edin's Hall once stood near Preston, and was allegedly the home of Red Etin, a terrible three-headed giant who kidnapped several young women, including the King of Scotland's daughter, turned two would-be rescuers to stone but got his just deserts at the hands of the third.

Two impoverished widows had three sons between them. One set out to seek all their fortunes, leaving his favourite knife with his brother. If its blade clouded over, it would mean something was wrong. At the castle, where he asked for shelter, Red Etin seized the boy and demanded answers to three questions. Was Scotland or Ireland the first to be inhabited by men? Was man made for woman, or vice versa? And which was made first, man or beast? The unfortunate youth had no answers, so the giant hit him over the head with a mallet, and the boy turned into a pillar of stone.

Meanwhile, back at home, the knife blade had turned rusty, and despite the entreaties of the widows, his brother set out to the rescue, only to meet the same awful fate. When he failed to return, the other widow's son packed his bundle, determined to do what he could to help his friends. On the road, he met an old woman with whom he shared his last bannock. In exchange, she gave him the benefit of her wisdom, so when the giant grabbed him and asked his three questions, the lad was able to whisper the right answers and Red Etin realised he was doomed. With one sweep of his axe, the boy removed all three of the giant's heads. The brothers were released from enchantment, the princess and her friends were rescued and married their saviours – but the boy never told anybody what he had whispered to the giant.

▶ *Just N of A1, 10 miles E of Edinburgh.*

SCOTLAND

⑫ Melrose, Borders

Although no monks have lived at Dryburgh Abbey for more than 400 years, ghostly cowled figures have been seen flitting among the secluded ruins, and unearthly chanting sometimes echoes through the tumbled-down remains of this once thriving community.

Founded in 1152 by Premonstratensian monks – who wore white robes and followed the Augustinian creed – the abbey was burned down twice and did not long survive the Reformation, but the apparition of a Grey Lady ensures that at least one episode in its history is not forgotten. In the 16th century, one of the monks had an illicit affair with a young woman from a nearby house. When the monk's betrayal of his vows was discovered, he was hanged in view of the house, so that his lover could watch. Driven mad with grief, she flung herself from a bridge into the River Tweed and drowned. Now her unhappy spirit returns to haunt the bridge and the hotel that was built on the site of her former home.

▶ *35 miles S of Edinburgh. Dryburgh Abbey is just E of the A68, 3 miles SW of Melrose.*

⑬ Jedburgh, Borders

The 12th-century abbey of Jedburgh, now ruined, was chosen by Alexander III, a widower, for his marriage to Yolande, daughter of the Count de Dreux, in October 1285. After the ceremony, a ball was held in the castle. A musical play had been composed, and dozens of masked dancers in fantastic costumes weaved in and out before the king and his bride. Suddenly a skeleton appeared among the company. It capered towards Alexander and thrust a bony finger almost into his face. Everyone was transfixed with terror and the queen buried her face in her hands. The skeleton vanished, but the splendid festival was ruined. The following March, the king, who had been feasting although it was Lent, was riding eagerly to rejoin his young queen when he and his horse fell from the cliffs near Kinghorn in Fife and were killed.

▶ *On A68, 45 miles S of Edinburgh.*

⑭ Hobkirk, Borders

A gravestone in the churchyard marks the burial place of an 18th-century minister, the Reverend Nicol Edgar, who is said to have laid to rest a troublesome ghost that haunted the church. This public-spirited action apparently gained the minister a supernatural reputation of his own, which persisted after his death. So, in order to deter his spirit from wandering, it was decided he should be reburied outside the village. While the corpse was being carried across the moor, the bearers slipped and the chill hand of the dead minister struck one of them, whereupon all fled in panic. The body lay where it fell until the next day, when it was returned to its original grave.

▶ *Just S of A6088, 7 miles SE of Hawick.*

⑮ Oakwood, Borders

Oakwood Tower, about 4 miles southwest of Selkirk, was the home of Scotland's eeriest enchanter, Michael Scot. Scot was an internationally famous scholar, who for several years in the early 13th century was physician and court astrologer to the Holy Roman Emperor Frederick II. His works on astrology, alchemy and the occult quickly earned him a reputation as a wizard, and in the opinion of his fellow countrymen, his years abroad had been spent not at the Imperial court but at the 'Black School', where he had learnt to control the powers of darkness and summon up the Devil. When he died in about 1234, his private *Book of Might*, in which he had recorded his spells and incantations, was buried with him, allegedly in Melrose Abbey.

Many stories are told about Scot's exploits. Once he sent a demon to split the Eildon Hill (see opposite) in three, and there are three peaks there to this day. The next night, he commanded the spirit to dam the River Tweed, and the ridge of rock at Kelso was the result. On the third night, he told it to spin ropes of sand at the mouth of the Tweed. More than 700 years later, the demon is still hard at work, to judge by the ridges of twisted sand that curl along the shore at low tide.

▶ *On B7009, 4 miles SW of Selkirk.*

GHOSTLY FIGURES FLIT

⑯ Hawick, Borders

One of the great border strongholds, Hermitage Castle stands in bleak isolation in the midst of open moorland, its imposing ruins haunted by the spirits of its violent history. Among the apparitions reported is the ghost of Sir Alexander Ramsay, who was starved to death in the castle's dungeons in the 14th century. Sir William Douglas, who held the castle at the time, was angry at being overlooked for the position of Sheriff of Teviotdale in favour of Sir Alexander and took action to rectify the situation. Prior to that, William de Soulis made himself so unpopular that legend says local people broke in, wrapped him in lead and threw him in a boiling cauldron. Unsurprisingly, his spirit can find no peace.

In 1566, when the Earl of Bothwell was laid up at the castle, wounded in a border skirmish, Mary, Queen of Scots rode all the way from Jedburgh to see him – and then back again, to avoid more scandal. It did no good. Scandal there was and both the Queen and Bothwell, whom she later married, came to unhappy ends. Mary's ghost occasionally revisits Hermitage Castle.
▶ *On A7, 45 miles S of Edinburgh. Hermitage Castle is 1 mile W of the B6399, 15 miles S of Hawick.*

⑰ Selkirk, Borders

A soutar – shoemaker – in Selkirk named Rabbie Heckspeckle was very industrious, and used to be at his bench long before dawn. Early one morning, a stranger came into the shop. He wore a long black cloak and a big hat pulled down over his eyes. The stranger picked up one of the shoes on the bench and tried it on. Finding it a perfect fit, he paid Rabbie in gold, and promised to return for the other shoe before cock-crow the following day.

Thinking it over, Rabbie became suspicious of his customer. His clothes had smelt mouldy, and his purse had contained as many worms and beetles as gold pieces. But, true to his word, the stranger returned next morning and paid for the other shoe. This time, however, Rabbie followed him. The tall, cloaked figure walked across the churchyard to a grave, jumped into it and disappeared. Later that day, Rabbie and a few neighbours returned and dug up the corpse. Sure enough, it was wearing the new shoes, which the soutar at once reclaimed.

Early next morning, Rabbie's wife heard him singing and banging away at his work, as usual, but suddenly his song ended in a screech. She rushed in, but her husband had vanished. When the grave was re-opened, the corpse was once more wearing its new shoes, and clutched in its right hand was Rabbie Heckspeckle's nightcap, but Rabbie himself had gone for ever.
▶ *On A7, 6 miles S of Galashiels.*

⑱ The Eildon Hills, Borders

Several places in Britain are claimed to be the resting place of King Arthur and his knights, including the Eildon Hills. The king and his entourage are supposed to lie sleeping there, awaiting the recall to battle in the hour of Britain's greatest need. Canonbie Dick, a horse-dealer, saw them. One night, riding home with a pair of horses he had been unable to sell, he was stopped by a stranger wearing old-fashioned clothes who asked to buy the horses. After some hard bargaining, he paid Dick in antique gold pieces. The episode was repeated on several nights until Dick suggested that, to seal the last bargain, they should go to the stranger's house for a drink. The man agreed but warned Dick that if he lost his nerve when he saw the dwelling, he would be lost for ever.

Dick was not easily frightened, so he followed his host to a hummock called the Lucken Hare, where they entered a huge cavern through a concealed door. Dick found himself surrounded by rows of sleeping knights in armour with their horses. On a table lay a sword and a horn, and Dick was offered the option of blowing the horn or drawing the sword – whoever made the correct choice, 'King of all Britain will he be'. Dick tried to blow the horn and a sudden mighty wind lifted him and threw him out of the cave. Next morning, he was found by some shepherds, and after telling his story, he died – the horn was evidently the wrong choice.
▶ *1 mile S of Melrose.*

AMONG SECLUDED RUINS
DRYBURGH ABBEY, MELROSE

SCOTLAND

CENTRAL & NORTHEAST SCOTLAND

Remnants of ancient pagan beliefs and devilish presences pervade the entire region, while Culloden field and the eerily beautiful Glencoe bear testament to a bitter history of betrayal and slaughter.

❶ Dunoon, Argyll & Bute

The Coylet Inn on the banks of Loch Eck was once used as a coaching inn on the main road from Glasgow to the port of Dunoon. It has had many ghostly sightings including the 'Blue Boy', whose spirit returns to the inn in search of his mother. It is thought that he was a young visitor who was known to walk in his sleep; one night he left the hotel, in a dream, crossed the road and wandered down to the loch, where he was drowned. Other paranormal manifestations include objects that have mysteriously disappeared from one area to reappear somewhere completely different, along with cold spots and wet footprints found in places and at times when there has been nobody there to make them.

▶ *Dunoon is on the A815 and can be reached by ferry from Gourock. Loch Eck is 8 miles N of Dunoon.*

❷ Loch Fyne, Argyll & Bute

The ghostly spectre of a gruagach – a small, long-haired spirit, known as the Green Lady – is said to have defended the inhabitants of Skipness Castle near Loch Fyne when danger threatened, and bewitched their enemies. The woods about the Claonaig stream, south of Skipness, were long believed to be sacred to the fairies, and hunters fled before the silent advance of horsemen dressed in green, for fear they should be spirited away. Another story tells how a woman was captured by the fairies and held prisoner for seven years. Her husband rescued her at last by lying in wait for the fairy host and throwing his wife's wedding dress over her head as she passed by.

Other supernatural hazards in the area include a holly tree that dances in the road to prevent people from returning home, and the sound of hoofbeats, which are a warning of impending death.

▶ *Skipness is at the mouth of Loch Fyne, 7 miles S of Tarbert.*

❸ Loch Awe, Argyll & Bute

About 1898, the driver of the mail coach was taking his team through the woods near the loch, when his sweetheart suddenly appeared on the box beside him, seized his whip and beat him so severely that he had to turn back. When he saw the girl again, he was extremely angry with her until she told him she had not been on the road at all. She had been very worried about him at the time of the incident, though, because she knew he was about to stop at a house where a fatal fever had broken out. Anxiety divorced her spirit from her body to save her lover.

▶ *Loch Awe is 8 miles W of Inveraray and can be reached by the A85, A819 or A816.*

❹ North Ballachulish, Highland

Sir Ewen Cameron of Lochiel (1629–1719) was a famous character in Highland lore, and a man of immense size and strength. On the road to the old ferry across Loch Leven at North Ballachulish he was overtaken one day by Gormul, a well-known witch. He ignored her and hurried on to the boat, trying to escape her attention, but she called after him, 'My blessings on you, Ewen.' He replied, 'Your blessings be on yonder grey stone, hag.' Instantly, the stone split in two. It was left where it was on the north side of the loch for many years.

The Scottish witches of the 17th century may have been a folk memory of ancient goddesses. An oak figure of a Cailleach, or Mother Goddess, was found beneath the peat near the Ballachulish ferry, together with the remains of a wickerwork shrine. The figure, 139cm (55in) tall and dating from between 730 and 520 BC, has eyes of inlaid quartz pebbles, which were believed to have magical powers. The statue is in the National Museum of Scotland in Edinburgh.

▶ *On A82, 13 miles S of Fort William.*

THE 'BLUE BOY' EMERGES FROM THE WATER

LOCH ECK

❺ Rannoch Moor, Highland

This sombre 20 sq miles of peat bog, ancient forest and water, surrounded by dark mountains, is associated with tales of legendary heroes, bandits and supernatural beings. William Wallace and Robert the Bruce in turn used it as a base from which to wage guerrilla warfare against the English, and for centuries it was a safe haven for the brigands who preyed upon travellers or stole cattle from the richer lands to the south.

It was once commonly believed that fairies, ghost dogs, water horses and other strange creatures roamed the moor or lived beneath the black waters of its lochs. A horse's bridle was once found near a loch, which local experts agreed was so beautifully made that it could only belong to a water horse, or kelpie.

Even in the 20th century, many people passing by Schiehallion – the 'Fairy Hill of the Caledonians' at the eastern end of the moor – reported being followed by a dog-like shadow that seemed to materialise from nowhere. Some stones on the hill's slopes mark the site of an old well, which was once believed to be inhabited by fairies who could grant wishes or cure ills. On May Day, girls dressed in white used to bring garlands as offerings to the wee folk – a ritual based on ancient well worship.
▶ *Crossed by the A82, 15 miles N of Tyndrum.*

❻ Glen Coe, Highland

The grim majesty of Glen Coe is a fitting backdrop to a tragedy. The massacre of February 1692, when 38 MacDonalds were murdered by their guests, a company of Campbell militia, has given birth to some enduring legends. To this day the nine of diamonds is known as the Curse of Scotland because the pips on the card bear some resemblance to the arms of the Master of Stair who, next to William of Orange, bore the greatest responsibility for the slaughter. There are also tales of fairy pipers leading Campbell troops astray in the mountains on their way back to Fort William, and of one soldier who, sickened by the order to murder a woman and her child hiding in the snow, killed a wolf instead and showed his bloodstained sword as proof of his obedience.
▶ *The A82 runs through Glen Coe, 16 miles S of Fort William.*

❼ Loch Earn, Perth & Kinross

On Dunfillan Hill, above the town of Comrie, St Fillan's Chair is a natural rock seat from which the 6th-century saint is said to have blessed his flock. Local people believed that anyone suffering from rheumatism of the back could be cured, provided they were prepared to climb up to the rock and sit on it, and then be hauled down the hillside by the ankles. Nowadays, most people are content just to sit for a while. A short way away is St Fillan's Spring, to which sick people would make pilgrimage every August in the hope of being cured of their ailments. According to tradition, the well moved itself there from the top of Dunfillan Hill.

▶ *The A85 runs along the northern shore of Loch Earn, 30 miles W of Perth.*

❽ Glen Lyon, Perth & Kinross

In the winding valley of Glen Lyon, at the turn into Glen Cailliche, a tiny stone house stands above a stream. This is the Tigh na Cailleach (or Cailliche), thought to be an ancient shrine to the pagan Mother Goddess, who is known in Scotland as the Cailleach. At the door of the structure, from May 1 to October 31 – Beltane to Samhain, the Celtic festivals that mark the beginning and end of summer – stand three strange stones, representing the Cailleach, the Bodach, or old man, and the Nughean, or daughter. Throughout the winter months, the stones, together with some others – thought to represent more children – are kept inside the house, but each year they are brought out to watch over the herds. During summer, the roof and walls of the house are repaired ready for the next winter, and the practice has continued, even though animals are no longer brought to the hills to graze.

At one time, a local legend sprung up that the three stones would guarantee good pasturage and fine weather, as they had done ever since a man and his heavily pregnant wife sought shelter in a bothy near the river. There, the woman gave birth to a daughter, and the couple vowed to stay forever and protect the glen that had given them hospitality. The stones were said to commemorate the family.

▶ *A minor road runs along Glen Lyon, W from B846, 5 miles W of Aberfeldy.*

FOR CENTURIES, A SAFE HAVEN FOR BRIGANDS

RANNOCH MOOR

❾ Scone, Perth & Kinross

The Stone of Scone, on which Scottish kings were required to sit to be crowned, was kept in Westminster Abbey from 1296 to 1996. Edward I removed it to London while attempting to unite the Scottish and English crowns. An old prophecy – 'If fates go right, where'er this stone is found, The Scots shall monarchs of that realm be crowned' – was fulfilled in 1603, when James VI of Scotland became James I of England.

Traditionally, the 66cm (26in) long block of red sandstone came from Ireland, where it was the coronation stone of ancient Irish kings. They called it Lia Fail, or the Stone of Destiny, and it was reputed to 'groan aloud as with thunder' if sat on by anyone other than the heir to the throne. The stone was brought to Scone by Kenneth MacAlpin, who defeated the Picts there in AD 843 and united Scotland under his rule.

Legend identifies the celebrated stone with Jacob's pillow (Genesis ch. 28, v. 11), and suggests that it was later given to a prehistoric Celtic king who married the daughter of an Egyptian pharaoh. Another story says that it was brought to Scotland by Joseph of Arimathea, and yet another that St Columba rested his head on it as he lay dying in the monastery church on Iona. Today the Stone is kept in Edinburgh Castle and will be loaned to Westminster Abbey for future coronations.
▶ *2 miles N of Perth.*

❿ Kirkton of Strathmartine, Angus

In a field 2 miles north of the village, a Pictish standing stone covered with carvings of strange animals may have been the source of a local legend. The 100cm (3ft) high boulder, known as Martin's Stone, marks the spot where that bold young man killed a dragon after a ferocious battle. Nine girls who had been sent to fetch water for their father had already been devoured by the monster.
▶ *On minor roads, 4 miles N of Dundee.*

⓫ Broughty Ferry, Dundee

Claypotts Castle is said to be haunted by a White Lady, identified as Marion Ogilvy, mistress of Cardinal Beaton. Every May 29, the anniversary of the cardinal's murder in St Andrews in 1546, she appears at a window, waving.

The castle was once home to another spirit, but this one was an industrious brownie who did all the household tasks at night, and asked no more in return than a basin of cream. Laziness offended his professional pride and, in the end, a slovenly kitchenmaid drove him out. He was so appalled by her wasteful methods of preparing vegetables for the pot that he beat her with a handful of kale stalks before leaving for ever, rather unfairly cursing the entire house and its inmates as he went. The castle is owned by Historic Scotland and has limited public opening.
▶ *3 miles E of Dundee.*

⓬ Arbroath, Angus

Parts of St Vigeans church date back to the 12th century and it was once used as a parish church for Arbroath, just over a mile away. However, no Holy Communion was held there between 1699 and 1736 because, according to one old story, people believed that, if it was, an underground lake over which the church was built would swallow up the congregation. Finally a minister took the risk, watched at a safe distance by his parishioners. Nothing happened and the spell was considered broken.
▶ *On A92, 17 miles NE of Dundee.*

⓭ Forfar, Angus

An iron gag in Meffan Museum and Art Gallery, Forfar, was used during the 17th century on those convicted of witchcraft. The unfortunate women, usually, were gagged while they were being taken for execution, presumably to stifle their screams. Most notorious was Helen Guthrie, who said she had eaten the flesh of babies to protect her from torture – if that was the case, her safeguard did not work.
▶ *1 mile E of A90, 14 miles N of Dundee.*

HER TORTURED SPIRIT COMES HOME, IN FLAMES

GLAMIS CASTLE

GLAMIS CASTLE

⑭ Glamis, Angus

If the legends about Glamis Castle are anywhere near the truth, the Bowes-Lyon family share their ancestral home with a terrifying medley of ghosts. From outside there are said to be more windows than can be found inside, and in a room so well hidden that not even the family now know its whereabouts, the 2nd Lord of Glamis, known as Earl Beardie, 500 years dead, plays cards with the Devil until the Day of Judgment. This may be the same room in which, long ago, a hideously deformed heir, said to look more like a toad than a man, was imprisoned for life. The Earl's spirit also wanders the castle and there are stories of children awakening to find him standing over the bed.

Lady Janet Douglas was burnt as a witch on Castle Hill in Edinburgh, on a charge of plotting to poison the king. Her tortured spirit is said to have come home, still wrapped in the flames in which she died. She may also be the Grey Lady in the chapel. A woman without a tongue and a gibbering madman on the roof are among the many unidentified ghosts that roam this ancient castle. The phantom of a young servant boy,

badly treated around 200 years ago, sits on a stone seat by the door of the Queen's bedroom.

Legend suggests that the castle is haunted as a result of an ancestral curse brought on the family by Sir John Lyon. He apparently removed a family chalice from the Lyon seat at Forteviot, where it was supposed to have been kept for eternity.

▶ *On A928, 12 miles N of Dundee.*

⑮ Kirriemuir, Angus

Cortachy and Airlie Castles have been in the Ogilvy family for more than 700 years. Apparently, a ghostly drum can be heard in Cortachy Castle whenever an Ogilvy is about to die. The drummer is supposed to have been thrown from a window in the tower after the discovery of an affair with the earl's wife. In another version, he was a Cameron who deliberately failed to give warning of the enemy's advance during the Wars of the Covenant, as a result of which Airlie Castle – 'The Bonnie Hoose o' Airlie' – was burnt to the ground. It was later rebuilt. The gardens at both castles are occasionally open to the public.

▶ *On A926, 4 miles W of Forfar.*

SCOTLAND

229

RUTHVEN BARRACKS

⑯ Tarfside, Angus

Near this village in Glen Esk, the hill of Rowan is allegedly where Robert the Bruce fought a battle against his arch enemy, the Red Comyn, and his battle cry of 'Row-in' has been associated with the place ever since. Although it seems doubtful if Bruce ever visited Tarfside, the cairns at the bottom of the hill have long been pointed out as the graves of those killed in the battle. In fact, they date from a much earlier period. The grave of an Iron Age chief was supposed to have been unearthed in the 19th century, but the site has since been lost.
▶ *7 miles NW from B966 at Gannochy, 5 miles N of Brechin.*

⑰ Glen Esk, Angus

The faint music of pipes can sometimes be heard in Glen Esk, reminiscent of a piper who was abducted by fairies years ago.
The piper lived in Locklee and his music was loved in all the glens of Angus. One summer evening, he was playing near Dalbrack Bridge when nine green-robed fairies came down the river in a boat. They stepped out on to the bank, one of them touched the piper's shoulder with her wand and he followed them back on to the boat. Three times the fairies sailed the craft round the pool called Pontskinnen Pot with the piper still playing, and then they disappeared upstream again. The piper had been taken to entertain them in the cave where they lived, and he was never seen again.
▶ *NW from B966 at Gannochy, 5 miles N of Brechin.*

⑱ Killiecrankie, Perth & Kinross

At the Battle of Killiecrankie in 1689, the Royalist general 'Bonnie' Dundee was killed as his forces defeated those of William of Orange. The next morning his phantom visited Lord Balcarres at Colinsburgh Castle (see page 216). In the wild gorge where he is said to have died, a spot known as 'The Soldier's Leap' was apparently the escape route of one trooper. Even with the encouragement of a Highland broadsword, the jump is a formidable one – down and across boiling waters and rocks.

▶ *On A9, 3 miles N of Pitlochry.*

⑲ Kingussie, Highland

In the 14th century, Ruthven Castle was the home of Robert II's younger son Alexander, a man whose ruthlessness rapidly earned him the title of the 'Wolf of Badenoch'. Despite the scandalised comments of the Church, he refused to abandon his mistress and return to his wife. As a punishment, he was excommunicated, to which the Wolf's reply, in 1390, was to burn Elgin Cathedral to the ground. He did penance and was received back into the Church, but the prince's piety was short-lived.

Alexander and his band of marauders became the terror of the district, pillaging by day and dabbling in witchcraft by night. Then, one stormy evening in 1394, watching villagers saw a sinister figure dressed in black ride into the castle. Creeping nearer, they peered through a window and there saw the stranger engrossed in a game of chess with the Wolf of Badenoch. The stranger moved a piece and laughed. 'Check!' he cried, and at once the scene was blotted out by a wall of fire. The villagers fled, and when they returned the next morning, they found the bodies of Alexander and his followers lying among the blackened ruins of the castle.

The first castle was actually destroyed in 1451 but rebuilt. Then in 1715 it was replaced by Ruthven Barracks, which were not finished until 1721 and fired by retreating Jacobites in 1746. Yet to this day, it is said, the Devil can still sometimes be seen among the ruins, endlessly playing chess for the soul of the Wolf of Badenoch.

▶ *On A9, 12 miles SW of Aviemore.*

⑳ Ben Macdui, Aberdeenshire

The savage grandeur of the Highlands provides an ideal setting for monsters, and Scotland has its own version of the Abominable Snowman in the terrifying shape of the Grey Man of Macdui in the Cairngorms. A grey figure, 3m (10ft) tall and wearing a black top hat, hovers near a cairn and bodes ill for all climbers and wanderers who meet him. He is reputed to have pursued wayfarers as far as the outskirts of Braemar, 11 miles away. A Banchory man claimed to have seen him in 1950.

▶ *12 miles SE of Aviemore.*

㉑ Banchory, Aberdeenshire

In 1562, the forces of Mary, Queen of Scots fought those of her cousin, the Earl of Huntly, chief of the Gordon clan, in the Battle of Corrichie. Huntly went cheerfully to war, bolstered by the witches of Strathbogie, who told him that after the battle he would lie in the Tolbooth of Aberdeen 'without any wound on his body'. The armies met on the Hill of Fare, 5 miles north of Banchory, and the Gordons were defeated. Huntly was captured unwounded but suddenly fell from his horse, dead from apoplexy. His body was taken to the Tolbooth, where it lay for the night, thus fulfilling the witches' prophecy.

There is a chair-shaped stone on the Hill of Fare on which Mary is said to have sat to watch the fighting. At the foot of the slope a modern memorial commemorates the battle.

▶ *On A93, 18 miles SW of Aberdeen.*

㉒ Methlick, Aberdeenshire

Ghostly piping is sometimes heard around ruined Gight Castle, 3 miles north of Methlick. The legend is that a piper was once sent to explore an underground passage leading from the castle, and never returned. Gight was the ancestral home of the Gordon family but had to be sold in 1787 by the 13th Gordon to live there, Catherine, to clear her husband's gambling debts. He was Mad Jack Byron, and their son was the poet, Lord Byron.

▶ *On B9170, 8 miles N of Oldmeldrum.*

BODIES LAY AMONG THE CASTLE'S BLACKENED RUINS

RUTHVEN CASTLE, KINGUSSIE

SCOTLAND

㉓ Aberdeen

One of the strangest hauntings in Aberdeen took place at the now demolished White Dove Hotel. A guest, an actress called Miss Vining, was stricken with a fever and a nurse was called in to tend her. The nurse noticed a strange atmosphere in the room and saw the seated figure of a small girl wearing a large hat that covered her face. She found herself unable to move and fell asleep in her chair. When she awoke, the child had gone. The next night she carefully locked the room, tended to her patient and again fell asleep. On waking, she saw the little girl as before. As the child rose and moved to the window, the nurse rushed at her, knocking off the hat. The face revealed was that of a beautiful Indian child, but her throat had been cut and the face was twisted in agonised death. The nurse fainted with horror. When she came round, the child had gone and her patient had died. As hotel staff packed up Miss Vining's belongings they found a photograph of a child. The nurse recognised at once the girl she had seen. On the back of the picture was written: 'Natalie. May God forgive us', but the child and the circumstances remained a mystery.

Other haunted buildings in Aberdeen include two more hotels, the Amatola Hotel, which is visited by the ghost of a Victorian lady, and the Ardoe House Hotel, where the spirit of a previous owner's daughter continues to wander. His Majesty's Theatre is frequented by the ghost of Jake, a stagehand who lost his head in an accident there before the Second World War. He seems to have stopped appearing following renovations in 1982, but when another round of repairs started in 2006, contractors heard the sound of someone in high heels walking around empty parts of the theatre. The spirit of a captain in the Gordon Highlanders, who committed suicide prior to an overseas posting, is said to be trapped in a building in King Street.

One of the most haunted houses is Leith Hall, in Huntley, the ancestral home of the Leith family, who lived there from 1650 to 1945. The ghost of a man identified as John Leith appears with a bloody bandage around his head. It seems that he was shot in the head – but whether during a brawl or in a duel is unknown. Other apparitions seen at the Hall include a young soldier, who has been glimpsed in the gardens, and an unhappy young girl. Numerous reports of poltergeist activity have been recorded, together with an uneasy presence, unexplained laughter, footsteps, cold spots, weird lights and strange smells.
▶ *On A90, 60 miles N of Dundee.*

㉔ Skene House, Aberdeenshire

This village was home to Alexander Skene, who lived from 1680 to 1724 and was known as the Wizard Laird. Even in the brightest sunlight, it was said, he never cast a shadow because it had been grabbed by the Devil while he was in Italy learning the black arts. The laird was often accompanied by four imps, in the shapes of a crow, a hawk, a magpie and a jackdaw. At Hogmanay, so the legend goes, the birds would sit beside their master in a ghostly coach drawn by black horses without riders or harness. The churchyard was usually the destination where the laird would open graves and remove the bodies of unbaptised babies as food for the four birds.

Often at midnight the laird would visit neighbouring glens in search of the herbs he used in his magic potions. He appears not to have welcomed competition, for he used some of his concoctions to poison witches.

One legend says the laird crossed the Loch of Skene in his coach, supported only by his magical powers and a thin coat of ice. He is said to have told his birds that he could make the crossing provided they proved true to him. The last night of the year was chosen for the feat and the laird told his coachman to have the carriage at the door by midnight. As there was no frost, the laird cast a spell to cover the loch with ice as thin as the finest glass. He told the coachman to keep the horses at full gallop during the crossing, with their heads towards the Hill of Fare. On no account was the coachman to look behind him.

The carriage sped across the ice with the four spirit birds flying alongside and encouraging the horses. The coachman, his terror barely suppressed, could not stop himself turning round as the horses touched land at the other side. There, seated beside his laird, was the Devil. In an instant the back wheels of the coach smashed through the ice and two black dogs, which had been chasing the carriage, plunged into the water. Nevertheless the horses took the laird safely home.
▶ *Just N of A944 near Dunecht, 12 miles W of Aberdeen.*

㉕ Inverness, Highland

The town has been the capital of the Highlands ever since the Pictish King Brude built his forts on the surrounding heights. St Columba performed many of his miracles there, and even 12th-century wizard Michael Scot contributed to the citizens' welfare by forcing demons to build them a bridge. However, it is to a large, rounded, tree-covered hill –

Tomnahurich, the hill of the yews, or the hill of the fairies – that the strangest legends cling. There, Gaelic adventurer-king Fionn escaped from an Irish king's enchantments by training his dog Bran to walk two of every species of animal round the hill (shepherding a pair of whales round the circuit was a particular achievement). Thirteenth-century seer Thomas the Rhymer is supposed to be buried there together with his men and his white horses, ready to rise again and save Scotland in her hour of need; and the Fairy Queen used to hold court there – still does according to some accounts. She was not the best of employers. Having paid two wandering fiddlers to entertain her guests for an evening, she kept them for 200 years, although they imagined they had been playing for only one night. When they were taken back to the hillside, they crumbled into dust. By eating fairy food and drinking fairy wine, they had fallen into her power.

Tomnahurich was used as a cemetery during the 19th and 20th centuries and has some imposing gravestones. A new cemetery has now been established farther out of town.

Although the Eden Court Theatre on the banks of the River Ness dates only from the 1970s, a number of ghosts wander around its environs. The most frequent visiting spirit is a Green Lady, who is thought to have once been the wife of a bishop. The gardens are haunted by a little girl, while on the banks of the river close by the theatre, the ghost of Duncan I is sometimes seen.
▶ *A9 from SE and NW, A82 from SW, A96 from NE.*

㉖ Culloden

The battle of Culloden Moor on April 16, 1746 was the final battle in the Jacobite Risings – and the last battle fought in Scotland. Charles Edward Stuart, better known as Bonnie Prince Charlie, was attempting to oust the Hanoverian George II in favour of the Old Pretender, the Bonnie Prince's father, who was the son of James II and also called James. James II had been deposed in the Glorious Revolution of 1688 and supporters had been trying to restore his line of succession, on and off, ever since. This was to be the Jacobites' last stand, and it was brutally put down by the king's younger son, the Duke of Cumberland, who earned himself the name 'Butcher Cumberland'.

In desperate, boggy conditions and driving rain, the 5,400 Jacobite troops were overwhelmed by a government force that not only had nearly twice as many men, but was also well rested and more effectively armed. More than 1,000 Jacobites died as against about 50 of the king's men, and most were buried where they fell, their graves marked by a stone or clan badge. Apparently, no birds sing on the battlefield or by the graves of the Jacobites, and no heather will grow over the burial sites. Each year, on the fateful day, the battle cries of the doomed men are said to ring out once again, along with the clash of steel on steel. The ghostly figure of a dead Jacobite soldier has been seen draped in a tartan cloth and lying on a grave mound, and a tall Highlander with a weary face says, 'Defeated,' to anyone he meets. Phantom Highland soldiers gather at nearby St Mary's Well.

Another Culloden legend is that of the Great Scree, an immense ghostly black bird that is said to be a harbinger of doom and bad luck. It was seen on the eve of the battle by the Jacobite commander, Lord George Murray, and was certainly an ominous sign for him.
▶ *Culloden Battlefield is just S of the B9006, 5 miles E of Inverness.*

㉗ Forres, Moray

Shakespeare placed Macbeth's three witches on the 'blasted heath' near here. Possibly he had heard the story, later related in a 17th-century book on witchcraft, of the mysterious sickness that afflicted King Duff of Scotland. Search parties discovered 'haggs roasting before a fire the king's picture, made of wax' at Forres. The witches were executed, and the king recovered – only to die in battle in the very same place, in AD 967, fighting the usurper Colin.
▶ *On A96, 12 miles E of Elgin*

㉘ Elgin, Moray

When the Devil took Sir Robert Gordon for his own in November 1704, he brought to a fittingly dreadful end the career of one of Moray's most deeply feared warlocks. Sir Robert had built himself a supposedly Devil-proof fortress in Elgin – the Round Square, now part of Gordonstoun School – and took refuge there with a parson, but at the last moment the parson persuaded him that he would be safer in Birnie church. On the way there, Sir Robert was caught by the Devil, who slung him over his saddle and galloped off with him to the fires of Hell. A huge demon dog ran beside them with its fangs buried deep in the warlock's neck. In fact, Sir Robert was a keen amateur scientist and inventor, which may have given him an unwarranted bad reputation, and the Round Square was a stable block.
▶ *On A96, 38 miles E of Inverness.*

NORTH HIGHLANDS & ISLANDS

This wild land, still scarred with the commanding ruins of its prehistoric past, is as raw and uncompromising as the battling clans that once roamed its lonely mountains and glens.

❶ Vallay, North Uist, Western Isles

Accessible by land only at low tide, this little island is now uninhabited but it was not always so. A woman there was once accused of being a witch and stealing milk by magic – a serious crime at a time when the cow was the most valuable of possessions. There were several ways for a witch to steal milk. One was for her to transform herself into a hare and suck the cows dry. Another was to recite spells while 'milking' the iron chain used to hang pots over the fire. Milk could be carried away in a needle, or in seaweed wrapped around her body. If these objects were damaged, the stolen milk would at once flow out. What method the witch of Valsay used, or how her crimes were detected, is not recorded, but a reminder of her terrible punishment still exists in the shape of a hollow pit. The chief ordered that she should be buried up to the neck in the gateway to the cattle-fold. There she remained, as the cattle passed over her, until her head was crushed. Now the pit can never be filled.

▶ *N from A865, 10 miles NW of Lochmaddy.*

CALLANISH STONES

❷ Harris, Western Isles

A legend attached to the many huge boulders scattered around Tarbert, the capital of Harris, has a Jack-the-Giant-Killer element to it. The stones are said to be all that remains of a giant's castle, where the ogre and his wife imprisoned a young girl, who had to spin cloth for their huge garments out of nettle leaves. When she had finished she would have been eaten but for her handsome young lover. He promised to give the giantess a string of enormous pearls if she would set the girl free. After many adventures and a dangerous journey down to the Sea King's palace, deep under the waves, the youth collected a string of wondrous pearls, and so won his sweetheart back.

A band of supernatural sea creatures were once said to prey on boats crossing the Minch – a stretch of sea between Lewis and Harris and the Shiant Islands. The Blue Men of Minch, as these kelpies were known, were blamed for churning up storms and luring sailors overboard.

The belief may have its origin in the memory of Berber slaves taken from Moorish ships by the Norse pirates who used to plague the islands. The Berbers always dressed in blue.

▶ *Ferry from Uig, Skye.*

❸ Callanish, Lewis, Western Isles

A prehistoric stone circle, 11m (37ft) in diameter, with avenues of monoliths radiating from it, rivals Stonehenge in mystery and grandeur. Inside the circle of 13 great stones, which are made of local gneiss rock, is a burial chamber, and bones found under a flat slab may be those of sacrificial victims. Legends link the stones with the Druids, who could turn men to stone, and the monoliths are called Fir Chreig, or 'False Men'. One theory is that the stones were a kind of astronomical calendar since the lines of construction appear to relate particularly to the position of the moon.

▶ *On A858, 15 miles W of Stornoway.*

4 Bettyhill, Highland

Just south of the town, where the River Naver flows into the sea, and 10 miles west of Strath Halladale, lies Loch ma Naire. The loch's curative powers have long been famous. Crowds used to gather on its shores on the first Monday in August, between midnight and 1am, when, apparently, the magical properties of the water were at their height. The tradition may well go back to pagan times. An essential part of the cure was the offering of some gift, such as a coin, and it was suggested that the Celtic festival of Beltane (May Day) was just as good a time to be immersed.

One 19th-century story tells how the loch obtained its power from a magic stone. A Gordon of Strathnaver coveted the stone, and tried to take it from its owner, an elderly woman. When she refused to part with it, he determined to drown her in the loch, but she ran into the water to get away from him, crying, 'May this stone do good to all created things – except a Gordon of Strathnaver.' He stoned her to death in the water. What happened to the wicked Gordon is not recorded, but the loch is said to have held the stone's powers ever since.

▶ *On A836, 28 miles W of Thurso.*

5 Thurso, Highland

In 1718, a man named Montgomery kept watch in his cellar to discover who was stealing his ale, according to a local story. A number of cats appeared and began to help themselves, whereupon Montgomery killed two with his sword and maimed another. As a result, two Thurso women died suddenly, and another was found to be minus a leg. She was forced into confessing herself to be a witch, and into implicating 20 others. Some were probably burnt on Gallahill, in a place marked by a large stone that always re-emerged, no matter how much earth was heaped on it.

▶ *A9 from S, A836 from E and W.*

6 Mey, Highland

The Castle of Mey, formerly Barrogill Castle, has a ghost. Legend says that Elizabeth Sinclair, daughter of the 5th Earl of Caithness, fell in love with a farm worker and was imprisoned by her father in the top room of the tower to prevent any possibility of a liaison. So that she could not even watch the man of her dreams at work, one window was bricked up. Subsequently, the unhappy girl fell from the other one, either accidentally when leaning out too far, or by design. Her mournful wraith is still said to drift about the place, and is referred to as the Green Lady.

The castle, originally built in the 16th century, was semi-derelict when, in 1952, it was saved by the late Queen Mother. In 1996, she gave it to the Castle of Mey Trust and the castle and gardens are now open to the public in summer.

▶ *Just N of A836, 12 miles E of Thurso.*

7 Canisbay, Highland

The parish church in Canisbay, a small town near the coast of the Pentland Firth, is the most northerly on mainland Scotland. In the churchyard stands a memorial stone to one of its most colourful ministers, Andrew Ogston, who died in 1650. Many of his flock believed that he had supernatural powers. On one occasion he fell foul of the Laird of Mey, who so terrorised Ogston's congregation that they were afraid to come to church. The minister responded by sending a piper round the parish on Sunday mornings and, as in the case of the Piper of Hamelin, the people felt compelled to follow him and so the church was always full.

Once, when he and a servant were a long way from home, he told the man to take the one horse they had between them, and ride back to the manse with all haste. The servant galloped home as fast as he could and was astonished to find the minister waiting at the door. The source of Ogston's spells was supposed to be a book of magic, but he made sure this was destroyed before he died.

▶ *Just S of A836, 16 miles E of Thurso.*

8 Murkle, Highland

A mermaid fell in love with a fisherman and lavished gold and jewels upon him, but discovered that he was using her gifts to court human girls. She invited him to her cave under Dwarwick Head, a point north of Castletown across Dunnet Bay, where she showed him the treasure of all the ships that had ever been lost in the Pentland Firth. While he gazed greedily at the spoil, she sang to him so sweetly that he fell asleep. When he awoke, he found he was chained to the floor with golden fetters, and there he remains, jealously guarded by his sea-mistress.

▶ *On A836, 3 miles E of Thurso.*

❾ Cromarty, Highland

Sometime around 1740, a Cromarty ship-owner named John Reid fell in love with Helen Stuart, but she refused to marry him. Walking sadly along the shore one morning, John was aroused from his reverie by sweet singing, and moments later he saw a beautiful, silver-tailed mermaid sitting outside the Dropping Cave. He crept up behind her and after a violent struggle, pinned her against the cliff. To win back her freedom, the mermaid granted him three wishes – that neither he nor any of his friends would drown, that Helen Stuart would change her mind, and a third that he never revealed. The first two, at least, came true.

▶ *On A832, 20 miles N of Inverness.*

❿ Loch Ashie, Highland

During the First World War, a traveller on the moors near the loch was startled to see a large number of men engaged in a pitched battle. Some of the combatants were mounted while others fought on foot, and although they hacked desperately at one another, they made no sound. When they suddenly vanished, the traveller realised that the armies were not of this world.

The phantom soldiers have been reported on several occasions, usually at dawn on May Day. There is a local tradition that the Irish hero Fionn mac Cumhaill once fought a battle hereabouts.

▶ *On minor roads, 6 miles S of Inverness.*

⓫ Invergarry, Highland

About a mile outside the town, on the west bank of Loch Oich, a curious monument was erected in 1812 to commemorate the gruesome killing of seven clansmen. This slaughter was the culmination of the Keppoch murders, which began in 1663 when, in a bid to claim the clan leadership for himself, Alasdair MacDonald of Inverlair and six accomplices – some say they were his sons – murdered the young chief of the Keppoch MacDonalds and his brother. Some two years later, another MacDonald chieftain, James MacDonald of Sleat, avenged the killings by sending a posse of men to Inverlair, where they killed and decapitated the murderers. The heads were taken to Invergarry to show to the Glengarry chief, who had refused to take any action, and on the way were washed in the spring. The place has been known as Tobar nan Caenn, the Well of Heads, ever since.

▶ *On A82, 42 miles SW of Inverness.*

MURDERERS KILLED AND DECAPITATED
THE WELL OF HEADS

12 Strathpeffer, Highland

In this quiet Victorian spa town, one of the churches is the focus of a prophecy by the Brahan Seer, or Coinneach Odhar. This Gaelic Nostradamus is said to have lived in the area in the early 17th century – although he is sometimes dated about a 100 years earlier, and there is some doubt whether he existed at all. Apparently, he said that when five church spires should rise in Strathpeffer, ships would sail over the village. The inhabitants, all too aware that a slight drop in the land would allow the Cromarty Firth to come rolling over their homes, were naturally opposed to more churches being built, and when the fifth, St Anne's, was proposed at the end of the 19th century, objections were raised. However, the funds were forthcoming, the church was built – without any sudden flooding – and it was finally consecrated in 1900, although some people went on brooding over an impending disaster. Then just after the First World War, a small airship flew over the village and the prophecy was at last fulfilled.

The seer supposedly possessed a magic stone, which was the source of his prophetical powers. It is said to lie in the waters of nearby Loch Ussie, where he flung it so that the loch waters would hide it for ever.
▶ *On A834, 18 miles NW of Inverness.*

13 Dingwall, Highland

In the Great Hall of Tulloch Castle, which overlooks the town of Dingwall, hangs a portrait of Elizabeth Davidson with her three children. Not much seems to be known about her past or how she died, but she is thought to be the Green Lady, the ghostly wraith that haunts the castle still, especially Room 8, causing a chill in the corridor and rattling the door at night. Why she should keep returning to her old home, and to that room in particular, is not clear, but she has, apparently, been seen by dozens of people, and may even have been captured digitally for posterity. In May 2008, a teenaged boy, who was attending a family wedding, took about 200 photographs at the event, and when transferring them to a computer, discovered a picture of a ghostly hand resting on the banister of the main staircase, surrounded by white mist.

Elizabeth was the daughter of Duncan Davidson, the 4th laird, who certainly made his mark during his 81 years. An MP and a favourite of Queen Victoria's, he always wore Highland dress wherever he went. He had 18 children with his five wives and probably fathered 30 more illegitimately. A prediction attributed to the Brahan Seer suggested that he would 'kill five wives in succession and the fifth will kill him', and he was survived by his fifth wife.
▶ *15 miles NW of Inverness. Tulloch Castle is just N of the town centre.*

14 Loch Maree, Highland

The loch, and one of its many islands, Eilean Maree, are named after the Irish saint Maelrubha, who founded a religious house at Applecross in the 7th century. From the scandalised accounts of 17th and 18th-century churchmen, it would appear that the saint's name must have long ago become confused with that of a Celtic god, Mourie. Certainly, the origins of rites that continued to take place on the island long predated Christianity. Bulls were sacrificed, a sacred well and tree were the focus of worship, and libations of milk were poured on the ground. A visitor in 1772 told how a lunatic was forced to kneel before a weatherworn altar and then to drink water from the well before being dipped three times in the loch. The process was repeated each day for several weeks in the hope of curing him. Similar rites were recorded in 1836 and 1852, at which time local people, who insisted that cures were most likely to be effective on St Maelrubha's Day (August 25), still constantly referred to the saint as 'the God Mourie'.
▶ *The A832 runs along the southern shore of Loch Maree, 2 miles NW of Kinlochewe.*

15 Torridon, Highland

The town lies at the head of Upper Loch Torridon among wild hill country. It has always had an eerie reputation, with tales of witchcraft, black and white, lingering in the area for a long time. As late as the end of the 19th century, a visitor recorded an extraordinary incident when a man mending a harness stuck a needle through the palm of his hand. A wise woman extracted the needle and blood spurted out, staining the opposite wall. Unperturbed, the woman pointed the needle at the floor and recited in Gaelic:

'Be your poison within the ground,
May your pain be within the hill.
Wholeness be to the wound,
Rest be to the hurt.'

The bleeding stopped immediately, and as far as any of the awestruck spectators could see, the wound was healed by the miraculous charm.

As in most places, iron was considered a powerful antidote to the supernatural. In Torridon it was believed that if an iron implement was used while gathering shellfish, these creatures would abandon the beach for ever. During clan feuds, it was alleged that people would plough their enemy's shellfish beaches by night in order to deprive them of an important source of food.

In the same district, the wood of the bird-cherry was considered far more powerful against evil than either rowan or elder. People used walking sticks made of bird-cherry as a charm against becoming lost in the mountain mists. The wood was also used when tethering a cow, to protect it from spells.

▶ *On A896, 10 miles SW of Kinlochewe.*

⑯ Loch Carron, Highland

The services of a wise woman who once lived at the head of the loch were often called upon. People from miles around would come to see her, in circumstances that may seem strange today but were perfectly sensible when belief in the supernatural was strong. A little boy from Applecross was wasting away, a victim of the evil eye, so his father went to the wise woman, taking an item of the child's clothing. She put a charm on it, and told him his son would be alive and well when he got home. Applecross is a remote village on the west coast. Land access is via the Pass of the Cattle on the highest road in Britain, and by the time the man got back his son was better. But the wise woman became ill, and lay near death for several days. This, she said, always happened when she fought the evil eye. It was as if all her strength went to cure another.

▶ *10 miles NE of Kyle of Lochalsh.*

⑰ Kyleakin, Isle of Skye, Highland

The ruined Caisteal Maol (bare castle) in the fishing village of Kyleakin is reputed to have been built by a Danish princess once married to a chief of the Mackinnon clan. Local people nicknamed her 'Saucy Mary', possibly because she charged vessels a toll for passing through the sea strait, Kyle Akin – by stretching a chain across to the mainland, according to one story. This sea channel is now spanned by the Skye Bridge, which since 2004 has been toll-free. The princess is said to be buried on the top of Beinn na Cailleach (hill of the old woman) nearby, with her face towards Norway. The castle was abandoned in the 17th century.

▶ *By bridge from Kyle of Lochalsh.*

⑱ Loch Cill Chriosd, Isle of Skye, Highland

The people living near the loch, in the parish of Strath, had cause to be grateful to St Columba when he visited the island in about AD 570. He chased away the evil spirit that lived there. Its power had been so deadly that anyone bathing in the water, or drinking it, would surely die, but after St Columba's intervention, the water became sweet and safe.

It seems that spirits could not leave the loch alone. Later, it became the haunt of a black water horse, or kelpie, that appeared in the form of a handsome young man. In this guise, he seduced young maidens, then galloped off with them into the loch. He met his match when, by mistake, he picked on a priest in long, flowing robes. The priest was safeguarded by his calling, and converted the pagan water horse to Christianity. Its ancient spirit has not troubled the area since.

▶ *On minor road, 3 miles SW of Broadford.*

A GHOSTLY WRAITH STILL HAUNTS THE CASTLE, RATTLING THE DOOR AT NIGHT
TULLOCH CASTLE, DINGWALL

Secrets of the loch

The dark, deep waters of Loch Ness are famous for a monster that continues to elude its dedicated investigators.

In the brooding, implacable Scottish Highlands, even the smallest expanse of still water can take on a life of its own. There is something in the nature of the northern light and the way the shadows of the mountains play upon the mirrored surface that draws even the most cynical observer to ponder what might lurk beneath. In Scotland, still waters run deep: around 228m (750ft) in the case of the country's most celebrated lake, Loch Ness, and around 305m (1,000ft) – close to the height of the Eiffel Tower – in the case of its smaller cousin to the north west, Lock Morar.

The monster appears

It is Loch Ness that holds the greatest volume of water of all the Scottish Lochs – more than the combined volume of all the rivers in England and Wales. The Loch is deep, dark and mysterious, even in modern times, with steep side-walls that defy easy investigation. It never freezes. And in the years since 22 July 1933, when Londoner George Spicer and his wife saw 'a most extraordinary animal' crossing the road along the shore, it has attracted tourists in their hundreds of thousands, each hoping to catch a glimpse of the elusive 'Nessie'.

The possible presence of a strange creature in the waters at Loch Ness fuelled a new interest in the search for animals unsubstantiated by science in the discipline of cryptozoology; the term itself meaning 'the study of hidden life.' Over the past 75 years, the search for the Loch Ness Monster – and for theories to explain its possible existence – have consumed more effort and expense than any other cryptozoological project around the world, yet even as NASA sends a probe to distant Pluto, scientists remain unwilling to rule out completely the idea that something extraordinary exists somewhere in the depths of the loch.

form of fish, or perhaps some naturally occurring (and as yet unknown) geothermal phenomenon that periodically disturbs or distorts the surface of the water.

The case for fish points to a shoal of sturgeon – the deep-water fish that, in their Caspian Sea habitat, produce caviar, and that in the Atlantic swim to fresh water each year to spawn. Given Loch Ness's separation from the sea, any sturgeon existing there today must be a sub-species that became trapped in the loch eons ago – or else the descendants of fish that were introduced to its peat-stained waters by human hand. Nevertheless, the largest sturgeon ever landed measured 8m (27ft) long and was estimated to be more than 200 years old, which goes a long way towards establishing the sturgeon's 'monster' credentials. Although no sturgeon has ever been found in Loch Ness itself, the spiny and strangely archaic-looking fish have been known to inhabit the Moray Firth into which the loch drains.

According to Devon zoologist and keen cryptozoologist Richard Freeman, the culprit is more likely to be an even less romantic creature: an eel. Normally, says Freeman, Scottish freshwater eels grow slowly over a ten year period before setting out for the Sargasso Sea in the North Atlantic Ocean to spawn and die. Freeman postulates that due to a freak genetic mutation, some eels are born without sexual organs and thus lack the impetus to spawn. Instead, in the absence of any major predators, they simply remain where they are, eventually growing to enormous proportions – in the region of 7.5m (25ft) long.

Not all marine biologists find Freeman's theory credible, although they admit that it fits the known facts better than most of the explanations put forward. These range from a family of plesiosaurs that survived extinction 65 million years ago to the effect on human consciousness brought about by the fault line near the loch.

Giants of the deep

Freeman points out that the 'giant eel' hypothesis could potentially explain a host of other Nessie-like sightings across the world, from the crystal-clear lakes of the Canadian Rockies to the icy waters of Lake Baikal in Siberia. Nor is Loch Ness the only Scottish loch to boast a monster: several others have made claims of varying, though largely dubious, credibility – including nearby Loch Morar, where one supposed sighting of a creature was later found to be the carcass of a stag thrown into the water by a poacher. Until proven otherwise, the existence of beasts in Scottish lochs will always be a matter of speculation. Staring into the inscrutable depths of Loch Ness, it is not hard to imagine how such beliefs arise.

The loch holds the greatest volume of water of all the Scottish lochs – more than the combined volume of all the rivers in England and Wales

LOCH NESS

ⓘ The Cuillin Hills, Isle of Skye, Highland

These wild hills are divided in two by the Glen of Sligachan – the Black Cuillins to the west are jagged and rough while the Red Cuillins to the east are more rounded and have some vegetation. They are all said to be haunted by the ghost of an outlaw named MacRaing. He committed one of his crimes at the old well called Tobar a' Chinn, the Well of the Head, at Torrin. The infamous outlaw is said to have robbed and then murdered a girl. When his son, shocked by his father's brutality, threatened to expose him, MacRaing killed him too and put his severed head in the well.

Torrin is where Flora MacDonald first brought the fugitive Charles Stuart, Bonnie Prince Charlie, in 1746, taking him to the House of Mugstot at Kilbride, before moving farther north to Monkstadt House and then Kingsburgh House on the Trotternish Peninsula.

As in other parts of Skye, the lochs and burns of the Cuillin Hills have long been associated with supernatural creatures. One such, a kelpie – the dreaded water horse – is said to live in Loch Coruisk. Well worship was not unknown, either. Childless couples, it is said, may drink the water of a well near Elgol, by Loch Scavaig, and invoke its guardian spirit to make them fertile. At nearby Strolamas the water of another fertility well is considered to be so strong that a couple who drink it will be blessed with twins.

Memories of Skye's ancient Viking rulers survive in the region. Beneath a cairn on Beinn na Caillich in the Red Cuillins lie the remains and all the treasure of a 13th-century Norwegian princess, who said she wanted the winds of her homeland to blow over her grave.

In modern times, drivers on the road at Sligachan have been frightened into pulling over by the headlights of a speeding 1934 Austin Seven, only for the car to vanish as it approaches.
▶ *10 miles S of Portree.*

⓴ Portree, Isle of Skye, Highland

Five miles north of Portree, on the east coast, just at the start of the Trotternish Peninsula, a natural stone pillar known as the Old Man of Storr has inspired several legends. Another column – the 'wife' – has fallen down, but the two great rocks used to stand side by side. Some say they were an old couple who 'saw something awful', or encountered a band of magical giants while searching for a lost cow. The couple ran away, but made the mistake of looking back and were turned to stone forever.
▶ *On A87, 30 miles NW of Kyle of Lochalsh.*

THE FAIRY FLAG OF THE MACLEODS

THE MOST TREASURED HEIRLOOM of the MacLeods of Dunvegan, on the Isle of Skye, is a tattered silk banner known as Bratach Sith, the Fairy Flag. No one knows for certain how it came to Dunvegan Castle. The story of a fairy wife giving it to her chieftain husband as a parting gift when she was recalled to fairyland – the place where she left him is still called Fairy Bridge – may have provided the flag's name, but a more likely theory is that a crusading MacLeod brought it back from the Holy Land as a relic, perhaps a saint's shirt. In fact, it probably comes from Syria or Rhodes.

It could even be the legendary Norse Land-Ravager, the magic standard that supposedly guaranteed victory to whoever possessed it. In any case, there is a tradition that if the clan are in desperate peril, they can become invincible by unfurling the Fairy Flag. The spell will work just three times, however, and the clan have already used it twice. The first occasion was at Glendale in 1490, when they were fighting for their lives against the MacDonalds. They unfurled the flag, the tide turned and the battlefield was soon piled with vanquished MacDonalds. The second victory was at Waternish in 1520. Again, the enemy were the MacDonalds and the MacLeods were hopelessly outnumbered, but as soon as the flag was unfurled, the MacDonalds were bewildered by the sight of a vast army marching down on them.

In all likelihood, the MacLeods often carried the flag into battle without unfurling it, and during the Second World War many young clansmen carried its photograph as a lucky charm. When Dunvegan Castle was seriously damaged by fire in 1938 many people were convinced that the Fairy Flag had prevented the fire from destroying the castle completely.

㉑ Trotternish, Isle of Skye, Highland

Far-off memories of the days when the Celts were head-hunters linger on in the legends of this most northern part of Skye – such as in the story of the malevolent ghost Colann gun Cheann, the Headless Body, who used to murder people in the area by flinging his head at them. He was banished to Arisaig, on the mainland, where he menaced travellers until a young man caught the head on his sword, and returned it only after making the ghost promise to return to Skye.

Another reminder of old habits lies in the local explanation for the Loch of the Heads at Cuidrach, on the west coast. The tale goes that a group of MacDonalds fought and decapitated a band of MacLeods, and rolled their heads down a hill into the loch. As they tumbled downhill, the heads cried out, 'Almost, almost, we almost won the day!' The hill is still known as Almost Hill.

Witches, too, are remembered. There is the story of the death of Iain Garbh, a powerful local laird who persecuted witches. On Easter Monday of 1625, he was drowned in a terrible storm – raised, they say, by the power of all the witches in Scotland.

▶ *N of Portree.*

㉒ Eigg, Highland

At first sight, a sandy beach on the rocky and desolate Isle of Eigg, off the west coast, appears to be like any other. But when the sands are walked upon or touched, they produce a musical sound. They sing, and not just one note. When slowly sifted through the fingers, the sands emit musical tones that can range from high soprano to low bass. These 'singing sands' are made up of tiny grains of quartz, ground to a rounded shape. When the grains are packed together, they are surrounded by a minute pocket of air, and the friction between the grain and the air sets off a vibration that creates a musical note. The note varies according to the amount of moisture in the atmosphere and the amount of pressure being applied. No dust or foreign matter can be present, as laboratory experiments have shown that even a minute pinch of flour halts the vibrations.

▶ *By ferry from Mallaig.*

㉓ Duart, Isle of Mull, Argyll & Bute

The castle at Duart is the ancestral home of the clan MacLean and, in the 17th century, one of their number was targeted by witches. His survival was due to local cattle rustler, MacIain Ghiarr, who had previously been a thorn in MacLean's side. They became firm friends from the night when MacIain was walking past the chapel of Pennygown, now ruined, and noticed a light. He found three witches, sticking pins into a clay image of MacLean, and grabbed it just as they were about to pierce its heart. After beating off the hags, he rushed to Duart Castle, where he found MacLean racked with pains. He told him the story, and as he removed the pins, one by one, so the pains diminished, until MacLean was well again.

▶ *3 miles E of Craignure which can be reached by ferry from Oban.*

㉔ Iona, Argyll & Bute

According to legend, St Bride lived on Iona until she was taken up by angels and transported to Bethlehem to be the newborn Jesus's foster mother. All the princes of the northwest wanted to be buried on this sacred island, partly because its blessed earth was thought to expunge all sin, and partly because of the ancient belief that when the second Great Flood came, only Iona would rise above the waves. Consequently, Reilig Odhrain, the graveyard named after Oran, a brother of St Columba, is said to contain the royal bones of 48 Scottish kings, from Kenneth MacAlpin, who united Scots and Picts, to Macbeth, the 11th-century usurper who inspired Shakespeare's play. Four Irish and eight Norwegian kings rest there, too, as well as many chieftains.

Stones and crosses play a large part in the island's lore. Highland chiefs took solemn oaths on the sacred Black Stones, and fishermen believed the Druid Stone helped them to navigate the treacherous waters around the island. Two fine crosses survived the Reformation – the 10th-century St Martin's Cross, near the abbey, and Maclean's Cross, which was hewn some centuries earlier and is said to be the earliest Christian relic in Britain.

▶ *By ferry from Fionnphort, Isle of Mull.*

ORKNEY ISLANDS

Great monuments to long-dead beliefs stand proud across the islands, defiantly guarding their secrets, while strange legends leave their supernatural mark upon coves, castles and ancient walls.

❶ Dwarfie Stane, Hoy

In an isolated, steep-sided valley between Rackwick and Quoys lies a 5,000-year-old block of hollowed-out red sandstone called the Dwarfie Stane. Inside this rock-cut tomb are two small cells, chiselled out using tools made of stone or antler, supposedly wielded by dwarfs.

Echoes that can sometimes be heard among the surrounding bleak cliffs, which are known as Dwarfie Hamars, were thought to be the dwarfs' voices. A later legend goes to the other extreme and makes the cells the beds of a giant and a pregnant giantess.
▶ *By ferry from Stromness and Houton on Mainland.*

❷ Stenness, Mainland

A few tall standing stones are all that remain of the original ring of 12 that were erected in a field in Stenness some 5,000 years ago, for purposes unknown. Two of the stones were wilfully destroyed in 1814 by the landowner, Captain Mackay, who was exasperated by the number of people tramping over his fields to visit one in particular, the Odin Stone. This monolith, which had a circular hole in it, had assumed enormous importance in local life. It was thought to possess healing powers and to bestow immunity from illness. Newborn babies were passed through the hole, sick people pushed affected limbs through it and gifts and offerings were left there. Contracts were sealed and lovers promises became binding when hands were clasped through the stone. The Odin Oath was unbreakable. The Stromness Pirate, John Gow, became engaged to the daughter of a local merchant at the Odin Stone. His short freebooting career ended in June 1725 with his body hanging in chains off Greenwich, little more than seven months after he seized the English ship in which he was second mate. So binding was the belief in their Odin pledge that the girl travelled to London to clasp her dead lover's hand so that she might be released from the oath.
▶ *5 miles N of Stromness.*

❸ Hestwall, Mainland

A mile southwest of Hestwall and 4 miles north of Stromness, Clumly Farm was the scene of a 19th-century murder and, as a consequence, is reputedly haunted – not by the victim but by the perpetrator, riding a ghostly white horse.

The story goes that a young woman from a nearby parish took a job at the farm and two men already working there became rivals for her favours. She played one off against the other until the two developed a deep mutual hatred. One day, when they were threshing sheaves of oats, standing face to face across the barn floor with heavy flails in their hands, one of them, goaded into blind fury by the other's taunts, smashed his rival's skull with a blow from his flail, and hid the body in the barn.

Later that night, the murderer took a white horse from the stable, secured his victim's body across its back and led the horse to the cliffs near Yesnaby, where he threw the corpse into the sea. As he rode away, he was gripped by a terrible fear that the dead man's ghost was following him, and he pushed the horse into a wild gallop for home. A dry-stone wall near the farm wasn't going to stop him but as the horse flew over it,

its hooves caught the top stones and brought them clattering down.

Some versions of the tale relate that both horse and rider were killed, others don't mention their fate, but whatever happened, no one has ever been able to repair the wall permanently. As though acting as a constant reminder of that terrible night, it always collapses again. On stormy nights, people have reported seeing a large white horse and rider leap over the wall to the sound of falling stones, and in the second half of the last century, a woman living near Clumly Farm answered a knock on her door to find a white horse and its rider standing outside. At her startled exclamation, the apparition vanished.
▶ *5 miles N of Stromness.*

❹ Noltland, Westray

The 16th-century castle, now ruined, was the home of the Balfours, and they shared it with a whole host of family phantoms. The castle used to be illuminated by a spectral light whenever a member of the family was born or married. Deaths were announced by the howling of a phantom dog, the Boky Hound. They also had a helpful creature, Broonie, who built roads and pulled boats to safety during storms.
▶ *By ferry from Kirkwall on Mainland.*

❺ Overbister, Sanday

Parallel grooves on a parapet of the ruined Kirk of Lady, near Overbister, are known as the Devil's Fingermarks, but no one knows why.

A girl who lived in nearby Broughtown was given a copy of *The Book of the Black Art* by a witch. This book, famous in Orkney tradition, contained magical recipes and conferred strange powers, but the possessor had to get rid of it by sale or gift before dying, otherwise the Devil would claim both the book and its owner. The girl, discovering its nature, flung it over a headland, only to find it again on her bedside table. At last, the island's Free Kirk minister, Matthew Armour, took possession of the book, and may still have owned it at his death in 1903.
▶ *By ferry from Kirkwall on Mainland.*

❻ Scapa, Mainland

A witch, angered by fishermen who would not take her son out whaling, buried her thimble on the beach and prophesied that no more whales would be caught in Scapa until it was found. It is still lost and the prediction is said to have come true.
▶ *2 miles S of Kirkwall.*

SHETLAND ISLANDS

Remote enough to be a refuge for smugglers and a haunt of pirates, the Shetlands are still a haven for sea birds – and for unknown spirits drawn to a ruined house overlooking a rocky shore.

❶ Yell

The ruined Windhouse stands on a hill in the middle of the island of Yell. The place was built in 1707 on the site of an ancient burial ground, but this is not thought to be the origins of the spirits that appear there from time to time. During rebuilding in 1880, the skeleton of a woman was found under the floorboards at the foot of the stairs. In life, she was said to have been the housekeeper, and possibly the owner's mistress, who fell down the stairs and broke her neck. Now, in death, she is the 'Lady in Silk' who rustles around in circles at the top of the fateful stairs, sighs and disappears. Other restless souls seen in the old house include a man in a top hat and long black coat, thought to be a murder victim, a servant girl who walks up non-existent stairs, a little dog and a crying baby.

▶ *By ferry from Toft on Mainland.*

❷ Busta, Mainland

The four sons of Thomas Gifford, the richest man in Shetland, were rowing across the voe, or inlet, of Busta one day in 1748 when the boat stopped dead. After prayers had been said, the boat moved again, but three strange creatures emerged from beneath the waves and swam slowly astern. One son was so scared that next day he refused to join his brothers in the boat when they went to see an uncle, and rode all the way instead. During the visit, his horse disappeared, so he joined his brothers in the boat for the return journey, and all four were drowned when it mysteriously capsized in a calm sea.

Later, a relative, Barbara Pitcairn, claimed to have secretly married the dead heir, John, and to be pregnant by him. The baby, Gideon, inherited the estate but his rights were challenged by a cousin. The case was long drawn out, but the protagonists' sons fought on, and in 1836 the courts decided against Barbara's grandson.

▶ *24 miles N of Lerwick.*

❸ St Ninian's Isle, Mainland

This peninsula, which is connected to Mainland by a tombolo, or sandbar, is popular with walkers and birdwatchers. It gained some fame in 1958 when a schoolboy, helping at an archaeological dig, uncovered a stash of silver bowls and ornaments, dating from around AD 800 and often referred to as St Ninian's treasure. The hoard was found under a cross-marked slab sunk in what had been the floor of a medieval chapel. This church stood on the site of an earlier place of worship, which is believed to have been Shetland's first Christian church and dedicated to St Ninian. A British bishop, St Ninian studied in Rome and afterwards made Pictish Scotland his missionary field. He established his first church on the Isle of Whithorn in Galloway in the 5th century. Although there is no evidence that he ever visited the Northern Isles, the church on St Ninian's Isle was always regarded as being of special sanctity, as was the nearby St Ninian's Well.

The treasure, which is in the National Museum of Scotland in Edinburgh, is described by the Museum as being 'both beautiful and mysterious; its craftsmanship is sophisticated, but its purpose, despite much investigation, is largely unknown.' Replicas are on display at the Shetland Museum in Lerwick.

▶ *16 miles S of Lerwick.*

ALL DROWNED WHEN THE BOAT MYSTERIOUSLY CAPSIZED IN A CALM SEA
BUSTA

❹ Fitful Head, Mainland

An inaccessible cave in the cliffs at Fitful Head, known as the Thief's House, is where, according to legend, Black Eric, a savage sheep-stealer, once lived. He had many fights but his main opponent was Sandy Breamer, an indomitable crofter. Once, as Sandy was gaining the upper hand, Black Eric's demon sea-horse, Tangie, whirled around the pair of fighters in a circle of unearthly light until Sandy fainted. However, Sandy eventually cornered Black Eric, and the villain crashed to his death over Fitful Head. Tangie continued to terrorise the district, harassing young women on the shore in his efforts to steal a mortal bride.

▶ *22 miles S of Lerwick.*

❺ Foula

This most westerly of the Shetlands is probably the most remote inhabited island among all the British Isles. On its rugged cliffs, near the top of Hamnafjeld hill, a narrow chimney is believed to descend about 300m (1,000ft) through the rock to sea level, but its exact position is unknown. The fissure was traditionally a hiding place of trows, spirit creatures, and anyone who visited Foula for the first time and dared to look down it would die immediately. About 300 years ago, so the story goes, two sceptical Dutch sailors were lowered into the hole. One was dead when pulled out, and the other died on the way back to his ship.

▶ *16 miles from Mainland, by ferry from Walls.*

RAIDERS OF THE NORTHERN SEAS

PIRATES, PRESS-GANGS AND SMUGGLERS were part of Orkney and Shetland life for centuries. The islands still hold memories of fierce Lewismen, raiders from the Hebrides. Such was the islanders' fear that when the Elizabethan explorer Martin Frobisher went ashore for water in 1577, the local people panicked and fled 'with shrikes and alarums'.

The most notorious pirate was John Fullarton, an 18th-century Orkney captain who was utterly ruthless and killed everyone who opposed him – even his own cousin whose ship he seized. His ending was as bloody as the rest of his career. After a running fight with the Scottish merchant vessel *Isabella*, he boarded her and murdered her commander, but he reckoned without the captain's wife, Mary Jones. She seized a pistol, put it to his temple and fired. The *Isabella* returned safely to Leith and Mary Jones became known as the Pirate Slayer.

Press-gangs, who were detailed to force able-bodied men to join the Royal Navy, were almost as great a scourge as the pirates. Scores of caves were used as hiding places by the hunted men, as well as secret cells in peat-stacks and hayricks. In Stronsay, Orkney, a man deliberately broke his leg to avoid being taken, and Barbara Wick of Deerness held a naval party at bay with a barrage of well-aimed stones while her lover escaped.

During the 18th and 19th centuries, smuggling was the most profitable of all island trades. Everyone joined in. Churches occasionally stored illicit alcohol and as late as the 1860s customers could buy smuggled gin over the counter of a Kirkwall bank. During the Napoleonic wars the guns of HMS *Norfolk*, lying at Kirkwall, were found to be loaded with tea and tobacco. Even at the beginning of the 20th century, French and Dutch fishing vessels regularly bartered a potent gin with the islanders for farm produce, such as eggs and butter.

Index

Acknowledgments

Back Cover Scottish Viewpoint/P. Tomkins/VisitScotland (Callanish Standing Stones, Isle of Lewis); **Front Cover** Pictures Colour Library/Brian Lawrence Images Ltd. (Kilchurn Castle, Loch Awe); **1** Mick Sharp and Jean Williamson (Mermaid of Zennor, Cornwall); **2-3** Photolibrary.com/Robert Harding Travel (Dunstanburgh Castle, Northumberland); **6-7** Scottish Viewpoint/P. Tomkins/VisitScotland (Callanish Standing Stones, Isle of Lewis); **8-9** Collections/Robert Estall (Hound Tor, Devon); **10** Alamy Images/Benjamin Volant; **12-13** www.ntpl.org.uk/©NTPL/David Noton; **14** Mick Sharp and Jean Williamson; **16** Mick Sharp and Jean Williamson; **18-19** Collections/Roy Stedall-Humphryes; **21** © Reader's Digest; **22** The Marsden Archive; **25** Mick Sharp and Jean Williamson; **26** Collections/John Tordai; **28-29** naturepl.com/Adam Burton; **30-31** The Marsden Archive; **32-33** Mark Bauer Photography; **34-35** Mark Bauer Photography; **38** Photolibrary.com/Britain on View/David Noton; **41** © Reader's Digest; **43** Photolibrary.com/Robert Jones; **46-47** © Oxford Picture Library; **48-49** Photolibrary.com/OSF/Peter Lewis (New Forest, Hampshire); **51** Fortean Picture Library; **52** English Heritage Photo Library; **54-55** Alamy Images/Tim Graham; **57** John Parker; **58-59** John Parker; **60-61** Alamy Images/Available Light Photography; **64-65** John Parker; **68-69** Alamy Images/Mal Smith; **70** John Parker; **73** © Reader's Digest; **75** www.ntpl.org.uk/©NTPL/Simon Tranter; **79** © Reader's Digest; **80-81** Alamy Images/Organics Image Library; **82** Mike Walker; **84-85** English Heritage Photo Library; **86-87** Photolibrary.com/Britain on View/Jeremy Walker; **88-89** www.jasonhawkes.com (City of London) ; **91** Alamy Images/Paul Debois; **93** Collections/James Bartholomew; **94-95** Collections/Malcolm Crowthers; **96-97** Photolibrary.com/Britain on View/Society of London Theatres/Pawel Libera; **98-99** Derek Adams & Dolly Whilems; **100** © Reader's Digest; **103** Mary Evans Picture Library/Peter Underwood; **104-105** John Parker (Mersea Island, Essex); **107** www.ntpl.org.uk/©NTPL/Joe Cornish; **108-109** John Parker; **111** © Reader's Digest; **112-113** The Marsden Archive; **114-115** John Parker; **117** John Parker; **118-119** www.ntpl.org.uk/©NTPL/Horst Kolo; **122-123** John Parker; **124-125** John Parker; **126** The Marsden Archive; **128-129** Corbis/Andrew Fox (Malvern Hills, Worcestershire); **131** Collections/Robin Weaver; **134** Collections/Quintin Wright; **136-137** Collections/Barry Payling; **138-139** English Heritage Photo Library; **140** Fortean Picture Library; **144** © Reader's Digest; **146-147** The Marsden Archive; **148** Photolibrary.com/Britain on View/David Sellman; **150-151** Mike Hayward- photoshropshire.com; **152-153** Collections/Roy Stedall-Humphryes; **154-155** John Parker; **158-159** Frank Lane Picture Agency/John Eveson (Forest of Bowland, Lancashire); **160-161** Photolibrary.com/Britain on View/Alan Novelli; **164** Fortean Picture Library; **166-167** Alamy Images/Tim Gainey; **168-169** Mick Sharp and Jean Williamson; **171** © Reader's Digest; **172-173** Jon Wornham; **174-175** Photolibrary.com/Britain on View/Rod Edwards (Hadrian's Wall, Northumberland); **176-177** Mike Kipling Photography; **179** www.ntpl.org.uk/©NTPL/David Sellman; **180** Collections/David Taylor; **185** Photolibrary.com/Britain on View/Joe Cornish; **186** DK Images/Joe Cornish; **189** © Reader's Digest; **190-191** The Marsden Archive; **192-193** Photolibrary.com/Britain on View/David Angel (Fairy Glen, Conwy); **195** The Photolibrary Wales/Peter Lane; **197** © Reader's Digest; **198-199** www.ntpl.org.uk/©NTPL/Andrew Butler; **200-201** Mick Sharp and Jean Williamson; **203** naturepl.com/Nick Turner; **204** Mick Sharp and Jean Williamson; **206-207** Collections/John Bethell; **208-209** John Parker; **212-213** Scottish Viewpoint/D. Cowie (Glen Coe); **214** Scottish Viewpoint/Garry McHarg; **218-219** Scottish Viewpoint/P. Dodds/VisitScotland; **220-221** Scottish Viewpoint/P. Tomkins/VisitScotland; **225** Scottish Viewpoint/Mike Clarke; **226-227** Scottish Viewpoint/Stuart Craig; **228-229** Collections/Robert Estall; **230** Scottish Viewpoint/Richard Nicholls; **234-235** Scottish Viewpoint/David Osbourne; **237** Scottish Viewpoint/VisitScotland; **240-241** Frank Lane Picture Agency/Jim Brandenburg/Minden Pictures; **244-245** Scottish Viewpoint/Gary Doak; **247** © Reader's Digest

Contributors

Project Editor Jo Bourne
Art Editors Austin Taylor, Conorde Clarke
Sub-editor Marion Paull
Cartographic Consultant Alison Ewington
Feature Writer Martin Preston
Additional material Marion Paull,
Lisa Thomas, Rachel Weaver
Picture Editor Christine Hinze
Proofreader Barry Gage
Indexer Marie Lorimer
Maps European Map Graphics Limited

FOR VIVAT DIRECT
Editorial Director Julian Browne
Art Director Anne-Marie Bulat
Managing Editor Nina Hathway
Prepress Technical Manager
Dean Russell
Product Production Manager
Claudette Bramble
Production Controller Jan Bucil

We are committed both to the quality of our
products and the service we provide to our customers.
We value your comments, so please do contact us on
0871 351 1000 or via our website at
www.readersdigest.co.uk

If you have any comments or suggestions about
the content of our books, email us at
gbeditorial@readersdigest.co.uk

Also available in this series:
The Most Amazing Birds to See in Britain
The Most Amazing Places on Britain's Coast
The Most Amazing Places in Britain's Countryside
The Most Amazing Places of Folklore & Legend
in Britain
The Most Amazing Places to Visit in Britain
The Most Amazing Places to Visit in London
The Most Amazing Places to Walk in Britain
The Most Amazing Scenic Journeys in Britain

The Most Amazing Haunted & Mysterious
Places in Britain Published in 2011 in the United
Kingdom by Vivat Direct Limited (t/a Reader's Digest),
157 Edgware Road, London W2 2HR

The Most Amazing Haunted & Mysterious
Places in Britain is owned and under licence from The
Reader's Digest Association, Inc. All rights reserved.

Reprinted in 2011

The Most Amazing Haunted & Mysterious Places in
Britain is based on material taken from Folklore, Myths
and Legends of Britain published by The Reader's
Digest Association Limited, London in 1973

Origination by FMG
Printed in China

ISBN 978 0 276 44542 2
Book Code 400-430 UP0000-3